VIKING FUND PUBLICATIONS IN ANTHROPOLOGY

edited by COLIN TURNBULL

Number Forty-Nine

THE DUGUM DANI

A young man. He wears a long penis gourd with a fur tassel, a nassa *shell chest piece, a dog fur arm band, and carries a pig tusk nose piece in his plaited arm band.*

The Dugum Dani

A Papuan Culture in the Highlands of West New Guinea

KARL G. HEIDER

ALDINE PUBLISHING COMPANY / *Chicago*

This volume comprises one of a series of publications on research in general anthropology published by the Wenner-Gren Foundation for Anthropological Research, Incorporated, a foundation created and endowed at the instance of Alex L. Wenner-Gren for scientific, educational, and charitable purposes. The reports, numbered consecutively as independent contributions, appear at irregular intervals.

Copyright 1970 by

WENNER-GREN FOUNDATION FOR ANTHROPOLOGICAL RESEARCH, INC.

First published 1970 by

ALDINE PUBLISHING COMPANY
529 South Wabash Avenue
Chicago, Illinois 60605

Library of Congress Catalog Card Number 70–106977
SBN 202–01039–2

Photographs copyright by Film Study Center, Peabody Museum Harvard University, Cambridge, Massachusetts 01238: Numbers 1, 2, 5, 7–11, 13, 14, 16–26, 28–41, 43–49, 56–59.

Photographs copyright by Karl G. Heider: Numbers 3, 4, 6, 12, 15, 27, 42, 50–55.

Photograph Credits: All photographs were taken by Karl G. Heider except Numbers 20, 21, 22, 25, 26, and 35, which were taken by Michael C. Rockefeller, Number 59, which was taken by Jan Th. Broekhuijse, and Number 13, which was taken by Eliot Elisofon.

The following photographs appeared first in *Gardens of War* by Robert Gardner and Karl G. Heider, published by Random House, 1969, and were copyrighted by the Film Center, 1968: Numbers 24, 32, and 48.

Dedicated to
the memory of
PROFESSOR CLYDE KLUCKHOHN

PREFACE

THIS study is a descriptive ethnography of the Dugum Dani, a Papuan society in the Central Highlands of West New Guinea (Irian Barat, Indonesia), based on research carried out in 1961–1963 and 1968. Despite the trend toward more specialized anthropological research and publication, I have chosen to present the Dugum Dani in a broadly descriptive format rather than to write only on a few specific problems from the standpoint of a specific theoretical position.

The basic approach of this study is holistic. Starting from the assumption that all traits in a culture are interrelated in some sense, the holistic approach proceeds to search out significant interrelationships on a broad front. The emphasis is not simply on describing as many traits as possible but on establishing the context of interrelationships of these traits. This holistic program is carried out most explicitly in the treatment of Dani warfare (Chapter 3), but it is applied to some extent throughout.

A second pervasive concern is with classification. The categories of ethnographic analysis have become sanctified by tradition. Some sorts of cross-cultural categories are essential, but often the traditional terms obscure more than they reveal. This problem is considered especially in the treatment of attire (Chapter 9) and art (Chapter 6). A closely related problem concerns the nature of the native Dani categories of various sorts. This is treated in the descriptions of arrows (Chapter 9), sweet potatoes (Chapter 1), and elsewhere.

This ethnography is divided into two parts. The first deals with economic activities, sociopolitical organization, conflict, the supernatural, language, art, and play; the second contains the more technical details of the material aspects of Dani culture.

NAMES—POLITICAL AND ANTHROPOLOGICAL

In many cases the anthropological use of names differs from the political use of these names. Since this study is anthropological, I have chosen to follow the anthropological usages. But to avoid misunderstandings, a few potential sources of confusion may be noted.

The Western half of the New Guinea island was called Netherlands New

Guinea until 1962, then West New Guinea, and after 1963 was administered by the Republic of Indonesia as the province of Irian Barat (West Irian), pending the final determination of its status in 1969. In August 1969, West Irian was officially declared a part of Indonesia. For the most part I have retained the politically inaccurate name of West New Guinea. The island itself is called Irian in Indonesian, but I have retained the traditional term of New Guinea. Politically the people are called Irianese, New Guineans, or Papuans, depending on which of three political jurisdictions they live in. I have followed the anthropological usage of Papuan for the non-Austronesian speakers of the Central Highland zone and Melanesian for the Austronesian speakers of the coast. Also, the people at the far western end of the Central Highlands are well known in the anthropological literature (especially through the works of Pospisil) as Kapauku, but by 1968 they themselves had rejected that name as a foreign term and insisted on the use of their own term, Ekagi.

ORTHOGRAPHY

The orthography used here for transcribing Dani words was established by missionary and government linguists at a conference in February 1961 (cf. van der Stap 1966:3). Generally the symbols have values close to English values, with these major exceptions:

j   is the Dutch *j*, the English *y;*

t   resembles the English stop except when occurring between two vowels, where it is "flapped" like a trilled *r;*

k   resembles the English stop except when occurring between two vowels, where it becomes a velar fricative, like a very soft Dutch *g*, or, in swift speech, disappears altogether;

dl is an alveolar implosive, made with a quick drawing in of the breath while pronouncing a *dl* sound;

bp is a bilabial implosive, made with a quick drawing in of the breath while pronouncing a *b* sound;

e   is never silent

a   as in English *father*, thus *wa* is *wah*

e   as in English *well*

i   as in English *keep*, thus *wim* is *yeem*, *Dani* is *dah-nee*

o   as in English *more*

u   as in *oo*, as in English *tool*, thus *Dugum* is *doo-goom.*

There are a few relatively unimportant modifications of the standard orthography which result from my own difficulties in distinguishing certain phonemes in certain contexts. No distinction was made between the vowels written *i* and *y* or between those written *u* and *v*. Also, in certain situations the following pairs were not accurately distinguished: *t* and *d*, *b* and *p*, *g* and *k*, *dl* and *bp*.

ACKNOWLEDGMENTS

So many groups and individuals have contributed to this study at various times that I can only mention a few by name.

I would like to thank the Government of Netherlands New Guinea, the United Nations Temporary Executive Authority, and the Republic of Indonesia for their gracious hospitality to anthropological research in a sensitive area. In particular, I would like to name Dr. J. V. De Bruijn, then Director of the Bureau of Native Affairs of the Government of Netherlands New Guinea, who first invited us to come to New Guinea and who eased our way in countless respects; Dr. Jan Pouwer, then also of the Bureau of Native Affairs, who gave us greatly appreciated support; and Drs. Anwas Iskandar of Universitas Tjenderawasih, who facilitated our visit in 1968.

Missionaries and anthropologists generally have such different backgrounds, educations, values, and goals that it is a wonder they can communicate at all. But like many anthropologists, I would like to pay sincere tribute to the missionaries in West New Guinea. They opened the Highlands, wrote the grammars, and maintained a magnificent communication and transportation network. I merely slipped in for a couple of years, taking advantage of what they had done, and they willingly aided and abetted me in this. I most gratefully acknowledge both their official aid and their personal friendships. In particular I would like to mention the Christian and Missionary Alliance; Father A. Blokdijk, Dr. Herman Peters, Father N. Verheijen, and the other members of the Order of St. Francis; the pilots of MILUVA (the Roman Catholic Mission air service, later called AMA), and those of the Missionary Aviation Fellowship. In 1968 our brief visit would have been impossible if Father Frans Verheijen had not invited us into his household at Jibiga, generously sharing his roof, his food, and his time. I would especially like to mention the assistance of two linguists, Dr. P. van der Stap, O.F.M., and Mr. Myron Bromley of the Christian and Missionary Alliance, whose grammars, word lists, and countless personal discussions enabled me to learn as much of the Dani language as I did.

To Robert G. Gardner, who conceived of the Harvard Peabody Expedition, organized and led it, and later, when I stayed on in the field alone, gave me constant support, go my warmest thanks. Also I would like to express my deepest appreciation for the friendship and the generous cooperation of the other members of the expedition: Michael C. Rockefeller, who gave of his talents, his goods, and finally his life; Jan Broekhuijse, who so often laid aside his own research in order to help the other members of the expedition; Peter Matthiessen, to whom I am indebted for much of the data on ecology; the Dani policeman Abududi and his wife Wamamogen, who did so much to assure our acceptance in the Dugum Neighborhood; Jusup Kakiay, the expedition cook; Samuel Putnam; Eliot Elisofon; the policeman Nawas; and Chris Versteegh, who has kindly furnished the plant identifications used here.

Professor J. O. Brew, then Director of the Peabody Museum of Harvard University, which sponsored the expedition, gave us the fullest support from his office on Divinity Avenue. Miss Carol Thompson (now Mrs. Hermann Bleibtreu), who was the secretary of the Film Study Center of the Peabody Museum, had the thankless task of watching us come and go and of handling the mail and film in between.

The expedition received generous financial support from the Government of Netherlands New Guinea, The Peabody Museum of Harvard University, and the National Science Foundation. During most of my time in the field I held a National Science Foundation Graduate Fellowship. I would also like to acknowledge additional research funds received from the National Geographic Society, the Norman Fund, Educational Services, Inc., of Watertown, Massachusetts, the Carnegie Corporation through a grant to the Cross-Cultural Study of Ethnocentrism Project, and the Foundations' Fund for Research in Psychiatry. I am also grateful to Brown University for faculty stipends during the summers of 1966, 1967, and 1968. The maps were drawn by Eric Engstrom.

During the six-month break in my field work, Professor David Owen, the late Master of John Winthrop House, Harvard College, generously sheltered me in the guest suite of the House.

Innumerable people have listened patiently to my discourses on the Dani during the past years. I am grateful to all of them and would like to thank in particular Denise O'Brien, Robert G. Gardner, Professor Andrew P. Vayda, my colleagues and students at Brown University, Jytte Boerge, my parents and brothers, Antonia Gerald, Frans Verheijen, O.F.M., Professor Douglas Oliver, and my wife and research associate, Eleanor Rosch Heider; these people through their agreements and disagreements have all given valuable help in formulating the ideas presented here and in disabusing me of many ideas which happily are not presented here. Each will recognize his or her own contribution; but needless to say, the responsibility for the whole is mine alone.

Finally, I would like to express my deep gratitude to Um'ue and to the other people of the Dugum Neighborhood, who are the subjects of this study. Their friendship and infinite patience with strange people doing strange things and asking strange questions is responsible for whatever accuracy this study contains.

CONTENTS

PLATES

(Photographs by the author except where noted.)

DIAGRAMS

MAPS

TABLES

INTRODUCTION

INTRODUCTION

HOLISM

THIS is an ethnographic study of a small group of Dani who live in the Dugum Neighborhood of the Grand Valley of the Balim River, some 1,650 meters high in the Central Highlands of West New Guinea, now the Indonesian province of West Irian at about Latitude 4° South and Longitude 138°50′ East.

This ethnography is holistic. It might better by specified as descriptive holism, to differentiate it from the synthetic or generalizing holism whose aim is to summarize a society in terms of a few themes or patterns. The holism in this case is the attempt to explore the interrelationships of traits within Dani culture.

Holism has an ancient and honorable ancestry in anthropology. Malinowski, in the Foreword to his first monograph on the Trobriand Islands, asserted that

One of the first conditions of acceptable Ethnographic work certainly is that it should deal with the totality of all social, cultural, and psychological aspects of the community, for they are so interwoven that not one can be understood without taking into consideration all the others. (1922:xvi)

Three years later, Mauss analyzed "the gift," or "prestation," as a "total social phenomenon," saying that

in these "early" societies, social phenomena are not discrete; each phenomenon contains all the threads of which the social fabric is composed. (1925; quoted from 1954:1)

But despite these brave words, holism has not had a totally happy career in anthropological research, for it is not without its disadvantages.

First among these disadvantages is the difficulty of actually achieving the holistic goal. Holism encourages the collection and presentation of more data than might be immediately relevant to a specific argument. It is especially difficult to organize the data satisfactorily. In attempting to recreate through lineal narrative in a few hundred pages the complex mesh of Dani culture, I have not tried to follow every line of interest through to the logical extreme of each relationship but have left many threads dangling, to be picked up in later chapters.

There are ways to avoid this dilemma to some extent. Early in my field work I considered writing an entire volume on the Dani Men's House, and starting from this central object, to trace its interconnections outwards until the entire culture had been described. This would have been a strained exercise, and I abandoned it.

Another technique would be to use an extensive graph or matrix in whose boxes the interrelationships of every trait or institution with every other could be entered. Elsewhere (Heider n.d.) I have explored the utility of such an approach to attack specific problems, and it appears that Malinowski used a similar device in his classes (Richards 1957:25). But useful as it is for directing research and pointing up specific problems, I fear it would prove too inflexible for the formal description of an entire culture.

Since no ethnography can be totally holistic and since even the most frag-mented ethnography cannot avoid it altogether, holism is not really a distinctive approach but simply a criterion for judging the adequacy of a descriptive ethnography.

A second shortcoming of the holistic approach is that it is essentially descriptive and not theoretical, and therefore it does not provide explanations. But this is a limitation, not a defect. I have not focused this study on a single theoretical proposition. But in dealing with warfare, for example, I have had to consider and criticize possible theoretical explanations of Dani phenomena. In this case, a single theoretical explanation of war along ecological lines is put into perspective by the holistic description of the extremely complex nature of war. This is the major advantage of the holistic approach: It provides the broad description of relevant interrelationships which must precede the theoretical explanation.

Since the categories of analysis direct and constrict the analysis itself, they must be carefully examined. Especially when the goal is holistic description, the restrictions of categories is crucial. For example, when dealing with objects such as penis gourds or carrying nets, the temptation is to put them in the category "clothing" and then mention that they also have functions similar to objects in the category "ornament." But in these examples it is conceptually restrictive to use clothing as a category. An alternative is to use clothing, ornamentation, communication, and the like as functional attributes of objects in a larger category, "attire." Then one can treat objects of attire in terms of the various relevant functional attributes of qualities (cf. Heider 1969a).

At first glance this may seem like quibbling. The preference for attributes rather than categories at certain levels is not based on truth or accuracy but rather on a desire to build a conceptual framework which will be maximally useful in directing research. It is quite conceivable that an analysis of the net or the penis gourd could begin by placing them within a limited single-function category such as clothing and then go on to examine other functions. But this would still necessitate working under the handicap of the limiting categories. Such an analysis would depend on its effectiveness on an implicit conceptual scheme working at cross-purposes to the explicit one. But a conceptual scheme that substitutes attributes for categories will force the analysis to take the broadest possible lines.

Often, as in the cases of arrows or war or ghosts, the English-language categories of traditional ethnography are quite appropriate. The task of the ethnographer is to describe the verbal and nonverbal behavior of one culture in cross-culturally relevant terms. In order neither to betray the reality of the native behavior nor to make a mockery of the concepts of ethnography, the categories of description must be adjusted for the best possible mutual fit.

FLEXIBILITY

In recent years much has been written about the loose or flexible nature of New Guinea Highland societies, with particular reference to their social organization. Specifically, the term "flexible social organization" is used to describe societies in which most of the behaviorally important groupings are constituted not on the basis of easily accessible and predictable principles like patrilineal descent, but on the basis of considerably more complex and subtle factors of personal motivation such as friendship. But since any social organization is based on a mixture of easily predictable rules and less accessible inclinations, such a term as "flexible" only has meaning if it can be carefully defined as one end of a scale of relative values.

One suspects that much of this Highland flexibility is a "discovery" by field workers who have had little experience in comparably unacculturated societies, and who are overwhelmed by the disparity between the orderly charts and tables in monographs and the swirling activity of a New Guinea village. (I hasten to include myself.)

Also, there is a danger of confusing the precise rules which might be quoted by an informant with the actual behavior on the ground. Hiatt (1967) has recently contributed to the understanding of Australian aboriginal social organization by showing that the mind-boggling complexity of the section systems was a legal fiction which, although some people followed, most found unworkable.

In a sense, New Guinea Highland studies find themselves at the opposite extreme, where an acceptance of "flexibility" or "vagaries of personal inclination" is used as an agnostic substitute for explanation. Two papers have been most influential in setting the tone for this position. In one, J. A. Barnes (1962) warned of the dangers of applying models based on the more rigid African lineage organizations to the New Guinea Highlands material, which seemed to be characterized by optation; in the other, Marshall Sahlins (1963) drew a contrast between the formal inherited chieftainships of Polynesia and the less powerful, more individualistic Big Man pattern of leadership which is found in New Guinea and Melanesia. These papers were important and necessary syntheses of the data, but in a sense they offered too easy a solution to the analytical problems presented by New Guinea Highland societies. The danger of the African lineage model is overformalization, a too-eager search for rules which might not actually be followed. But the danger of the flexible model is that it discourages the search for rules and promotes an interpretation of social behavior as simply the result of idiosyncrasies.

The problem of flexibility is not unique to New Guinea Highland scholars. Barnes himself, while questioning the utility of the African models of lineage systems which were developed in East and West Africa, drew from his own acquaintance of the Lake Region of Central Africa where optation seemed important (cf. especially Mitchell 1964 and van Velsen 1964). Many observers of Thai society have been struck by its "loose structure" (cf. Phillips 1969), and Navahos' social organization has been also characterized as flexible, especially in contrast to their Pueblo neighbors (cf. Aberle 1963). In the Dutch work on West New Guinea, particularly the lowland regions, there has been a concern with this problem ever since Held wrote his book on the Papuan as culture improvisor (1951); this concern, which has had little effect on the English-language works on the rest of Melanesia, was brought to a climax in the extended debate between Pouwer (1960a, 1960b, 1961) and van der Leeden (1960).

Probably the use of terms such as "flexible" has caused more confusion than clarification. Phillips, in his discussion of how the concept had been used with regard to the Thai materials (1969), emphasized that it is at best a descriptive generalization and in no sense an explanation. He points out that its main value lies in directing attention to the varying degrees of flexibility which may exist in different areas of a culture.

The concept of flexibility refers to two different aspects of behavior. One is the existence of alternatives or variants, and the other is the explicitness of rules which may lend some degree of predictability to the behavior. To the extent that the available alternatives of behavior can be easily predicted, the use of the term "flexibility" would cause no confusion. It is when there are no apparent rules, implicit or explicit, to govern behavior and allow prediction that flexibility becomes a problem. Aberle has likened these two situations to the linguistic concepts of conditioned variation and free variation (1963:3). The trap here is assuming that there are no rules when neither the statements of the actors not the observations of the ethnographer have yielded rules. But Barnes, in his 1962 article, was deliberately using the term optative, and not random, to describe some aspects of New Guinea Highlands social structure. A philosopher of science has discussed the difference between the falling of an object in a vacuum, which may be predicted by the use of the law of gravity, and the falling of a leaf from a tree, which is subject to many principles and may at times violate the law of gravity.

If one is accustomed to expecting explanatory devices on the order of the law of gravity (or patrilineal descent), then the more complex behavior of the leaf (or a Highland Papuan) may well seem unfathomable. The recruitment to membership in a Dani sib can be explained as the result of the rule of patrilineal descent. But, while the recruitment to membership in a Dani neighborhood can be described as flexible or the result of optation, this is no explanation. The more flexible the focus of investigation, the more difficult the explanation, and the extent to which one presses for explanation depends on one's theoretical interests and research abilities. In retrospect, I regret that my treatment of local residence and leadership recruitment go little beyond the generalization that they are flexible. It would be possible to make the kind of detailed analysis which would permit not true prediction but at least a more precise statement of the mixed lot of factors which influence Dani behavior in these fields. But this limitation does not affect the validity of the judgment that in these fields the Dani are flexible, relative to other societies.

The question of whether the Dani are flexible or not in the sense of free variation is a misleading question, if free variation means only those principles or norms of behavior which have not yet been discovered. The question might be posed in terms of the degree to which the norms of Dani behavior are explicit. Here I have the definite impression that the Dani are relatively inexplicit about their norms, but I cannot support this with a quantitative measure which has cross-cultural validity. The question can also be framed in terms of the other sense of flexibility, namely in terms of available alternatives of behavior.

The answer is illusive because, as Phillips (1969) has emphasized, the degree of flexibility within a culture varies from part to part, and because it must be made relative to a cross-cultural scale which is not available. For example, Dani marriage rigidly follows the principle of moiety exogamy, but the choice of mate (and for men, number of mates) within the opposite moiety is extremely flexible; residence is normally within the confederation or at least the alliance of birth, but choice of compound is highly variable; adult male public attire invariably includes the penis gourd, but its shape, size, and ornamentation vary considerably. But despite their limitations, these two concepts of flexibility help to bring out important principles of Dani behavior.

THE DANI OF THE DUGUM

The culture of the Dugum Dani is one of the countless variations on the general Highland Papuan theme which stretches across central New Guinea for 1,200 kilometers, from the Wissel Lakes in the west to the Owen Stanley range in the east.

The Dani will be described as they were in the ethnographic present of 1961, when regular warfare was still going on, but frequent reference will be made to subsequent events.

The well-built houses of the Dugum Dani cluster in compounds on the high, level floor of the Grand Valley. Here live some 350 of the estimated Grand Valley Dani population of 50,000. They are accomplished swineherds and gardeners, producing mainly sweet potatoes in complex ditched garden beds which they work with simple digging sticks. In April 1961, when this study began, their technology was primarily stone age, in the sense that iron and steel had only begun to replace polished stone adzes and axes. Also, in the early months of this study the area was not pacified by government forces, and war was being waged against their neighbors, the Widaia. Dugum Dani society is organized along lines of territorial political units and nonterritorial patrilineal sibs and moieties.

There are other aspects of Dani culture of particular interest: flexible political and social system; great spatial mobility within the framework of permanent settlements; an egalitarian society whose leaders have influence rather than power and which has minimal social distance between top and bottom of the society; stable population with low birth rate and low infant mortality; minimal social and economic importance of the family; minimal explicit interest in sex; minimal formal legal structure; minimal intellectual and artistic elaboration; and all of this taking place in a geographical setting which is characterized by the almost unique absence of predictable climatic changes.

An early problem in the field research was to choose an area of focus for the study. It was very soon clear that one compound, with perhaps a dozen people but a very unstable population, would be unsuitable. The "villages," or groups of compounds, soon turned out to be just clusters of compounds with no separate social reality. The next larger real territorial unit of political organization, the confederation, was too large for close attention. I finally settled on the neighborhood around the field camp. This Neighborhood is not a unit recognized by the Dani, but it is of a useful size for description. I have named it Dugum after the Dani name for the small hilly salient cutting into it from the mountain wall. On three sides the boundaries are unambiguous: to the east, the mountain wall, the edge of the Grand Valley, and the uninhabited forests; to the south, the low ridge of the Dutoba and the kilometer or so of uninhabited forest that forms the border with the friendly Walalua Alliance; to the southwest, the no-man's-land that forms the war frontier with the Widaia; only to the west and northwest is the boundary of the Neighborhood open to the rest of the confederation, and therefore in question. The Neighborhood is conceived of on the basis of interaction: it is a geographical area of gardens and compounds, and it is a group only in the loosest sense of that term, including people who live and work more within the area than outside it and who interact with each other more than with people of different areas. We may draw a geographical boundary, but the group has no corporate meaning and can be defined only as those people more associated with the neighborhood than with any other neighborhood.

This is specifically the ethnography of a single group, and only occasional references will be made to Dani societies in other areas, based on published material, casual personal observations, and personal communications from other field workers. Studies of other Dani groups which will help to clarify a "Dani pattern" are beginning to appear: Jan Broekhuijse on the Dugum and Southern Valley Dani; Denise O'Brien on the Konda (Swart) Valley Western Dani; Gordon Larson on Ilaka Western Dani; Anton Ploeg on Bokondini Western Dani; Herman Peters on Grand Valley Dani; Anwas Iskandar on the Grand Valley Dani; Herman Lantang on the Southern Dani; Myron Bromley on Grand Valley and Southern Dani; and Klaus-Friedrich Koch on the closely related Jale. A history of research in the greater Dani region appears as Appendix I.

Culturally and linguistically we may describe the people of the Dugum Neighborhood as Central or Mid-Grand Valley Dani. It may be useful to point out a few factors that have particular influence on the people of the Dugum. Their position on the edge of the Grand Valley, near an important brine pool, gives the Dugum people several advantages over their neighbors living along the Balim River in the center of the valley. Since the neighborhood includes both valley floor and the slopes of the valley wall, the Dugum Dani have both bottom land and slope gardens. Also they have ready access to the high forest, where they can easily obtain wood and vines for construction, fibers for strings, pandanus nuts, and many other products which are scarce and difficult to come by in the deforested center of the Grand Valley. The brine pool is less than an hour's walk away, and the path lies (or did until 1966) through allied confederations, so salt is readily available and is extensively used for trading with other, less fortunate groups. Further, the Dugum Dani have ready access and close relationships with the people of the Central Jalemo region, three days through the high forests to the east, from whence come valuable woods, feathers, furs, and shells. Also, the Dugum Dani fields are not subject to the periodic devastation caused by the flooding of the Balim River. While the floods can sometimes cause famine along the Balim itself, there is no indication that the food supply of the Dugum is ever threatened.

LANGUAGE

The Dani are Papuans. Until recently this was a category formed by intuition and filled by default. All cultures in New Guinea and the eastern islands *not* Melanesian divisions of Austronesian in race and culture, and especially language, were called Papuan, or non-Austronesian.

New linguistic evidence primarily from work with East New Guinea languages points to the linguistic reality of Papuan. Wurm considered nearly all the languages spoken in the Highlands Districts of East New Guinea to belong to a single phylum, the East New Guinea (Micro-) Phylum and about 96 per cent of all Highlands people to belong to one stock, the East New Guinea Highlands stock (1964:77). On the basis of a grammar for the Western Dani dialect spoken in Bokondini, just to the north of the Grand Valley, Wurm considers Dani closely related to the Stock (1964:91). Following Bromley (1967), there appears to be a single West New Guinea (Micro-) Phylum consisting of four language families: (1) Wissel Lakes-Kemandoga Language Family (including Kapauku or Ekagi, Woda, and Moni); (2) Uhunduni-Amung Language Family; (3) Dem Language Family; and (4) Greater Dani Language Family.

The Greater Dani Language Family includes the Wano Subfamily; the Ngalik-Nduga Subfamily (spoken by the Jale in the Jalemo and the "Pesegem" to the south of the Grand Valley); and the Central Dani Subfamily. The Central Dani Subfamily includes the Western Dani language and the Grand Valley Dani language. The people of the Dugum Neighborhood speak a dialect of the Grand

Valley Dani language which corresponds closely to Bromley's Mid-Grand Valley dialect.

"Dani" is a convenient term, but like so many such names, somewhat inappropriate. The Dani themselves have only recently begun to use the name, and the group referred to by the name is a linguistic group and not in any sense a political or social unit.

The origin of the name Dani is uncertain. It may be derived from the Moni or Uhunduni term *Ndani*, which they use for the Western Dani who live to the east of them. Van Nunen (1966:45) has suggested that it may be related to the Moni term *ndao* (stranger), while Bromley says that it "is derived from bilingual mispronunciation of the Western Dani indigenous term Laany for the Western Dani language" (1967:297n). ("Lani" is a Grand Valley sib name.) Ndani was used instead of Dani in some of the earlier literature. In fact, a better term for them would probably have been *aguni*, the word for people in many dialects. However, the term Dani is by now well established and there seems to be no reason not to use it. (It is, of course, conceivable that the Dani themselves will come to prefer some term of their own, in the way that the Ekagi now use that name rather than Kapauku, the more familiar but foreigner's name for them.)

DANI PREHISTORY

The problem of reconstructing Dani history is immense. Neither the Dani nor their neighbors had any written records, and they share the general New Guinea highlanders' indifference to oral historical traditions. Archaeological research should eventually produce some general indications of the Dani past, but elsewhere (Heider 1967a) I have suggested that Dani remains are meager and misleading to the archaeologist.

At first glance the very sophistication of Dani horticulture suggests that their present culture has existed in the Grand Valley for a very long time. But Watson (1965a, 1965b) has argued that the sweet potato-based Papuan cultures reached the Highlands only recently. It may turn out that Dani culture as pictured here has only existed for a century or two. Proceeding from the hypothesis that the Dani represent an incomplete and perhaps recent shift from nomadic hunting and gathering, I have speculated on functional grounds that some aspects of Dani culture seem more suited to a previous, more mobile form of culture than to their present state (cf. Heider 1967b).

CIRCUMSTANCES OF FIELD WORK (The Harvard Peabody Expedition)

The field work on which this study is based was carried out over twenty-seven months in three periods during the 1960's. I first went to the Grand Valley as a member of the Peabody Museum of Harvard University Expedition from 1961–1963 and in 1968 returned for a brief period with my wife, Eleanor R. Heider.

The present study represents one part of the results of the Harvard Peabody

Expedition. The expedition was organized and led by Robert G. Gardner, Director of the Film Study Center of the Peabody Museum, Harvard University. Gardner conceived of the expedition as the broad study of a small group, combining the traditional anthropological approach with the literary layman's impressions and the fullest possible use of modern recording instruments, still and movie cameras, and the tape recorder.

All of these approaches have been tried and proven. There are innumerable ethnographic accounts of tribal peoples; there are a few films, a few unobjectionable laymen's accounts, extensive recordings of tribal music, and many photographs. The Harvard Peabody Expedition was an attempt to focus all these different approaches at once on the same small tribal group of people.

Gardner's own role in the expedition was the cinema, and his film *Dead Birds* (1963) is in distribution. Peter Matthiessen, novelist and naturalist, has written a journal account, "Under the Mountain Wall" (1962), of the same events of war and peace which figure in the film. Michael C. Rockefeller was responsible for recording all the sounds of Dani life and also did a major portion of the still photography. After completing his part of the expedition, he undertook another expedition to collect the Asmat art of the southwest coast of New Guinea for the Museum of Primitive Art in New York, and it was there that he met his tragic death. Samuel Putnam joined the expedition briefly to assist in the still photography. Jan Broekhuijse, then a doctoral candidate in sociology and anthropology from Utrecht University, who had served in the Dutch government as District Officer in the Grand Valley and had some knowledge of the Dani, was attached to the expedition. He introduced the expedition to Dani culture and acted as interpreter, at the same time carrying out his own research for his dissertation on the Dani. The writer, at the time a doctoral candidate in the Department of Anthropology at Harvard University, also carried out anthropological research. This book represents an extensive revision of his dissertation. Eliot Elisofon, a professional photographer and Research Assistant of the Peabody Museum, joined the expedition for one month to assist with still photography. Chris Versteegh, government botanist at the Manokwari Experimental Station who had first entered the Grand Valley with the Archbold Expedition in 1938, spent a week with the expedition to identify the plants used by the Dani.

The Harvard Peabody Expedition to New Guinea began to take shape in the spring of 1960. Gardner had been making preliminary plans for an expedition and was approached by Rockefeller and Putnam, who expressed their interest. At this time Dr. J. V. De Bruijn, Director of the Kantoor voor Bevolkingszaken (Bureau of Native Affairs) of the Government of Netherlands New Guinea, visited Harvard and invited Gardner to do his field work in Netherlands New Guinea.

During the next year, while preparations for the expedition were going on in America, Broekhuijse was relieved of his administrative duties so he could carry out preliminary survey work for the expedition.

At that time Broekhuijse determined that the Gutelu area would be the most favorable in the Grand Valley for research because of its relative isolation from the influences of government and missionary activity. However, when he visited the northern part of the area and attempted to set up a long-term camp, the people asked him to leave.

Broekhuijse then turned to the southern Grand Valley, to a region called Minimo, closer to the main government post at Wamena. With the help of the policeman Abududi, the son of an important man of the Minimo area, Broekhuijse was able to spend three profitable months gaining basic knowledge about the Dani culture which would be of help to the expedition. In 1958 Abududi had been one of the first Dani to be recruited into the police force. He knew some Indonesian, and although he tended to project his own southern Grand Valley dialect and culture into his explanations of events in the midvalley area, he played a major role in the success of the expedition.

In February 1961 Gardner arrived in New Guinea to begin the main work of the expedition. Together with De Bruijn and Broekhuijse, he discussed the local situation in the Grand Valley with the government and missionary personnel, and it was determined to make another attempt to get in to the Gutelu region.

This time Gardner and Broekhuijse, with the policemen Nawas and Abududi and Abududi's wife, Wamamogen, who was also a Dani, entered the southern Gutelu region from the Christian and Missionary Alliance post at Tulem. The small party was met at the frontier by the warriors of the Gutelu, and there was some discussion about whether or not to receive the strangers. Um'ue, an important man of the Wilihiman-Walalua Confederation, seeing that this intrusion might be turned to his advantage, offered the group camping ground near his villages.

A temporary camp was established on the Anelatak Ridge. The area seemed ideal for the field station. A small grove of araucaria, a placed called Homuak, at the foot of the Dugum hill, was decided upon for an expedition campsite. It had the advantage of excellent water; it was uninhabited and large enough to absorb the camp of six or eight tents without disrupting life as thoroughly as it would have had the camp been pitched in a Dani compound.

After a week Gardner left, followed two weeks later by the rest. Rockefeller and I arrived in New Guinea in March 1961. Expedition equipment which had been shipped from Boston the previous November, together with canned and dried food bought in Hollandia, capital of Netherlands New Guinea, was flown into Wamena, the chief government and missionary settlement in the Grand Valley, some ten kilometers south of the Dugum.

On April 1, 1961, the camp at Homuak, in the center of the Dugum area, was set up. The expedition was now augmented by Jusup Kakiay, an Ambonese from Sorong, who served as cook and later made a collection of bird skins for Dr. S. Dillon Ripley, then of the Peabody Museum of Yale University. The supplies were brought by boat from Wamena, a trip of a couple of hours up the Balim and the Aikhe rivers, and then by a twenty-minute walk from the head of the Aikhe River.

In mid-April 1961 Matthiessen arrived for a four-month stay in the Dugum area. Elisofon joined the expedition for the month of May. In June and July, Rockefeller left the Grand Valley to spend several weeks, accompanied by Putnam, on his first trip among the Asmat peoples of the south coast, collecting art for the Museum of Primitive Art in New York. They returned to the High-lands in early August, and Putnam spent that month with the expedition. At the end of August 1961 the other members of the expedition left the Grand Valley and I stayed on in the Dugum. In June 1962 Gardner made a two-week visit to the Dugum.

I spent twenty-six months in the Dani area during two periods: eighteen months from April 1961 to October 1962, and eight months from April until early December 1963. During most of this time, about twenty-two months, I lived in the Dugum Neighborhood, but I also visited the Konda Valley, the Pass Valley, the Gilugui Valley, and every week or two went to Wamena. During the intervening six months in 1962–1963 I returned to Harvard to catch my breath and work over my field notes. In July 1968 my wife and I spent six weeks in the Grand Valley. We lived at the Roman Catholic Mission post at Jibiga, an hour's walk from the Dugum Neighborhood.

The expedition numbered at various times up to ten people, so to disturb local life as little as possible, a tent camp was pitched in Homuak, a few moments' walk away from three settlements. An important trading path led through the grove, and people from different areas had ready access to the camp. The major part of our food was imported in cans, but vegetables, bananas, and firewood were bought from the local people, usually for small amounts of salt or a shell or two.

After the others left, I consolidated the tent camp and continued to live in Homuak. However, toward the end of the first year the tents were beginning to rot, and Um'ue encouraged me to build a house at his compound of Wuba-kaima and move there. By then I felt a need for closer, more continuous contact with one compound. A house with sides of plaited bamboo and mosquito netting and a thatched roof was built in Wubakaima by the men of the Neighborhood, and there I lived for the final fourteen months of my field stay (cf., Pl. 45).

In 1968 we lived in a mission building at Jibiga, part of the small settlement which included a mission school, airstrip, first aid station, and police, military, and government posts just a few minutes' walk from the large Dani settlement of Jibiga, where Gutelu and other important men of the region lived.

The Grand Valley was not physically difficult. In 1968 we did suffer a series of minor ailments, but during the first two years I had remarkably good luck in this respect; and even during wartime there was never any real danger to our lives.

Although the Dugum Dani live only a couple of hours from four airstrips with their mission and government stations, in the early 1960's they had had relatively little contact with outside influences. The war frontiers made much travel tantamount to suicide, and even travel into a friendly area was potentially dangerous. These restrictions never applied to us, and we moved freely across all boundaries. During the first five months the expedition used a motorboat to bring supplies and mail to within twenty minutes of the camp. While I was alone I walked into Wamena, a two- to four-hour walk depending on the wetness of the trails, every ten days or two weeks to pick up supplies and mail and to spend the night in the small prefabricated settlement.

INFLUENCE OF THE EXPEDITION

Heisenberg's Uncertainty Principle in vulgarized form is applicable to ethnographic field work. It suggests that the observer alters the observed; that the closer one tries to observe, the more change one effects in the subject of observation. Even a single ethnographer is bound to cause some disturbance in the ethnographic situation. An expedition of ten people will necessarily cause more disturbance in the local situation. Since this influence is one of the prime factors determining the validity of the data, it is necessary to at least attempt to evaluate it.

Direct economic influence was especially obvious. Although the Dani themselves were not accustomed to direct buying of goods or services with a standard currency, they had no trouble or hesitation in accepting our use of cowrie shells and salt as money. Vegetables, especially sweet potatoes, were bought for the expedition table. People were paid for carrying supplies from the boat landing to the camp. The expedition contributed to the debasement of the cowrie shell relative to other goods such as pigs and nets which we did not provide. This debasement had been going on for several years as a result of the government and missionary posts in the Grand Valley, and especially at Wamena where several different government agencies and missionary groups were competing for the relative scarcity of food, firewood, and services. Dubbeldam (1964) has described this process in the Wissel Lakes to the west. Some indication of the Grand Valley situation is hinted at by the figures for the cowrie shell exchange value in 1938 given by Archbold. Then ten kilograms of sweet potatoes could be bought for one "average" cowrie shell, and "6–10 good ones would purchase an ordinary pig" (Archbold, Rand, and Brass 1942:253). Twenty-five years later I could buy one or two sweet potatoes for a shell, and it was impossible to buy a pig for cowrie shells at all. However, it is not very meaningful to speak of inflation of the basic subsistence part of the economy. The Dani produces all the goods he needs to live on. The cowrie shell serves decorative and religious functions. It plays a central role in the Dani ceremonial life, but only when sewn on the knitted bands used in ceremonial exchange. The production of the shell bands is limited by the time necessary to knit the band.

Other trade goods used by the expedition were Nassa (snail) and Cymbium (bailer) shells and, especially toward the end of my stay in 1963, quantities of iron and steel axes, knives, and machetes. The actual changes in the way of life made by these introductions seemed surprisingly slight.

On the other hand, the fact that most of the expedition goods were being funneled into a relatively small area certainly influenced the balance of political power in the Gutelu Alliance and perhaps beyond. The success of Um'ue and then Weteklue in gaining control over the expedition resources gave them a great edge in the struggle for political power which was politely being waged within the alliance and perhaps contributed to the temerity shown by Weteklue and Sula when in May 1961 they withheld battle trophies from Gutelu and in November 1963 actually tried to force the *ebe akho* ceremony through over Gutelu's head. (This is described in more detail on p. 78).

To what extent did the expediton influence the immediate daily life of the Dani? We shall never know, of course. The ideal anthropologist can become invisible at will in order unobtrusively to watch events. Lacking this skill, we can only watch and speculate. It is my best judgment that our presence had a minimal effect on the Dani. It was extremely easy to fade into the background of an event. When an event got under way, we were usually thoroughly ignored. We were just there. We were never specifically excluded from observing any event, but we were rarely told about an event beforehand. Apparently little was concealed, but certainly little was pointed out.

This raises the question of the relationship between the expedition and the Dani. Quite simply, we were just accepted. We were never "initiated into the tribe" or even "considered just one of them." Our status, at least at the beginning, was neutral; friendly, but above all neutral. In battles we were not shot at by either side; between battles we could travel through enemy country without being suspect; in even the most sensitive religious ceremony we did not need to be purified. A radio was a mild curiosity at first, but even that was soon ignored. Besides the regular trade goods, our flashlights, matches, mirrors, and umbrellas were appreciated and coveted for their obvious utility. We never explained the function of cameras, or showed them pictures of themselves, but this would probably have had no effect.

The Dani are above all a pragmatic and satisfied people. Those aspects of our technology which were of use to them, such as steel axes or wooden matches, were traded for; the rest ignored. Our presence was interesting and even beneficial, but no Dani ever asked, "Why are you here, what are you doing?" This attitude was reported by the first explorers to contact the Dani. Wirz describes (1924:37) the calm with which the Swart Valley Western Dani took the coming of the 1920 expedition, and a similar attitude was noted in 1938 by the Archbold expedition, which was the first expedition to enter the Grand Valley. As they descended into the Grand Valley, they walked

through many more villages and across acres of highly cultivated fields. Here the natives seemed to take our party for granted. Some stood by and watched the long line of carriers file by, while others, digging in the gardens of rich black earth, did not even look up. (Archbold, 1941:336)

I am often asked if I liked the Dani. The answer to this question is a complicated yes. I liked many individuals, particularly Um'ue and his family. But we were never friends in the usual Western sense of that term. They never understood why I was doing what I was doing, and I was always conscious of the fact that I was using them as my subjects and that the more they revealed themselves to me, the more important it was to record their words. To them I represented outside power, and they always overestimated the influence which I had with the Dutch and Indonesian governments. In 1968, when Um'ue was maneuvering to hold a pig feast apart from Gutelu, both sides tried to enlist my support, and only by living in the mission and government post of Jibiga could I maintain any sort of neutrality. Finally, I must admit that I did not really empathize with much of Dani culture. Although I was close to individuals and was excited by the theoretical problems which emerged from the study of their culture, the culture itself deemphasized aesthetics and intellectuality and emphasized war, farming, and pigs in reverse proportion to which I value those aspects of my own culture.

Although our relations with the Dani were excellent, during the first months our activities were misunderstood by some government and mission personnel. We had assumed that anthropology in general and the goals of our expedition in particular were familiar to the Europeans in the Grand Valley. Unfortunately, during the months before we arrived this information had not traveled beyond the capital at Hollandia, and we arrived in the Grand Valley preceded by more rumors than information. Assuming that what we had told Hollandia had been passed on to the Grand Valley, we proceeded directly to our field camp. In retrospect we might have spent a few more days in Wamena explaining ourselves, but at the time we did not feel the necessity for it. We sought out the most untouched part of the Grand Valley—that is, where warfare was still going on—and did not identify ourselves with either government or missions. Our desire for neutrality between the forces of change and the Dani was misinterpreted, and we were suspected of encouraging warfare in order to make a film. We had not encouraged warfare, but neither had we tried to end it. A political storm blew up that reached even The Hague. We were investigated and exonerated, but it was some months before relations with government and missionary personnel became really cordial.

In a sense, the anthropologist is in an untenable situation. In order to understand war and ritual he must be a neutral observer. But in a situation like the Grand Valley in 1961, when most Europeans and Americans were working to change the Dani way of life, it was difficult to explain this neutrality to either the Dani or the outsiders. No matter what we said or did not say, our mere interest in an activity which other outsiders were trying to suppress seemed to give support to the Dani and to work against the activities of change.

The moral of this incident is simply that an anthropologist has the responsibility to establish rapport not only with the people he is studying but also with the outsiders living in the area.

Knowledge of the Dani Language

Someone has written that the true test of fluency is to be able to understand an overheard argument between two brothers. By this criterion I was never fluent. Broekhuijse and Abududi were able to help me with the language at first, but when they left the lack of bilinguals removed the temptation to rely on interpreters and I used the Dani language exclusively. After the first few months my control of the Dani language grew to the point where I was able success-fully to handle controlled conversations.

The only linguistic data we had before arriving in the Grand Valley were some taped and transcribed words and phrases kindly furnished by the Christian and Missionary Alliance (CAMA). Once in the Grand Valley we were led astray by the simplified Police Dani developed by the Dutch and coastal New Guinea government men. Unlike such people as the French, the Dani seem to have no chauvanistic investment in the proper speaking of their language. They were quite willing to speak the simplified Dani and in fact learned it much faster than we did. I suspect that they either felt we were not capable of learning their language or that it was much simpler for them to learn our version.

This simplified language of course created great problems for the field worker. The cultural nuances possible to express by the highly inflected verb forms—van der Stap has estimated (in a personal communication) 1,680 different forms for most verbs—are obliterated by the use of one form for all situations, as in Police Dani. (Significantly, this is the present singular imperative.) Also the vocabulary is condensed into a few key words with quite an uncontrollable range of meaning which hardly reflects the complex reality. And finally, since this simplified Dani was developed in the Wamena region where the Southern Valley dialect is spoken, many of the words are different from those used in the Mid-Valley dialect spoken in the Dugum area. This Dani is indeed a primitive language, as pointed out by a recent explorer (Harrer 1963:30). He did not realize, however, that he was speaking of Police Dani rather than the language actually spoken by the Dani.

Van Nouhuys, who wrote the first ethnographic description of any Dani group on the basis of only four days' contact with the Pesegem Southern Dani in 1909–1910, suspected that the Dani did not actually use the word for sweet potato for the verb "to eat," but had simply taken over the expedition's misuse of it (1913a:253).

Simplified Dani is better than nothing, however, and I used it unwittingly until, after being in the field for nine months, I was given a grammar of the Southern Valley dialect prepared by P. van der Stap. Then I was able to begin systematically to learn Dani grammar, albeit that of a slightly different dialect. A few months later Myron Bromley of the CAMA gave me a grammar for the Mid-Valley dialect prepared in English. During the rest of my stay in New Guinea I struggled to overcome the bad speaking habits learned in the first few months. With great effort I was able to convince the people of the Dugum that I really wanted to learn the proper Dani, and a few would sometimes try to correct my grammar and vocabulary. Normal spoken Dani is very fast, and many phonemes tend to be slurred over. This makes accurate transcription difficult; and there were several phonemes which I never did control.

In the four and a half years between my second and third trips I had little opportunity to use Dani, and the prospects for a return trip were so uncertain that I spent little time reviewing the language. But to my great surprise, within a couple of weeks of my return in 1968 my knowledge of the language revived and my command of it was nearly as good as it had been five years before.

FIELD APPROACH

By far the greatest part of my time during the first twenty-six months of field work was spent in observation and recording. Sometimes this was at a ceremony or other event; usually it meant simply sitting in a house or garden, watching. Most of this observation was done in the Dugum Neighborhood.

I sometimes questioned informants systematically but with relatively little success. Until very recently there has been no other culture with which the Dani could compare their own culture. It may be that the long isolation of the Dugum Dani, the fact that they never came into contact with other cultures or other languages, is an important factor in this apparent lack of introspection. Also, they do not make their culture explicit in teaching it to their children. As we shall see later, there are no schools, no formal instruction, no wise old men sitting around relating the lore of the group. Children learn their culture primarily by observation and rarely through verbalized instruction. Thus, while I had unusually free opportunity to observe the events of Dani culture, I was unusually handicapped in eliciting formal statements about the culture.

The bulk of my formal questioning sessions in 1961–1963 was spent with Um'ue, an important man of middle age of the Wilil sib. But very little of the data here relies solely on Um'ue's testimony, and that which does is so noted. Most of the data presented here have been checked over by observation, by the use of informants in the informal settings of their homes, or conversations held with them at different places.

In 1968 I administered formal questionnaires on ethnocentrism to four men (cf. Le Vine and Campbell 1965) and Eleanor R. Heider administered psychological tests on numbers, colors, and emotion terms to several hundred people.

We plan to return to the Dani in 1970 to pursue in a more rigorous manner some of the unresolved problems which were turned up by the earlier research. In retrospect I realize how unfocussed and inefficient my first field work was. I would not want to proceed that way again myself, and I doubt that I would encourage others to try it. But this broad approach to field research did contribute to the holistic viewpoint which I have used in describing and analyzing the Dani.

In returning to the Dani I have violated the anthropological norm of doing research in a second culture as soon as (or even before) one's basic work on the first culture is written. In my own case, so many specific and general problems arose from the first work that it seemed most sensible to follow them up among the people who had generated the problems and whose language and culture I already knew. The efficiency of this strategy is considerable, and many months of ethnographic and linguistic groping have been by-passed. And, of course, I was able to gather information in 1968 which necessitated a drastic revision of my earlier work, especially on Dani warfare. Every field worker must expect and hope to be challenged and corrected by later investigators, but it is good when one can be one's own first revisor.

PART I

1

SUBSISTENCE

EACH family or compound, provided that it includes both a man and a woman, is relatively independent in terms of the subsistence economy, which is based on intensive sweet potato gardening and pig husbandry. Although there are spare-time specialists, they do not possess exclusive and necessary knowledge not available to other members of the community. The Dani of the Dugum trade mainly for nonessential, ornamental, or ritual objects, and for finer examples of materials which are available close at hand, such as fibers or wood. The only important exceptions are adze and axe blades, which must be imported. But otherwise the demands of the basic economy can be satisfied by the woods, gardens, or brine pool close at hand. However, the accessibility of these resources depends on the state of peace. The people of the Dugum have easy access to both field and forest, but the brine pool lies in the territory of a neighboring confederation, and their access to it depends on the condition of their relations with that confederation. To this extent the basic economy of the household may be considered dependent on the state of the larger group.

In contrast to the apparent economic independence of the family or compound, one is struck by the great extent to which the Dani is involved in the multiple social ties of his gregarious culture, expressed especially in the ceremonial exchange system and in the fighting patterns.

DIVISION OF LABOR

The only major divisions of labor follow the lines of sex and age. Individual importance or talents make very little difference in a person's normal range of activities. Men's work tends to be either concentrated spurts of heavy physical labor or else light craft work which can be done casually at the man's convenience, often at the same time he is visiting and gossiping with his friends. Women's work is likely to be long, tedious, and lonely.

Both the heaviest and the finest work is done by men. Cutting wood, shaping tools, construction, and the digging and maintenance of the garden ditches are done exclusively by men. Men also weave the shell bands and plait the fine women's skirts.

Even though most women have lost all but two or four fingers as funeral sacrifices, they make carrying nets and ceremonial nets; they also harvest vegetables. Men tend to do the heavy garden work, such as breaking the soil, while women usually do the planting, weeding, and cooking and have most of the responsibility for children and pigs. Otherwise, work may be done by either men or women.

Children participate in most work chores and by the age of ten may be given the care of household pigs and babies during the day. However, these responsibilities are often a point of conflict, and a child may move from his parents' household into another household because he feels he has been given too much work to do.

There is no full-time specialization among the Dani, other than in terms of age or sex, although certain people are noted for special skills at certain jobs and their help is often requested by others. As spare-time specialists, they may receive minor compensation. Some men are especially good at making arrow tips or removing arrow tips from wounded men or performing bleeding operations or leading ceremonies as an *ab wisakun* (male-curing specialist). Some women are known as *he phatphale* (female-curing specialist) or as midwives, and some are said to know how to perform abortions.

MOVEMENT OF GOODS

Movement of goods within the Dani social network may be considered under four headings: casual gifts moving within close circles of friends and neighbors; ceremonial exchange or presentation; trade; and legal restitution.

CASUAL GIFTS

Among the members of a single compound and even among close friends of different compounds there is fairly free giving and taking of minor items and usage of major items. Since ownership is clearly recognized, this is not some vague communal ownership but rather lightly held individual title. In part this may be considered hospitality, as when casual visitors are offered baked sweet potato or tobacco. Both potatoes and tobacco can be clearly traced as the property of one man or woman from the time of planting, through preparation, up to the point of consumption. But both food and tobacco are offered to whomever happens to be present in a compound at mealtime.

Small items such as feathers or a new penis gourd are often given on request, with no thought of repayment, although if the object is not consumed it may be returned to its original owner. Even the use of more valuable items such as tools or garden land is frequently transferred or loaned without ceremony or restitution.

CEREMONIAL EXCHANGE

Most circulation of goods takes place within the sphere of ceremonial exchange. This occurs primarily at various stages in the funeral and marriage ceremonies (see pp. 150-2).

RESTITUTION

Restitution constitutes a minor but steady means of circulation of goods (see pp. 150-1).

TRADE

Numerous ancient trails connect the Grand Valley Dani with Dani groups in neighboring areas. Small groups of men, women, and children laden with goods often make trips of several days through the high forests to other valleys where they have friends and relations with whom they can live while they exhange goods. The Dani have neither regular markets nor professional traders, but most people make at least one long trading trip every few years. Major trading areas are shown on Map 1.1 (p. 26).

The full extent of the trade network in the New Guinea Highlands is not yet known, but it is impressive. No cultural group has been found anywhere in the Highlands which did *not* have at least two kinds of ocean shells, the cowrie (Cypreae) and the snail (Nassa).

We can view the trade in New Guinea as flowing along the strands of a vast network of social relationships. It seems likely that every valley in the Highlands is part of this network, but it is also likely that some branches of the network are much more active than others. It may even be possible to describe spots of exceptional network activity as regional trade areas, or trade pools. Because my own research was limited to one area, I do not have the perspective necessary to recognize such trade pools. Some individual objects move in clearly defined areas, though. Adzes are a prime example of this. Adze blades from the Nogolo Basin quarry circulate eastward through the Grand Valley to the Jalemo, and although the Jalemo also gets adzes from the Star Mountain region further to the east, these Star Mountain blades do not come into the Grand Valley, even though there are trade connections between the Jalemo and the Grand Valley. The fact only emphasizes the importance of dealing with trade as a network of social relationships and not just in terms of what goods may happen to move or not move along the network.

The Grand Valley Dani trade extensively with the people to the northeast, in the various valleys of the Jalemo; on the west, they have trade connections with the Western Dani on the Upper Balim River and through them with the Dani groups of the Swart (Konda) and other rivers draining to the north (Map 1.1, p. 26 and Map C.2, p. 299). The Western Dani border on the west with the Uhunduni and Moni peoples, who in turn have close contact with the Ekagi (Kapauku), living around the Tigi-Paniai (Wissel) Lakes.

Highland trading is relatively short range. Objects are traded from hand to hand and from valley to valley. Each group has trading relations with neighboring groups, and trading parties move back and forth between neighboring groups. But few people make really long-range trading trips that pass through

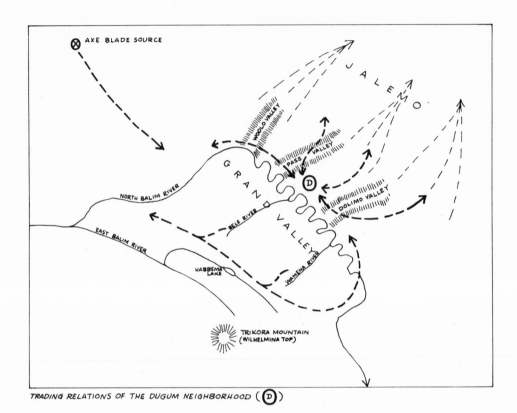

AXE BLADE SOURCE

NORTH BALIM RIVER

EAST BALIM RIVER

HABBEMA LAKE

BELE RIVER

WAMENA RIVER

GRAND VALLEY

WOOLO VALLEY

PASS VALLEY

DOLIMO VALLEY

JALEMO

TRIKORA MOUNTAIN (WILHELMINA TOP)

TRADING RELATIONS OF THE DUGUM NEIGHBORHOOD ((D))

MAP 1.1
TRADING RELATIONS OF THE DUGUM NEIGHBORHOOD

several different populations. It would be rare for an Ekagi to reach the Grand Valley on a trading trip. Undoubtedly the constant warfare inhibits long-range trade, for such traders would have little security beyond familiar territory.

There are, however, trade routes that cross long stretches of uninhabited and often very high country. Between the Grand Valley and the Central Jalemo are two or three days of uninhabited forest, and the route past Trikora Mountain (Wilhelmina Top) between the lower and upper Balim is said to take many days over the high plateau area.

The major items traded are stone, salt, and forest products. Stone for axes and adzes is from what seems to be the only quarry in the area, lying in the Nogolo Basin. Salt from the few brine pools scattered throughout the area is rare enough to be an important trade item. Forest products, such as woods, fibers, furs, and feathers are traded from thinly populated valleys to those where dense population has overexploited the forests.

The Dugum Dani have significant trading advantages over their neighbors only in respect to salt, for they have ready access to the important brine pool of Iluekaima. Those areas which do not have the advantages of quarry, forest, or brine, must rely on pigs for their trade items.

Trading Friend. There is often a special relationship between two men in different areas. This seems to have none of the formal aspects of the trading partner, which has been described from elsewhere in New Guinea (for example, Mead 1938:321 ff). The term *atek* is used as both term of address and reference by both men, and it resembles kin terms in having a plural form (*atugui*).

These trade friends do not necessarily have any traceable kin tie; theirs seems to be simple friendship with the practical advantage of providing a man with a base when visiting a neighboring area. Men of the Dugum Dani may have one or more *atugui* in the Jalemo and even in various regions of the Grand Valley itself.

Intra- and Interregional Exchange. Although there is a great deal of circulation of goods within a local area, it is primarily in the context of ritual exchange at funerals and secondarily in the form of more casual gifts and loans between friends. Circulation of this type is what Mauss called "prestation" (1925); it involves delayed exchange and has considerable effect on social solidarity in terms of ties and obligations formed by as yet-unreturned gifts.

Interarea trade is in the form of direct exchange, and although some social ties are established, especially in the form of the trading friend relationship, it is basically different from the intraarea exchange.

It is not possible to exactly define the area, but most prestation takes place within the confederation and most trading between alliances.

The Dugum Neighborhood: Surplus and Scarcity. The major surplus item used in trade by the Dugum Dani, and indeed, by all those in the Gutelu Alliance, is salt from the Iluekaima brine pool, an hour's walk from the Dugum in the territory of Gutelu's Dloko-Mabel Confederation.

Although there are a couple of poor brine pools in the southern Grand Valley of the Balim, the only other major pool in any Dani area lies far to the west, in the country of the Western Dani. Thus the people around the Iluekaima pool have an important monopoly on a valuable and necessary trade good.

The people of the Dugum prepare this brine as a bundle of hard ashy salt. They may actually take the bundles to other areas, or they may simply keep them on hand for trading to parties from elsewhere who come to their compounds.

The Dugum Neighborhood borders on the flanking forests of the Grand Valley, but these forests are regularly searched and hunted and are no longer very productive for the large population of the Grand Valley. The raw materials of the forest are imported from other areas, mainly the Jalemo. Major imports are various kinds of fibers from bushes, a thick bark cloth which is picked into fibers for net making, and bamboo, used especially for knives and containers. The most important imported wood is *dlugu*, a laurel (*Lauracea actinodaphne*), which is used for the light-colored fighting spears.

Also imported from the Jalemo are the feathers of the cassowary, various birds-of-paradise, the cockatoo, parrot, and others; and the femur of the cassowary, which is used as a knife for splitting the red pandanus fruit.

Since the Dugum Neighborhood has only sandstones, limestones, and very rarely flints, some stones must be imported, including blades for axes, adzes, and chisels, all of which come from the Nogolo quarries; large flat slaty stones used to exchange or sacred stones which come from the Jalemo; flint, from the west across the Balim and upstream; and finally, river pebbles for hammer stones, which are perhaps not actually imported but were often carried three hours from the Wamena River when Dugum people accompanied me to the government post at Wamena.

Certain manufactured goods are also imported by the Dugum Dani, notably fine nets and arrow points. Nets from the Jalemo are particularly noted for their coloring and nets with bright orchid fiber wound around the strings come from the southern and the northern Grand Valley. They are common in the Western Dani regions and may actually originate there.

Local nets are rarely as well made or colored and are practically never decorated with orchid fiber, although it is available in the forests and used in the women's skirts made by the Dugum men.

Likewise, arrows made locally are recognized by their simple barbs and lack of incised decoration. Elaborate barbed and decorated arrows are usually from the Jalemo or the Pass Valley.

In both these instances it is difficult to explain the Dugum Dani's apparent lack of craftsmanship. Certainly the raw materials are available. Poor quality nets and arrows are made, while better quality nets and arrows are desired and traded for. Once one has acquired the basic skill of net weaving or arrow carving, it would seem to be a minor step to the better kind. But the Dugum Dani do not make this step.

Rappaport has made the very interesting suggestion that trade of this sort has a sound ecological basis (1968:106). He points out that if trade were limited to necessities, salt and adzes, it would be vulnerable to accidents of supply and demand of these items alone. One area could get salt only when their trading partners needed axes, and vice versa. But if the trade also involves a substantial amount of perishable luxuries such as decorated nets and feathers, the trading activity can be maintained on a high level despite the vagaries affecting the more basic items.

It is significant that the people of the Dugum and the others of the Gutelu Alliance are the producers of salt, which has unique properties: it is both a necessity and, since it is rapidly consumable, it is in constant demand by others. The one other item that might well be called a necessity for Highland life, the stone adze blade, is not quickly consumed and so the demand for it is erratic.

If trade involved only salt and adzes, the people to the west and south of the Gutelu, who have adzes but no salt, would be able to get salt only when someone in the Gutelu happened to need an adze blade. The people of the Jalimo, who need salt and adzes, would be in an even more unfavorable position. But the people of the Gutelu desire the fine handicrafts and higher quality raw materials of the other areas, and a brisk trade is maintained.

SHELLS. The Grand Valley Dani have three sorts of shells, the small snail shell (Nassa), the cowrie shell (Cypreae), and the large bailer, or moon shell (Cymbium). Informants agreed that Nassa and cowrie shells came through the Jalemo from the north and east and bailer shells came from the south and west. Since 1909 expeditions have been entering the West New Guinea Highlands, releasing considerable numbers of shells into the local economies, and thus creating at least temporary "sources" of shells. Also it is likely that the expeditions unwittingly opened up many trade routes from the coasts into the Highlands. The establishment of permanent government and missionary posts in the Wissel Lake (Ekagi) area in the mid-1930's created an important source of shells which may have affected some of the Dani areas and at least partly obliterated former trade routes.

It is conceivable that at least some of the Cymbium shells came from an eastern trade route. Many of the old, precontact Cymbium shells worn in the Grand Valley have a perforation at the lower tip that is certainly not explainable by any current Dani use. Some informants claimed that formerly women wore these shells horizontally to hold up their breasts. Others said that before European contact, when there were not enough Nassa shells to make the long neck strips on which the Cymbium shells are now mounted, men wore them simply suspended from a neck string through a hole in the other end. However, Blokdijk reported (in a personal communication) that Cymbium shells of this sort worn by the people to the northeast of the Grand Valley, in the Ubrup-Jaffi area south of Humboldt Bay, have such a hole at the tip for suspending decorations.

Also, in the region from Western Dani to Kapauku, Cymbium shells are not worn as long scooped plates, but are cut into small rectangular pieces, so it does seem unlikely that the Dani shells could have moved unscathed and uncut through the western area.

Circulation of some goods follows a stable regional trade gradient: salt always moves away from the brine pool areas; furs and feathers always move away from the heavily forested, thinly populated areas. But some items, especially pigs, and secondarily adze blades, circulate in a more random manner, according to temporary personal or regional conditions. Pigs are traded both to and from the Jalemo by the Dugum Dani.

Jalemo. To the northeast of the Grand Valley lies a series of valleys draining down the northern slopes of the Central Highlands into the Idenburg River, which meanders through the swampy Meervlakte, or Lake Plains. The Dugum Dani call these collectively the Jalemo, and distinguish between the Amenoko Jalemo, which is a day's walk to the north through the Pass Valley, and which I call the North Jalemo; the Jalemo that is three days' walk to the east, and which I call the Central Jalemo; and the Delok Jalemo, which I call the South Jalemo, and which lies to the southeast and is so called because the men wear *delok*, multiple bamboo waist hoops which serve as armor in battle and noise makers in dance.

A major trail passes through the Dugum Neighborhood, under the Mountain Wall, into the Walilo-Alua area to the south and then runs east, leading up the narrow side valley of the Solimo. Then leaving the population behind, the trail crosses the ridges and finally drops into the Central Jalemo. To the south is a route to the South Jalemo, and to the north trails lead out both the Pass Valley and the Wodlo Valley into the North Jalemo (the upper Hablifuri), where the people called Gem live.

This central trail leads from the Solimo to the Central Jalemo, where apparently people are predominantly Grand Valley Dani, or closely related. Many Grand Valley Dani live there, and several of the people in the Dugum Neighborhood have gone to live there for a year or more. Most of the people of the Dugum Neighborhood have *atugui*, or trading friends, in the Central Jalemo and have been there on a trading trip at least once, and some go every few years. There are no specialized traders, however.

The Jalemo valleys have much greater range in altitude than the Grand Valley. Where they drop below about 1,200 meters sago grows, in addition to the cultivated sweet potato. Women from the Jalemo are readily distinguishable in the Grand Valley by their dress, a thick brushlike bundle of *gem*, grass, one in front and one behind. The few Jale women who have married into the Grand Valley retain their distinctive skirts.

Because there is more forest, fewer people, and ready access to more varied ecological zones, the Jalemo has many items that are scarce in the Grand Valley. But there is considerable demand for salt in the Jalemo, so the people of the Dugum, who are only an hour away from a large brine pool, can use salt as their main trade item with the Jalemo people.

Western Dani. Trade connections between the Grand Valley and the Upper Balim were the route by which hard adze blades were moved from their quarry area in the Nogolo, north of the Upper Balim, into the regions to the east.

At the upper, or northwestern, end of the Grand Valley there is a clear break between speakers of Grand Valley Dani and speakers of Western Dani. The most obvious trade connections lie along the Balim Valley itself. There are also long-range trade routes which lead from the upper Balim over the high, unpopulated plateau past Lake Habbema, over the flanks of Wilhelmina Top (Trikora), and enter the Grand Valley through the Bele or Wamena valleys, or actually meet the westward-flowing Balim below the Grand Valley and move back up it.

Larson has told (in a personal communication) of meeting Grand Valley Dani at Ilaka who have used this route, spending twenty days or so away from the village areas. The Archbold Expedition of 1938–1939 followed the trail on the stretch between Habbema Lake and Wilhelmina Top, reporting that in one spot it crossed a 3,800-meter pass and that the trail at places was worn shoulder-deep into the ground.

In 1963 when visiting the Gilugui Valley, which lies some ten kilometers below the Grand Valley, Denise O'Brien found that her Western Dani dialect, which was useless in the Grand Valley, was readily understood by the Gilugui people because of their close trade connections over the high trail.

At least one important innovation, the *hesilum* dance, which has sexual overtones, spread from the Western Dani on the upper Balim to the Grand Valley not simply downstream, but over the high route and then upstream into the Grand Valley. Van der Stap, who observed its progress, reported (in a personal communication) that it was then stopped at Wamena by a district officer who was concerned by its moral implications.

HORTICULTURE

Crops

The staple food of the Dani is the sweet potato (*hibiti*). This accounts for about 90 per cent of the Dani diet. The sweet potatoes fall into two major categories: some have grayish or cream-colored meat, and others, called explicitly *hibiti modla* (light), have yellow to orange meat. The sweet potatoes range in size from small ones fed to pigs to the large ones eaten primarily at ceremonies and which may weigh as much as two kilograms. The tuber is practically never eaten raw but is either roasted in the coals or steamed in the steam pit. The leaf of the young vine is also eaten steamed and tastes somewhat like spinach. However, those vines growing in the Neighborhood are *wusa*, taboo, and cannot be eaten. The leaves that are eaten in the Neighborhood come from gardens along the Elogeta River.

Two other tubers are also eaten: taro (*hom*), a larger, drier tuber, and yam (*bain*), a smaller tuber whose vines are trained up poles. Like the sweet potato, yam and taro are both roasted and steamed. In neither case are the leaves eaten, although the broad "elephant ear" leaf of the taro is used for wrapping bundles, and by the men as a temporary head covering when working, or in bad rain or hot sun.

Two plants are cultivated especially as greens but are not a staple part of the diet: *hela*, a mallow, grown commonly near or in villages; and *wenali*, a pea whose leaves and pods occur rarely in compound gardens. Both are steamed.

Ginger (*hide*) is the only vegetal condiment. It is grown in village gardens and is eaten raw, often with salt or brine. A small cucumber (*gilu*), grown most frequently in the hill gardens, is eaten raw, casually between regular meals.

Two closely related kinds of gourds are grown. One produces the long thin fruit used for penis gourds. The other produces a squatter fruit used for water flasks. Either of these may be steamed and eaten.

Tobacco (*hanom*), which is cured and smoked in a cigarettelike wrapper, is usually grown in the compound gardens.

Banana is the only regularly cultivated fruit. It is grown exclusively in the village gardens, where it grows tall and treelike, shading the houses and breaking the force of the winds which often sweep up the valley from the south. The fruit of the banana is usually eaten raw but is occasionally roasted or steamed. Practically the entire banana plant is utilized in some way. The dried outer bark (*gisakpel*) is the universal wrapper. Soft and flexible, it makes small envelopes for feathers or large bundles for pig meat or trade goods. The packages are tied with a strip of the same bark. The trunk of the banana plant may be cut into sections as a pillow or other support for a wounded or sick person, and is used to make the frame for a corpse to sit in during the morning of the cremation if the corpse is not laid in a chair in the yard. Thick segments of the trunk are peeled apart, dried, soaked in the brine of the salt well, again dried, and finally burned to produce salty ash. Banana leaves are also used as wrapping, in particular for bundles which are steamed. They are used at certain levels in the steam bundle to hold in the steam; they are used as temporary rain hats or to keep rain from freshly butchered meat. The bud of the fruit stalk is sometimes dragged around on a string by little girls, who call it *wam-wam*, or pig-pig. Some kinds of bananas are taboo for one moiety.

The trees of the *daik* pandanus, which yield a large red fruit whose juice is eaten on tubers, are sometimes planted in village gardens. However, the *daluga* and *duge* pandanus, which have nuts, grow wild in the forests. Each pandanus tree is owned by a particular man and tended and eventually harvested by him.

As would be expected of a culture where agriculture is a major occupation for the entire population, the vocabulary of agriculture is enormous. There are generic names for the fourteen different cultivated plants, and also specific names for varieties of these plants:

			Named varieties
sweet potato	*Ipomoea batatas*	*hibiti*	70+
taro	*Alocasia* sp.	*hom*	21
yams	*Dioscorea* sp.	*bain*	13
(a mallow)	*Abelmoschus manichot*	*hela*	1
(a pea)	*Psophocarpus tetragonolobus*	*wenali*	4
ginger	*Zingiber officinale*	*hide*	1
cucumber	*Cucumis satavis*	*gilu*	2
gourd	*Cucumis* (?)	*gijo*	2
tobacco	*Nicotiana* sp.	*hanom*	9
banana	*Musa* sp.	*hagi*	16
red pandanus	*Pandanacea*	*daik*	1
nut pandanus	*Pandanacea*	*duge, daluga*	2
sugar cane	*Saccharum officinarum*	*el*	8
thick-stemmed grass	*Setaria palmifolia*	*doa*	18

It is difficult to account for the large number of names for sweet potato varieties. It is well known that New Guinea Highland peoples have many names for sweet potato, and to some extent this is hardly surprising. Languages may be expected to elaborate vocabulary in areas of special interests. Just as Eskimos and skiers have several words for different sorts of snow, and Arabs for different sorts of camels, so Dani have several words for sweet potatoes.

In 1968 I performed a simple experiment to see how consistently the terms for sweet potato varieties were used. A woman who seemed unusually competent was asked to name each tuber in a pile of several dozen. Twenty-eight different kinds were found and labeled with numbers. Then four groups of two or three women and girls were asked to name each of the twenty-eight sweet potatoes. Although sometimes a group would momentarily disagree on a particular sweet potato, in every case the disagreement was quickly resolved and a single name firmly agreed upon. Earlier in a similar experiment I had used men and boys. They had been often hesitant, carefully examining each tuber and sometimes scratching into the flesh before making an identification. But the women were confident and made their identifications on the basis of surface appearances alone.

So twenty-eight tubers were identified five times by the sweet potato specialists in a culture which specializes in sweet potatoes. But these five groups were unanimous on only five tubers; four of the five groups agreed on another five; and eighteen tubers were identified with less consistency. So, although there are more than seventy terms for sweet potatoes, they are used with considerable imprecision. Even the figure of seventy is more a reflection of collective vocabulary. Individual women seem to use only forty to fifty names. But it is hard to explain even forty names. A few kinds of potatoes are recognized as tasting especially good and a few as being only fit for pig food. If the different varieties had different susceptibility to flood, drought, or disease, there would be an obvious insurance value in growing a large number of varieties; and if the Dani were aware of this, then names for the different varieties would be useful for planning the planting. But they explicitly deny that the different varieties have different susceptibilities; and in any case, as we have seen, the names are not used consistently for the varieties. In short, the large number of names and their use raise tantalizing questions about Dani language and horticulture.

Types of Gardens

Within the Neighborhood there are three main types of gardens: the extensive ditched gardens on the low, level floor of the Grand Valley; the gardens at the compounds; and the hill slope gardens. (Occasionally a few tubers or gourds or ginger are grown in tiny plots by the watchtower shelters.)

Valley Floor Gardens (Plates 2, 3, 4). The flat gardens are the source of most of the food. They are laid out in large low-lying level areas on the floor of the Grand Valley stretching out in front of the villages. Through this area, separating one group of gardens from the next, are several meandering, causeway-like features. Geologically their origin is uncertain. They are called *dom ake*, mountain tail. Ranging from twenty-five to one hundred meters broad and two

PLATE 2. The Dugum Gardens. Looking from the Dugum Hill across the sweet potato gardens of the Dugum Neighborhood towards the southwestern wall of the Grand Valley. To the right are the compounds of Mabilatma.

to four meters above the level of the gardens, they are made of soil free of stone or sand and support high grass and occasional bush. They are frequently burned over so the grass cannot be used as cover for an enemy raid, but they are not cultivated. Most of the watchtowers are situated on this high land, and where it extends into no-man's-land it is the scene of battles. From the air they resemble a pattern of streams that drain into the Aikhe River and the Balim, but from the ground they are seen as the reverse of a stream bed, a raised flat-topped ridge.

Below and between them lie the valley floor gardens, cut by a labyrinth of ditches. The major crop of the flat gardens is sweet potato; also taro, yam, and very rarely, tobacco are planted here.

Compound Gardens. In the compound areas, crops are grown in three places: the *hagiloma,* the banana yard between the inner and outer fences of the village where bananas, sugar cane, gourds, and sometimes small amounts of the other crops are planted; in the *maikmo,* the area inside the courtyard immediately adjacent to the houses and fences, are grown taro, tobacco, and gourds. Sometimes small gardens of a few dozen square meters are cleared and fenced just outside the entrance to the compound and grow tobacco, and sometimes mallow and yam.

Slope Gardens (Plate 5). The mountain gardens are on the hill slopes behind the villages. These are classic slash-and-burn gardens, hacked out of the forest, often with the skeletons of the larger trees left standing. Poles pegged to the ground act as retaining walls. Here the same crops are grown as in the flat gardens, but with more emphasis on taro and cucumber than sweet potato.

Ownership

In the flat garden areas a few men have vague residual rights over large areas of land. This land is loaned without compensation to other men or women who work a garden. Most men, some women, and even a few boys have such gardens which are in practice their own, but the ultimate ownership of the important man is recognized. This ownership usually passes from father to son.

Other, smaller pieces of land may be passed quite casually and without compensation from one man to another. Disputes arising over land use are rare.

Women do much of the work in a garden owned by a male relative, husband, son, or brother; women may also have a garden area of their own and call their men to do the heavy work for it.

Although usage and harvesting rights are held by individuals, because of the pattern of hospitality the produce from a particular garden will eventually be eaten by many people outside the household of the person whose garden it is.

On the hill slopes, gardens are chopped from the forest. Ownership of these hill slopes is much less clearly defined. It is said that a certain sib has control of a certain mountain; in practice, the hill garden belongs to the man who clears and works it. The only limitation is that a man would not attempt to

PLATE 3. Air view of gardens. Most beds have newly-planted sweet potato mounds, and others are about to be planted.

PLATE 4. Air view of gardens. On the left, fallow land with traces of old garden ditches; in the center, cleared land; at bottom, the soil has been turned, and on the right are newly-planted beds.

37

PLATE 5. Slope Garden. Men work on a large slope garden high above the Valley floor.

PLATE 6. Terraced gardens on the lower Balim where, some 20 kilometers below the Dugum Neighborhood, the Grand Valley ends and the Balim River cuts through a steep gorge.

clear a garden in an area where he had enemies who might object to his presence.

Each person will have gardens in several different areas and in different stages of development. Most adults have two or three active gardens in the flat area, specialized village gardens, and often one or more strips in the hill area. In most cases the garden areas of those living in the Dugum Neighborhood are in the Neighborhood, but a number of people have gardens outside the Neighborhood, in the Elogeta region. These latter are important as a source of sweet potato leaves, for the leaves from the neighborhood gardens cannot be eaten because of supernatural restrictions.

Division of Labor

Three stages of the garden cycle are done exclusively by men: chopping the heavier trees and shrubs in clearing, and fence building, both of which involve the use of the adze, which is rarely handled by women; and the mudding and ditch clearing. Women never enter the ditches, apparently because of supernatural restriction.

The only task done exclusively by women is the harvesting. In theory, women also do the planting (an unmarried man will ask a female relative of his to plant his gardens); but in fact I often saw men planting.

Generally the men use the heavy digging stick to break the soil and women use their own digging sticks to maintain the garden after it is planted, loosening the crusted top soil, weeding, and thinning out the sweet potato vines. Men and women often work in the same garden at the same time, but rarely do the same job or even talk with each other. A group of men or a group of women will talk freely, laughing and joking among themselves, but they almost never sing.

No men in the Neighborhood are exempt from garden work. Even Weteklue, the most important man of the confederation, whose name implies that he never works, does work in gardens. (The people of the Neighborhood claim that Maikmo, an important Himan on the Elogeta, and Gutelu, the most important man of the alliance, do not work in gardens. However, in 1968 I saw Gutelu doing garden work.)

Jogo (Cooperative Work Party)

When a man has broken the soil of his garden, and just before or just after the planting, the garden is smeared with mud dug from adjacent ditches. This is usually done by a work crew (jogo) summoned by the man. The crew may be as large as fifteen men and boys. About noon the wives or compound women involved in the garden steam sweet potatoes and bring them for the workers to eat. There is no other payment, but those who have worked for the man are able to call the man to help with similar work on their own gardens. Such a work crew is not a stable group. Rather, a man will call those living near him and those with nearby gardens.

VALLEY FLOOR GARDEN CYCLE

On the valley floor, gardens have at one time or another occupied all suitable land. Perhaps half of this land at any one time lies fallow. To start a new garden, the first step is to clear the cover, grass, bushes or small trees off the old, fallow gardens. This work is done by men. First, with adzes, they chop the trees and bushes near the base; then with heavy digging sticks they cut the grass at the roots and dig out the roots of the trees and bushes.

If the garden approach is through other gardens, bridges over the ditches will probably have to be rebuilt. Such garden bridges are temporary, maintained only as long as the intensive work on the garden continues. Bridges usually are simply logs thrown from bank to bank; occasionally they are supported in the center by a crotched pole sunk in the mud of the ditch bottom, and some-times a pole is stuck in the mud beside a bridge as a handhold when crossing.

The cleared vegetation is allowed to dry for a few days, then heaped together and burned. The sod is broken and the top layer turned with the heavy digging sticks. This is primarily men's work, although women often help, and may involve a cooperative project (Plate 7).

Mudding may take place before and/or after the planting, and it is usually done by a work crew. During the fallow phase of the garden cycle, the ditches have filled up with a muddy mixture of washed off topsoil and rotting vegetal material. This solution is put onto the garden beds to refertilize them and to clear out the ditches. Some men stand in the ditches, up to their waist in water and mud, cutting into the mud with the broad-bladed digging sticks and heaving it onto the banks with their hands; other men or women on the banks then spread this mud out evenly with their feet.

Planting is usually done by women, using a slender, short digging stick. A small mound, about forty centimeters high, is scraped together; a shoot of sweet potato vine, cut that morning from another mature vine, is then tucked into the earth; two vines are usually planted per mound. Taro shoots, the tubers having been cut off, are planted by making a shallow hole in the ground and inserting the root. Taro is planted primarily on the edge of the ditch, above the water level, though some taro may be planted in the mud of the ditch.

Mud is usually spread over the newly planted mounds. Then a few days later, when the mud has dried and cracked, a woman with a light digging stick breaks the soil. During the following months women make occasional visits to the garden to dig up weeds or, when the vines grow large, to thin them out by trimming off the ends of the vine creepers.

Harvesting continues over a period of several months. Usually a woman or girl will stop at the garden on her way to another, prod in the mounds with her thin digging stick seeking large tubers, and dig them up. When the harvesting is finished, pigs are often let run in the gardens to eat the remaining small tubers. These may be the pigs of the user of the garden or, by explicit agree-ment, the pigs of someone else.

PLATE 7. A cooperative work crew of men and boys open a garden, using heavy fire-hardened digging sticks to turn the sod.

Now the field is let lie fallow for some time. There is no standard time of fallow: some fields are reused when they have only been covered with high grass; other fields, covered with small trees, are not opened although they are in a safe area and owned by a man who is opening other fields with shorter fallow time.

Although about half the ditched land in the Neighborhood is fallow at any one time, it is all used. Most of the land in use between 1961 and 1963 was fallow in 1968, and vice versa. Although I did not attempt to measure the relations of carrying capacity of land to population, it appears that there is a favorable balance and that the Neighborhood is neither underpopulated nor overpopulated.

There is no standard time or schedule for any of these operations; often the field will be cleared, burned, dug up, and then simply let lie. Planting in particular tends to be staggered even on the same plot. Often as the field is being dug up a few taro and a few mounds of sweet potato are planted, usually along the ditch; rarely is a single plot planted at once, but even in an area of several dozen square meters the planting may continue in spurts over a period of several weeks.

GARDEN DITCHES

Nowhere does the sophistication of Dani agriculture become more apparent than in the system of ditches that interlace all the valley floor garden beds. These ditches, filled with fertile mud and often standing water, constitute some 20 to 40 per cent of the total flat garden area. Aerial photographs give a good idea of the great extent of the ditch systems (Plates 2, 13). In some parts of the Grand Valley garden ditches are laid out with great regularity, but in the Dugum Neighborhood they wind and turn in labyrinthine fashion.

The ditches are rarely less than two meters broad, and often the main ditches are five meters in breadth. Because of the muddy bottoms of the ditches in use, the depth is hard to measure exactly, but often the head of a man standing in a ditch does not reach above the adjacent garden bed.

Probably the ditches were originally dug to reclaim the land from the swamps of the valley floor. In the southern corner of the Dugum Neighborhood this process is still under way, and after peace was established in 1961 by the government along the Widaia frontier, men of the Dugum reopened old gardens in no-man's-land and pushed garden areas into the swampy Hetaie area. By 1968, after several years of continuous cultivation, the garden beds in this area were firm and dry.

The ditches also serve for both drainage and irrigation. During long periods of rain the ditches collect the run-off and protect the sweet potato beds from flooding somewhat. During dry periods the few streams that run into the ditch systems can be channeled to bring some moisture to the sweet potato roots.

Probably the most important function of the ditches is fertilization. The topsoil washed from the sweet potato beds, together with garden trash, sweet potato vine cuttings, and the weeds growing in the ditches, combine to form a rich mud deposit. When this mud is smeared onto the sweet potato beds at the time of planting, it does much to restore and maintain the fertility of the none-too-fertile soil.

GARDEN MAGIC

Some ceremonial activity relating to gardens is described elsewhere: the "ghost bridge" structure to ward ghosts away from gardens (p. 138); the various rituals designed to control rain (p. 214); and the mock garden battle (p. 163). Other ritual activity, which is unique for gardens, is described below.

Cave-In Knots. Often when a new garden area with especially steep ditch sides is finished, several reeds, with their leaves knotted, are planted in the garden beds beside the ditches.

Informants explain that these are to dry out the newly mudded walls of the ditches so they will not cave in. One informant said the knotted reeds were especially directed at a spirit named Domakei that lived in the ditch water and would pull at the ditch walls.

Garden Arch. When a new garden area is opened or an old fallow area reopened, an arch of saplings about 1.5 meters high is erected by the most important man involved in the new garden at one edge of the area just before the planting. A bundle of various kinds of grasses is put between the legs of the arch and pinned to the ground by hoops of thin branches.

Although I often came across the arch itself, I never observed the ritual involved in erecting it. However, one informant explained its symbolism: The grass bundle constitutes a kind of home (*ai*) for the soul, or essence (*akotakun*), of the sweet potato which is about to be planted. The grass is called *al ega* (*al*, anus; *ega*, leaf) and corresponds in name and function to the grass laid under a baby in a carrying net. When the ghosts and spirits come to look, they find the *akotakun* in place, and they are satisfied; and the sweet potatoes grow large. If the *akotakun* has no home, the sweet potatoes do not grow. Then as the sweet potatoes grow their soul essence moves to the tubers themselves in the gardens.

There is an obvious symbolic analogy between the baby in its grass-lined net, which slowly develops a soul matter called *edai-egen*, and this description of the sweet potato.

The garden arch, although similar in form to the funeral arch (p. 159), resembles it functionally only to the extent that both are related to ghosts and vaguely with food.

First Fruits. Near the garden arch a mound is prepared and many sweet potato cuttings planted in it before the new garden beds themselves are planted.

The ritual involving the harvesting of this first produce was described by one informant. Women dig up the tubers and steam them. The men eat the largest, and the smallest are given to the women and pigs. These sweet potatoes are called *hibiti juguk*, but they are also referred to as *ninakoja*, our mother, because they feed people the way a mother does.

TOBACCO

Tobacco (*hanom*) is grown and cured primarily by men but is smoked by both men and women. Nearly every adult Dani smokes. The only exception are the senile men. Tobacco is usually grown in small fenced-in gardens in or by the compounds, although rarely it is planted in the garden areas proper.

After the leaves are plucked they are brought into the house. The medial vein is stripped at the tip but left attached at the basal end, and the leaves are strung on short bamboo splints, several to a splint, and hung on a pole in a house to dry for several days. Then they are taken down and laid on a broad board, usually the door board; each leaf is laid out carefully to make a mass of leaves; then these are kneaded, matted down with the palm of the hand

and then with the feet (the man crouching over because of the low ceiling). Then the mass is rolled up, starting at one corner and twisted tightly. It may then be left as a long roll, or may be wound around a bamboo length to make a coil and tied for a day or so. The roll is then wrapped in banana bark and hung behind the fireplace for a few days to cure further.

Tobacco is made into cigarettes wrapped in one of various leaves, usually a spurge, *lisaniga* (Euphorbiacea *Acalypha*, sp.) gathered in the forest and dried in presses. To make the cigarette, the leaf is first licked and then rubbed on the thigh; one corner is folded to make a trough; a pinch of tobacco is scraped with the thumbnail from the tobacco roll; the leaf is then folded over and over; then pressed, often inside the knee. When a man is going out of the house, he may take his tobacco roll and leaves; but he usually makes up several cigarettes which he puts under his arm band, in his ear hole, or in the hair above his ears. The cigarette is usually lighted by being held to a burning coal. Seldom is it held in the mouth while lighting. When a Dani smokes, he takes smoke into his mouth, allows some to escape, then draws the rest drawn back with a quick snap, *hut!*, inhaling some tobacco. When the cigarette is smoked down to about one centimeter, he throws it into the hearth ashes and covers it up. At some curing ceremonies the butts are carefully saved, since the smoke would disturb the nearby ghosts, and only later burned in a fire behind the men's house.

SALT

There are two source of salt for the Grand Valley Dani: one on the western slopes of the Southern Valley, in the Gutima region; another, called Iluekaima (*ilue*, salt; *ai*, water; *ma*, place) in Mid-Valley, on the eastern slopes of the territory of the Gutelu Alliance.

There are several access routes to the brine pool. One from the floor of the Grand Valley, passing through the territory of the Dloko-Mabel, is safe only for those who are allied with the Wilihiman-Walalua. There is also a mountain route from the Pass Valley, to the northwest; a mountain route from the Jalemo to the east; and an alternative route from the Grand Valley, from the south, which passes above the mountain wall.

The people of the Neighborhood, being allied to the Dloko-Mabel, have free access to the brine pool by the easiest route, that across the valley floor. It is possible for them to make the round trip to the pool in three or four hours.

Preparation of the salt is left exclusively to the women. Men or youths may and usually do make the trip to the pool with the women, offering companionship and protection, and often carry containers for brine, but otherwise salt is women's work.

Usually several women of one compound or a couple of compounds make the trip to the pool together. The route leads across the gardens for an hour, to the place where the narrow valley debauches steeply into the Grand Valley.

PLATE 8. Women stand in the Iluekainma brine pool soaking up the brine in strips of banana trunk.

Here the trail climbs steeply for a twenty minute walk over rocks smoothened by countless bare feet, crossing back and forth over the small stream, slowly rising high into the moss forest above the Valley floor. The brine pool, which lies beside the stream, is 10 meters in diameter and less than a meter deep.

Most brine is collected by soaking the salt water in banana trunk at the pool. The trunk of the banana plant is cut down and beaten to separate the sheaves of the trunk, which are thick, honeycomblike structures. These are dried in the sun for several days, then bundled up and carried to the well. The women wade into the pool and stand there, working the brine into the spongy banana trunk strips (Plate 8). Carried back to the compound, the strips are laid out to dry on fence and house thatch. After a few days of sun, the strips are taken to one of several rocks in the bush away from the compounds and here set afire. They slowly burn down to ash. The ash is put into a bark dish. The women sprinkle water on the ash and knead it into cakes, which they wrap in banana bark (*gisakpel*). After a few days these cakes are rock hard. When they are to be used, the wrapper is peeled back and a bit of the cake is scraped off as powder on the meat or vegetable to be eaten. The cakes are used locally or traded.

Especially if men accompany the women to the well, the briny water itself is brought back, either in gourds, or in lengths of bamboo. The brine is usually consumed by men, who either drink it straight from the container or wrap spinachlike leaves thoroughly soaked in the brine in bundles, steam these in a steam pit, then eat them in the men's house. Usually ginger is also eaten with the brine-steamed leaves.

PLATE 9. Men lay the base grass in the steam bundle pit.

PLATE 10. Women and girls build up the steam bundle with alternating layers of grass, pork, vegetables, ferns and heated rocks. Water is poured on the rocks to make steam.

FOOD PREPARATION

Dani meals, eaten in the compounds in the morning and evening, consist simply and monotonously of roasted sweet potato. When people go to work in the gardens during the day, they usually take along a baked sweet potato or two to eat cold at midday. In addition, every few days the women of a household cook potatoes and greens in a small steam bundle; and most people attend a ceremony of some sort every week or two, where they eat a few chunks of pork.

Roasting or baking is the common manner of cooking the ordinary meal. Pig meat is sometimes simply roasted over a fire; sweet potatoes and other tubers are briefly roasted on the coals and then thrust into the ashes to bake for thirty minutes to an hour.

Food may also be steamed with heated rocks in a grass-wrapped bundle set in a pit (*bakte*). The rocks are fine grain limestone collected from the Dugum hillsides. The rock fire is made up with large logs set crosswise in the yard. First a layer of stones is laid down on the ground, then the logs built up and another layer of rocks laid down over it. This fire is lit, and allowed to burn down for about an hour.

Meanwhile, the pit is prepared; if a new pit is to be dug, it is dug by the men with digging sticks. If an old pit is used, the grass from the last steaming is removed and any collected water is scooped out. A layer of long grass is laid down from the center of the pit, overlapping the edges and extending out a meter or so beyond the hole (Plate 9); this grass is eventually bunched over the top and used to bundle up the steamings.

When the rocks are hot and the food assembled, the process of building up the steam bundle is begun. This is usually done by both men and women. Long tongs (*hibpa*) are used to carry the hot rocks from the fire to the pit; rocks, ferns, meat, leaves, are laid down in alternating layers; at several stages banana leaves are laid down to capture the steam; sometimes water is poured on the rocks from a gourd to make them steam (Plate 10). When the mass has been built up above the ground level, the grass is flipped in, over the top, and the first binding is made. A digging stick is planted in the ground at the edge of the mass and heavy vines are tied around it and then wound around the mass several times. Then this is fixed, the grass is opened up again, and the building up of alternating layers continues. When this is finally finished, the grass is again flipped over the top of the bundle, the binding is continued up to the top, and perhaps a board or two is laid on top to hold in the steam and keep off rain. The process of building up layers may take an hour; the steaming usually continues for another hour. When the steam bundle is opened, it is unwound, the binding removed, the stones, now cool enough to be handled, are tossed to the side and the food set out for distribution.

THE TOTAL PIG

Pigs are basic to Dani culture. That the pig is the only important domestic animal of the Dani and the only regular source of meat is almost incidental. It may even be, as Rappaport has suggested for the Maring (1968:62), that although pigs convert carbohydrates into valuable protein and fat, their total contribution of energy to men is less than the energy men expend in raising the pigs in the first place. But to consider pigs only in terms of their contribution to the Dani food supply is to miss the total impact of pigs on Dani life.

One of the first words the Dani baby learns after *pa-pa* (father) and *da-da* (mother) is *ma-ma*, a baby's version of *wam*, pig. Small pigs are his companions on the floor of the common cooking house and the first creatures with which he can deal as equals. His first important responsibility, when he is a few years older, is the herding of his family's pigs.

Although the importance of a man cannot be judged solely by the number of pigs in his herd, the possession and presentation of pigs is essential to his importance.

Nearly every ceremony involves eating pig meat, and pigs are rarely eaten except in ceremonial contexts. The desperate squeals of dying pigs are markers in Dani life, for the ceremonies of birth, marriage, curing, and death all necessitate the giving and eating of pigs.

The general word for pig is *wam*. Another word, *akho*, is used with the bound possessive pronoun (*nakho*, my pig) and in certain ceremonial contexts. The major ceremony that climaxes a ceremonial cycle is called *ebe akho*. *Ebe* means body, or perhaps main or principal.

DESCRIPTION

Pigs are distinguished in terms of color: *modla*, or light-skinned pigs; *mili*, dark or black pigs; and *bima*, which are generally reddish-brown. When young, *bima* pigs have lateral strips down the back, rather like a chipmunk, which gradually fade with age. *Bima* are fairly rare, but pigs are not preferred on the basis of color.

Spotted black and white pigs are called *dakabe*, and dark pigs with white bellies are called *wilehasu*.

Pigs are given individual names around the time they are weaned. Sometimes litter mates receive the same names. The pigs rarely have names of people.

OWNERSHIP

Pigs are said to belong to individual men, women, or children. Often a man will at least nominally transfer ownership of a small pig to one of his children who does most of the herding. However, the eventual decision of the disposal of the pig—that is, the decision to kill it at a particular ceremony—lies with the man of the household. All the pigs of a single household are kept together in a single herd, live in the same pig sty, and are driven out together.

CARE

Pigs spend the night in the stalls of the pig sty in the compound itself. Each pig has its own stall, except for unweaned shoats and small litter mates. The exception is shoats that are ill or whose mother has been killed, which are cared for during the day by women and left in the small stall inside a woman's house during the night.

In the morning the pigs are let out of the sty. Usually they circulate around the yard, eating potato skins that have been thrown out of the houses from the first meal of the day; then, between seven and nine o'clock they are driven out of the compound, usually by a child but often by an adult, to the place where they are currently rooting. If it is raining or if for some reason such as a ceremony the people are busy, the pigs will not be taken to root, but they are usually let out of the compound for a few moments to defecate. They also defecate in the courtyard, but seldom in the sty itself.

For several hours they root either in a fallow field or in the woods. Usually someone stays close by. The pigs may be near a working man; or a child may be delegated to stay with them, keeping them from straying. Usually the child himself strays, to play with other children or just to relieve his boredom. Such negligence is a major cause of friction between parents and children.

In the afternoon the pigs are herded back to the compound where they may be put directly into the stalls or allowed to wander around the courtyard. By dusk they are shut in the stalls, where usually a few kilos of the smallest potatoes are thrown in for them to eat.

A few compounds have special pig runs, fenced areas in the banana yard where pigs can run and root. These are quickly worked out by the pigs and in fact are seldom used.

In many paths there are mud holes, fifty centimeters deep and up to one meter long, which are dug with heavy digging sticks by men. During wet periods these fill with water and mud, and pigs wallow in them.

The chronic ailment of pigs is sores in the skin from the bites of rodents at night. It is common in the morning to see pigs with several of these sores, several centimeters wide, raw but not bleeding. These are treated (by either men or women) by plastering araucaria pitch over the wound and then sprinkling the pitch with ashes from the fire.

The ears of pigs are usually cut with bamboo knives after they are weaned, often in connection with some ceremony or with castration. Ear cutting is said to help the pigs grow. Most of the ear is left, to be removed during the butchering. There are four different patterns of ear cutting. The first, simply called *balek* (cut), is the cutting off of the tip of the ear. All female shoats are treated in this manner. Male shoats' ears may be cut in three different ways: (1) *gakalhek* (split)—the ear sliced in two, but no piece removed; (2) *asuk ganok balek*—a cut starting from one side and then bending out to the tip, leaving a kind of tail; (3) *ideak oba bpialek* (cut to the *ideak*, or mandible)— the tip of the ear cut off and then a slice made into the base.

Several men use each pattern in cutting their pigs' ears, and some men use more than one. The patterns are not unique owners' marks but do help identify the pigs.

Most male pigs a few weeks old are castrated. The stated reasons are to make the pig grow larger and produce large tusks, to keep it from running away after female pigs, and to remove it from the breeding pool.

The pig is held head down in the yard; usually it takes several people to hold it still and hold its mouth shut to reduce its squealing. The operator, a man, slices through the scrotum with a bamboo knife just to the rear of one testicle, removes the testicle with a bone awl, cuts the cord with the knife, lays the testicle on a leaf on the ground, pushes the end of the cord back into the cut, and pins the scrotum together in a couple of places with bamboo splints. The operation is repeated for the second testicle. Ashes are sometimes sprinkled on the wounds; if the ear tips have not already been sliced off, they are now sliced; and the pig is put on the ground, to run off its pain, ignored. The testicles and ear pieces are roasted in the coals of a fire and eaten without ceremony, usually by any children who might have been watching.

Another operation, whose effect I cannot explain at all, is performed on female pigs after they have been weaned: The pig is laid on the ground on its back; at a point midway down its belly, between the midline and the teat line, a man using a bamboo knife makes a lateral incision about two centimeters long through the skin; with a bone awl he probes into the cut and finally draws out a thin white cord from the body; this is severed, and the ends are pushed back into the cut; the same operation is performed on the other side of the stomach of the pig; accumulated blood is smeared on the stomach; mud or ashes may be smeared on the wounds; if the pig has not previously had its ears sliced, this is now done; and the pig is released and ignored.

The Dani say that this operation makes the pig grow larger. When I asked if it sterilized the pig, they laughed, saying of course not, they wanted the pig to bear as many young as possible. It may be that the operation has no utilitarian effects. But both times I saw it done there were no signs of any ritual; and of course, it is done by the same men who castrate male pigs for biologically impeccable reasons.

Breeding

The Dani are quite aware of the principles of pig breeding, and they practice selective breeding. Only the largest and most promising male shoats escape castration, and there are only one or two boars in the Neighborhood. Sows are brought to the boars to be serviced at no charge. In the 1960's large boars of better meat-bearing stock were flown into the Grand Valley by government and missionary groups and strategically distributed to the Dani. Because of the selective castrations, these boars should have a rapid effect on the quality of the Grand Valley pig population.

When the sow is close to littering, she is taken from the stall into nearby woods, where she stays while she gives birth and for a few days thereafter. She is moved so she won't crush her shoats in the cramped stall. Her owner visits her every day or so in the woods and soon brings her back to the sty.

It sometimes happens that a sow must be killed for a ceremony before her shoats are fully weaned. Then a woman takes charge of the shoats, feeding them prechewed sweet potato and carrying them in a net or hobbling them to a house pole with a braided cord (*gupi*). Popular accounts of Highland Papuans often state or imply that women carry such pigs in the same nets with their own children and breast feed them, and in fact Meggitt shows an Enga woman doing this (1965:Pl.10). However, it was never observed in the Dugum Neighborhood and all informants denied it emphatically.

Use

The most obvious use of pigs is as food. But the eating of pigs serves a purpose beyond the purely culinary one. Unless a pig dies accidentally or of a sudden disease, in which case it is eaten on the spot by whoever happens to be around, it is saved for a ceremonial use; in funeral ceremonies the pigs are brought as important objects in the ceremonial exchange which involves also nets, shells, and exchange stones, and eaten by the entire company; pigs are also killed and eaten by the subject of curing ceremonies. In the rain ceremony a pig is killed and its blood used, but its flesh is burned, not eaten.

On the morning of a ceremony, the largest pigs to be killed are driven to the compound of the ceremony; smaller pigs are flung upside down over the shoulders of young men, who hold them by the snout and carry them in this relatively helpless and silent manner. Sometimes the pig is killed before it is brought into the compound, but usually pigs are presented alive and killed by one of the important men directing the ceremony.

There is a standard position for pig killing, common throughout the Western Highlands of New Guinea: The pig is held by two men, one grasping it by the ears and the other by the hind feet; a third man approaches from the side with bow and bamboo arrow, goes into an exaggerated crouch as he draws back the arrow (Plate 12), and releases it into the squealing pig, penetrating just behind the front elbow; the arrow slips between the ribs and usually goes in the full ten to twenty centimeters of its blade. The bowman grasps the arrow by the hilt, perhaps jabs it in a bit further, and then removes it. The pig is set on the ground by the holders. If the shot has been good, the pig will immediately topple. Usually it runs a few wavering meters and finally drops, kicking. A particularly lively pig may have to be chased by the men and boys in the yard and knocked over; then several of them place their feet on its side, pressing the blood out; occasionally the bamboo arrow is reinserted in the wound, plunged in and out to enlarge the wound. The pig finally falls silent and dies. If it is a large ceremony with many pigs, their desperate screaming may rise above the noise of the crowd for half an hour or more.

A particularly large pig may be shot on the ground, not held (Plate 11); or poles may be slipped under its body between the legs, one towards the front, one towards the rear, the pig lifted off the ground and then shot.

As soon as they are still, the bodies of the pigs are laid out in a line extending from just in front of the men's house toward the entrance of the compound, along the axis of the compound. First they are laid on their sides, feet toward the entrance, heads toward the left, or cook house, almost touching each other. If it is an important ceremony with many pigs, the men confer over them for a while, sometimes rearranging the order. This moment, which passes almost unnoticed by the guests and is hardly emphasized by the principals, is one of the symbolic climaxes of the entire ceremony. Most Dani ceremonies are symbolic statements communicating to the ghosts the concern of the living for the dead. By laying out the pigs, the people say to their own ghosts, in effect, "Look what we have done for you." Sometimes a man walks the length of the line of pigs, pausing at each and shouting the name of the donor to emphasize this message. Then, quickly, whatever momentary ritual mood had been created is broken, and the men turn to the business of preparing the pigs for human consumption.

The pigs are turned on their stomachs, legs stretched out as if in a flying

PLATE 11. A man shoots a pig with a bamboo arrow at a ceremony.

PLATE 12. Wali (Um'ue) shoots a pig at a curing ceremony. The patient crouches in the entrance of her house. The pig's blood will drain onto the leaves below and then be daubed on the patient's forehead, knees, elbows, and shoulders.

gallop. The ears and tails are carefully cut off with bamboo knives, laid on a leaf, and taken into the men's house. The tails of smaller pigs are simply cut off at the base; with large pigs a circular patch of skin and fat is cut off around the tail.

A fire is built in the yard and the pigs laid over it, and as the hair and outer skin singes it is scraped off with sticks.

The butchering proper is now begun. Banana leaves are laid on the grass in front of the men's house, the singed pigs are brought to it, and various men begin the butchering. There is no definite protocol as to who is to do the butchering. If not enough men come forward, more must be asked. Butchering is done by men, usually married men. Often several men and boys sit around a single pig, watching, helping; sometimes two or three can work at the same time. Young boys and girls watch and are sometimes allowed to hold ends of pieces while the older ones cut.

Even in 1968, when steel knives were plentiful, men preferred the easily sharpened bamboo knives. The sequence of butchering is the same for all pigs. First a cut is made on either side of the mouth, down the stomach just inside the legs, and two cuts meet at the anus. The mandible is freed, usually with great difficulty, cutting the masseter muscles with a knife while bracing one foot on the palate and wrenching upwards with both hands grasping the mandible; as it is freed, it, together with the belly strip of skin, is removed and set aside.

The *meb egen*, the clotted blood lying between the rib cage and the intestines, is pulled out and deposited in a leaf or gourd; this is usually used for magic. The organs are removed, separated, and set aside. The pelvis is broken at the pubic symphisis with an adze, allowing the remaining parts of the pig to lie flat on the ground, and the ribs are broken at their proximal ends with the adze. The ribs are removed, usually each side in one piece. The meat of the shoulders and the haunches is cut away carefully to make long strips of flesh, which are hung on horizontal poles erected above the fences between the houses. The vertebral column is removed. The skull is broken open with an adze and the brains removed and rubbed in ferns, which are bound up in a bundle.

Meanwhile the intestines have been entrusted to children, who take them to a nearby stream and wash them out, turning them inside out and reaming them out with thin poles. Then they are brought back to the courtyard and draped over the meat poles.

If this is a part of a ceremony where a steam bundle is used, the pig's skin, ribs, vertebral column, and organs are usually put directly into the steam bundle; the flesh strips and intestines are kept on the poles in the men's house and roasted over coals later.

After cooking, the skin is held up by one or two men and cut with a bamboo knife by a third man in a sequence and pattern of cuts which is standardized not only for the Neighborhood but, as far as I could observe, for the entire Grand Valley. Then the skin is handed out to the guests. The flesh and the skin are eaten; the fat is rubbed on the body; the larger bones are broken open with rocks and the marrow extracted and eaten. The bones are thrown on coals and burned.

Pigs furnish much more than meat; nearly every part of the pig is utilized: skin, flesh, organs (except for the gall bladder, which is thrown away), gristle, ears, and the marrow of the larger bones are eaten; mandibles of larger male pigs are broken open to remove tusks which, with back sides removed, are used as scrapers or tied in pairs butt to butt and worn by men through the nose septum in battle or dance; mandibles of medium-sized pigs and large females are hung on a bar inside at rear of the men's house; fragments of the femur shaft are ground down to make needles or awls; ribs may be saved and used by the fireplace to scrape off the ashes from baked potatoes; the ilium may be ground down to serve as a spoon for pandanus sauce; the tail tufts are used for magical purposes: tied to a neck piece, or on a tobacco net, or shell band, or funeral net, they give protection against ghosts, as does the scrotum-cum-penis which is tied around the arm of a man or child; the *meb egen* (blood clot) is either mixed and cooked with the brains and eaten, or, in some ceremonies, rubbed on joints, palms, and forehead of mourners or, in curing ceremonies rubbed on patients.

In short, the only nonutilitarian parts of the pig are the gall bladder, the bristles, and those bones too large to be chewed and eaten, and not otherwise converted into implements.

HUNTING

Every man hunts on occasion, but most hunt rarely. Game does not form a regular part of anyone's diet. The forests that edge the Grand Valley are fairly well hunted out, and unlike many other regions of Highland New Guinea, there are no feral pigs at all. In all the time I spent in the Grand Valley, I saw only one live bird-of-paradise. The few men who do keep dogs and hunt the more spectacular birds and marsupials must go far into the high forests for their game.

Bows and arrows are the only tools used in hunting. The bow is the same as the one used in war; the arrows are special ones.

FOREST HUNTING

The marsupials of the forests behind the villages are sought for several things: their flesh is eaten without ritual; their furs are used in headdresses, on shell bands, and as tassels on the end of penis gourds. The mandibles of some are used as gravers for incising lines in shifts and arrow tips. The mandibles of all sorts of marsupials are hung casually by fireplaces where they slowly blacken from the soot. They are trophies of the hunt and are occasionally considered as magic to influence runaway women to come to that men's house. These forest creatures are usually hunted during the nights of a full moon. Dogs are used to corner an animal that has been hit with an arrow, or to dig them out of burrows.

FIELD RODENTS

The small rat-like rodents of the fields and villages, *bugale* and *gobpa*, are frequently hunted. They are used in several rituals, such as augury to determine whether or not a wounded man will recover or whether a missing pig has been eaten or not; also at a certain stage in a funeral they may be roasted and eaten. They are seldom eaten for food, and when one is found in the course of clearing a garden area, it is usually released. *Bugale*, especially, are scorned by the men, who say that only women eat them. However, rodents are some-times specially hunted and given alive to young dogs, to train them as hunters. The rodents which are constantly heard around the villages are ignored or tolerated, although they have considerable nuisance value. At night they attack pigs confined in the narrow stalls; they also chew holes in greased nets or consume pig fat that is not carefully closed in a gourd. However, unlike the Ekagi (Kapauku) of Enarotali who assiduously hunt down any rodent heard around a village (L. F. B. Dubbeldam, in a personal communication), the Dani are uninterested in such minor game. Occasionally cats are traded in from the direction of the government post. They are kept for the few weeks necessary to clean out the rodents in a compound and then traded on toward the north.

When it is necessary to obtain rodents for a ceremony, several men and boys, as many as several dozen, go to fallow gardens armed with short spears and digging sticks. They beat through high grass and thickets or dig around promising-looking roots, and eventually, after an hour or two, come back with a couple of rodents.

BIRDS

Birds are prized particularly for their feathers and only secondarily for food. The feathers are used in men's decorations and in several sacred objects: for decorating shell bands; for the feather wands that remove *wusa*, or taboo, after a contaminating job. However, most of the more important feathers are traded in from the Jalemo, because the cassowary and birds-of-paradise are lacking in the Grand Valley. Parrots, mountain pigeons, hawks, egrets, and herons abound in the Grand Valley but are seldom hunted. Birds are also used in some curing ceremonies.

The smaller birds are hunted by masses of men and boys armed with branched sticks. They are surrounded and then, as they fly from the grass and bushes, they are barraged with the sticks. Occasionally one is hit. But even on unintentional meetings with birds, there seems to be an almost moral obligation for every man and boy to throw anything at any bird that comes within range, usually without success.

Birds are also hunted with special bird arrows by both boys and men. If killed, a bird is quickly plucked, roasted over a fire, and eaten.

Two elaborate bird blinds were observed in the forested hills. A stick led from a small domed shelter across a pool, or to a hole in a tree trunk in which rainwater collected. Above the stick where it emerged from the shelter was a short bamboo tube. The hunter, crouched in the shelter, would shoot an arrow through the tube at a bird sitting on the stick drinking. The bird would be impaled against a wad of ferns at the far end of the stick. Wagner has described a similar bird blind in the Karimui area, six hundred kilometers east of the Grand Valley (1968:15).

BATS

Bats and flying foxes flapping on their great leathery wings come to the compounds at night to feed on ripening bananas. Occasionally when the moon is full they are hunted with bird arrows, although I never actually saw this. They may be eaten; the fur is not used; the mandibles are hung by the fire of a men's house. In the Southern Valley bats are considered to be ghosts, and it is dangerous to kill them (Broekhuijse, in a personal communication), but there are no such connotations in the Neighborhood.

DOGS

There are a few domestic dogs in the Neighborhood. In 1961 all the dogs were of a distinctive barkless type whose howling at night sounded like the crying of a woman or child. They were apparently related to the Australian dingo. But by 1968 interbreeding with introduced dogs had all but obliterated the aboriginal strain. Each dog is the personal property of a man or boy and is given a personal name. The dogs live in the compound and enter the common cooking house freely, but seldom the men's house. There is some difference of opinion as to whether or not dogs have an *edai egen*, or soul, as humans do. Dogs are given or bought as puppies and encouraged to be hunters by feeding them rats and mice. Dogs can be a nuisance when they chase and fight with pigs, and generally they are not particularly valued.

Although dogs are eaten by the Dani of the southern Grand Valley, in the Dugum area they are strictly taboo. The people explained this in terms of the dog's close relation to the original ancestor, but this does not explain why dog flesh should be taboo in the midvalley and not in the southern valley. However, even in midvalley dogs are killed for their fur, which is worn by men as arm bands.

INCIDENTAL COLLECTION OF FAUNA

Several other kinds of fauna are also collected casually, usually by children. Small crayfish, rarely more than ten centimeters long, can be found in streams and garden ditch systems. Boys dive for them, feeling around in the mud. They are then roasted and eaten. (The crayfish of the Balim grow to great size— twenty or thirty centimeters—and the people living along its banks catch them with hand weirs.)

Snakes are very rare, but once I saw one roasted and eaten. Stink bugs, which live in the young trees of the fallow gardens, are savored by boys who wrap them in leaves and eat them. A child may catch a cicada to play with it, holding it in his hand, swing it around furiously, and then releasing it, letting it fly its wavery dizzy path. The rhinoceros beetle may be caught and kept for a while as a pet; one horn is broken off, the end of a grass stem forced in the hole, and the beetle led around as if on a leash.

Although fish are not native to the Grand Valley, they have been introduced by the government since 1960. By 1968 the fish were driving the crayfish out of the streams and ditches and Dani were being encouraged to dig special fish ponds. In the future, fish will probably come to be an important source of protein for the Dani.

GATHERING FOOD AND SUPPLIES

The uninhabited forest within one or two hours' walk of the compounds yields many of the necessities of Dani life. Gathering in the areas close to the compounds is done by anyone, but usually by men, or women accompanied by men, who venture into the forest where there is always the chance of meeting an armed enemy.

The Dani are technically a stone-age culture. Stone tools are important, but in fact, the Dani culture is based on wood and string and could be called a String Culture. The fabric of Dani material culture is fiber, plain or rolled into string. The women's skirts are braided of fiber and tied with string; the girls' skirts are held together with string; the women's carrying nets are of string; the men's penis gourd is held on with string; the exchange system at the core of the ceremonialism centers on knitted string bands and string nets.

Fiber for string is obtained either from the inner core of certain plants or from the inner bark of certain trees. The best plant fiber, and all the bark cloth that is pulled apart for fiber, is traded from the Jalemo. However, fiber for basic needs is obtained from the local forests.

As with all forest goods, the better quality is farther from the dense population of the valley itself. Usually a party of several people goes off on a few days' collecting trip. They return with bundles of 1.5-meter-long stalks weighing several kilos. The outer bark is scraped off by the women with a bamboo splint and allowed to dry in the sun or in the smoke of the common cooking house. Then the stalks are beaten with a wooden mallet on a stone, the fibers are loosened, removed from the inner core, and made into a bundle. They may be used in this form or rolled into string.

Wood is used in houses, fences, tools, weapons, and for fires. It must also be gathered. Construction wood is cut by the men with the adze. Poles and planks come from the forests between the villages and the mountain wall. Although this area is closest to the compounds of the Dugum Neighborhood, other people of the alliance are free to use it. The bark is stripped off, planks are split and hewn at depots, usually rock shelters, in the woods, and then carried down to the compounds.

Wood for cooking, and especially for making the rock fire and the cremation fire, are logs, cut and carried by the men, or simply dried branches collected by men, women, or children, bundled up and carried down to the villages at the end of the day's work.

Except for stone blades, almost all the tools, weapons, and implements of the Dani are made of wood. In addition, bamboo is used for knives, for lashing, for mouth harps, and for fire thongs.

The Dani use no nails or spikes. All construction is lashed together with vines gathered in the forests. Vines range from the long, heavy vines that bind the watchtower to the supple ¼-centimeter vines that lash the reed floor of the sleeping loft. Vines are worn loosely around boys' waists or necks as a sort of decoration.

Little food is gathered from the wild, except pandanus and ferns, which are steamed with vegetables. Raspberrylike berries (Rubiacea *Rubus*), though fairly sweet and juicy, and growing along paths, are seldom eaten. There are no other common wild fruits.

Lisaniga, a spurge, is gathered from the forest in quantities, dried, and used as the wrapper for cigarettes.

Grass is gathered for thatching and for floors; and also for lining the steam bundle. .

POPULATION AND LAND USE

In discussing the nature of Dani land use, the question arises of the relationship between Dani subsistence technology and population density. Density alone, as an absolute factor, can be expected to have some effect on social structure and the nature of leadership within the group. It makes a difference if there are two hundred or two thousand people per square kilometer. But it may well also make a difference, particularly in the nature of conflict behavior within and between groups, if the land is overpopulated or underpopulated—determined by the relationship of population density to carrying capacity of the land. But neither density nor carrying capacity of land can be expressed unambiguously.

Population density is roughly figured by dividing the number of people by the number of square kilometers involved. But Dani land use varies in degree from the relatively intensive use of the settlement sites to the relatively nonintensive use of forest areas, with the use of garden areas an intermediate on this scale. The Dugum Neighborhood's 350 people use about two square kilometers for dwelling and gardening. These figures give a population density of 175 per-

sons per square kilometer. For the Grand Valley as a whole, figuring about
50,000 people living in about 315 square kilometers, one gets nearly 160 persons
per square kilometer. (However, the population figure is only a guess and may
be off by 50 per cent.)

But what of the several square kilometers of forest behind the Dugum settlements that provide rooting grounds for pigs, lumber and vines for houses, minor
food from game and pandanus, not to mention shelter for ghost houses? Even
without proving that the forests are indispensable to the Dugum Dani, it is
obvious that they are used. If the immediate forest area is to be calculated, the
population density of the Dugum Dani could well be about fifty persons per
square kilometer.

The determination of the carrying capacity of land is no less vexing a problem.
If the basic sweet potato and pig subsistence were maintained but the population
gradually increased, it is logical that eventually there would be too many people
for the land. A good measure for overpopulation would be whether or not the
Dani food supply was adequate in terms of minimal standards of protein, calories,
and the like. A comprehensive study would be needed to determine standards
relevant to the Dani, to measure the food values of the present Dani diet, and
to discover the maximum potential production of food on the Dugum land by
present Dani methods.

And in any case, overpopulation is not merely a technological state, referring
to carrying capacity of land, but has also a psychological aspect, referring to
the feeling of being too crowded. This is what might be called the Daniel Boone
Complex, after that semilegendary American frontiersman who is supposed to
have moved on when another family settled within a day's walking distance of
him. Unless the attitude is explicitly expressed, psychological overpopulation
would be difficult to recognize, much less to evaluate.

Since overpopulation may influence behavior, it is of some theoretical importance. Perhaps crowding increases conflict within a group; perhaps an overpopulated group seizes land from an underpopulated neighbor. Both of these
propositions are reasonable, but they must be treated as hypotheses, not as assumptions. Internal conflict or war cannot be taken as evidence of overpopulation.
In Chapter 3 a hypothesis is considered which would link population pressure to
incidence of warfare, and whose validity depends on being able to establish a
criterion for carrying capacity of land. In a crude way, technological overpopulation might be indicated by periodic hunger and malnutrition, and psychological overpopulation by what the people themselves say. But since the Dugum
Dani have no shortages of food; seem as energetic, strong, and healthy as any
population I know; and never expressed concern about crowding, I would say
that they are not overpopulated. Of more general interest is whether or not
the evidence from the Dugum Dani helps to establish criteria for determining
population pressure among other Dani in other places. Such criteria would permit
us to deal with hypotheses relating conflict and other behavior to population
pressure. Unfortunately, I am not able to suggest precise criteria.

CONCLUSIONS

In gross terms, there is a remarkable uniformity in Dani subsistence activities. All adults are horticulturists and herders. The only people who are not continuously engaged in the cultivation of sweet potatoes and the tending of pigs are the young, the senile, and, temporarily, the sick and the wounded. Although a few people engage in minor, spare-time specialization, the Dani approach the bare minimum human division of labor where age and sex are determinant.

But the light demands of subsistence in the Grand Valley permit considerable flexibility in carrying out the details of these activities. A man may work a garden bed alone or he may cooperate with others in the heavier labor. He may open gardens on the hill slopes to supplement those on the valley floor. He may plant several crops in succession in the same bed or he may shift to a new bed after each crop. Crops are planted irregularly but harvested daily. Although the meals are monotonous, there is never a shortage of food; casual visiting at meals is common and there is no strict accounting of where the produce actually ends up.

In addition to this variability of subsistence activity, there is a degree of implicitness to the norms of agricultural behavior that is unusual for a horticultural society. Because of the uniformity of climate, there is no planting season and no harvest season. Perhaps because of the plentifulness of arable land, ownership of land is not relevant and usage rights are transferred easily and without compensation.

It is tautological to observe that any culture represents a successful technological adaptation to its environment, but the Dani have achieved a particularly successful adaptation to their particularly advantageous environment in the sense that the nature of their technology provides surpluses of time and land which allow flexibility of behavior.

2

SOCIAL ORGANIZATION

MUCH Dani activity takes place in the framework of two different sorts of groups, one organized along the lines of patrilineal descent and the other organized in terms of residence. These groups are nonterritorial (or nonlocalized) patrilineal descent groups and residential, territorial (or localized) political units. There are also other kinds of groups, such as those formed by a compromise between the principles of descent and residence and which include those members of a descent group who live in a certain area. These groups are only the basic, idealized framework of Dani social structure, however. There is practically no behavior that involves any group in its entirety, and most activities, even when done in the name of some one group, include participants from other groups. In part this is because of the balanced cross-cutting nature of the groups, so people who are in different groups on one dimension will find themselves in the same group on another dimension.

The two kinds of descent units are named, noncorporate, patrilineal moieties and sibs whose members are dispersed throughout the Grand Valley and beyond. Smaller descent units such as lineages and families are vague, unnamed, and, with few exceptions, unimportant. The two important political, land-occupying units are what I call the alliance and the confederation. The neighborhood is a concept I use for descriptive convenience. Houses form compact compounds, but these compounds usually have little stability as social units.

DESCENT GROUPS AND LOCAL SEGMENTS OF DESCENT GROUPS

The Patrimoiety

The most important area in which membership in a moiety determines behavior is in choice of spouse, since each moiety is exogamous; moiety membership also effects use of kin terms, some food restrictions, and participation in some ceremonies.

Every Dani is a member of one or the other of the two moieties, Wida or Waija. The moieties are exogamous and patrilineal. Moieties are found throughout the Grand Valley and are present to some extent in the Western Dani region. Ploeg (1966:264) reports a pale reflection of the moiety system from the

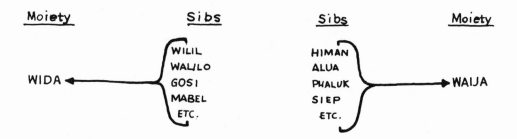

DIAGRAM 2.1
NONTERRITORIAL (PATRILINEAL) DESCENT GROUPS

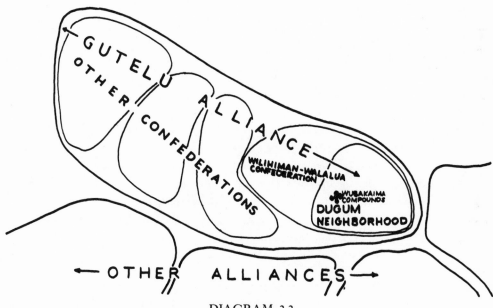

DIAGRAM 2.2
THE TERRITORIAL POLITICAL UNITS

Western Dani of the Bokondini region, just a few kilometers north of the Grand Valley, where the two two groups, called Woda and Weja, are ideally but not actually exogamous. Although Wirz (1924:46) described a Wenda and a Woja moiety among the Panaga Dani of the lower Swart Valley system, Denise O'Brien found only the barest traces of moieties during her research in 1961–1963 in the Konda Valley, part of the upper Swart Valley system (personal communication). Gordon Larson (1962:32) reports that the far Western Dani, in the Ilaka Valley, have moieties. The Jale, who are part of the Greater Dani Language Family, also have moieties (Koch 1968:87). The Dani and their neighbors to the west, the Uhunduni (Damals), are apparently the only people in the entire New Guinea Highlands with a moiety organization (cf. Ellenberger 1962).

The norm of moiety exogamy is rarely violated (see below). Kinship terms which are used in one sense between people with traceable relationships may also be extended in a classificatory manner to the limits of the pertinent moiety. Thus, *opase* refers in one sense to ego's father and father's brothers but may be extended to refer to any male of the older generation and of ego's own moiety. Likewise, *ami*, which refers basically to ego's mother's brothers, can be extended to refer to any male of the older generation and of the opposite moiety to ego.

In certain rituals there are roles which are prescribed in moiety terms. For example, in funerals, members of the dead person's own moiety are responsible for certain acts, members of the opposite moiety (that is, ego's mother's moiety), for other acts.

Participation in a funeral is determined by informal factors such as nearness of residence and personal friendship. But even those participants who have no traceable kinship with the dead person have a role in terms of their moiety affiliation. Everyone has a place in the system. An older man is considered either an *opase* or an *ami* of the dead person and can act accordingly.

Food Taboos. Food restrictions are usually based on moiety membership. The Wida members are not supposed to eat one kind of banana, and one kind of bird. Waija members, on the other hand, are prohibited from eating more than a dozen kinds of birds and mammals and two kinds of bananas. There is no obvious explanation for the imbalance. Breaking of the restriction is said to be punished by ghosts, who cause the stomach to swell and the transgressor to die. Although the prohibitions are widely known, they are not rigorously observed. I have frequently seen people in a group refuse to eat a certain prohibited food, but then show no hesitation to eat it when alone with me.

The prohibited foods do not seem to have any further, totemiclike relationship to the moiety members, nor are other beings or objects associated with the moieties. However, even this limited association is noteworthy, for Peters (1965: 25) states that no comparable moiety relationships exist in the Southern Valley.

I was not able to find a Dani explanation for the moiety systems. The one informant who told me of the origin myth said after much probing on my part that the first man was Wida, but this seemed to be nonessential to the myth, and he himself was Wida.

Moiety Boundary-crossing. Although the division between the two moieties is particularly important in patterning Dani marriage, the line between them is not absolute and may be crossed in two special circumstances.

All children are born into the Wida moiety regardless of the moiety of their father. At the time of the Pig Feast (*ebe akho*), which is held every few years, those boys who have reached an age of responsibility since the last ceremony and thus are about three to six years old, and whose fathers are of the Waija moiety, are "made Waija" (*waija hakasin*). I did not observe this ceremony and could learn only the broad principles involved. Apparently the girls of the same age with Waija fathers became Waija at the same time, but without ceremony. This patrilineal principle, which is evoked not at birth, but several years afterward, is a most unusual manner in which to run a moiety system. However, it has mainly theoretical significance. The only really basic way in which moiety membership effects behavior is in marriage choices, and the children of Waija fathers are "made Waija" long before marriage.

Another sort of boundary crossing in the Dani moiety system is the status held by four men in the Neighborhood who are part Wida and part Waija. They are described as *golek*, or *widbalek*, but it is not clear what this means. Apparently all these men were born into and are of the Walilo sib, which is a Wida sib, but for some reason they disliked this Wida status and chose to become part Waija. I could discover no reasons for or ritual involved in the change. It was said that their feet and penises were Waija, their heads Wida. (Peters [1965:22] describes the same phenomenon from the regions south of the Dugum but reports the reverse details: There the lower half of the body is Wida and the upper half Waija. The same situation was reported in the Jibiga area.) In the Dugum Neighborhood all such men are married to Waija women and generally function in ritual situations as normal Walilo sib members, which is to say, Wida. Peters also reports that they marry Waija women. Folk explanations were offered for both cases. About the former, it was said that the men were really Wida because their *uguloak* (literally, skull, head, or sib) was Wida; in the other, it was pointed out that the penis, being Wida, had to marry a Waija woman. None of the men who are part Wida and part Waija are important leaders, and in fact they do not seem to be exceptional in any other way.

A third possible example of moiety boundary-crossing is reported by Peters (1965:23) from the southern Grand Valley. There, members of two sibs (Molama and Hisako) may be either Wida or Waija, although Peters' informant clearly disapproved of the situation. Neither of these sibs is represented in the Dugum area. Also, an informant at Jibiga insisted to me that the Widikpo sib is Wida in Mid-Valley and Waija in the Southern Valley.

Moiety "Precedence." There is a use of the basic kinship terms that treats the people of the Waija moiety as older than the people of the Wida moiety. For example, there are two pairs of reciprocal terms used by males of the same moiety which indicate difference in age. One pair (*opase-abut*) is used by men of adjacent generations and the other pair (*oe-akot*) by men of the same generation. (These terms include the English pairs father–son and older-brother-younger-brother respectively, but they are used for all men of one's moiety rather than only for specific consanguineous relatives.) In this special use of kinship terms, a male of the Wida moiety would address a Waija male as *opase* or *oe* regardless of their relative ages.

I was never able to obtain a satisfactory explanation of this usage, and it seems to contradict the fact that all Dani are born Wida and half become Waija only when they are a few years old. Use of terms in this pattern was observed occasionally in casual moments during ceremonies. It may be partly ritual, but there also seems to be a joking element to it. I also once heard this pattern used in a very tense but painfully polite confrontation between leaders of enemy groups.

The Local Segment of a Moiety. Each moiety comprises tens of thousands of Dani who never act as a group. However, men of the Waija moiety who live in one local area and who thus form what may be termed a local segment of a moiety do cooperate in performing the initiation ceremony for their sons at the time of the major Pig Feast held every few years. I did not observe a Pig Feast, but informants spoke of it and Peters (1965:114 ff) has described one from a nearby area.

The Sib

Patrisibs have been reported from all Dani regions, and a few of the Grand Valley Dani sib names can be traced into the Western Dani region. People living in the Dugum Neighborhood between 1961 and 1964 represented eleven sibs of the Wida moiety and thirteen sibs of the Waija moiety. An additional six Grand Valley sibs were mentioned in genealogies that had no representation in the Dugum Neighborhood (See Table 2.1). Several other sib names are known from distant parts of the Grand Valley and beyond, and Peters (1965:23) lists another twenty-four sib names (eleven Wida, thirteen Waija) from the southern Grand Valley. Since he omits only five sib names found on the Dugum list, it is unlikely that his names are only local variants of the same sib. Thus, there must be well over fifty sibs in the Grand Valley.

Sibs are patrilineal, and one is a member of one's father's sib from birth. This is different from the moiety system, where everyone is born into the Wida moiety and some are later taken into their father's moiety (Waija).

Sibs are nonterritorial, and members of the same sib living in different parts of the Grand Valley may never meet. There is not necessarily any traceable relationship between members of the same sib, and I could discover only the slightest hint (in an origin myth episode, p. 141), that the members of a sib were eventually descended from any common ancestors. Thus, although these Dani units are patrilineal and nonterritorial, they lack the clear recognition of original filiation which is usually associated with sibs (cf. Murdock 1949:47). But rather than add another term to the complexities of kinship literature, I am using sib as the most satisfactory existing term for referring to these units.

In most cases the etymology of Dani sib names is not clear and cannot be explained by the Dani.

Sib Associates. Each sib is associated with a specific topographical feature, in most cases a promontory of some sort; with a kind of bird; and in a few instances with some furry mammal (*bpake*) or with an insect or reptile (*wato*). Most people disagree about the names of the birds of sibs other than their own. Lists from different informants usually disagreed in some 40 to 60 per cent of particular cases.

A mythological explanation of these associations lies in the origin myth (p. 141), which, as related by one informant, states that

In the beginning, birds and people were together, living in sib groups, and each sib had pigs. Then they asked Nakmatugi, the first man, who they were, and he said: "You are people, you are birds." The birds said, "We don't like people, we'll go off and be

TABLE 2.1

ADULT POPULATION OF THE DUGUM NEIGHBORHOOD BY SIB AND SEX

	Sib Name	Males	Females
Major Sibs of Confederation	Wilil *	31	22
	Himan	3	10
	Walilo *	17	19
	Alua	17	26
	Phaluk	11	14
Sibs Represented by Adult Males	Dloko	4	5
	Gosi *	4	3
	Widipo *	3	8
	Dutabut	3	9
	Matian *	1	9
	Dlogobal	1	2
	Atudama *	1	0
Sibs Represented Only by Women Who Have Married into the Area	Siep	0	9
	Mabel *	0	7
	Hilabok	0	5
	Loka	0	4
	Eloktak	0	3
	Jokobi *	0	2
	Babiga *	0	1
	Halidopo	0	1
	Atoba	0	1
	Oake	0	1
	Idlai *	0	1
	Wadik *	0	1
		96 (in 12 sibs)	170 (in 23 sibs)

Other Sibs Mentioned in Genealogies but Not Represented: Isiba, Wuga, Maduan, Dlapi, Huwi, Waliagen

* Sibs of Wida moiety. Others of Waija moiety.

Other sib names known—*Wida:* Honamput, Helakmelama, Gagolik, Toi; *Waija:* Gedata, Dabulai, Hiluga, Dodlidopo, Mosip, Gilugua, Widikpo.

Other sibs mentioned by Peters (1965:23)—*Wida:* Wamu, Aso, Gutesi, Elokbete, Lakoban, Lani, Molama, Hisake, Galhulik, Lega and Gerda; *Waija:* Jukusu, Walela, Ndawi, Hutugalek, Mulia, Eginia, Molama, Hisake, Oakai, Meake, Jeli, Dibo, and Heselo.

birds." The pigs became *bpake* [ground mammals] and the *wato* [insects, etc.] also went off to be *wato*.

The bird of a person's sib is his *akalak*, brother, and he cannot eat it, although others can. For example, a man of the Wilil sib is called *ab wilil* (*ab*, man), and the *jubuti* bird is called *due wilil* (*due*, bird), suggesting the common sib membership of the two.

There are no restrictions against eating the sib *bpake* or the sib *wato*, if they are gastronomically palatable.

The word for mountain or hill, *dom*, when used in the sib context, is one of the few nouns which take a possessive prefix. Thus, a Wilil might refer to the Wilil sib hill as *nadom* (my hill) or *ninadom* (our hill), *n*—being the first person singular possessive prefix. This form of the possessive is generally limited to kin terms, and suggests a special relationship between man and mountain.

Some sib hills are mountains outside the Grand Valley, where the sib members have special rights to pandanus trees and hunting; others are minor hills in the Grand Valley, with no apparent economic advantages. There seems to be no particular ritual conecting sib and hill, although at one time the hills may have been the sites of sib ghost houses.

The question of Dani sib totemism involves two sets of problems. In the first place, Lawrence and Meggitt have stated that except for one dubious case, "totemism is not reported from the Highlands" (1965:11), but they refer only to the Highlands of East New Guinea. Pospisil has mentioned a "simple totemism" for Ekagi (Kapauku) sibs (1958:74), and elsewhere he expanded his description, saying that

The native tradition claims that Ugatame, the Creator, founded all the sibs and determined that each of them should be mystically related to two or more animal or plant totemic species, which the members are forbidden to consume under the penalty of deafness. (1963:38)

Ellenberger reports a similar totemism for the Uhunduni (Damal), who live between the Ekagi and Western Dani (1962:10). However, since Pouwer has not mentioned any such features in the Star Mountain region to the east of the Dani, it appears that, like moieties, totemism in the New Guinea Highlands is limited to the far western cultures.

But more important is the problem of totemism itself. Lévi-Strauss, in his critique of the concept, has said that

The supposed totemism eludes all effort at absolute definition. It consists, at most, in a contingent arrangement of nonspecific elements. (1963:5)

In Lévi-Strauss' terms, the Dani totemism has two features: a belief in the mystical relationship between a cultural group (sib) and a natural particular (hill) and a belief in the mystical relationship between a cultural group (sib) and several natural groups (bird, animal, and insect species). Particularly in the cases of sib-bird and sib-animal relationships there is a belief in an isomorphism between the divisions of the cultural world and those of the natural world.

The relationship between Dani sibs and species of birds may be understood in terms of Lévi-Strauss' insight into the symbolic basis of this sort of relationship. He suggests that these relationships are not based on the symbolic identity of cultural and natural groups but on the isomorphism between sets of cultural groups and sets of natural groups. For the natural groups we look to the Dani mortality myth, where the bird, representing mortality, is opposed to the snake, which represents immortality. Because the bird prevails, says the myth, men are mortal. Transformed into a Lévi-Straussian equation:

bird:snake :: Dani (mortal) : what Dani might have been (immortal)

The value of this equation lies in forcing us to consider the total context. Dani are associated through their sibs with birds not just because birds are mortal, but birds and Dani are mortal vis-à-vis snakes and something. What is the something? Perhaps, non-Dani humans. There is no indication that the Dani themselves traditionally completed the formula, either with ghosts or with non-Dani humans of whom they had only vague knowledge. But now, in a mythic revision, the white man fits the empty space. In various areas for various reasons (the Dani have never seen a dead white man; the Christian message talks of immortality) the Dani consider the white man to be immortal (cf. O'Brien and Ploeg 1964). That this is not pure anthropological speculation is suggested by the fact that some Dani actually call white men "snake people," using the term *helal*, which is a kind of snake in the *wato* category. (This was reported to me by J. Vehling, a Dutch patrol officer, and Herman Lantang, an Indonesian anthropologist.)

Power of the Sib Name. Often, when a person has a minor accident such as knocking something over, or giving himself a minor bruise, he says, under his breath, the name of his sib. The significance of this is not at all clear. It may be related to the practice of others to say, when a person slips on a path, "*Hakotakma!*" ("May your soul stay in place!").

Terms for Moiety and Sib. Generic terms for both moiety and sib refer to body parts. *Ugul* (head), *ugul oak* (head bone, skull), *ugul isi* (head hair), and *ilaka* (eyebrow) all refer to sib, while *ebe* (body) refers to moiety. Thus, the question, "*Hugul oak edaka?*" (Your skull is called?)" elicits the name of the informant's sib. This is quite explicit symbolism and the term is often accompanied by the touching of the appropriate body part. The breast is used by a woman to indicate her children or their sib members (which are, of course, of her husband's sib) and by a man to indicate his sib members. The penis gourd is also used by a man to represent his sib members.

Van der Stap (in a personal communication) suggested that in the southern Grand Valley dialect these same terms may be used in a more complicated and specific manner, indicating lineages in addition to sib and moiety.

Sib Boundary-crossing. In a few cases sibs within a moiety are closely associated. For example, two Waija moiety sibs, Alua and Phaluk, are sometimes confused when a person refers to another person whom he does not know well. An example of changing sib affiliation was provided in the Dugum Neighborhood. According to one story, some thirty years ago, as a result of a fight, a small group of people moved into the Dugum area from the Pugima area, ten kilometers to the south. Among them were several important men of the Phaluk sib, one of the dominant sibs in the Pugima but quite unimportant in the Dugum. These men associated themselves with the Alua sib, the dominant Waija sib in the Dugum area. Other informants insist that these men were born in the Dugum

Neighborhood. One of these men, Weteklue, is the leader of the local Alua group and is in fact the most important man in the Dugum area. When asked, people were as likely to say that Weteklue is Alua as they are to say that he is Phaluk.

This move from the Phaluk to the Alua sib could be seen as an opportunistic move to gain a power base, but it is difficult to reconstruct the exact sequence of events. Now people recognize Phaluk and Alua sibs as closely related, but this may equally be the cause enabling Weteklue's move or the result of the move. Similar relationships are recognized between other pairs of sibs such as Alua and Maduan, a sib not strongly represented in the Dugum area.

THE LINEAGE

Lineage, consisting of immediate, traceable relatives, is relatively unimportant for the Dani. (Peters suggests that in the southern Grand Valley, lineage is more important [1965:27].) There is no name for it, and the broad, classificatory nature of kinship terminology overrides the line between lineage relatives and one's comembers of the sib or even moiety.

The Dani are typical of the New Guinea Highlands in having little interest in genealogy; that is, they have shallow genealogies. A person can trace only his immediate relatives. A grown man remembers those whom he has known as a child, but rarely more than one generation beyond that.

A group of sacred objects usually belongs to a sib segment—that is, men of the same sib but not necessarily with traceable relationship. However, in several instances the men claim descent from a common ancestor, although the actual links with the ancestor are not known.

FAMILY

The importance of the family as a social and economic unit is limited by several factors. The members of the polygynous and even the monogamous families tend to be scattered in different compounds and sometimes even in different neighborhoods, and interaction may be rare. Even small-scale interaction and cooperation tends to take place in terms of impermanent and informal groups usually composed of members of more than one family who happen to be living in a single compound.

The socialization of children after the age of two or so, when they no longer lie in their mothers' nets and are in effect weaned, takes place increasingly in terms of larger groups, first the compound and then peer groups. By eight or ten most children spend long periods away from their parents, joining in the activities of other compounds. There is little formal instruction, and nothing corresponding to regular schooling. Children learn the pattern of Dani life from early ages by watching and gradually participating.

This is not to say that the Dani have no family pattern. There are a few nuclear families in the Neighborhood that do have unusual cohesion. But in terms of both ideal and observed norms, the family must generally be considered a relatively unimportant social or economic unit of Dani society.

Residence. The family as a residential group consists of the husband, one or two wives, and the younger children. By the time they are ten years old or so, many boys and girls will spend long periods away from their parents, living with friends or relations. Commonly children go to live with a mother's brother or other older man of the mother's moiety, but there does not seem to be a particular preference for living with the actual brother of the mother. It is also common for older married people to separate and live in the household of one of their children.

Residence is highly mobile. It is rare for one person to live for any length of time in a single compound with the same people. This may be seen in part as the withdrawal reaction to interpersonal stress, discussed below (p. 101). When stresses develop between people in the same compound, and even the same family, it is easier to move to another compound than to stay on and accommodate the stress.

It is difficult to speak of Dani residence in terms of the traditional categories of patrilocal, matrilocal, neolocal, and the like, partly because of constant, kaleidoscopic changing of residence, and partly because of the settlement pattern: many small compounds relatively close to one another.

Marriage and Divorce. Regular marriages take place only during the *ebe akho* ceremony, which occurs every four or five years.

In theory cross-cousin marriage is possible, but in fact no cases were known, and informants had no opinions about its desirability. Even marrying into one's mother's sib was not particularly common. An exchange of women was suggested by statements of some informants, but the groups on which this was based were vague, and certainly they were not families. Each of a pair of men of opposite moieties might marry girls of the same sib as the other man, and they would consider themselves more closely tied than the ordinary in-law relationship, but this pattern was not particularly emphasized.

At the time of the *ebe akho* ceremony, all girls who have had a *hodalimo* ceremony (marking the onset of regular menstruation) since the last *ebe akho* ceremony are married. Men of ages eighteen to twenty-two marry for the first time, and other men may take additional wives. All women except the hopelessly crippled and all men except the hopelessly *gebu* (cf. pp. 90-1) marry.

Although many marriages go through periods of separation, especially when there are cowives involved, there is also a regular divorce-and-remarriage ceremony which may be performed at times other than the *ebe akho* ceremony. The one time I observed it, it involved the plucking of the woman's eyebrows and burying them at the roots of a newly planted banana plant beside the woman's house in her new husband's compound.

Polygyny. Polygyny is common. Table 2.2 gives the crude figures.

The three bachelors are considered *gebu*, of least importance (p. 72); the term *dloni* is regularly applied to their confirmed bachelorhood and only jokingly to that of the fifty-three males who are too young for marriage. Approximately half the adult men are polygynous, but the figures contain some obvious error. Some of the forty-nine men with only one wife are young and can expect to accumulate other wives later. On the other hand, the figures do not discriminate between full polygyny, where the husband lives and works with all his wives; displaced polygyny, where the cowives live in different compounds and the husband spends time with each in turn; and what is in fact monogamy, where the man marries again only after he is effectively divorced from his first wife. Most Dani polygynous families shift frequently between full and displaced polygyny as friendships between cowives wax and wane.

TABLE 2.2

DUGUM NEIGHBORHOOD MALES: MARITAL STATUS

Status		N
Not Yet Married		53
Never Married (permanent bachelors)		3
One Wife		49
More Than One Wife		43
2 wives	23	
3 wives	14	
4 wives	5	
9 wives	1	
Total		148

There is no tendency for cowives to be sisters or even to be of the same sib. Theoretically there is no limit to the number of wives a man may have. Practically, he is limited by his ability to enter into the extensive economic exchange involved in marriage and by his personal ability to attract and hold a woman. It should be noted that the independence and individualism of the Dani women make it very difficult for even the most important man to maintain more than one or two wives in the same household. Those men with more than two wives must in most cases maintain several compounds or allow some of their wives to return to their parents' compound, or run the risk of desertion or divorce.

Levirate. The Dani explicitly approve of the sib levirate, where, on the death of a man, his brother or close friend in his sib marries his widow. This is emphasized by the fact that a woman is called by the same term by both her husband and by other men of her husband's age and sib, that is, her potential husbands via the levirate. There were fourteen cases noted where a woman remarried after the death of her first husband, and in only four of these cases she remarried a man of a different sib. However, often even young widows do not remarry at all.

Of 170 married or widowed women in the Dugum Neighborhood, thirty-four, or just 20 per cent, had been married more than once for the reasons indicated in Table 2.3.

Incest. Moiety exogamy is strictly observed, and there were no known cases

TABLE 2.3
Reasons for Women Having More Than One Husband

Reason	N
Natural Death of First Husband	4
Violent Death of First Husband (warfare, feud, brawl)	14
Divorce or She Ran Away	3
Unknown	13
Total	34 [a]

a. Representing 28 double and 3 triple marriages.

of intramoiety marriage. Incest is called *itu oati* (*itu*, the term used by a man for a woman of the same generation and the same sib or moiety; *oati*, term for testes or blunt term for fornication). Informants could describe only a single instance of incest in the Neighborhood. They said that when this was discovered, the man's father beat him and his wife left him.

Incest is *wusa*—that is, prohibited by supernatural sanctions—but the precise nature of these sanctions was not clear. In the one case mentioned, it appeared that the beating by the father was an outcome of sudden rage rather than a normal punishment. There was obviously no general disapproval of this affair. Most informants considered it rather amusing.

The Dani have no restrictions on marriage between two people who live in the same area. This is noteworthy, for there is a general pattern of local exogamy (based on village or political unit) in many East New Guinea Highland societies.

Children. Women rarely have more than two children. The distribution for the Dugum Neighborhood is described in Table 2.4. These figures are minimal figures, since the data came primarily from male informants, and undoubtedly not all children who died in infancy were remembered and reported.

TABLE 2.4
Number of Children per Woman in the Dugum Neighborhood

Married Women Having Borne:	N	
No children	13	(all young married women who have not yet begun to have children)
1 child	86	
2 children	57	
3 children	13	(includes two women with twins)
4 children	1	(woman with two children by each of two husbands)

Dani men say that women simply do not want more than one or two children because of the work and bother involved, and that they frequently practice abortion by manual manipulation. Men usually want more children and when talking to me they often spoke bitterly of abortion. However, there is no indication that abortion actually occurs, and it did not seem to be a cause of tension in normal husband-wife relations.

Role of Sexual Intercourse in Marriage. Certainly sexual abstinence is an important factor in the low birth rate, but it was not possible to learn details about it. Although a married man usually sleeps in the men's house, he does sometimes join his wife in the woman's house for the night. There is no feeling that intercourse is dangerous and can weaken men, which is the explicit rationale for the men's clubhouse in so many Eastern Highland groups (cf. Meggitt 1964). A few men sleep regularly with their wives, but these women do not necessarily have more children.

A Dani couple is supposed to observe an extraordinarily long period of sexual abstinence after the birth of a child. Since they do not measure time in terms of years, it was not possible to determine exactly how long. However, informants were asked to describe this duration in terms of the relative ages of siblings, and from this I estimate the period of postpartum sexual abstinence to be about four to six years.

Postpartum sexual abstinence is not just an ideal norm; to the best of my knowledge it is actually observed. Among the several hundred Dani whom I knew personally and whose genealogies I had collected there was only one instance where siblings with the same mother were closer in apparent age than about five years. (It is conceivable that contraception or abortion rather than actual abstinence would account for this, but I have no solid evidence for the former and the latter seems to be quite rare. In 1968 at Jibiga a few men spoke of the use of contraceptive plants by women, but this was denied by the women I asked. Further research on this subject is necessary.) The one exception to this age separation was the result of unusual circumstances: Shortly after a young woman had given birth, her husband was killed in battle, and she lived for a while in another alliance area where she remarried and had a second child only a couple of years after the first.

Although some period of postpartum sexual abstinence is common throughout the world (cf. Whiting 1964), the Dani period of four to six years is exceptionally long. The Cheyenne were reported to abstain from intercourse for ten years, but it is clear that this was considered an unusual and virtuous act and was certainly not a strictly observed rule (cf. Grinnell 1924:149). However, the Dugum Dani period is not unique, for Koch has reported a four-year postpartum sexual taboo from the closely related Jale of the Southern Jalemo (1968a:90).

The Dani had no specific explanation for this abstinence. Children do nurse occasionally into their third or even fourth year, but after the second year nursing seems less a source of nourishment than an occasional search for comfort at the mother's breast.

It is further striking that the Dani show no overt signs of sexual anxiety during this period of sexual abstinence. Of course, the high incidence of polygamy means that some men would have access to another wife while one was prohibited, but this does not account for the women or for the monogamous men. And in fact, if one of a polygynous man's wives has a baby, he tends to live with her and not with another wife to whom he would have sexual access.

Similarly, the general prohibition on extramarital sexual intercourse seems to be observed. It is clearly dangerous to make such statements about the absence of sexual behavior, for that is one of the most private spheres of life. However, the norms are explicit, and Dani life is in fact so public that there is little opportunity to keep illicit sex secret. Twice during my twenty-six months' stay extramarital affairs were discovered, and they caused great communal stir. And since the Dani do gossip, and since I was friendly with many people who told me quite scurrilous things about each other, I feel fairly confident that I would have been aware of it if much extramarital sexual activity was going on. On the basis of his four and one-half years in the Grand Valley, Peters comes to similar conclusions (1965:29).

On the other hand, in 1968 when I questioned Dani men at Jibiga, they claimed that premarital sexual intercourse was very common and that few girls were virgins at marriage. I tend to doubt this for several reasons. The informants were unable (or unwilling) to give specific instances of premarital affairs. Too, they knew of no children born out of wedlock (but explained this on the grounds that continual sexual intercourse is necessary for conception, and that premarital affairs were brief). Since marriages take place only every five years or so, toward the end of that time there are many unmarried girls who would seem to be quite fecund. In any case, the possibility that my informants are right cannot be completely ruled out.

But if long postpartum sexual abstinence and the virtual absence of extramarital sex is accepted as fact, we are faced with explaining the mechanism for enforcing such seemingly abnormal behavior. In theory enforcement would be possible in any society, of course, if the control system was strong enough. However, with the Dani not only is there no apparent legal mechanism but there seems to be neither concern nor anxiety about it. Here the observations of the anthropologist come into direct conflict with the assumption of a basic human sexual drive. It would seem either that the Dani are genuinely casual and unconcerned about sex or that they have a most remarkable mechanism for repressing their concern. This is clearly one of the problems raised by the Dani data that demands further research.

KINSHIP TERMINOLOGY

The Dani use two sets of kinship terms, defined in Table 2.5. Roughly speaking, one set is broadly classificatory and is used for blood relatives; the other set is descriptive and is used for affinal relatives. However, the persons in the first set are by no means always traceable blood relatives. Perhaps it would be better to say that the first set of terms categorizes people according to ascriptive statuses, namely descent group (moiety), age, and sex, while the

TABLE 2.5
Dani Kinship Terms

Term	Sex of Alter	Moiety	Generation	Dani Term Includes English:
Ascriptive ("blood," classificatory) Terms				
opase	M	=	+1	father
he opase	F	=	+1	father's sister
akoja	F	≠	+1, 0	mother, mother's brother's daughter
ami	M	≠	+1 [a]	mother's brother
ejak	M or F	≠	0, −1, etc.[b]	child (female speaking), father's sister's child, sister's child
oe	M	=	+½	older brother
akot	M	=	−½	younger brother
itu	F	=	0	sister
abut	M or F	=	−1, −2, etc.[c]	child (male speaking), brother's child
opa	M	=, ≠	+2	grandfather
opa	M or F	=, ≠	−2	grandchild (male speaking)
akona	F	=, ≠	+2	grandmother
akona	M or F	=, ≠	−2	grandchild (female speaking)
Achieved (affinal, descriptive) Terms				
ake [d]	F	≠	0	wife, brother's wife, wife's sister
akun	M	≠	0	husband, husband's brother
akobak	M	≠	0, −1	sister's husband, wife's brother, son-in-law
akhoan	F	=	+1	mother-in-law
akhami	M	≠	+1	father-in-law
akalho	F	≠	−1	daughter-in-law (male speaking)

Key: Moiety =, ego same moiety as alter, ≠, ego opposite moiety from alter; Generation, alter same generation as ego (0), alter older or younger in same generation as ego (+½, −½), alter one generation older or younger than ego (+1, −1), etc.

a. And male descendants of this category through male links.

b. And descendants of this category through male links; except that a woman uses *akona* for her grandchildren.

c. Except that for biological grandchildren, a man uses *opa*, a woman *akona*.

d. The terms *ake* and *akun* are descriptive in that they refer to ego's specific spouse or potential spouse under the levirate or sororate.

second set of terms categorizes people according to achieved relationships, namely affinal (or in-law) status. I have called these two sets ascriptive and achieved kinship status terms.

The ascriptive terms usually denote sex of alter (but rarely of ego); whether ego and alter are of the same or opposite moieties; and generation of alter vis-à-vis ego.

The Dani usually use the ascriptive kinship terms in a broadly classificatory manner without regard for the actual genealogical relationships. But they are quite aware of genealogical relationships, at least within a few linking generations, and can use the same terms in a descriptive way. For example, in normal conversation any man of ego's moiety and older than ego by a single generation would be called an *opase* of ego. On the other hand, the question "Who is ego's *opase?*" would elicit the name of ego's actual father.

The two sets of terms, ascriptive and achieved, are in part overlapping. The ascriptive terms are not reserved for blood relatives but are extended to moiety boundaries. Achieved kinship terms are used only for real affines and usually take precedence over the blood terms. For example, when a man marries, he calls his father-in-law by the affinal term *akhani* rather than by the more classificatory blood term *ami.* Marriages between persons of known consanguinity are most unusual (although they are not discouraged in any way), so this pattern may merely reflect preference for the more descriptive term.

Some terms have behavioral connotations that go beyond kinship relationships. For example, when a child is born, and at other critical points in its life, its mother's brother or another *ami* presents it with cowrie shells. The proper reply is "*nami wa!*" (*n-* being the first person singular possessive prefix and *wa!* simply an exclamation). By extension the proper reply or thanks for any gift of cowrie shells is "*nami wa!*" regardless of the actual relationships of the individuals involved.

Kinship terms are used both as terms of reference and frequently as alternatives to personal names, as terms of address. All kinship terms have an initial vowel and are usually used with a personal possessive prefix. (Peters gives somewhat different kinship terms for the Dani immediately to the south of midvalley [cf. 1965:47–49]).

TERRITORIAL UNITS

THE ALLIANCE

The alliance is the maximal unit within which ceremonial, political, and social activity takes place. People of different alliances refer to each other as *dili-mege,* which means foreigner, outsider, person of another alliance, and contrasts with the term for people of one's own alliance, *aguni juma-mege,* literally, people of this place, local people. Fighting between alliances is war and has ritual implications lacking in any fighting within the alliance. Although the alliances are clearly bounded, they are inherently unstable, and the history of the Grand Valley Dani is one of kaleidoscopically shifting alliances.

These strict political boundaries are neither cultural nor linguistic boundaries. Some major and many minor differences in material culture, in ritual, and in language occur from area to area within the Grand Valley; but generally speaking, adjacent alliances, whether friendly or enemy, have cultures and languages so similar as to be completely mutually intelligible.

In the Grand Valley there are about a dozen of these alliances. In 1961 people of the Dugum Neighborhood were part of the Wilihiman-Walalua Confederation which, together with the Gosi-Alua, Wilil-Himan, Dloko-Mabel, Dlabi-Mabel, Phaluk-Matian, Widipo-Alua, and a few other confederations, made up a major alliance of perhaps five thousand people living in about forty square kilometers of the northeastern corner of the Grand Valley. Both alliance and confederation are composed of members of many sibs.

There is no Dani term, generic or specific, for the alliance, nor is there a term for the area the alliance occupies. For its own convenience, the Dutch government used the name of the most important man, Gutelu (Plate 14), for the name of both alliance and territory, and the Dani themselves are gradually adopting this usage.

Alliance boundaries are defined by frontiers where two alliances meet. The territories of alliances that lie at the edges of the Grand Valley gradually shade off into the unpopulated mountain forests. Interalliance frontiers may be war or peace frontiers, depending on the current relations between the two alliances.

In 1961 the Dugum Neighborhood, which forms the southernmost part of the Gutelu Alliance area, shared frontiers with the friendly Walilo-Alua and the enemy Widaia (Map C.3). The Walilo-Alua frontier was a kilometer-broad strip of broken, forested slope through which passes a major trade route. The Widaia frontier, on the valley floor, was a two-kilometer strip of no-man's-land, overgrown gardens, abandoned villages, and several battlefields. In time of peace, the people of the two alliances push out to farm and live in the no-man's-land.

Two major activities take place within the alliance as a whole. Warfare, with its ritual, involves the entire alliance. Although battles are initiated and fought on the confederation level, groups from other confederations usually join in. The ultimate responsibility for war ritual lies with the most important man of the alliance—with Gutelu, in the Gutelu Alliance.

When Gutelu was at the peak of his influence, all trophies taken from enemy killed in action on any front of the Alliance were given to Gutelu to be kept in one of his sacred compounds. By May 1961, however, the leaders of the Wilihiman-Walulua Confederation, notably Weteklue, perhaps in part emboldened by the presence of our expedition felt that their importance was great enough that they could withhold from Gutelu the trophies captured in action by their confederation.

Two years later, however, these confederation leaders were at first hesitant to take the more drastic step in usurping Gutelu's role in initiating the *ebe akho* ceremony (the ceremony held every few years, when all outstanding funeral ritual is concluded, marriages are made, and boys are initiated into the Waija moiety). It is an alliancewide ceremony, and it must be initiated by the most important man of the alliance.

CONFEDERATION

The confederation, which is a territorial, social, and political unit within the alliance, is perhaps the most important unit of Dani social organization. The confederation is the frame for much more group activity than is the alliance.

While people frequently move from compound to compound, and even from neighborhood to neighborhood, they tend to stay within the boundary of the confederation. Although a Dani would rarely make this explicit, it seems clear that his basic allegiance is to the confederation rather than to larger or smaller units. When one Dani wishes to identify another, he is concerned about his sib affiliation first (and thereby, of course, his moiety) and his confederation second.

There are some thirty confederations in the Grand Valley, varying considerably in their degree of discreteness. Some, like the Gosi-Alua in 1963, are recognized as discrete units with clear boundaries. Others, like the Dloko-Mabel and the Dlabi-Mabel around Jibiga in 1968, are recognized as being to some extent politically and ritually independent, but they occupy a common territory and for a time the leaders of the Dloko-Mabel were recognized as the leaders of the Dlabi-Mabel also. The Wilihiman-Walalua Confederation, which includes the Dugum Neighborhood, presents an even more ambiguous case. Its name includes four sib names—Wilil, Himan, Walilo, and Alua—and suggests that two confederations, the Wilil-Himan and the Walilo-Alua, merged into one. However, there is no basis for distinguishing two separate confederations in terms of territory, or political, ritual, or social behavior. (Until 1966 there was another separate Wilil-Himan confederation on the Elogeta River, neighboring the Wilihiman-Walalua.)

The Wilihiman-Walalua Confederation, which includes the Dugum Neighborhood, occupies some eight square kilometers in the southern end of the Gutelu Alliance area. The population of the Confederation is about one thousand people. Most of the men, and all the more important men of the confederation, belong to one of the four named sibs (Wilil, Himan, Walilo, and Alua). A tendency to patrilocal residence in terms of confederation boundaries is shown by the fact that most adult males are native to the confederation.

The independence of the confederations is in constant flux as wars wax and wane, alliances form and collapse, and important men emerge and fade.

Although the Grand Valley Dani have no name for confederation per se, each confederation has a name, usually compounded from the names of the two dominant sibs of the confederation. In most cases one of the dominant sibs is of the Wida moiety and the other of the Waija moiety. However, in one confederation to the south of the Dugum Neighborhood, the Siep-Eloktak, both sibs are Waija.

Membership in the confederation is dependent on residence, but there are no formal residence requirements. People often leave their original confederation, usually because of interpersonal friction, and come to another confederation where they live first with friends, participate in the activities of their new confederation, and eventually build their own houses and even compounds. After a few months or a year or two, they are considered part of their new confederation. Even when moving across alliance frontiers, they may be accepted by their former enemies.

The confederation can only be considered a loose group, since there are no activities limited to the confederation in which everyone, or even every man, is required to participate. However, there are a few activities which are generally participated in by most of the people of the confederation. Since the confederation itself does not actually own goods of any sort, it cannot be considered a corporate group in the usual sense of the term. It does occupy a territory, but as will be discussed below, it does not actually own the land.

War is conducted on an alliance level, with alliance fighting for several years against alliance. But the separate one-day battles are fought primarily by the confederations. A battle is initiated by the important men of one confederation, who challenge the important men of the contiguous enemy confederation to fight on one of the battlegrounds in the intervening no-man's-land. Most of men and older boys from each confederation will then join in the battle, even if only to stand in the rear ranks as noncombatants. Frequently they will be joined by individuals or groups from other confederations in their respective alliances, but the battle remains the responsibility of the initiating confederation. Similarly, in the *edai,* or two-day dance ceremony that follows the killing of an enemy, people from other confederations always join in the ceremony, but it remains an *edai* of the confederation responsible for the kill.

The *je wakanin* ceremony (p. 139) which occurs midway in time and size between the individual funeral cremations and the alliance-wide *ebe akho* ceremony is for the most part a confederation ceremony. Both the Wilihiman-Walalua and the Gosi-Alua held a *je wakanin* ceremony in November 1961, and on one day held a joint ceremony at Wakawaka, the home of the very important man Sula.

In November 1963 there was another ceremony at Wakawaka, again including the Wilihiman-Walalua and the Gosi-Alua, but excluding Gutelu's confederation, the Dloko-Mabel. Gutelu, who was supposed, as leader not just of his own confederation but of the entire alliance to initiate the *ebe akho* ceremony, had delayed for months, and the leaders of the other confederations in the alliance attempted to usurp his privilege and initiate the ceremony themselves. After Gutelu made various physical and supernatural threats, a compromise was reached and he agreed to the immediate beginning of the *ebe akho.*

These ceremonies involving more than one confederation but less than the entire alliance represented a step in the division of the alliance into two separate alliances. The break-up of the Gutelu Alliance had its roots in friction between the two factions which was apparent even in 1961, and the events of 1963 hastened the end despite the apparently amicable settlement of the *ebe akho* dispute in 1964. The alliance was finally shattered in 1966, when one faction of the alliance attacked the other faction. By 1968 the two sides were in different alliances, recreating the situation which had existed a generation before, and of the two confederations which had lain along the line of fracture, one was split in two and the other had been dispersed.

THE NEIGHBORHOOD

The Neighborhood is an analytical construction which I developed after several months' observation out of a need for some unit smaller than the confederation on which to focus my study. In 1961–1963 it was a convenient unit, but the events of 1966 caused so much turmoil that by 1968 it was not. Here it is described as it was in the early 1960's.

The people of the Dugum Neighborhood are considered to be those who actually lived (rather than visited) for more than a week or so in compounds in the Neighborhood. The Dugum Neighborhood does represent a real unit in a geographical sense. However, there is no Dani term for the concept of neighborhood, and it seems unlikely that a Dani would consider himself a "member" of a "neighborhood." No formal activity involves the entire neighborhood and only the neighborhood, but most close friendships and informal working or playing takes place within groups living in the same neighborhood. It may be said that the neighborhood approximates the maximal area of regular face-to-face contact. No compound in the Neighborhood is more than about twenty minutes from any other.

The Dugum Neighborhood covers roughly two square kilometers (Plate 13, Map C.4). Over the course of the thirty-two months between early 1961 and late 1963 at least 361 people lived in 39 compounds grouped in 16 compound clusters in the Neighborhood. However, the number of people and compounds at any one moment during this period was somewhat lower than these figures. Table 2.6 breaks the population down in terms of sex and age relative to marriage (which occurs for men when they are roughly twenty, for girls at about fifteen).

TABLE 2.6
POPULATION OF THE DUGUM NEIGHBORHOOD BY AGE AND SEX

	Male	Female
Too Young For Marriage (males under 20, females under 15)	53	41
Never Will Marry (defectives)	3	2
Married (males over 20, females over 15, married or widowed)	92	170
Total	148	213

On three sides the boundaries of the Dugum Neighborhood are formed by unpopulated areas, and only on the West is there real ambiguity about the boundary. However, I suspect that elsewhere in the Grand Valley where there

PLATE 13. The Dugum Neighborhood. An aerial view from the northwest, with the Dugum Neighborhood in the center of the photograph. On the left, the mountain wall swings around to end in the small knoll of the Dugum Hill. In the foreground is the Eloketa River. The far boundary of the Dugum Neighborhood is marked by the Aikhe River running along the base of the Dutoba Ridge. (Photograph by Eliot Elisofon)

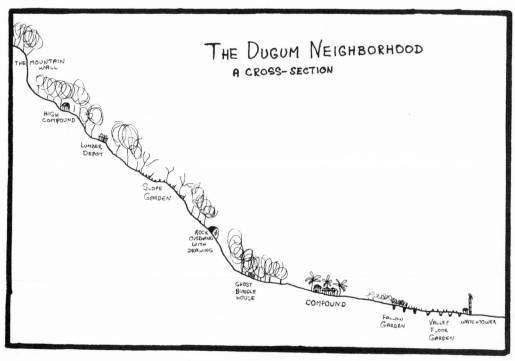

DIAGRAM 2.3
THE DUGUM NEIGHBORHOOD: A CROSS-SECTION

are no such conveniently bounded areas of similar size the neighborhood may not be a useful frame of reference.

The Dugum Neighborhood has a range of features lacking in other less favorably situated areas in the Grand Valley. The Dugum includes both flat valley floor and slope gardens, both larger valley floor compound clusters and isolated compounds on the forested hilly flanks where people take pigs for fresh rooting ground.

The sib representation in the Dugum Neighborhood was described in Table 2.1 (p. 67). A total of 82 per cent of the men and 54 per cent of the women in the Neighborhood belong to one of the five dominant sibs, Wilil, Himan, Walilo, Alua, and Phaluk. The difference between the men's and women's figures is some indication of the degree of patrilocal residence in terms of the Neighborhood. Adults of other sibs have for the most part moved into the Neighborhood in their own lifetimes. The fact that the Neighborhood women represent nearly twice as many sibs as the men, also indicates the degree to which women tend to marry into the husband's area. But because the Dani moved so much and it is difficult to establish a home area for most, I did not gather specific figures on exogamy.

COMPOUND

The compound is the smallest territorial unit of Dani social organization and the focus of Dani activity. It consists of several buildings of specialized design linked together like pearls on a necklace by fences, and laid out so as to open to an elongated closed central courtyard: the long common house, where cooking and other daily activities take place; the large round men's house, where men and boys and sometimes younger girls spend hours talking, working, and sleeping; several smaller round women's houses where women, girls, and the youngest children sleep; and one or more pig sties. Behind the houses are banana plants and often small vegetable gardens, pandanus tres, gourd frames, and pig runs. The whole is enclosed by an outer fence. This is the basic residential unit, the compound (Pls. 44–47). Often several contiguous compounds have common banana yards; sometimes a smaller tributary compound will open on to a major compound. The structures of the compound will be described in Chapter 9.

In the Dugum Neighborhood the compounds range in population from three (a single nuclear family) to a maximum of about forty. Generally, each compound is composed of parts of several extended polygynous families. In only a few cases these extended families are linked by real or at least sib relations.

It is perhaps better to speak of the interaction that goes on within the compound not as interaction primarily of the residents of the compound but of the entire Neighborhood. During the course of a normal day the men's house and even the common house will have as many visitors as residents. These visitors come to gossip, smoke, and often casually share in the meals.

Funerals, curing ceremonies, and most other ceremonies take place in the compound (*silimo*), and for an important ceremony, the courtyard is likely to be filled with several hundred men, women, and children from the Neighborhood and beyond. It is in fact rare that the entire compound will be involved in some activity that does not also include people from other compounds.

The individual compounds do not have names, although they are often referred to in terms of the most important man: "*Hat koma lakadik?*" ("Where are you going?") "Um'ue *wetekma*." ("To the place of Um'ue.") Of the thirty-nine compounds in the Neighborhood, only six stand by themselves. The others are attached to and enclosed by a fence common with one to four other compounds. To call such clusters of compounds villages or hamlets would be misleading. Geographically they form one unit; but in terms of social, political, or ritual interaction, they are independent of one another, and in most cases there is no greater degree of interaction between contiguous compounds than between compounds of different clusters.

The Dani make no lexical distinction between the compounds and the compound cluster. The term *sili*, or *osili*, refers to an area where there are houses. Although each compound cluster may be referred to by an individual name, this name is not strictly the name of the compound but rather the name of the area where the compound is located.

WATCHTOWER GROUP

A more ephemeral and secondary territorial group is formed by the men responsible for a certain watchtower. These watchtowers are in the garden areas on or close to the edge of no-man's-land, between the Wilihiman-Walalua and the Widaia areas. Each tower provides a small platform seven to ten meters above the ground, from which the man can watch for an enemy raid while the women are working in the gardens (Plate 49). Each watchtower commands a strip of the garden area, and the men with interests in those gardens take the responsibility for maintaining the watchtower. In the Dugum there are no special-status young bachelor sentries such as Peters reports from the southern Grand Valley (1965:83).

Beside each watchtower is a low shelter with thatched roof, open on the sides. Here during the day men gather to gossip, smoke, knit shell bands and sleep. These shelters are *wusa*, or taboo, for women to even approach, and they form a sort of secondary men's house. The watchtowers were maintained and manned during wartime, but after September 1961 and the advent of peace, they were allowed to decay and by 1968 no watchtowers were left.

RITUAL GROUPS

The territorial units described above have an intermeshing variety of social, political, economic, and ritual functions. However, there are also two kinds of groups that do not fit conveniently into the categories used to describe the other groups. These exceptions, while territorial to some extent, are defined only in terms of their ritual function. They are the *ganekhe* group, holding the sacred stones of its members, and the *wagun* group, responsible for the grass bundles symbolic of the dead and kept in a house or cave in the forest.

Ganekhe Group. Much of Dani ceremonial activity centers around the *ganekhe*, certain sacred objects that are stored in the cabinets at the rear of certain men's houses (Plate 59). These objects include the *sugan*, very sacred slate stones that lie, wrapped, on the floor of the cabinet.

Ganekhe were kept in ten different men's houses in the Dugum Neighborhood. Most of them were owned by three to seven men of the same sib, and one group was owned by fifteen men of the Wilil sib. In all cases the men lived in the Neighborhood.

Basically the *ganekhe* are owned by individual adult men, and if one man moves to another area he may take his *ganekhe* to a more conveniently located men's house. However, when ritual involving the *ganekhe* objects takes place, the *ganekhe* group acts together and all its members are expected to participate.

The *ganekhe* group are all members of the same sib who generally live in the same or adjacent neighborhoods. Some men who spent most of their time in compounds of the Dugum Neighborhood actually kept their *ganekhe* in compounds in other parts of the confederation, and a very few of the newcomers to the area had their *ganekhe* in distant places.

Except in the cases of those sibs with only a few local representatives, the *ganekhe* group does not include all the men of one sib in the confederation, or even the Neighborhood.

Women have only indirect interests in these objects through their brothers or husbands.

In a few cases the men are related to one another through known genealogical links; but in most cases, and especially with the larger groups, the common sib membership is the formal link, although sometimes vague relationship through a distant ancestor is cited. It is tempting to see these as small lineage groups, each holding its own sacred objects. However, the Dani are not particularly concerned with genealogical relationships, and emphasize common sib membership over blood ties. Thus, at the present time, these *ganekhe* groups are better described as local sib segments which may incidentally be lineages, than as lineages which may be especially complex. Formerly the *ganekhe* objects may have been held only by groups of brothers and cousins, but such projection is not supported by any data.

Mogat Ai Group. In the Dugum Neighborhood are three *mogat ai* (literally, ghost houses), wooden structures containing grass bundles representing dead people, placed in the structures at the time of the funeral. One structure is used for members of three of the four major sibs in the confederation, Wilil, Himan, and Walilo, another by three minor sibs, and the third by two minor sibs. The other major sib of the confederation, Alua, uses a *mogat ai* in the territory of the allied Gosi-Alua.

PLATE 14. Gutelu, the most important man of the Gutelu Alliance.

This pattern may represent former sib confederations which have since been rearranged. The only joint activity involving the *mogat ai* is in connection with the *ebe akho* ceremony.

SUPRAALLIANCE TRIBUTE SYSTEM

The alliance is the largest territorial unit within which there is organized social, political, and religious activity. The only regular interalliance activity is warfare between enemy alliances and trade between friendly alliances.

However, there is some activity on a supraalliance level, which may be considered tribute systems. They involve payments of pigs by the leaders of some alliances in return for certain rights of access to areas controlled by leaders of other alliances or by Grand Valley leaders to their counterparts in the Jalemo for sacred red paint.

According to information gathered by Father van der Stap and related to me in a personal communication, Wasin, the very important leader of the Siep-Gosi Confederation in the Mid-Grand Valley, receives a regular payment of pigs from the people of the Delok-ugu, the Southern Jalemo, for allowing them to live in that area. The details of Wasin's rights over that area were not specified.

This arrangement is apparently contradicted by data from a Dugum Dani informant concerning the baked red clay (*bimut*) that comes from the Jalemo and plays an essential role in boys' initiation into the Waija moiety at the *ebe akho* ceremony. The red is painted on the initiates and is also used for the red series of rock paintings. The red pigment, used throughout the Grand Valley for boys' initiations, comes into the Grand Valley by two routes. The first is from the Northern Jalemo through Gutelu, the most important man of the Dloko-Mabel Confederation and of the alliance which includes the Dugum Neighborhood. This red goes to all the groups in the northern half of the Grand Valley. The second source of red is the Delok-ugu, or Southern Jalemo, which supplies red to the groups in the southern half of the Grand Valley. The Welesi, in the upper Wamena Valley, get their initiation red from a separate source.

The Waija men of each confederation, including those of Gutelu's own alliance, give Gutelu one or more pigs for the red. Likewise, the Waija men of the southern half of the Grand Valley, including Wasin of the Siep-Gosi, send pigs to the Southern Jalemo in exchange for their their own initiation red.

In a sense this circulation of goods is a form of trade. However, because of its obligatory and ritual aspect, it may also be called tribute.

A third sort of tribute is payment of pigs to Gutelu by groups outside his

PLATE 15. Wali, or Um'ue, who by 1968 was a very important man of the new alliance.

alliance for free access to the Iluekaima brine pool. Members of the Gutelu Alliance have free access to the brine pool.

Gutelu and his Dloko-Mabel Confederation physically control access to the brine pool, but, more important, they also control the *wusa*, or sacred power of the pool itself.

Apparently Hatateak, the important man of the area across the Balim River, paid Gutelu at the time of his *ebe akho* two pigs for access to the brine pool and one for the initiation red. The pigs given for salt access are called *wam wude*, and those for the red pigment are called *wam usakun* (*usakun* has many shades of meaning, all connoting sacred, powerful status). But knowledge of these intraalliance relationships is not widespread, and even in 1968, when I was in close contact with Gutelu, it was difficult to learn about them.

LEADERSHIP AND INFLUENCE

The difficulty of defining the Dani concept of leadership is like that faced by other anthropologists in Melanesia. Oliver has described (1955:xvii ff.) his original problem of finding out about the leaders of the Siuai of Bougainville; Pospisil relates that when he went to the Ekagi (Kapauku) of West New Guinea he had been assured that there was a "virtual absence of authority and leadership" (1958:77), and Brown has described the pre-European situation of the Chimbu of East New Guinea as showing "an absence of any fixed authority ('anarchy')" (1963:3) and "no formal office of leadership existed for the tribe or any segment of it" (Brookfield and Brown 1963:8). Closer examination does of course reveal a pattern of leadership which seems to be fairly uniform throughout the Melanesian region. Sahlins has described the Melanesian leader (in contrast to the Polynesian chief) as a man of achieved influence rather than of inherited power, who functions through consensus rather than proclamation (1963). As Sahlins points out, the term for leader in many Melanesian societies is translated literally as "big man." Salisbury, in his penetrating analysis of New Guinea leadership (1964), suggests that while most leaders are of the generally democratic "Melanesian big man" pattern, the men at the very top are in fact despots. The aspiring leaders of the second rank, who function within the egalitarian ideology, are more numerous and more visible to the anthropologist, while the really big men are in fact outside the system and tend to be written off as anomolous. Salisbury's analysis of these two rather different sorts of leaders does seem to fit the Dani situation: the confederation-level leaders are of the big man pattern, while at the head of most alliances is a leader of a significantly different caliber, although the term despot may be too strong. My own observations were primarily of confederation-level leaders, and certainly this picture of Dani leadership would be somewhat different if it had been based on the behavior of Gutelu, the most important man of the Alliance.

Dani leadership is highly informal. Leaders gradually emerge, reach a peak of leadership, and then gradually decline. Leadership is not marked by elections, inaugurations, material symbols or rank, or other dramatic forms of public recognition. There is public implicit acknowledgement rather than an explicit recognition of leaders. The leaders act through influence, by persuasion rather than by wielding coercive power.

DANI TERMINOLOGY

On the Dani gradient of influence, there are two concepts: *ab gogtek* and *gebu*.

Ab gogtek. Ab gogtek means literally "big man." This term or its Southern Valley equivalent, *gain*, is translated by the government and missionaries as "chief." This is inaccurate on two counts. The concept of chief implies an institutionalized authority with coercive power. This is lacking among the Dani. Further, *ab gogtek* is a very broad term. It was, during my stay among the Dani, applied to nearly every man at one time or another. Of the hundred or so adult men in the Neighborhood, informants were willing to call all but one or two *ab gogtek*. In this sense the term may be better understood as normal men, men who fight, farm, have at least one wife or are only temporarily bachelors.

The terms for leader that mean literally "big man" throughout New Guinea and Melanesia (cf. Sahlins 1963) are usually much more restricted in usage. Since the Dani term has such a broad reference, I prefer to use "leader" or "important man" when describing Dani of special influence.

In addition to the broad term *ab gogtek*, there are several other terms that apparently indicate status of greater and perhaps more specialized influence. Informants varied greatly when describing and differentiating between the attributes of these various statuses, and no two informants agreed on who occupied any particular status. It seems probable that these statuses are roughly synonymous for persons with relatively more influence than the other *ab gogtek*.

Terms of address for an especially important man is *namene* or *najege*, both of which mean "my dog" and which refer to the *anini* quality of the dog, a kind of reckless bravery.

On the other hand, there are two men in the Alliance with kinds of status which seem to be more than just quantitatively different from the *ab gogtek* status, but which do not seem to have a special name. First, Gutelu himself has the unique authority to initiate the *ebe akho* and thus is the only confederation leader with real alliancewide influence.

The attempt by Sula, Weteklue, and Polik in November 1963 to usurp this power and to initiate the *ebe akho* on their own was an explicit challenge to Gutelu's prerogative. The ultimate failure of this attempt in the face of Gutelu's displeasure supports the suggestion that his is a special although perhaps vulnerable status.

Gutelu's status was inherited from his father. It has a strong supernatural foundation, based on his control of the brine pool at Iluekaima and the house of the sun at Wadlagu, and other particularly powerful sacred objects.

To use Salisbury's terms (1964), Gutelu is a "director," while Weteklue is merely an ordinary man who has risen by ordinary means to the top of the "executive" category. In every alliance in the Grand Valley there is one such man who can initiate the pig ceremony. The names of these men are known throughout the Grand Valley.

The second unique status was that of Maikmo, the important man of the Wilil-Himan, a minor group which broke off from the Wilihiman-Walalua Confederation, probably in the 1950's. They lived on the Elogeta River, adjacent to the Wilihiman-Walalua, with whom they had friendly but somewhat distant relations. Peters mentions that in the southern Grand Valley members of the Himan sib (to which Maikmo belongs) have a special relationship with the sun. Maikmo's Wilil-Himan were caught in the middle of the attack of June 1966 which destroyed the alliance, and afterwards they dispersed. By 1968 this group could hardly be said to exist, and Maikmo was living almost as a refugee in the far end of the old alliance area.

Maikmo has a special relationship with the sun and the moon. The details are not clear. Some people say that he is the child of the sun. A general euphemism for the sun is *ninakoja*, our mother; while it is recognized that for most people this is just a manner of speaking, there may be some genealogical mythology behind Maikmo's use of the term. In any case, Maikmo seems to have much closer relationships with the sun and moon than even Gutelu, and by virtue of this relationship Maikmo is said to be particularly effective in controlling rain. These two men seem to have the sort of extraordinary position of leadership which was described by Salisbury. Unfortunately I had only casual contact with both of them and was unable to get extensive data on their activities.

Gebu. At the other end of the power scale are those men who are called *gebu*. The *gebu* are the rare permanent bachelors and are noticeably subnormal both physically and mentally. In the Dugum Neighborhood there were only three of them, compared with ninety-two married men. These are the only men who are never called *ab gogtek*, or big man. My questions about whether these three could be called *ab gogtek* always met with amused but firm denial. The *gebu* are the men who do not fully participate in the normal male activities: they do not fight, they have never killed, they are not married, and any suggestion on my part that they might eventually marry was met with scornful laughter; they are less than men in the sense that they do not carry a man's burden in the compound's economic or social life; but none of the *gebu* observed in the Neighborhood take on any aspects of the woman's life. There is no transvestism. They are simply a little outside the system. But they are not worthless; their prestige is low, but they are tolerated, even with affection.

Hubugaijo is a prime example of *gebu*, and the first on every list of *gebu*. A withered middle-aged man, about forty, he is very clumsy, and perhaps feeble-minded. He has no wives, no pigs, no gardens. Yet he never lacks a place to sleep or food to eat. Often he visits Um'ue's compound for a few days or weeks. He sits quietly in the rear of the men's house, rarely joining in the conversation. When he enters, men whisper to me in a stage whisper, "*Hubugaijo gebu!*" He is the frequent butt of jokes, most of them sexual, on the part of the younger men. They snatch at his testicles or flip off his penis gourd as he is slowly changing into a new one. Sometimes he is blamed long and elaborately for running off with a pig or a wife. The teasing is abruptly ended just as he seems about to burst into tears. But despite his uselessness, and his clumsiness, he is often treated with regard. He may be drawn aside for a serious consultation during a ceremony. When the men of the compound where he is staying participate in joint work effort, Hubugaijo joins them. During one of his stays with Um'ue he built and planted a small tobacco garden outside the compound on his own initiative.

SYMBOLIC SIZE

Despite the broadness of the term *ab gogtek*, it is possible to ascertain the real leaders by asking who are the *really* large men. *Gog* (big) refers not to physical size—indeed, many leaders are of normal height—but to symbolic size, a concept implicit in the idea of leadership. Sometimes the relative influence of leaders is described by indicating relative heights above the ground with the hand. Also, the *wap*, the brightest stars and planets in the night sky, are said to be the heads of particularly important leaders touching the sky. These men are also described as *edaka pokot*, literally "called sky" in reference to their symbolic association with the sky.

THE IDEAL DANI LEADER

Dani statements about leadership are worth noting, even though they do not particularly correspond to observable reality. The invariable Dani answer to the question, "Why is (X) such a big man?", is "He has kill many people in war." Secondary replies mention his many wives and pigs. But in fact, the lists of killings attributed to the various men of the Neighborhood are greatly inflated or at best describe general participation in a killing. (If they were real, one would have expected that their enemies had long since been completely eradicated.) The number of wives a man has is more a result of influence, especially economic influence, than a cause of it. And leaders in fact often have fewer pigs on hand than many less important men.

Skill in oratory, which figures so prominently in the leadership pattern of nearly every other New Guinea society, is quite unimportant to the Dani. There are no speeches at public events. The leaders of a ceremony will mumble incantations at ghosts or shout names to identify givers or receivers of goods, and at battles it is most often the young and unimportant men who shout the most hilarious obscenities. The persuasiveness of a leader is exercised privately, in small groups or tête-à-tête.

The confederation-level leaders are all gentle men of strength and skill. To some extent these Dani leaders correspond to Read's (1954) description of the leaders of the Gahuku-Gama in East New Guinea. But while Read suggests that this gentleness is a mark of autonomy, of standing somewhat outside a system in which the primary male virtue is aggressiveness, in the Dani case it is this gentleness which seems to be the dominant virtue. Read has said of New Guinea Highlanders in general that

they seem to be continually on the verge of some more or less violent and unexpected outburst, and continual close association with them becomes a strain. (1954:6),

This description certainly does *not* fit the Dugum Dani. Their aggressiveness in warfare is a different matter. It is not so much interpersonal aggression for the purpose of domination, but much more a tactical skill whose result may be the death of an enemy. The Dani simply do not live in the tense, aggressive atmosphere that Read and many others since have reported from the Highlands of New Guinea.

I think that when the Dani describe their leaders as killers with many wives and pigs, they are referring to a general quality of skill or competence: Personal aggressiveness and brutality, even against an enemy, is not valued; but one often hears the cry "*Hat hotiak*" ("you are clever") said approvingly to both children and adults, referring to this skillful competence.

MEANS OF GAINING INFLUENCE

There are no formalized requirements or institutionalized paths to leadership and influence. Likewise, there is no status or rank that a man at some point in his career assumes and later relinquishes. All normal men are big men (*ab gogtek*) to some degree. Those I call leaders are those with the greatest influence. The Dani themselves have no comparable term to separate out this category of leaders.

Since the means of increasing one's influence are implicit, we must look to those men who have greater or less influence and attempt to discover the reasons for their position in the continuum.

Pospisil has stated of the Ekagi (Kapauku) that "pig breeding constitutes the only way to become rich and to acquire prestige, achievements which in turn enable a man to become an influential politician" (1958:14) and that "wealth and skill in oratory constitute the prerequisites for assumption of the political leadership of a village" (1958:15). For the Dugum Dani wealth is certainly a factor in achieving leadership, but skill in oratory apparently does not play an important role. There seem to be four major factors in the development of influence for the Dugum Dani.

Skill in Warfare. Skill in warfare is a major factor in the prestige of a man. The number of kills a man has to his credit, is probably not so important. Rather, his bravery or his fearlessness is important. This quality may be demonstrated in different ways. A man like Wejaklegek, or the cripple Alheto, demonstrate it on the front line of battle, never retreating and courting enemy arrows. On the other hand, the powerful Um'ue is rarely seen on the front lines—he fights on the side, in the bush, where cleverness is more important than brute courage.

The younger men are judged by their skill and courage in the face of the enemy. For those men who have enough influence to call a battle or raid, much of their prestige rides on their skill in assuring the success of the venture.

Economic Competition and Household Size. Economic power is gained not so much by accumulation of wealth as by skillful manipulation of wealth in the complex exchange system—in participating in the exchange which takes place at funerals and other ceremonies. An unimportant man such as Egali happens to have many more pigs but less prestige than an important man like Um'ue.

The number of wives a man has does not directly effect his prestige; rather the number of women—wives, older relatives, and young girls—and boys in his household has a direct effect on his economic power: The pigs are cared for primarily by women and boys, and so if a man has few women and boys, his ability to maintain a large heard is diminished. In practice this is not a limiting factor: Egali, with one wife and one son, maintains a herd of about fifteen pigs; Um'ue, although there are perhaps ten women and boys in his household, is never able to increase his herd much beyond ten because he is involved in so much exchange at funerals. Women are further important because, salt, which is traded for feathers, furs, exchange stones, and net materials from the Jale, is prepared exclusively by the women; too, the exchange nets are made exclusively by women.

An indication of the influence of a man is the number of youths—boys and sometimes even girls—who come to live in his compound on the basis of the kinship structure, and in particular the *ami* relationship. The *ami* is the mother's brother, but also includes all men of the mother's sib or even moiety. The *opase*, strictly the father, but extended to all men of the father's sib and even moiety, functions similarly. A youth can claim either *opase* or *ami* relationship with any man of the area, and, if there is a friendly relationship, can live in that man's compound, sharing the work of the compound, and eventually expects the man to assist in the marriage exchange, or in exchange at the cremation of one of the youth's closer relatives, and even in disputes. These youths, between age ten and the time they are married (around the age of twenty) lead highly mobile lives, drifting from one compound to another. An important man like Um'ue may have up to three or four such youths staying in his compound, but there is nothing formalized in these relationships.

Heredity and Inheritance. An important factor in prestige not recognized explicitly by the Dani is heredity. Heredity has an indirect effect on prestige: A man is not important simply because his father was a leader; but several factors make it easier for such a man to rise in importance, make it more likely that a leader will be the son of a leader.

Since the more important men tend to have more wives and therefore more sons than the less important men, perhaps probability favors an important man having an important father. But more significant is the fact that the important man will be able to give his sons pigs, and his sons will have a share in his other wealth. When the time comes for them to marry, they will have easier access to wealth for the marriage exchange than the son of a poor man.

Charisma. The factor of charisma is easy to exaggerate in a situation such as the Dugum Dani, where the other factors are so vague. However, it is certainly present. Personal charisma must be a factor in almost any culture except where there is a purely hereditary kinship or a leadership based on certain special talents such as shamanism.

In the Dani case, charisma is not demonstrated by the orator, but rather by the man acting within the small group—in his conversation in the men's house or the watchtower shelter.

There is no Dani term for charisma, but it is related to the Dani concept of *edai-egen,* the physiological heart; also the soul of the living man; and, most pertinent in this sense, it may be described as the "goodness" of a person. A man with a short temper, who is easily provoked into hurting people within his group (as opposed to the valued killing of the enemy), is described as *edai-egen dlek,* having no heart. The leader is also the man with a great *edai-egen,* a man kind to children, hospitable to all.

This concept contradicts to some extent the category of *hunuk balin,* in which are found those who are particularly ruthless in war and who are also sometimes said to have no *edai-egen.* For example, Husuk, an important leader of the Gosi-Alua, is *hunuk balin* but is also noted for his kindness.

Prestige and Influence. Prestige does not necessarily imply influence as a leader. For example, Asikhanedlek (Plate 36) has prestige because of his fighting ability, but he has little influence. Like his father before him, he is relatively poor. He has one wife, and rarely more than one pig. Most important, he is a loner. He lives with his wife and daughter alone in a compound, one of the two one-family compounds in the Neighborhood. He chooses solitude, which is rare among the highly gregarious Dani.

Oaklia also has prestige without influence. Although he also has only one wife, his compound attracts several other older women, a girl, and several youths. He is a member of the powerful Wilil sib. Economically he is well off. But he does not excel in warfare. Although other men often come to his men's house, he rarely visits other men's houses.

LEADERSHIP AND SPHERES OF INFLUENCE

Leadership among the Dani may be reduced to influence; the extent to which a man is a leader is determined by the kinds of activities in which he can exercise effective influence on the behavior of others. The spheres of influence pertinent to the Dani are cooperative work projects, warfare, and various ceremonies.

Cooperative Work Projects. Most work is done by men working alone or together with the men of a single household or compound. However, there are some jobs—in particular, thatching a roof and smearing mud on a garden—that are usually done by a larger group of men, a dozen or more. If the man or men who own the house or garden have enough influence to call (*jogo*) the group together it is a sign of influence.

In the case of house building, influence is never a problem. Any man with enough influence to have a house of his own will have enough influence to summon the necessary helpers. This is not always true in the case of a garden. Even boys as young as ten may have their own gardens. Most boys from the age of fifteen or so do have their own gardens. Most men, and even some boys of fifteen, are able to call a crew of men and boys to help them in the mudding. There are a few exceptions: Asikhanedlek does most of his own mudding, although he is occasionally helped by his cousin, Huoge. One man, even more of a loner than Asikhanedlek, had no help at all in mudding his large garden. However, nearly all men have enough influence to call a mudding crew together.

Warfare. War itself is an alliance affair, but the events of war, the raids and battles, are usually carried out on the confederation level.

The leaders in warfare are those who have the influence to initiate, or call (*jogo*), a raid or battle. The members of a raiding party are usually drawn from among friends living in a single neighborhood; the participants in a battle are drawn from the entire confederation. However, both the raid and the battle are called by leaders of confederation stature—men whose influence extends beyond the neighborhood. There is considerable disagreement as to how many men are able to call raids. But in practice, raids are called only by a few men in the confederation. Of these, only Weteklue or Nilik call battles. However, since in a battle called by a Wilihiman-Walalua leader, the warriors are usually joined by the allied Gosi-Alua, this man may be said to have influence beyond the federation.

Ceremonies. The only man whose influence is alliancewide is Gutelu (Plate 14) of the Dloko-Mabel Confederation. Some men from the Dloko-Mabel often drift over to battles on the southern front, and occasionally Wilihiman-Walalua men participate in battles on the northern fronts. However, only one event is truly alliancewide. This is the *ebe akho,* the great pig feast that takes place every four or five years. In 1963 Gutelu proved to be the only man able to initiate this ceremony.

Another ceremony, intermediate in size between the *ebe akho* and individual cremations is the *je wakanin* (carrying of the exchange stones) which, in October 1961, involved the Wilihiman-Walalua, the Gosi-Alua, the Phaluk-Matian, and several other confederations, but not the Dloko-Mabel. This was initiated by Sula, the leader of the Phaluk-Matian, and Weteklue of the Wilihiman-Walalua.

A further indication of influence is the custody of war trophies. Until 1961 all trophies captured by any members of the alliance were taken into custody by

Gutelu. By May 1961, however, the influence of Gutelu in this matter over the southern members of the alliance was weakening, and Weteklue took custody of trophies captured by the Wilihiman-Walalua on the southern front.

Funerals provide a frequent opportunity for the public exercise of leadership on the confederation or even neighborhood level. A cremation is held in the compound in which the person died. To some extent, the number of mourners and the number of gifts brought to the cremation and the later *ilkho* ceremony terminating the mourning period are determined by the influence of the dead person and the circumstance of death. The cremation of a person killed by an enemy will draw considerably more attention than that of a person who has died of natural causes, because of the greater need to placate the ghosts after a war death. For example, although the cremation of the young boy Wejakhe, killed in a raid, was held in the compound of the unimportant Halihule and was run by Asilanedlek and Huoge, both uninfluential young men, a large number of gifts was brought because of the circumstances of the death.

To some extent, however, the number of gifts is determined by the influence of the men in whose compound the cremation is held. At the cremation of Asikhanedlek's father, in his compound, there were pitifully few gifts; at the cremation of Jagik, formerly an influential man and father of two influential sons, Nilik and Elabotok, held in Nilik's compound, there was an exceptionally large number of gifts. During a period of six months, in 1961–1962, there were seven cremations in the neighborhood, five of them in Um'ue's compound. Of these, three were for people who did not live in the compound but who had come there a few days or weeks before they died. It was said that they expected there would be a better cremation if it were run by Um'ue. This reflects both the financial ability of the host, who must sacrifice more of his own pigs than the visitors, and his influence in being able to call gifts to a cremation for which he is responsible.

To the largest cremations, gifts and visitors come from most of the neighborhood, and a few may come from outside the neighborhood.

INFLUENCE GROUPS

Within the groups of Dani social organization described above, it is possible to speak of three separate but interrelated realms of influence and leadership: men, children and boys, and women. The mainstream of social leadership, which is confined to the men, has been described above.

The leadership of children's play groups lies with boys up to an age of about fifteen. Until this age children have no influence in the economic or any other aspect of the culture. They do participate to the extent of herding pigs or helping with minor jobs around the compound such as baby-sitting, but they work in a strictly noninfluential capacity. Groups of boys in a neighborhood frequently play together, in more or less organized play. The core of these groups are boys ten to thirteen years of age, but the groups also include smaller brothers and sisters on the fringes. Play is often war games—mock battles with grass spears, or shooting at rolling hoops with wooden spears; *waik*, where spears are skidded along the ground to achieve the greatest distance; or expeditions to kill birds with sticks or crude bows and arrows. In this play the leaders are primarily the boys with the greatest skill—such as Juwa, the twelve-year-old son of the unimportant Loliluk.

Leadership Among the Women. Women seldom act as a group. They tend to stay in their compounds or to work individually in gardens. Thus there are no women with broad neighborhood or confederation influence comparable to that of the men. However, women do exert considerable influence on their husbands and even on their grown sons. This influence is related to the important role of women in the economy. They have the primary responsibility for maintaining the gardens, cooking food, and tending the pigs. The degree of independence of Dani women, and therefore their influence, depends to a great extent on their personality. Generally speaking, Dani women are highly independent. In many instances a woman prefers simply to leave her husband or father's household rather than to remain in a stressful situation where influence is necessary. In most cases, however, the women will stay and exert influence even on an influential husband. Um'ue (Plate 15), for example, who in 1963 already had considerable influence in the affairs of the Neighborhood and the local Wilil sib members, was in turn subject to the active influence of his wife Egabue (Plate 40), (It was she who insisted he build a compound in the mountains so she would not have to live with two other of his wives). His strong-willed old mother, Aneakhe (Plate 39), and his young daughter Hagigake both could publicly win their way over him in minor matters of daily life.

Exceptions to the generally limited influence of women in Dani culture are the women with special curing powers, the *he phatphale*. During a curing ceremony a *he phatphale* takes charge of the ceremony, entering the men's house and directing the activities of even the most important men.

CONCLUSIONS

Although the patrilineal ideology expressed in moiety and sib membership and in kinship terms is a prominent and explicit feature of Dani social structure, it has little coercive effect on Dani behavior. The one area where ideology is definitive is in marriage, in which moiety exogamy is rigidly observed. Attendance at ceremonies is not defined by descent, although the forms of the prestations are. Residence is a matter of choice, and although most men live in a confederation which has a strong representation of their own sib, the sibs have considerable geographical distribution, so even this limitation leaves room for option.

Like the economic aspect of Dani life, the social and political aspects show little specialization; that is, there are no classes and there is little concentration of power in the hands of the leaders. However, while economic production is

so generalized that there are virtually no specialized kinds of goods to be exchanged for other specialized kinds of goods within the society, moiety exogamy
creates a social specialization which assures a complex network of social ties.
Along these ties flow gifts valuable because of their general scarcity, not because
of their specialization. Dani society, if one takes the 5,000-person alliance as a
unit, consists of a large interacting group, but it is not a complex group in the
sense of containing much division of labor in an absolute sense. The ties that
make up the social network are an arbitrary socially defined division of labor.
For example, moiety exogamy rules say in effect that one's own moiety produces
no marriageable women, and wives must be obtained from the opposite moiety.
At a funeral, shell gifts are necessary and they must be obtained from the sib
of the dead person's mother. In short, the Dani social network is widespread but
egalitarian.

3

CONFLICT

THE previous chapter, which dealt with the social organization of the Dani, exaggerated a sort of timeless equilibrium of the alliances and confederations. In fact, Dani life is shot through with social conflict that keeps the alliances in a state of constant turmoil. But this turmoil is more that of a glacier than of ocean waves. Changes take place over a period of years and decades and are marked by a long period of stress, leading up to a sudden convulsive rearrangement of the political grouping, and then another long period of slowly building stress.

The focus of this chapter is on interalliance warfare. Since Dani wars begin at the level of individual conflict, a general model of conflict is proposed; then feud and war are described; and finally a detailed holistic analysis of war is presented.

In my earlier field work I was misled by the events which I saw and the inaccessibility of those which I did not, and so misjudged the nature of Dani conflict. During the first months of 1961 I could observe the ongoing ritual aspect of war, which involved little loss of life, no shift of population, no taking of land, and was directed primarily toward placating the ghosts. It was clear that alliances shifted, but the events were never described in great detail. During my entire field work I had the greatest difficulty eliciting satisfactory information from any Dani informant about events which I had not myself seen or already knew specific details about. It was only when I went back in 1968, just two years after a major split of the Gutelu Alliance, that I could put together a picture of the long-term pattern of Dani warfare. The observations of the early 1960's had produced a picture of war that was not so much wrong as only half right.

A MODEL OF DANI CONFLICT

Dani conflict may occur on many different levels. It may be between individuals or between groups of various sizes, from a few men to confederations and alliances. But the source of all Dani conflicts is on an individual level. Neither the confederation nor the alliance has the group power, coordination, or ambitions necessary to formulate and carry out policies that could result in conflicts being precipitated directly on a higher level.

Acts causing friction lead to conflict which, if not resolved, leads to greater conflict. Resolution is a diminishing, even if only temporarily, of conflict.

If conflict is not resolved, it may escalate in terms of the number of people involved and the seriousness of expression. In the Dani situation the maximal extent of the conflict is determined by the sizes of the political groups of the individuals concerned. Conflict may be expressed in personal tension; through name calling; in violence between the two principals; or in intergroup fighting, which takes the form of brawl, feud, or war.

Conflict does not spread beyond the minimal common political group of both principals. Conflict between men of a single neighborhood may eventually split the entire neighborhood, but it will be confined to that neighborhood. Conflict between men of different confederations of the same alliance may involve the two confederations, but even if the conflict breaks into open fighting and men are killed, it is only what the Dani call *umai'im,* and what I call feud. Finally, conflict between men of different alliances may involve both alliances in prolonged hostilities which the Dani call *wim* and I call war.

Neither war nor feud was observed in a formative stage by me, so the accuracy of the conflict model is open to question. It seems unlikely that conflict between two men in an otherwise peaceful and friendly context could in itself escalate into feud or war, unless perhaps the men were of exceptional importance. It seems more likely that a series of interpersonal conflicts would create a hostile atmosphere in which a single additional conflict would then be sufficient to precipitate the feud or war.

SOURCES OF CONFLICT

Among the sources of conflict, pigs and women are primary, and land rights run a poor third. Pigs, by their nature and through the carelessness of the children often assigned to herd them, are frequently missed. If a missing pig is not found, the suspicion quickly arises that it has been stolen. This may often be the case, but the problem remains of determining who was the thief. Accusations wrongly directed created a second righteously aggrieved party, and even accurate accusations increase conflict.

Women are also frequent causes of conflict. Adultery *in situ* is probably rare; at any rate it seldom comes to the public notice. But when it does, it is a source of conflict. Forcible abduction or rape seems rare and unlikely in view of the strong-willed independence of most Dani women, but women do often leave their husbands on slight provocation. This separation, which is a common way of resolving intrafamily conflict, often leads to conflict between the husband and the man to whose compound the wife has fled.

Use of disputed land occasionally leads to conflict. However, there is little evidence of population pressure, even in the relatively densely populated Grand

Valley, and land does not often become an explicit subject of contention between groups. Sometimes, though, one person begins to open a garden area which another was planning to use, and conflict results. It is remarkable that in the origin myth (episodes two and three, pp. 140-1), Nakmatugi, the first man, has disputes over land with both his brothers, and he kills and eats one brother. The prominence of land as a source of conflict in myth is certainly not reflected in the actual cultural pattern.

Thus, while disputes over pigs, women, and land are common causes of conflict, the conflict is often maintained or escalated by the repetition of the offense or by other offenses, of which the most important is killing. War, which is described below in detail, keeps up its momentum by killing, which in turn prompts killing.

RESOLUTION OF CONFLICT

WITHDRAWAL

Withdrawal is a means of resolving conflict by diminishing or eliminating contact between the two parties. This is a common Dani solution and is practiced both by individuals and by groups.

The emotional and social ties holding a nuclear family together are relatively loose, and they can and are broken at will. Discipline and quarreling are rare in the family group, but this apparent peace is bought at the price of family stability. It is easy for a person to detach himself from his nuclear family and move in with another family group. When friction arises, be it between husband and wife, between cowives, or between parents and child, the person with less power and influence—the wife, or the less favorite cowife (not necessarily the junior), or the child—simply moves. Withdrawal seems always to be voluntary and is not a matter of being sent away.

Children of six to eight and older rarely spend much time with their parents; if a man has more than two wives, they rarely live in the same compound. Probably most of this moving falls under the category of withdrawal from a conflict situation. In most cases, where the move is made before the conflict has reached an acute stage, the move is not far; friendly relations are maintained, and the people easily reunite for important work or ritual events.

The term withdrawal seems more appropriate than exile or flight because it suggests the voluntary choice among available alternatives. In exile or flight the individual or group is ejected and finds a new location as best it can. But for the Dani individual or group there is a relative balance among several areas (compounds, neighborhoods, or even confederations) in terms of availability and desirability of residence. While staying may sometimes be difficult, moving is always easy.

Withdrawal is also used by groups of dozens or hundreds of people or even by entire confederations to avoid feud or war.

As a result of a brawl involving most of the Wilil sib men in the Dugum Neighborhood in January 1963, one man was killed, and the less powerful faction moved to new compounds over the crest of the Dutoba Hill, a few kilometers to the southeast. Polite relations were maintained between the two groups, and the sacred objects were kept together, but the separation reduced face-to-face contact to a minimum and there was no further conflict.

Movement of this sort, which is judicious withdrawal, is different only in degree from common flight of defeated groups. For example, about 1950, relations between a group of Dutabut sib members living on the Elogeta River and the other members of the Gutelu Alliance reached a breaking point. A major fight resulted in the death of many Dutabut. The survivors abandoned their land and took refuge on several areas along the Balim River. Since then they have been called Asuk Balek, or "Cut Ear," because it is said that the victors sliced off the ears of the vanquished dead on the battlefield. There are several similar instances of the renaming of a vanquished group with a more or less deprecatory term. But the flight of the Asuk Balek, or Dutabut, was not considered permanent, and after the realignment of forces in 1966 many Asuk Balek moved back to join the Wilihiman-Walalua in their new alliance.

RESTRICTIONS AND LAW

In most societies it is easy to isolate and describe a formal mechanism for social control which includes an explicit normative code, a system for deciding trouble cases, and a means of enforcing the decisions. This formal social control has generally been handled apart from the other kinds of social control under the heading of law. By these formal criteria, the Dani have a minimum of law.

A few cases were observed in which valuable goods were given as restitution for assault or theft. The assault was always performed by a younger, less important man or youth against an older, more important man. Restitution was either a shell band or a small exchange stone. The cases of theft involved the stealing and eating of a pig by a youth, and the restitution was one or two pigs paid by the youth or by his father.

Not more than a dozen of these cases were noted, and no case was observed in its totality. Informants mentioned them casually, and all efforts to learn the precise principles involved, or the detailed behavior, failed. Thus, the critical judicial moment at which a legal decision was apparently made remains obscure. This gap in my data is particularly frustrating because it is just here that the Dani legal structure is to be found.

Anthropologists such as Hoebel, Bohannan, and Pospisil have rejected the idea that formal courts and elaborate legal procedures are prerequisites for a legal system. In general they agree that legal principles must have some general application, and that in legal systems the behavioral norms (or laws) are supported by pressure which has group approval. Hoebel (1954:28) limits this legal pressure to force or threat of force; Pospisil (1958:29) suggests that it should be extended to such nonforceful pressures as social disapproval and ostracism when they are used by the group against an individual as the result of a legal decision. But apparently they are agreed that the description of certain societies as lawless is false, and that all societies do have a legal system.

I do not suggest that the Dani have no legal system. But it is clear that the great part of Dani behavior directed toward resolution of conflict is not legal in the sense outlined above. I have assumed that the decision-making process involved in the payment of restitution is legal behavior, but can offer no data based on direct observation to support this. At best one can say that in the total range of mechanisms for conflict resolution, the Dani legal system plays only a minimal role.

The Problem of Dani Law

We can focus our search for Dani law by pointing out some common legal forms that the Dani lack and some common Dani patterns that are clearly not law.

Legal code. I had the greatest difficulty isolating what could be considered a legal code. There are names for certain crimes, such as various kinds of theft, but statements describing an abstract principle of crime and punishment do not seem to be made by the Dani. Dani informants would say, "X gave Y a pig as restitution because X's son stole and ate Y's pig," as a statement of fact but not in the form of an abstract principle with predictive value. And the few statements which were predictive were not consistent with each other, especially in terms of severity of punishment.

Courts. As stated above, the actual legal decision-making process was not observed. It was certainly brief and involved a few of the important men of the Neighborhood. There was no formal court, but at most an informal meeting of men whose authority depends on a consensus of opinion which Bohannan has called a moot (1963:291).

Corporal punishment. Pospisil has stressed that legal behavior exists on various levels in a society and states that "every functioning subgroup of the society has its own legal system" (1958:272 ff). In this sense, the physical punishment of a wife by a husband or of a child by a parent is a legal act of corporal punishment.

Overt disciplining within a nuclear family is very rare, but parents occasionally hit a child who has refused to go to a spring for water or has been negligent in pig herding. On one or two occasions a husband beat his wife, ostensibly for not cooking meals properly, and once a woman was speared in the thigh by a supporter of her husband for suspected adultery.

Punishment of this sort is administered within the family by a senior to a junior member. Others show much interest but do not take sides. This is legal punishment in the sense that it is administered by an "approved agent of the society" (cf. Hoebel). Following Pospisil's important distinction of different levels of legal action, this is legal action on the family level.

But on the higher levels of organization, such as the neighborhood, confederation, or alliance, corporal punishment or the threat of it against an individual on behalf of the group is apparently absent. The interpersonal fighting is private retaliation or vengeance and cannot properly be considered legal.

TYPES OF CONFLICT

Conflict between individuals or groups often takes the form of tension, which may be expressed in various forms short of physical assault. The opposite number is usually avoided where possible, and ignored when ceremonies or other events make avoidance impossible. Conflict may be expressed verbally with the large and colorful repertoire of insults, usually obscene, in the Dani language. These insults often have a tinge of humor which prevents more serious conflict.

Physical conflict between two persons may take the form of punishment, which is one-sided, or it may be a mutual exchange of blows. Both forms are rare. But assault involving two people occurs especially between cowives.

Physical punishment is ambiguous and may be seen as both resolution and conflict. It is an attempt to resolve conflict, to correct a conflict-causing situation. But unless the punishment is accepted in this sense, it is also itself a conflict episode which must be resolved.

Fighting between two men often escalates into fighting between two groups. It may be confined to a brawl, which is short-lived fighting within the bounds of the confederation. It may become a feud, if the two men are of different confederations, or it may become war, if the two men are of different alliances.

In the theoretical model of conflict escalation there is a critical point, a point of transition as the conflict escalates from interpersonal conflict to feud or to war. I did not actually observe this point, and unfortunately informants' statements about it were vague. Thus, the mechanism that takes the conflict from the hands of the individuals and turns it into the concern of the confederations as corporate bodies in the case of feud, or of the alliances as corporate bodies in the case of war, is not known. It seems that at least in the case of war, the leaders of the opposite sides perform some ceremony to invoke the aid of the alliance ghosts and in some manner "declare" war.

BRAWL

One brawl in the Dugum Neighborhood was instigated by the repeated adultery between an important young man and the young wife of an older man. Once the couple was discovered in the woods by boys and quickly half a dozen men had gathered on each side, shooting arrows at each other. When I arrived on the scene the brawl had just ended. One man was wounded and the best surgeon present, who happened to be on the other side, dropped his weapons and followed the wounded man home to remove the arrow.

The second act also occurred in my absence a few months later, when the same couple was again found *in flagrante*. A brawl again ensued and one man, a friend of the adulterer's, was killed. The conflict was then resolved when the friends of the husband sent especially valuable goods to the funeral and the other party subsequently moved to a new compound and garden area beyond the southeastern boundary of the Neighborhood. Unfortunately I did not observe any of the major events of this brawl.

FEUD

Sometimes prolonged states of fighting take place between confederations of the same alliance. This fighting is called *umai'im*, in distinction to a brawl, which is "just fighting," and war (*wim*), which is fighting between alliances. The ghosts are not concerned with feud, and it has none of the supernatural implications of war. The Dani also point out that the enemies in a feud are just *aguni juma-mege*, local people, while the enemies in war are *aguni dili-mege*, foreigners, or people of another alliance. As alliances shift, so do the terms.

WAR

Dani warfare proceeds through a cycle involving two rather different sorts of events. There is a long period of relatively low-key fighting between two alliances, in which the main emphasis is on the ritual aspects of war. But each alliance is a basically unstable grouping of confederations. After several years, perhaps ten or twenty, the alliance explodes in a major battle, new alliances are formed, and the ritual warfare is resumed along the new frontiers.

In the Grand Valley there are only 50,000 people, but the feuds and wars, the alliances forming and disintegrating, the confederations shifting over a few kilometers or simply vanishing, constitute a history fully as complex in fifty years as that of Europe during two millennia. The political and military history of the Grand Valley could be written, of course; but the events before 1954, when the first missionaries arrived, are prehistory, and the task of the historian in sorting out the facts from a wealth of contradictory oral reports would be stupendous. The Dani are somewhat less than ideal informants about events past or hypothetical, and this, combined with my own incomplete command of their language, seriously limits the value of much of the following historical data. However, the account of ritual warfare is based on my own observations of it in 1961, before the area was pacified, and the explosion of 1966 as witnessed by missionaries whose stories helped me to get to the core of those events.

During the childhood of the present important men, in the 1930's, there was a war frontier along the Elogeta River splitting the groups which were later to join in the Gutelu Alliance. The Wilihiman-Walalua were allied with the Widaia to the south, and the Dloko-Mabel wih other groups to the north. There are now many different versions of what happened next, but all agree that the Wilihiman-Walalua broke with their allies and joined forces with the Dloko-Mabel. Broekhuijse (1967:69) tells that a secret arrangement was made between the Wilihiman-Walalua and the Dloko-Mabel and that one day in battle the Wilihiman-Walalua turned on their erstwhile allies and, supported by the Dloko-Mabel, inflicted a major defeat, driving the Widaia to the south and opening a new no-man's land. Other informants said that the leaders of the Dloko-Mabel convinced the leaders of the Wilihiman-Walalua that it was foolish for the two groups to keep on fighting each other. At any rate, by the mid 1940's the Gutelu Alliance had been formed. It lasted, despite growing internal problems, until 1966, when an unannounced attack by the Dloko-Mabel against the Wilihiman-Walalua broke open the alliance and restored the pre-1940 alliances. During the periods when the alliances were relatively stable, ritual warfare was carried on between alliances until 1961, when the government pacification program became effective.

Previously, during 1958 and 1959, the District Officer in Wamena led several patrols into the Gutelu Alliance area. After an engagement in the Dugum Neighborhood in which a group of warriors attacked a patrol and one Dani was shot and killed, the Pax Hollandia was successfully imposed on the southern frontier of the Gutelu and Widaia. During this time trade was carried on across the frontier, people moved freely back and forth, and joint compounds were established in the no-man's-land and frontier areas. After December 1959 apparently only an occasional patrol came near the area, and none entered it. Effective government control had disappeared, and eventually fighting broke out along the frontier again. The joint compounds were abandoned and a state of war was resumed.

The first clear date is January 1961. Then an important pig feast was being held in the Widaia area. Three women and a man, relatives of Maikmo, an important Himan, went to the feast and were killed by Widaia. During the next weeks there was constant action between the Gutelu and Widaia alliances.

Fighting was observed between the Gutelu Alliance and the Widaia Alliance along the southern front from April through August 1961:

April 10	Battle called by Widaia
April 15	Battle called by Gutelu
May 4	Battle preliminaries, nothing developed
May 11	Gosi-Alua raid Widaia, kill one
May 26	Battle called by Widaia
May 29	Widaia raid disrupts dance
June 4	Widaia raid, wachtower burned, brief skirmish
June 5	Battle called by Widaia, men out, but no engagement
June 7	Widaia raid burns watchtower shelter, uproots potato vines, cuts dam
June 10	Widaia raid, Wejakhe killed
June 22	Battle called by Widaia
July 5	Raid on Widaia foiled, Jenokma killed
August 2	Pig stolen from Widaia, ambush by Gutelu, battle
August 6	Battle called by Gutelu
August 16	Battle, preceded by raid on Widaia
August 25	Asuk-Balek man visiting Gutelu killed

early September   (not observed) Widaia raid, Digiliak killed
                   Gutelu raid kills two Widaia
                   Police post established
October 13   Peace conference among government, Widaia,
                   and Gutelu

Thus, in one 5½-month period there were nine battles, of which two did not develop into full affairs, and nine raids, of which five were made by the Widaia and four by the Gutelu men. (One of the battles was not announced in the regular way, but developed out of a raid.) Two men died of wounds received in these battles; six men and boys were killed outright in the raids.

A more detailed chronology of the events of war between April 10 and early September 1961 is given in Appendix II.

THE RITUAL PHASE OF WAR

The long periods of ritual warfare are marked by announced, formal battles and surprise raids. The following account is based on the events of 1961, when the Gutelu Alliance still included the Wilihiman-Walalua of the Dugum Neighborhood.

Battle. The ritual immediately preceding a battle was never observed by me, but an informant described it. When an important man has decided to call a battle, he holds a feast for the men of his confederation. A large pig is killed and steamed together with sweet potatoes. If, on opening the steam bundle, the sweet potatoes are found to be not well cooked, it is considered a bad omen for the coming battle. Only the males eat pig, and a portion is laid in the rear of the men's house for the ghosts to eat.

This ritual is called *elak gabelhatek*, which refers to the sharpening of spears and arrows. It seems quite likely that the sacred stones of the man calling the battle are also involved, but this was not made clear.

The enemy is not notified, and presumably does not know, that a battle will be called on the following day.

Early the following day the important man who has taken the responsibility for the battle sends young men to the frontier to shout a challenge across to the enemy. The challenge is accepted on behalf of another important man. The place of the battle is agreed upon, and soon the whooping imitation of the call of the large cuckoo dove (*jokoik*) sends the news of the impending clash from compound to compound across the alliance. Men prepare for battle: grease their bodies, don furs and feathers, take up their weapons. In small groups they drift toward the site of the battle.

Actual fighting begins sometime between nine and eleven in the morning and continues until rain or dusk sends the warriors home.

Weapons are the bow and arrow, long thrusting spears, shorter throwing spears, and at times even any throwable stick. Battles take place on any of several long narrow strips of land bordered by swamps. The front extends across the dry land of the strips and may even stretch in a more tenuous way into the swamp (Plate 17).

PLATE 16. Men watch a battle from a nearby ridge.

PLATE 17. In the bushy swamp, on the fringe of a battle.

PLATES 18, 19. The front lines of a battle. (Photographed from a hill with a 500 mm. lens)

The front is generally stable, but sometimes one side will gain momentum, pushing the other back several hundred meters until the front is again stabilized.

Battle grounds. On the southern front, battles are held either on the Dogolik or the Watabaka. The Dogolik is one of the geologically enigmatic strips of ground, about fifty meters wide and raised some two to four meters above the bordering swamps, that run from the Dugum Hill to the Dutoba Hill, a distance of about three kilometers. The only vegetation on the strip is grass and an occasional clump of reeds; it is a flat, level area along which the warriors from front line to rear positions may extend a kilometer or more. Often men move off the strip into the swamp, stalking the enemy through high grass and bushes.

The Watabaka is a rocky L-shaped ridge about thirty meters above the level and about 1.5 kilometers long. The outside of the ridge drops off into knee-deep swamp; the short arm of the L is extended by low, dry land; inside the L are the overgrown gardens and abandoned banana plants of a former settlement area.

During a battle on the Watabaka, the front usually lies across the inside slopes of the L, extending to the dry, open level ground on the inside of the L. The two terrains impose two different, fighting conditions: dodging among the rocks of the slope, or the free movement possible on the level ground. These two arms of the front stay on the same line; if one drops back the other will drop back with it. Although battles on the Watabaka usually begin at the crotch of the L, the front can fluctuate, and at various times each side has been pushed off the L completely.

Battle Formation. The men on either side are strung out for a kilometer or more back from the actual front, along the narrow battlefield. Groups and individuals move up to and back from the front, and the formations are generally in flux. However, the Dani recognize four positions at a battle.

The first battle position is front rank, not more than twenty or thirty meters deep, composed of younger men and youths actually engaged in battle (Plates 18 and 19). These are the active warriors, most of them between eighteen and thirty. A few of the braver boys are as young as fourteen or so; and a few men in their thirties will stay in the front lines, shouting encouragement and perhaps solidifying their positions as leaders. There are seldom more than a dozen men on the actual front. Fighters move up, shoot arrows or throw small spears, and then drop back. Arrow wounds are frequent, especially for those who have come closest to the enemy and are dropping back, their backs turned and their eyes not covering the entire enemy front.

The mass of men behind the front includes men who are resting just before advancing to the front or just after leaving the front itself. Also in this battlefield position are the important men, the battle leaders, who shout unheeded directions at the front. The men in this area are still within range of high-shot arrows, and the careless are often wounded.

Beyond the range of arrows circulates a large group of noncombatants who watch the battle: warriors recovering from recent wounds; men in their forties and fifties who are too old to fight and not important enough to lead; and young boys not yet old enough to fight but who often carry tobacco or cigarettes for a man who has gone forward (Plate 16).

Far back from the front, often out of sight of the battle, a few old men sit around a fire smoking and listening. A line has been gouged in the earth from their hearth a few meters toward the battlefield, which informants explain is to direct the ghosts toward the battle.

Dani women never approach a battlefield, and in fact often work in the gardens apparently unconcerned, only occasionally looking up when a particularly loud cry comes from the battle. This behavior is in contrast to Kapauku warfare, where the women, enjoying complete immunity, wander across the battlefield collecting spent arrows. Pospisil has explained this participation in battle on the grounds that

Since incessant shooting readily exhausts the supplies of ammunition, and since the warriors find no time to collect stray arrows, it is the task of the women to collect the ammunition for their husbands. (1958:91)

However, Dani men, even in the heat of battle, were often observed stooping to retrieve an enemy arrow.

Battles can be a bloody business, but they are seldom fatal to the warriors. In the course of eight battles I observed on the southern front, no one was carried away dead, although two men died later—ten days to nine months—from wounds received in battle.

Though battles are fought as part of the war, the sportive element in them seems to be very strong. There is a good deal of joking, even across enemy lines. Except for one or two tense moments, no one was ever in real danger of being overrun by an advancing enemy line.

Battles are casual. Often during the noonday heat both sides simply withdraw and sit in groups, smoking, talking, and resting for a while before resuming hostilities. Once, late in the afternoon, fighting ceased altogether and both sides sat on comfortable rocks hurling insults at one another, picking out certain of the enemy by name. A choice remark would be greeted by both sides with roars of laughter.

Individualism is all-important in battle. Occasionally an important man shouts advice from the rear lines, but this is rarely heeded. Individuals move to the front, fight for a time in their own way, and then retire.

Once, during a particularly slow battle, a large cuckoo dove flew back and forth over the lines. All fighting stopped as the warriors, boisterously laughing, threw sticks and stones at the bird.

Raids. In contrast to battles, which are mainly sportive, raids are the effective means of killing the enemy. A raiding party consists of only a few men, between a dozen and fifty. They slip through the high grass and bush over the frontier, across no-man's-land, hoping to escape being sighted from an enemy watchtower. Then they lie in wait for a single person or small group at a drinking place, or try to surprise a lone man or woman in an unprotected garden area. If the battle is inefficient in killing, the raid is highly efficient, its purpose being to kill an enemy. There are risks for the raiding party, though: On July 5, 1961, a raiding party was spotted by the Widaia lookouts, a counterambush was set up, and one of the raiding party was caught in the trap and killed.

Raiding is not always successful; when such customary means of killing an enemy have failed, and pressure to kill is felt, other means may be used. On August 25, 1961, after the Gutelu had been unsuccessful in several attempts to kill an enemy, a man from a group allied to the enemy Widaia was killed as he came on a visit to Abulobak.

Ceremonies: The Edai Dance. The death of an enemy initiates a two-day ceremony of dancing called *edai.* If the enemy has been killed outright in a raid, the *edai* begins on the following day. If he dies from wounds after a battle, the news is shouted across the frontier on the morning of the funeral. Thus, the funeral on one side of a frontier is echoed by an *edai* on the other side. Both ceremonies have a degree of ambiguity. The funeral combines mourning for the dead and apprehension for his ghost, but there is also the knowledge that his ghost will assist against the enemy. On the other side, the *edai* is dominated by rejoicing that the local ghosts have been placated by a killing, but there is also an awareness that another dangerous enemy ghost is at large.

During the first morning of the first day of the *edai,* small groups gather at dance areas near watchtowers to dance and sing. Around noon the groups converge at the main dance ground (*edai-ma*) of the Neighborhood, and for the rest of the day they dance, running in groups back and forth and around in circles, shouting and singing. The dance is exuberant but repetitive. There are no special steps; the dancers simply run in a normal fashion.

On the second day the people return to the *edai-ma* and continue the dancing and singing. The most recent battle trophies, called *ab watek* (*ab,* man; *watek,* killed, dead) are displayed. During these two days all people dress in finery; this is the only time women wear the shell, feather, and fur ornaments normally worn only by men (this does not appear to be a significant transvestism).

The *edai* is not so much a victory dance, or even a ceremony of rejoicing, as it is a ritual of communication with the ghosts in which for two days the people inform the ghosts with noise and movement that they have killed an enemy.

The participants come mainly from the three nearest confederations, those which are most involved in the fighting along the southern front; but usually all parts of the alliance are represented.

Ghost Participation in War. The Dani consider that the ghosts of their own dead are potentially malevolent towards them. Most Dani ritual concerns these ghosts and is negative, designed to prevent or to negate action taken against them by their own ghosts. The only major exceptions to this pattern are certain rituals connected with war. In war, one's own ghosts can be beneficial, acting both defensively and offensively against the enemy. Thus, war ritual is positive, designed to encourage action by the ghosts in their own favor. Some of the rituals connected with war are described below.

Miniature bow and arrows are placed in the base of the watchtower at the time of construction as a defensive measure to encourage the ghosts to watch for enemy raids.

Raiding parties often come to attack the Dugum Neighborhood through the forests along the Aikhe River. Along this route is a small structure hidden in the forests beyond the watchtower defense line. It is a house, about a meter square and fifty centimeters high, raised a meter above the ground on stilts. In the narrow space inside the house lie arrows, penis gourds, and other unidentified wrapped bundles.

Informants explained that these goods are especially attractive to the ghosts and served to lure the ghosts to the lonely frontier area and to encourage them to give warning of enemy raiding parties. One informant said that if an enemy were to approach, the ghosts would make the treetops wave back and forth.

The ghosts are said to cross into enemy territory on the night before a battle to symbolically throttle an enemy in his sleep, or to attend the battle itself and spear an enemy on the field. This does not immediately kill the enemy, but it makes him vulnerable to killing by the spears of the warriors the next day.

The youth Jenokma, who lived in the Dugum Neighborhood, was killed on a raid into the enemy country in July 1961. It was said later that the night before, an enemy ghost in the guise of a *sijo* bird visited him and throttled him. Then, when he went on the raid, the ghost preceded him, looking at him over its left shoulder, and the enemy killed him.

The Privilege and Responsibility of War Leadership. Only a few men of the confederation have the stature to initiate a battle or raid. Informants generally agreed that five or six of the most important men of the confederation could, but there was considerable disagreement on whether or not the younger men of the next rank could.

Apparently Weteklue had moved from the north into the confederation area to take charge, or to participate as a leader, in the war which ended in September 1961. There seemed to be no resentment on the part of the other leaders of the confederation. If anything, they were grateful for the help his supernatural power, or *wusa*, brought to the confederation.

It is the function of the leader to initiate a battle or raid, and also to take the responsibility for the possible death of one of his own men in the action. If such a death occurs, presumably his own supernatural power is endangered, although this was not made explicit. On a material level, he is expected to contribute substantial goods to the funeral of the killed man.

Emotional Attitude toward War. The Dani seem particularly matter-of-fact about war. There is excitement before a battle and tension before a raid. But there is no horror or indignation at killing and no fear of being killed. The Dani consider the enemy fully human. In fact, because of the contact, friendships, and even intermarriage between the Gutelu and the Widaia during times of peace, the people of the Widaia are known personally to those of the Gutelu. In battles, personal names and personal joking insults are thrown back and forth along with the arrows.

In August 1961 on two different occasions we took a man from the Dugum Neighborhood down to Aikhe River to Wamena. Each time we dressed the man in Western clothes to disguise him and avoid any incident. On one of the return trips, the man stripped off his clothes, greeted the men on the riverbank with kin terms—men whom we recognized from the battlefields of a few days before—and finally asked us to stop the boat so he could talk with some of the enemy.

This of course was in the context of the expedition. In the context of war they would kill without mercy and expect no mercy. When the young boy Wejakhe was killed in a Widaia raid, there was much grief but no indignation at his death. In August 1961, when the Asuk Balek visitor was killed at Abulobak, there was general rejoicing. As his body was dragged to the dance area, young boys ran alongside it, piercing it with their toy spears. On the dance ground, under the light of the full moon and a few meters from the corpse, men, women, and children danced with joy.

Under the constant threat of enemy raids there is no terror. Usually care is taken to man the watchtowers, and women wait for the smoke signaling an all-clear before they move out into an exposed garden area. Yet on the day that Wejakhe and a few friends went to the Aikhe River to drink, though the Widaia had been raiding the area during the past week, the watchtowers were not manned. The boys were foolish—not in their fear, but in their confidence.

Even during the height of a battle, when several hundred men were engaged in the fighting, noncombatants carried on their daily routine. Women often continued gardening within easy earshot of the battles, and once a man and his son quietly weeded their tobacco garden a few hundred meters from the fighting.

DEFENSE: THE WATCHTOWER

The compounds of the Gutelu are well back from the enemy Widaia, under the slopes of the mountains which rise abruptly at the edge of the Grand Valley. Stretching out in front of the villages are the gardens. Along the outer edge of the gardens, either immediately in the gardens or on higher, grassy strips just beyond (Plate 49), is a line of watchtowers commanding strategic strips of no-man's-land, looking towards a particular enemy area. This line is the defense perimeter, the true frontier. Beyond it, between the watchtowers of the Gutelu and the Widaia, lies the empty no-man's-land (Map 3.1). The watchtower is made of strong logs, the bases sunk into the ground about one meter and bound tightly together to form a column about 50 centimeters in diameter. This column supports a narrow platform 5 to ten meters above the ground which is simply a board seat on which a single man can sit with comfort. Often a framework of thin sticks supports a crude thatch roof which serves as shelter against the elements and, if it is full enough, conceals the presence or absence of a watcher.

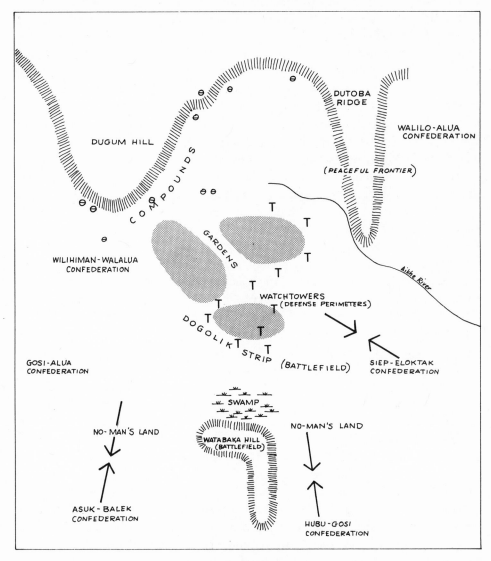

MAP 3.1
SOUTHEASTERN WAR FRONTIER OF THE GUTELU ALLIANCE, 1961

On the ground a few meters away from the watchtower is a low shelter with thatched roof and open sides where men can sit talking, smoking, and doing small jobs, ready to grab their weapons and fend off an attack at the call of the man in the tower.

The watchtower is not actually the property of any one man; it is built and maintained by all men whose women work the gardens under the protection of the particular tower. However, each tower is referred to in terms of a particular important man with large gardens in the area who has prime responsibility and who takes the initiative both in maintenance and in watching.

During times of danger men always precede women into the garden area.

In the midmorning, by nine or ten o'clock, as the women watch from the compound area, one or more men move out to the farthest towers, usually stopping at a tower or shelter in midroute to smoke a cigarette and gauge the possibility of an ambush. When they have reached the farthest tower and satisfied themselves that there is no danger of attack, they light a smoke fire, signaling the women that it is safe for them to follow.

Someone is sent scrambling up the tower to keep watch—maybe a young boy or maybe the important man himself. Every hour or so the watcher climbs down and his place is taken by another. Or, if there are enough men around and the danger seems slight, the tower may remain empty.

During the morning and the early afternoon men drift in and out of the shelter. Some will be the regulars; some will be passersby who stop to visit. The shelter by the watchtower is forbidden to women and serves as a daytime men's house. Except when there is heavy garden work to be done—such as breaking the sod or working on the ditches—the garden work is left to the women, and the men sit around the shelter. They may sleep on the dried grass; make cigarettes and light them on the fire which is kept intermittently blazing and smoldering under the shelter; they may pluck each other's facial or body hair; make a spear or bow or arrows; knit a shell band; play a mouth harp; but all day there is conversation and joking. In midafternoon when the women have finished their work and have headed back to the compounds with their heavy nets full of the day's harvest, the men pick up their weapons and drift back also.

CONSTRUCTION

The construction materials are first assembled: ten or twenty strong poles, of the largest ten to fifteen centimeters in diameter, and lengths of heavy vine lashing. Then the base hole is dug with digging sticks, about a meter in diameter at the mouth and perhaps a meter deep. The first poles are set into the hole, jammed and lashed together. Gradually the column is built up, setting poles into the uneven top and lashing the entire mass together every seventy centimeters. The lashings serve as footholds and two or three men work their way upward, lashing. When the desired height has been reached—this depends on the terrain to be surveyed and ranges from five to ten meters—boards are handed up and a platform lashed to the top. Four poles are extended above the platform a meter or two. Cross-poles are lashed to them, and grass is draped over them to form a shelter from the sun.

The tower is now finished except for the magical appurtenances. A miniature bow about fifty centimeters long together with plain reed arrows of the same length are set between the poles behind the lashing at the base of the tower, on the side toward the enemy (cf. p. 113). A bundle of *lugaga* grass is cooked on a fire and the grass laid in a careful circle around the new watchtower. Those who take part in the building and the consecration of the tower have been in contact with the sacred power and their hands are ritually cleansed by a wave of a feather mounted on a small stick. The tower and the surrounding garden area is now vacated and for the next day remain taboo. No man or woman is supposed to approach the area. The ritual is to assure the efficacy of the watchtower. While men are watching, they are assisted by the ghosts. The magic is to assure that the ghosts will give their support and to assure against the danger of the watcher becoming blind and not seeing an enemy attack.

Function of Watchtower. The primary function of the watchtower is, of course, defense. In theory it serves as a safeguard against a surprise attack on the gardens; and in case of such an attack, its detachment serves as a ready means of blunting the effect of such an attack. The efficacy of the watchtower system is supported by the vigilance of its men, and by the ghosts.

In fact, the watchtowers are not always effective. Often they are undermanned; for periods during the day the tower itself may be neglected and its men may don their short penis gourds and go into the gardens to help the women. In the raid of July 5, a party from the Gutelu Alliance surprised a man in a Widaia watchtower and killed him; another man working nearby in a garden escaped. The death of Wejakhe by a Widaia raid on June 10 could probably have been prevented if Wejaklegek's watchtower at Buauguloba had been manned that afternoon.

A very important secondary function of the watchtowers is social. They provide a sort of daytime men's house away from the village, where men and boys who happen to be in the area congregate to talk and to listen. The core of regulars who frequent a shelter and cooperate in the work of maintenance constitute a social group, tenuous but real (p. 84).

The *gaijo* and its shelter present a target both strategic and accessible for an enemy raiding party that crosses the frontier but finds no human victims. During the five months of observed battle, several towers were uprooted and thrown down and several shelters were burned. On the day after the destruction, the men responsible for the tower or shelter assembled and quickly rebuilt. A new hole may be dug for the tower, but any old lumber still in good condition is utilized. The ritual is renewed. Apparently there is no blame cast on the ghosts for allowing the destruction; no fear that the ghosts may have assisted.

The Regulation of War

Although the Dani do not have an explicit code of war, it seems clear that at least in the ritual phase of war both sides observe certain restrictions. For example, there is no fighting at night. Even the raids, which rely on maximum surprise for their success, take place only in daytime. Perhaps the belief in ghosts which are especially dangerous after dark, inhibits night raids. But of course these same ghosts do not have any effect on the considerable amount of peaceful activity which does take place outside the compounds at night, especially on those nights when there is a bright moon.

Also, it would presumably be very easy to make more effective weapons by fletching the arrows and enlarging the bows. But the Dani do not make innovations of this sort. There is no "arms race." On the battlefield arrows would be much more effective if they were shot in volleys, instead of at individual whim.

It is difficult to tell how much these patterns represent general Dani conservatism and how much they are really the result of restrictive norms. I hesitated to probe into these matters for fear that my questions might in themselves contribute to making Dani war more deadly, but my guess is that they would not have. The Dani reaction toward our guns may be significant. They knew that we had shotguns which we used for hunting ducks, and they knew that the government police patrols had killed Dani with guns, yet no one ever suggested, even jokingly, that we use our guns on their behalf in battle.

BATTLE DRESS

Dress for raids is simple. No special headdress is worn. Shell ornaments, ordinarily hung around the neck, might attract attention of the enemy, or catch in the underbrush, so they are usually swung around to lie on the men's back during a stealthy advance. But in battle all possible personal ornaments are worn: feather and fur headdresses, sometimes surmounted by a meter-long bird-of-paradise plume; snail shell and bailer shell chest pieces; back ornaments (a net or gourd decorated with feathers). Most men either grease their bodies and blacken their faces with ash and pig grease, or sometimes paint their legs with light-colored mud. Many men wear a double pig tusk through their nasal septum to give them a ferocious appearance.

Warriors carry feather hand ornaments; perhaps a whisk made of the thigh bone and feathers of the cassowary bird, or a long wand decorated with the white feathers of the egret. These are waved tauntingly at the enemy.

THE NONRITUAL PHASE OF WAR

In many ways the ritual phase of war seems more like a medieval tourney than like what we usually mean by war. Of course, there are sneak raids, and people are killed, but that phase of war is dominated in terms of time and energy investment by the arranged battles fought in elegant attire and the emphasis on supernatural, rather than economic, effects. The nonritual phase of war is just the opposite: short, treacherous, bloody, and with major economic effect.

In 1966 the Dugum Dani were involved in a nonritual war episode, which I learned about in 1968 from the Dani participants and missionary observers. The events of June 4, 1966 could only be called a massacre. At dawn that day warriors from the northern part of the Gutelu Alliance crept through the ground fog to launch a well-planned attack on the compounds to the south of the Elogeta River. The attack lasted only an hour or so, but nearly 125 men, women, and children were left dead or dying, and dozens of compounds were in flames. Other alliances had been informed of the attack and joined in, not so much to kill and burn as to plunder pigs.

The attack caught the men of the southern compounds completely by surprise, but they were able to put up some defense and harassed the attackers as they pulled back across the Elogeta. The corpses were hastily cremated on mass pyres without the usual ceremonies.

During the next days the survivors made a series of counterattacks on the north, in conjunction with governmental forces who were trying to reestablish order. During the counterattacks many of the northern compounds were burned, but since the attacks were anticipated and the people had fled, only twenty or so people were killed.

The origin of the first attack probably lay in the origin of the Alliance itself, when the Wilihiman-Walalua broke with their old allies, the Widaia, and joined the Dloko-Mabel. Although Gutelu was recognized as the ultimate leader of the Alliance, by 1961 the leaders of the Wilihiman-Walalua and the Gosi-Alua had begun to press their own ambitions. Their attempt to start the pig feast by themselves in 1963 failed, and the feast of 1964 was carried out under Gutelu's leadership. Also, by this time the government police post, which had been established in the Wilihiman-Walalua area in 1961 to make friends with the Dani and to keep the peace, was itself a source of friction. It was inevitable that the police came to know and trust the Dani living closest to the police post—that is, those of the Wilihiman-Walalua, Wilil-Himan, and Gosi-Alua confederations living south of the Elogeta. When trouble arose between the Dani south of the river and those north of the river, the police tended to intervene on the side of the southerners. At least, so it seemed to the northerners. In any case, the behavior of the police, or the Dani's perception of the police behavior, aggravated an already tense situation.

It is not at all certain that Gutelu himself was involved in the planning of the attack, or whether he was simply handed a *fait accompli* by the younger leaders of the Dloko-Mabel, Dlabi-Mabel, and other confederations north of the Elogeta. The attack must have been planned in great detail, and it was carried out at a moment when the missionary at Jibiga and all the police but one had gone to Wamena for a few days. The compounds attacked were for the most part those directly to the south of the Elogeta River. The Dugum Neighborhood, at the far southern end of the Gutelu Alliance, was spared except for the compounds of Mapilatma.

The attack was called war (*wim*) and not feud (*umai'im*). I had thought that since it took place within an alliance it would be considered feud, but it seems that the attack itself ended the alliance, and so was an act of war.

Apparently the attackers had tried to enlist the aid or at least the passive support of other alliances. If this had been completely successful, the attack would undoubtedly have wiped out the Wilihiman-Walalua, Wilil-Himan, and Gosi-Alua. However, an alliance to the south led by Obagatok came to the aid of the victims (who had been their allies twenty years before), and so the same

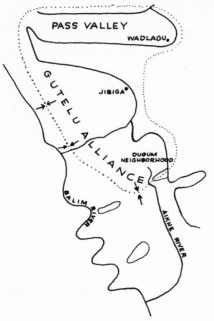

1. WAR FRONTIERS OF THE GUTELU ALLIANCE

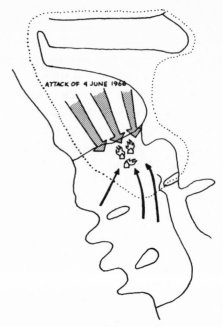

2. ATTACK OF 4 JUNE 1966

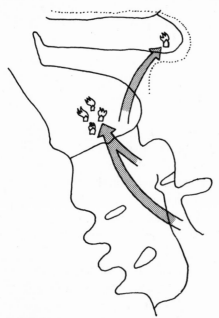

3. COUNTER-ATTACKS

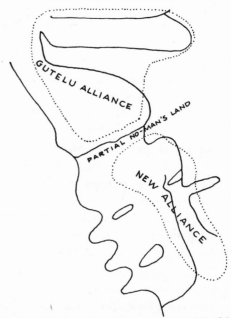

4. ALLIANCE BOUNDARIES AFTER JUNE 1966

MAP 3.2
FRONTIERS BEFORE AND AFTER THE ATTACK OF JUNE 4, 1966

act which split the Gutelu Alliance was responsible for forming a new alliance made of the southern Gutelu and the people of the Solimo.

The immediate effect of the attack was a major population shift. Most of the survivors left their burned-out compounds on the southern banks of the Elogeta River and moved into the Dugum Neighborhood, or beyond to occupy the old no-man's-land. About half the population of the Dugum Neighborhood moved south, fearing new attacks, and their compounds and gardens were then taken over, with permission but without compensation, by the refugees from the Elogeta. Thus in 1968 the Dugum Neighborhood had about the same population as in 1961, but about 50 per cent of the people were newcomers from the zone of attack. The no-man's-land during the warfare in 1961 had already begun to be used for gardens by 1963, and by 1968 it was densely populated and the old gardens were open and in use. But the burned-out compound sites and gardens on either side of the Elogeta were for the most part deserted, and the no-man's-land which had existed there twenty years before had begun to reappear. Even though the government police and military were able to maintain pacification as far as ritual battles and raids were concerned, the Dani feared that no force would be able to halt another secret attack like the one in 1966.

It is impossible to make precise comparisons between the attack of June 4, 1966 and other such events. There is no reason to suppose that this attack differed from others in the history of the Grand Valley except in the details of police involvement and the use of steel bush knives instead of spears and bows and arrows. Both in form and in intensity it was probably typical of the violent phase of war which, together with the ritual phase, form the normal pattern of Dani warfare. But it is clear that this explosive phase of war differs dramatically from the ritual phase. Even though it lasts only days, compared to the years of ritual war, in many respects its effects are more far-reaching.

The Dani do not have separate words for ritual and nonritual phases of war, but they do distinguish an extreme form of fighting, *mugoko*, which involves the driving out and massacre of an entire alliance. In form it is a sudden massive attack typical of the nonritual phase of war; however, it involves not previously peaceful confederations within the same alliance but different alliances which had been engaged in the ritual phase of war. Dani informants insisted that *mugoko* is different from *wim* (war.) However, the behavioral resemblances seem more relevant than the lexical distinctions, and so I have chosen to override the native categories and include the *mugoko* in the discussion of war.

One instance of *mugoko* happened about 1952 to the Wio Confederation, which was then living at the present site of the government post, Wamena. The Wio were surrounded by enemies who at a certain moment joined forces and attacked them from all sides, killing people, burning villages, and stealing pigs. At that time, so the story is told now, the important man of one of the attacking groups said that the Wio would be made like the *mugogo*, the great gray white-faced heron, to fly from one end of the Grand Valley to the other without a home. At present the Wio are called Mugogo and in fact live scattered throughout the Grand Valley. After the fight some enemy groups moved in and occupied parts of the Wio land, but most of their former home area remains a deserted area except for the presence of the government post.

In September 1962 the Idlai-Phisake group to the southeast of the Dugum Neighborhood suffered a similar fate. Their frontiers had become war frontiers on three sides. In June 1962 a party of Walalua camped along the Walalua-Idlai-Phisake frontier on their way to the Jalemo were attacked and slaughtered. The Walalua victims were related to an important man. In September the important man called battle for his own group, the groups along the Aikhe, and those in the Bugima Valley. They attacked the Idlai-Phisake from three sides. Informants returning from the scene reported that some people escaped; many others were killed; villages were burned; and pigs were driven off and later eaten.

Events leading up to the *mugoko* were not observed in detail, but the general principles involved seem clear. The Idlai-Phisake Confederation had lost the war-and-peace balance in their relationships with the various groups surrounding them. Through some series of circumstances they had allowed all their boundaries to become war frontiers at the same time that the boundaries between their various neighborhoods became peaceful. At this point they were in a perilous position. The killing of the relatives of the important leader of one enemy group, which ignited the total war, was perhaps committed by a few Idlai-Phisake who had not comprehended the total position.

A third instance of *mugoko* was reported by Myron Bromley (via L. F. B. Dubbeldam in a personal communication) for the Wodlo Valley, a tributary valley at the north end of the Grand Valley. In the late 1930's one part of the Wodlo population was driven out by the other. Some of the refugees fled to the Grand Valley and others toward Archbold Lake. In April 1962 these two refugee groups made a joirt attack on the Wodlo inhabitants living around the Protestant mission station there, driving them out and leaving the area at least temporarily uninhabited.

ENDING WAR

It seems likely that until the Dutch and Indonesian governments began their programs of pacification in the 1960's there was no appreciable period of peace in the Grand Valley. All alliances were at war with at least some of their neighboring alliances.

But specific wars do run their course and are altered or ended after ten or twenty years. It is possible to conjecture about how this happened before 1960. One pattern is suggested by the events involving the Gutelu Alliance: Alliance A is at war with Alliance B, the ritual phase of war is going on; then as that war ebbs, or perhaps while it is still in full swing, Alliance A can no longer hold together; it splits, and one half joins with B in a new alliance to resume or continue warfare with what remains of A.

Another hypothetical model for the events ending a war may be suggested.

When the incidents which began the war between alliances A and B have long been forgotten, a feeling for peace grows. In the meantime relations between A and another bordering alliance, C, become less and less friendly. The ghosts of A still demand killing, but at one moment Alliance A kills not a member of Alliance B, its enemy up to that point, but a member of Alliance C, its friend up to that point. Now the fighting is shifted from the A-B frontier to the A-C frontier. No data were obtained that either support or discredit this theory, but it does have an appealing logic.

AFTER WAR, WHAT?

At the end of August 1961 I left the Dugum Neighborhood to spend two weeks on the coast. During my absence the Gutelu killed two enemy, and the enemy had raided deep into the Dugum Neighborhood and killed a local youth. The next day the District Officer at Wamena had led a police patrol into the area to pacify the frontier and to establish a police post fifteen minutes' walk from the Dugum Neighborhood. The Dani knew the power of the police guns and had accepted pacification without argument.

In view of the prominent role of ritual war in Dani life, I predicted that pacification would only rechannel the violence. Even though the final series of killings between the Gutelu and the Widaia would have placed the Dugum Dani in a slightly more favorable position vis-à-vis their ghosts, it seemed that there would be an increase in ghost anxiety. And since pacification had ended the ritual phase of war as an outlet for hostility, it seemed likely that there would be a striking increase of within-group fighting and that perhaps suicides would occur. In the Wamena area to the south, which had been pacified since 1958, suicide was common (cf. Peters 1965:36), and it seemed that this inner-directed violence had replaced the forbidden war violence.

I was wrong. During the following two years there were no suicides and apparently no abnormal within-group violence in the Dugum Neighborhood, no sudden increase in ritual aimed at placating the ghosts. Perhaps most significant, although the people came to me with every other imaginable complaint against the police stationed in their midst, they never complained to me about the stopping of war. (Peters, working in the southern Grand Valley, did hear many complaints from the Dani there that the stopping of the wars was to blame for drought, flood, and blindness [1965:71, 79]. I was present when one of his informants told of these things and was quite astonished, for I had never heard anything similar in the Dugum Neighborhood.)

How can this Dugum Dani attitude be explained? Is the importance of war perhaps only an illusion?

First, it must be said that the data on incidence of ceremonialism and within-group fighting are not conclusive. The observation of only five months of wartime may be too brief a period to form a base for comparison with the twenty-one months of observed peacetime activity. Also one might argue that the frustrations caused by breaking off the ritual phase of war in 1961 were finally released in the attack of 1966.

Perhaps the answer lies in the pragmatism of the Dani. The accommodation of the Dani to unusual patterns is striking—for example, in the area of language. As mentioned above, the Dani were so willing to accept the simplified version of their own language developed by government personnel that it was months before I realized that the language which they were using with me was rather different from that which they used among themselves.

It will be clear from the discussion of the supernatural which follows that while the ghosts are the subject of much ritual attention, they are on the whole not unreasonable. I would suggest that the threat of the ghosts, which is the explicit motive for war, adjusts to the means available to placate that threat. When war is available as a means of placating the ghosts, war is necessary for placation. When war is not an available means of placation, then the threat of ghosts diminishes and the normal amount of other means suffices.

The 1961 pacification turned out to be less effective than it at first appeared. Five years after the pacification, and despite the presence of the police, war erupted again briefly. It would seem that while the Dani can accommodate to the absence of the ritual phase of war, the factors that lead to intraalliance explosions are more powerful and less easily controlled.

Is *Wim* War?

Can the Dani fighting behavior called *wim* actually be considered war? This is a terminological question which does not affect the present analysis, but a consideration of the question may bring out certain useful points.

The anthropological literature on war is rather scanty. Certainly one reason is that by the time most anthropologists have arrived on the scene, war has disappeared. Even in the present case, the bulk of my field work was done after pacification, and only a glimpse was caught of the Dani at war.

In his book on primitive war Turney-High lays down certain criteria for calling any particular fighting pattern "war" (1949:39). These are purely formal criteria modeled on modern international warfare and so have limited usefulness. Turney-High approaches primitive war as an isolated phenomenon, apart from the context of conflict and conflict resolution.

Schneider's (1950) approach to the problem is contextual, or functional. He points out the importance of distinguishing war from feud and crime and punishment. He emphasizes the importance of specifying the degree of independence between the groups involved in fighting. By his criterion, the fighting between the independent Dani alliances is indeed war.

The objection might be raised that the Dani *wim* is merely group vengeance, an alternating series of killings, one prompted by the next. However, it should be clear that *wim* is a long-term institutionalized pattern of behavior between independent groups, whose momentum is characterized by but not dependent on strict alternation of killings.

It is worthwhile to reemphasize that what I call war, and what the Dani call *wim*, involves two rather different sorts of activities, the ritual fighting and the explosive attack that ends an alliance. I have presented them here as different phases of the same general behavior. However, since the events of the 1960's suggest that even if the ritual fighting is successfully suppressed the explosive attacks may still occur, it is clear that the two phases of war are not necessary conditions of each other.

HOLISTIC ANALYSIS OF DANI WAR

Finally, war may be described holistically, in terms of its interrelationships with other features of the Dani culture and environment. I have chosen a holistic approach rather than a functional analysis in the specialized sense of Vayda, who, in one of his many contributions to the anthropology of war, limits the concept of functionalism to "maintenance of a specific variable within a specific range of values in a specific system" (1968a:105). Thus, for example, he is interested in the possibility of showing that a function of war in a tribal society is to maintain population density at an optimal level by providing a means for an overpopulated group to seize land from an underpopulated neighbor (1968a:86).

Unfortunately, the kinds of data necessary for applying such specific hypotheses to Dani warfare are not available, and because of the difficulty of accurately reconstructing data even for the immediate past, they are not likely ever to be available.

A holistic analysis is essentially descriptive rather than explanatory. Where the two phases of Dani war, the ritual and the secular, differ, they are treated separately. Diagram 3.1 illustrates schematically certain conditions that contribute to the pattern of Dani war behavior and certain effects of that behavior. It has seemed useful, also, to distinguish between those conditions and effects that are explicitly stated as motives or explanations by the Dani themselves and those that are recognized through ethnographic analysis.

I have been intentionally conservative in listing conditions and effects. In cases when an effect is desired, this desire may be a contributing factor, or condition, of war. In the case of leadership, war does have an effect on the allocation of personal influence and the emergence of leaders within a group; but it may also be that the desire of some individuals for influence through war is a condition for war. However, since I have no data to suggest this, I have refrained from proposing it myself.

War is a complex institution intricately embedded in Dani culture, and a holistic analysis is a convenient way of showing the behavior of war in its complexity. It leaves open the question of functional or causal explanations of war, and most important, it avoids the tendency of the functional hypotheses to prematurely narrow the search for explanation to a few of the many possible factors. Finally, the holistic approach is certainly not in opposition to the functional approach when that approach emphasizes multiplicity of functions (as in Vayda 1968b:470).

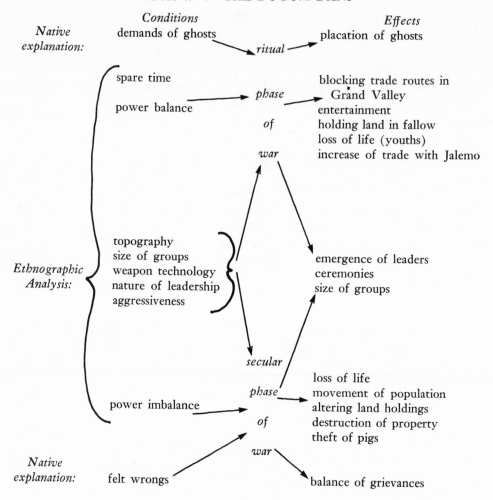

Native explanation:

Conditions

demands of ghosts

Effects

placation of ghosts

ritual

spare time

power balance

phase

of

war

blocking trade routes in
Grand Valley
entertainment
holding land in fallow
loss of life (youths)
increase of trade with Jalemo

Ethnographic Analysis:

topography
size of groups
weapon technology
nature of leadership
aggressiveness

emergence of leaders
ceremonies
size of groups

secular

phase

of

war

power imbalance

loss of life
movement of population
altering land holdings
destruction of property
theft of pigs

Native explanation:

felt wrongs

balance of grievances

DIAGRAM 3.1
HOLISTIC ANALYSIS OF DANI WARFARE

RITUAL PHASE OF WAR

Conditions. The weapons technology of the Dani probably has a limiting effect on warfare. The bows are relatively weak, and the arrows are not fletched, which limits their accuracy, and are never shot in volleys, which limits their effectiveness. The spears are used mainly for killing at short range. Steel bush knives, which came into use in the 1966 attack, are probably more efficient killing weapons than wooden spears, but their range is even less than that of the spears.

A factor effecting the pattern of warfare in the Grand Valley, as distinguished from that carried on by Dani in the narrower valleys to the west and north, is topography. The broad flat plain of the Grand Valley permits a heavy concentration of population, and therefore more men can reach a fighting ground here on a couple of hours' notice than is possible in the thinly populated narrow valleys. Also, Grand Valley topography provides many broad, flat areas for the grand battles. Such sites are rare in other Dani areas, where most of the land is hillside.

But population size alone could not produce large armies if the cooperating political groups were small. So, the large political alliances of several thousand people in the specific setting of the Grand Valley must be counted as a factor contributing to the form of Dani warfare.

Because of technological ease of food production and the cultural circumstance that no great food surpluses are desired, Dani subsistence is easy and requires relatively little time, especially for the men. Thus there is a surplus of time and energy, which is spent on the ritual phase of war. Other activities that might utilize this surplus in the realms of art or ceremonies are absent or minimal.

Berndt has pointed out that warfare in the Highlands of East New Guinea was to some extent limited by the importance of permanent exchange relationships between groups, which suffered in time of war (1964:203). It is difficult to judge how great a role exchange plays in inhibiting Dani warfare. The many personal ties across alliance boundaries are indeed disrupted during wartime, but this does not seem particularly to concern the Dani. Interalliance trade is routed through middlemen in mutually friendly alliances. Enemies of the Gutelu Alliance were denied direct access to the important brine pool in the Gutelu area, but they could still obtain salt from the pool through indirect means. In general it seems more likely that disrupted personal ties and trade relations do not have any great effect on warfare itself, but their quick resumption at the end of a war makes for an easy peace.

The informal nature of Dani leadership has an influence on the pattern of warfare, but in a minimal or even negative sense. Dani leaders initiate war actions but do not have the power to force warriors to participate; they cannot even exercise much direction on the field of battle.

The role of aggressiveness in Dani warfare is particularly hard to evaluate. At first glance Dani warfare appears to be typical of the general New Guinea Highlands pattern of regular, endemic, institutionalized fighting between local groups. Together with pigs, sweet potatoes, and patrilineal descent ideology, warfare has been reported from every Highland culture. Highland warfare has been considered the normal result of the standard Highland personality, which is generally characterized as violent and aggressive. Yet the Dani are not an overtly violent and aggressive people. This seems to pose a paradox, for they are involved in regular fighting and killing. But if the Dani warfare were to be understood as the expression or result of a high level of Dani aggressiveness, then we would expect to see more signs of aggressiveness in the general atmosphere of Dani life, especially in the battles themselves. Further, it could be expected that if war had served as an outlet for aggressiveness, aggressiveness would have found other dramatic and noticeable outlets when warfare was ended. It might be argued that the attack of 1966 was the sudden outbreak of aggression which had been successfully repressed since 1961. The question of

aggression and the measuring of aggression are ultimately psychological questions which most anthropologists are not prepared to handle. But I do think
that the naive impressions of those of us who have lived with Highland groups
are valid as far as they go and can be used, with some caution, for comparative
purposes. So I feel confident in saying that the Dani present no overt signs of
aggression, barely pent up violence and tension which are so often mentioned
in the reports of anthropologists who have worked amongst the Highland
groups to the east of the Grand Valley.

There remains the possibility that the Dani have simply managed to repress
their aggressiveness to a remarkable degree, or that my own account of these
people has been skewed by my own personality and ideology. Certainly Bromley's picture of the Southern Valley Dani, who live only 10–20 kilometers
south of the Dugum Dani, suggests a more typical Highland New Guinea
aggressiveness. However, I feel that we both may be right and that the Southern
Valley Dani *are* significantly more aggressive than the Dugum Dani. One indication of this is that cannibalism and suicide, both known in the southern Grand
Valley, are to the best of my knowledge not practiced at all by the Dugum Dani.
In the end, the possibility of subjective distortion is difficult to handle.

It is significant that in the ritual aspect of Dani wars there is never a victor,
for the single killings alternate so as to keep the two sides relatively in balance.
I would suggest that the important psychological features of Dani warfare are
skill and competence and exuberant exhibitionism, with rapaciousness, aggression,
and drive for dominance playing only a minor role. In 1968 I heard in considerable detail about the attack of 1966 from both instigators and victims, but I
could not recognize either pleasure or indignation in the accounts. In other
words, there seemed to be aggressive behavior without aggressive emotion.

Effects of the Ritual Phase of War. Land use is affected by the ritual phase
of war in several ways. In the first place, the broad strips of no-man's-land
between antagonists in the ritual phase of war reduce the amount of land
available for horticulture. However, any particular no-man's-land zone is withdrawn from horticulture for only a decade or so, until the alliance boundaries
shift, and then it is likely to become available again for cultivation. This was the
case in the southern Gutelu area, where approximately the same amount of
land was under cultivation in 1961 as in 1968, but the no-man's-land itself had
shifted. In other words, the ritual phase of war—or more properly, the changes
of alliances in warfare—serve to hold large strips of land in long-term fallow.
This mechanism does not affect all cultivable land, and the Dani normally allow
land to lie fallow anyway, so war is only one factor regulating the fallow cycle.

The loss of human life is an obvious and striking feature of Dani warfare.
The statistics presented earlier are certainly suspect, but they give some idea of
the extent of the ritual war death: .48 per cent of the population killed yearly
in ritual war; 6.25 per cent of three confederations killed in the attack of June 4,
1966; 28.5 per cent of the males and 2.4 per cent of the females die bloody
rather than natural deaths.

It may be that war mortality is lower in the Wilihiman-Walalua and Gosi-Alua areas than elsewhere in the Dani region. N. Verheijen O.F.M. has reported (in a personal communication) that in two consecutive days of battle in 1959, 34 of the 434 people living in the twelve compounds of Musatfak, in the western Grand Valley, were killed. Bromley has estimated that between 1954 and 1956 the Aso-Logobal Confederation of the southern Grand Valley lost 1 per cent of its population per year through war (1962:23).

The great sexual disparity in war deaths has an effect on the pattern of polygynous marriage. The Dani have a rare situation in that there are virtually no bachelors over the age of 25; and a large percentage of the men have more than one wife. This is possible with an imbalanced sex ratio, which the Dani achieve through disproportionately high male mortality in the ritual phase of warfare.

The sportive aspect of ritual war is certainly important. Dani adults have no organized sports, and there are few amusements except conversation. There can be no question that Dani men find the battles great fun. The exuberance, the joking, the ornaments, and even the risks and the daring are all indications of this sportive element. But Dani ritual warfare is much more complex than just a game.

The field of war is one of the important places for proving manhood, and for the emergence of leaders. The most commonly voiced attribute of an important man is his success in killing; the reason given for a man's being unimportant is that he has not killed; he is *gebu*, coward. In actual practice this is an exaggeration. Actual killing may not be the major criterion, and certainly skill in manipulating the economic system is also of great importance. But no man becomes a leader who has not proven himself in war: on the front lines, facing the spears and arrows of the enemy; or on the flanks where the dirty war is fought around bushes; or in raids.

In broader social terms, the battles and raids of a war are an important cohesive element among the men. War provides one of the few times when a large number of men gather. Other group activities such as gardening and house building seldom involve more than a dozen men. Through war, hundreds of men establish regular, face-to-face contact. Through war, men who would otherwise remain leaders of only a small neighborhood group emerge as important men in the wider area of the confederation or even the alliance.

To some extent ceremonies also afford opportunities for such large gatherings. But generally only the cremations of men killed by the enemy draw more than a few dozen people. The other large ceremonies take place infrequently. Thus, since war and the direct consequences of war, the fresh-blood funerals, are the only regular, frequent events that bring large groups of people together in cooperative effort, war seems to be at once the sole creator and the sole benefactor of larger social cohesion.

A final affect of ritual war is on trade, the intersocietal transactions that result in the balancing of regional specialties. From an ecological standpoint, the most obvious feature of trade is that it gives the Dugum Dani access to goods which are not available in their own immediate environment and deprives them of goods which are. Major imports into the Dugum Neighborhood are seashells, adze stones, furs, feathers, and fine woods and nets: that is, goods from the ocean, goods from a quarry one hundred kilometers to the northwest, and goods from the dense forest. (The forests in the immediate vicinity of the Dugum Neighborhood are thinned out and no longer very productive.) The exports are salt from a local brine pool, which is the best in the entire Grand Valley, and pigs. Most of the trade was between the Dugum Dani and the people of the Jalemo, a densely forested area three days' walk to the northeast. The Dugum Dani exchange basic foods (salt and pork) with the Jalemo for luxuries (fur, feathers, orchid fiber, the best spear and bow woods) whose main use is in warfare and whose demand is maintained by warfare.

The subject of trade introduces another interesting ecological factor of warfare. While I do not see any real ecological effect of the trade on the Dugum Dani, it does seem that warfare in the Grand Valley provides the peoples of the Jalemo with staple food items. It is possible that this flow of staples to the Jalemo has a significant effect on the density of population there.

The Native Explanation of the Ritual Phase of War. The Dani themselves explain the ritual phase of warfare in terms of ghosts: "We must kill an enemy, for otherwise the ghosts will be angry." Dani ceremonialism is chiefly concerned with placating the ghosts, the omnipresent ghosts of their own dead which constitute a constant threat to the Dani's health, economic welfare, and even life. The ritual phase of war can be seen as an extension of ceremonialism. To paraphrase Clausewitz, "Dani ritual war is simply the continuation of religion by other means." This is particularly evident in the two days' dancing that follows the killing of an enemy. The dance does not celebrate a victory over the enemy but calls the attention of the ghosts to the death of an enemy.

Bromley, who is very familiar with Dani culture, has written of the Dani's "sacred obligation to fight" (1962:24). While this may be true for other Dani areas, I feel that it is too strong for the Dugum Dani. There is not really a contractual obligation between the Dani and the supernatural; rather the Dani feel that when the threat from the ghosts is increased because of an enemy killing, it may be decreased by killing an enemy. In other words, the Dani themselves have an understanding of war that conforms well to Vayda's criterion of functional explanation cited above. Within the system of man-ghost relations, at any time the ghosts may be more or less placated or angry. For the Dani the function of the ritual phase of war is to keep the ghostly threats to their well-being at a tolerable level. When the enemy kills one of their own people, the ghostly threat rises; the greater the felt threat, the more the people strive to kill an enemy, which act alone will reduce the threat. The general working of this system can be seen as a compound homeostatic feedback system (see Diagram 3.2).

THE SECULAR PHASE OF WAR

Conditions. For the most part, the conditions of the explosive attacks which make up the secular phase of war are similar to those of the ritual phase. One

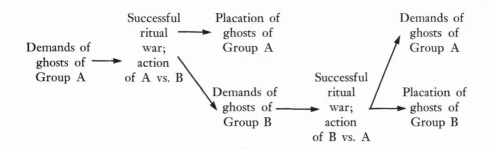

DIAGRAM 3.2
DANI WARFARE AS A COMPOUND HOMEOSTATIC FEEDBACK SYSTEM

major difference is in terms of relative balance of power. During the ritual phase of war the power of the two sides may be in relative balance; in the secular phase the attacking side presumably at least thinks it is more powerful than the other side. The cultural restraints of the ritual phase probably make any but the most extreme differences of power irrelevant. There are far fewer restraints during the secular attacks, and it seems unlikely that a group would risk an attack unless it was fairly confident that it could withstand any counterattack.

Effects. The effects of the short, violent secular phase of war are quite different from those of the more leisurely ritual phase. During the ritual phase of war an occasional watchtower may be toppled and a few sweet potato gardens trampled, but material destruction is minimal. On the basis of the 1966 attack, however, it is clear that the secular attacks result in the burning of many houses, personal belongings, and ritual objects, together with the plunder of many pigs. These losses are limited to the area of attack and not spread out over the entire area involved.

Loss of life in the secular attack is considerable. In 1966 about 150 of 2,000 people were killed in the first few hours. While the ritual phase of war culls out a low but steady portion of the young male population, the nonritual, explosive phase takes a sudden and heavy toll of males and females of all ages from a small area. (The people of the Dugum Neighborhood had not been the subjects of such an attack in living memory, and they did not bear the full brunt of the 1966 attack.)

Shifts of population commonly occur after the explosive attacks. Both the withdrawal of individuals and groups to distant areas in the face of minor conflict and the retreat of defeated groups serve to open land, which the dominant or victorious groups often occupy. Several reports suggested that the Dloko-Mabel once were confined to the Pass Valley, but in the course of a generation or two they established a foothold at the edge of the Grand Valley and then gradually extended their lands toward the Balim River as they triumphed in a series of wars and feuds. The latest of these was in the 1950's, when the Dutabut (or Asuk Balek) sib members were defeated, driven out, and their lands occupied by the Dloko-Mabel and their allies. Also, when the Wio (or Mugogo) were dispersed from their lands around the present site of Wamena, the Hubigiak Alliance expanded to the south, occupying several square kilometers of former Wio territory.

It has often been suggested that in other parts of the New Guinea Highlands war is a means by which an overpopulated group can adjust its boundaries at the expense of an underpopulated one. However, in order to drive out a neighbor, a group needs not density of population per se, but military power. It is not necessary, for example, to assume that the Dutabut were less densely populated than the Dloko-Mabel, but only that they were less powerful. In fact, it seems likely that war and feud, by creating refugees, may generate more local overpopulation problems than they solve. Unfortunately, I do not have the demographic data with which to support or refute this demographic-adjustment–power argument. Even in the 1960's census figures for the Grand Valley Dani were little more than guesses, and it would be practically impossible to reconstruct figures for the period before 1960 which would have the accuracy necessary to answer this question. It is conceivable that the population figures could somehow be assembled. But they are only meaningful to this argument if they can be related to some measure of population pressure. When does a Dani group become overpopulated? The technical question of carrying capacity of land is far from straightforward. The Dani system of ditch horticulture is too flexible to yield an easy formula. And unless one conceives of population pressure purely in this technical sense, one must ask, "At what point does a Dani feel overpopulated?" In short, I am not prepared to deal with the population hypothesis and feel confident only in stating that more powerful groups do displace less powerful groups.

But whatever the facts of demographic balance resulting from war, some peoples of the East New Guinea Highlands explicitly say that they are fighting for land (for example, Meggitt 1965:256). The Dani in their own statements never suggest land as a motive for war.

The Native Explanation of the Secular Phase of War. The Dani emphasis on ghosts is unusual among New Guinea Highland cultures, and the Dani view of the ritual phase of warfare as a human means to effect ghostly revenge has not been reported from elsewhere in the Highlands. When explaining the secular side of war, however, the Dani ignore ghosts and refer only to their grievances against the enemy. Informants were quite explicit that the attack of 1966 had nothing to do with ghosts or even murders, but was a retaliation for a long history of more minor wrongs.

Here again the Dani's own explanation of a cultural pattern suggests a self-regulating system. When the felt wrongs become too great and the tension within an alliance becomes too high, the aggrieved party attacks the other. The attack itself is revenge, a balancing of accounts. The alliance is broken, and the two parties put physical distance between them, creating some degree of social and physical barriers to further inhibit conflict-producing interactions.

SUMMARY

The holistic description has indicated the complex embeddedness of Dani warfare. Because of this complexity and the indeterminate nature of the various factors involved, I am reluctant to isolate any factors as self-regulating systems. It seems significant that the Dani themselves perceive war in simple cause-and-effect terms.

Although this holistic analysis is concerned with the ways in which war is embedded in Dani culture, it suggests the related question of the degree to which it is embedded. Elsewhere (1967) I have suggested that the ritual phase of Dani war was not deeply embedded in the culture on the grounds that it resembled in many respects an earlier hunting pattern and that it was apparently so easily given up in 1961 under government pressure. However, the secular attack of 1966 took place in the face of the government pressure.

The ultimate criterion for strength of embeddedness is the degree of ease with which a trait is given up by a culture. Unfortunately, the Dani case is not an ideal test, since the ritual and secular phases of war were not comparably effected by the government pacification program. The ritual phase, because of its open and regular nature, was much easier to control than the secrecy and suddenness of the secular attack. While the Dani calmly abandoned the ritual phase, they did stage the attack of 1966; so the attack was in some sense more necessary, more embedded, than the ritual battles.

4

MAN AND THE SUPERNATURAL

HE Dani conceive of the world as inhabited by a host of supernatural beings. A very few of these supernatural beings are nonanthropomorphic, such as the snake of the rainbow and the monsters of the whirlpools. Among the anthropomorphic beings some are remote and have little relevance to human behavior, like the people of the sky, the sun woman and the moon man, and the spirits that live in special places. But most immediately effecting Dani behavior are the ghosts of dead people, which stay near the living people and pose a constant threat to them. In Dani terms, the *edai egen* or soul matter of the living are vulnerable to attack by the ghosts of the dead. The theme that runs through Dani ritual is the placation of these ghosts and is manifest in such ritual activities as bringing goods together, killing pigs, and killing enemies. As these acts are performed, the ghosts are informed by displays of goods, shouting, singing, and dancing.

It is often suggested that a culture develops ritual around those areas of life that are most uncertain, that cause the most anxiety. This is largely true for the Dani. The Dani are a healthy people living in an extremely mild environment and enjoying an unfailing food supply that demands relatively little effort on their part. There is only minor ritual connected with sickness, weather, and agriculture.

Death, which is an uncertain state, though inevitable, is compounded by warfare, and it is in the funeral that the Dani have their most elaborate ritual. But in a sense there is a vicious circle at work. Funerals and war are interdependent rituals: The deaths from war cause the largest funerals and prompt further fighting, which results in more deaths, and so on.

The second part of the hypothesis, concerning the relationship of ritual to anxiety, seems less convincing in the Dani case. As a naïve observer I will suggest that the Dani are remarkably free from anxiety. In the face of war, death, and ritual—three areas where one most expects overt signs of anxiety—the Dani seem calm and relaxed.

GHOSTS (*Mogat*) AND SACRED POWER (*Wusa*)

1. Mogat (Ghosts and Spirits)

The basic elements in the supernatural world of the Dugum Dani are the *mogat*, which are both the ghosts of their own dead and various spirits that live in particular areas and behave like ghosts. There seems to be no explicit conception of the *mogat* shared by all members of the society. Basically, the ghosts are explained as follows: When a person dies, the ghost emerges from his corpse and after a few days goes, with the encouragement of the various funeral rituals, to the *mogat ai*, the ghost house (which is also called *wagun ai*) in the woods where the ghost bundles (*wagun*) are stored. This is the place of the ghosts, where they stay all the time; but at certain times they approach the compounds. At night, especially, they are likely to way-lay and throttle a passerby who has no torch. Ghosts are also present at battles.

Ghosts retain some human attributes. They may be pleased or displeased; they are able to hear requests and demands shouted at them; they are able to eat, in a symbolic way: during the ilkho ceremony of the funeral, when the mourners eat food passed under the arch, an old man shouts to the ghost of the departed, "You eat this!" At the *mogat ai* ghosts come and eat, again symbolically, the sweet potato laid there for them. The ghost of a recently departed person may even come at night to wander around his old compound.

Ghosts represent an ever-present threat to the well-being of the living. They are the ultimate cause of death, illness, and pig diseases; they come with the rain and have basic control over the weather (cf. p. 214). On the other hand, the *mogat* may be of assistance in war: they may warn of an enemy attack; before battle they may "pre-kill" an enemy; and they may actually assist the forces in battle.

Although the ghosts are discrete anthropomorphic entities, the Dani make no attempt to identify a specific ghost with a specific person. Occasionally a person will describe an encounter with the ghost of a particular remembered person, but usually ghosts are referred to anonymously as simply *mogat*.

Informants listed five to ten names of spirits but rarely agreed on all the names. However, all informants agreed that the spirits could be either male or female, that they live in special areas, and that they are controlled in some manner by specific men.

Spirits are physically more remote from people than are the ghosts, and they have little influence on human behavior. They apparently do not have the same human derivation as ghosts, although the distinction between ghost and spirit does seem analogous to the distinction between the ghosts of recent and remote dead, which Lawrence and Meggitt mention as characteristic of East New Guinea Highlands groups (1965:11). There is nothing in Dani belief that corresponds to a supreme being or to gods, although the sun woman and the moon man do have a special status.

2. Wusa

Wusa corresponds to the taboo and mana of anthropological literature. *Wusa* is the attribute of sacredness, the association of an object or class of object or act with the supernatural world. *Wusa* is used in one sense to mean "prohibited for sacred reasons," such as the eating of certain foods by certain people, or performing certain acts such as defecation or collecting firewood in certain areas; or the area belonging to a man who has marked it out with knotted grass signs. *Wusa* also refers to the power inherent in certain things of ritual significance—a power not in itself inimical if limited to the ritual context. But *wusa* must be ceremonially negated when the ritual is over; for example, men who have handled a corpse in the course of preparing it for the pyre or men who have worked on the building of a watchtower have come into contact with *wusa*, which must be removed from the men by a feather (a process called *duesi balin,* feather cutting) before they resume normal activity (Plate 20).

The antonym of *wusa* is *weligat,* profane. In other contexts *weligat* is also used to mean "it is just there, it has no particular meaning," or "it is given free, there is no obligation to repay."

Wusa (Sacred) Places. Wusa as sacredness or potentially dangerous power may be associated with places in different ways. There is the permanent *wusa* attached to the araucaria grove, Homuak, and to the single lone-standing

PLATE 20. A small feather mounted on a stick is waved over hands which have just done ritually dangerous work to cleanse them. (Photograph by Michael Rockefeller)

araucaria tree called Mabile near the compound Mabilatma. There are areas which have been declared *wusa* by placement of the knotted grass sign, the *silo*. These are primarily the areas around the *wagun ai*, or ghost houses, in the forest. But *silo* may also be placed to protect a wooded area from being searched for firewood; a man who plans to make a garden outside a compound entrance often puts *silo* around the plot to prevent people from defecating there. Also, certain structures are considered *wusa*: the *wato leget* and *oak leget* enclosures behind the men's house (p. 271); and the *gagok* cabinet in the rear of the men's house, where the *wusa* objects are stored (p. 258).

But in no case is the *wusa* area strictly maintained as a sacred area, apart from any profane uses. There is no Dani equivalent of a temple or similar area which must always be treated with respect.

Wusa as Restrictions on Human Behavior. Various norms which restrict certain kinds of human behavior have supernatural sanctions. The word *wusa* is used to describe the restricted behavior, meaning behavior restricted or prohibited on pain of punishment by ghosts.

Many of these norms are exclusive, restricting certain behavior only for members of a particular sib or moiety. In particular, members of a sib are restricted from eating the bird of their sib; a number of foods are restricted for members of the Waija moiety, and a few are restricted for members of the Wida moiety; bananas and cucumbers grown in the compound gardens where one's sacred objects are kept are also restricted.

Sexually exclusive restrictions are those prohibiting women from entering men's houses or from working in gardens after certain rain ceremonies.

Inclusive restrictions, which effect all people, are those against whistling indoors; against eating sweet potato leaves from the gardens of the Dugum Neighborhood (but not from other neighborhoods); against throwing banana peels away instead of drying them out and burning them; and against a husband and wife having sexual intercourse for several years after the birth of a child.

Symbols of restrictive *wusa* are *silo*, knots of grass placed waist-high on trees and bushes every 20–50 meters around an area which is to be entered with special care. These areas are particularly the immediate vicinity of a *mogat ai*, a structure in the woods containing bundles which represent individual dead. *Silo* indicate that it is *wusa* to drink water, collect wood, urinate, or defecate in the area.

Silo are also used in a non-*wusa*, or profane, manner to prevent people from urinating at night directly outside a compound entrance, or to gather firewood from an area claimed by a particular person, or to block a path into a garden area. In these cases the sanctions are not supernatural but are carried out by human beings.

In all cases of *wusa* restrictions, the sanctions derive from generalized fear of the ghosts who enforce them. Often informants would specify that ghosts would cause the stomach of the transgressor to swell, and he would die.

A similar but not serious use of *wusa* in this sense is made by adults in disciplining young children. Generally the Dani are very permissive toward their children, but when a child has hopelessly tangled a coil of thread or comes too close to a fire, he is gently removed with the warning that it is *wusa*. In these cases there is no involvement of supernatural powers.

Wusa as a Restriction on the Activity of Ghosts. Much Dani activity can be seen as an attempt to restrict or control the activity of ghosts, usually by pleasing the ghosts, as in the funeral ritual. But there are some rituals that use magical objects to prevent ghosts from approaching a person or a compound or a garden. In these cases the supernatural power which is *wusa* does not derive from the ghosts, nor is it sanctioned by the ghosts, but it is directed against the ghosts.

Some of these magical objects are carried on the body. For example, a person who is sick or wounded, and whose *edai-egen* is thus weak, sometimes wears a few of the pungent seeds of the *dogalit*, whose odor is supposed to keep away ghosts. A malformed child may wear a necklace of crayfish claws, which are also supposed to keep away ghosts.

Other magical objects are stationary symbolic barriers, usually feather-studded reeds or hoops placed by a path to prevent ghosts from approaching a compound where a sick or wounded person lies.

The *mogat agu*, literally ghost bridge, is a more elaborate object also placed by a path to prevent ghosts from attacking the compound of a sick man, or a pig sty where there are sick pigs, or a new garden. The *mogat agu* is an N-shaped structure of two-meter-high poles about one meter apart, with a diagonal brace, standing upright beside a path. The essential element in addition to the frame is a stalk of sugar cane tied across the two upper points of the frame legs.

The *mogat agu* and its position have symbolic reference to the ritual directions or vectoring mentioned in the origin myth episode (p. 142). In the Dugum Neighborhood, the base of the sugar cane is directed toward the cave where the first man emerged, the leaf end toward the western quarter, the direction taken by men and ghosts as they dispersed from the origin cave (see Episode 8 of the origin myth, pp. 141-2). The *mogat agu* is placed alongside a path on the side toward the compound or garden being protected.

The usual meaning of *agu* is bridge, and is used both for the simple poles over garden ditches and for the complex lashed structures over wide streams. But the *mogat agu* is not a bridge facilitating access of ghosts to the compound or garden. Rather, it is a deflector, inducing ghosts to continue along the path and not to turn toward the protected objects. The sugar cane has special powers in this respect; the ghosts, on approaching the *mogat agu*, are supposed to slip along the sugar cane from the base out past the leaves and thus directed past the protected area.

ATTITUDE TOWARD THE SUPERNATURAL

Despite the pervasive presence of powerful, threatening ghosts, and despite the frequent contact with *wusa* objects, the Dani are in no sense pious. Though all their ceremonial activity and all their pigs are used in placating the ghosts, there seems to be no actual fear of ghosts. The Dani could only be called matter-of-fact about the supernatural world. There are certain minimal rituals which must be performed; these are performed, the subject is dropped, and normal life is resumed.

The Dani recognize the potential evil of ghosts, but they do not take unnecessary or uncomfortable steps to divert this evil. For example, it is recognized that if one travels abroad at night without a light, one is subject to attack by the ghosts. During our first days in the Neighborhood, Dani visitors to our camp would usually ask to borrow a flashlight to return home, "or the ghosts will kill us." At first we cooperated, but it soon became clear that our flashlight supply would not hold up. When we refused flashlights, there was obvious and great distress. But when it finally became clear that we would not loan them flashlights any more, their evening visits to the camp did not drop off at all.

For another example, the ghost of the recently killed youth Jenokma once was heard at night shuffling around in the men's house in which he had last slept. The story was told the next morning with great enthusiasm and a little mirth, but no fear.

Foods that are *wusa* for members of one moiety are generally not eaten, but if a person is hungry, and he is not observed by an older person, he will eat the supposedly restricted food without qualms.

The knitting of the band for the shell band is considered *wusa*, and the *wusa* must be removed from the knitter before he goes about his normal activities. If a feather is handy, a man will purify himself by waving the feather over his hands before eating or smoking. But if there is no feather at hand, he will not hesitate to lay down the band and take up a sweet potato or cigarette in his "polluted" hands.

Conduct at ceremonies is marked by this same attitude. Mourning is very intense; at certain moments, men and women grieve loudly, wiping their eyes and rubbing their thighs. During the dirge the atmosphere is intensely sad. But as soon as it is over the mourners quickly return to their normal conversation, laughing and joking. The only exceptions will be perhaps a parent or spouse of the dead person.

Ritual itself shows the sharp break between the sacred and the profane. For example, in the *je wakanin* ceremony (p. 80) nets, stones, and shell bands are brought from a great distance, discussed, laid out, and then shouted over. As soon as the shouting is finished the ceremony is over. In a most unceremonious manner everyone packs up his own bundle and leaves for home. There is no accompanying drama. A certain thing must be done; it is done, usually in an atmosphere of concentration for the actor and attention on the part of the onlookers, but as soon as it is accomplished the atmosphere immediately returns to normal.

There is no sense of fear in the Dani's relationship with the supernatural. Ghosts and spirits, although omnipresent and ever threatening, are not prone to irrational vengeance. For example, in the forest around the *mogat ai,* or ghost house, are *silo* to warn people not to gather firewood or to defecate in the area. It is all right to drink if the water flows through an area from a spring farther uphill. The punishment for those who violate the *silo* warning is ghost-inflicted death. However, small children and pigs are not in danger. They may transgress without being punished, for they are not able to understand the meaning of the *silo.*

MYTHOLOGY

ORIGIN MYTH EPISODES

Dani mythology is not very elaborate, and not particularly prominent in Dani life. The bulk of Dugum Dani mythology consists of a multiepisodic myth concerning the first man, Nakmatugi, and the origins of various things. Apparently this myth is not generally known, but is considered extremely sacred and only told to males after they are married. Only after countless attempts, and using certain key words from the word lists of van der Stap and Bromley, did I manage to get the story from the Dani. Even then, the great bulk of the myth was obtained from a single informant, the important Wilil man Um'ue. It was never possible to elicit a continuous relation of the myth. Questions were necessary at each step. I have no reason to believe that the myth as given by Um'ue is not the accepted version. On the other hand, I can offer neither continuous text nor secondary verification.

This is the myth as pieced together.

Episode 1: Sky and Earth

In the beginning, the sky lay on the ground. Nakmatugi the first man lived in the Huwainmo Cave. He made thunder, and the sky separated from the earth, rising to its present position.

COMMENTARY. The Huwam Cave lies on the outer northern flank of the Pugima Valley, about five kilometers southeast of the Dugum Neighborhood in the territory of the Phaluk-Meduan Confederation. It is a limestone cave about 15 meters high and 5 meters broad from which issues the Huwam River, which flows into the Lower Aikhe River.

The possible sexual symbolism of sky lying on earth, rising, and people issuing from a cave is complicated by Um'ue's statement that the sky is female and the earth male.

Episode 2: Origin of Cannibalism

Nakmatugi had a fight with his younger brother Phuba over ownership of land and killed him. Nakmatugi cut up Phuba's body with bamboo knives, roasted and then ate the pieces.

COMMENTARY. Ritual cannibalism was probably practiced in the Huwam region and generally in the southern Grand Valley until recently. Hitt quotes a missionary witness account of butchering the corpse of an enemy (1962:126ff.), but as Peters pointed out (1965:105, n. 1), the missionaries turned away at the last moment and did not actually see the eating of the flesh. In any case, the people of the Dugum believe that the Southern Valley people did practice cannibalism, although they deny that they themselves did. However, in 1968 at Jibiga, informants claimed that their fathers or grandfathers ate human flesh.

The bamboo knives used by Nakmatugi are called *dakdak* and are distinguished from ordinary bamboo knives, called *wim ugul*. Many collections of sacred objects (*ganekhe*) include *dakdak* attributed to Nakmatugi. They are used in the pig castration ceremony preceding the *ebe akho* ceremony.

Episode 3: Footprints

Nakmatugi had a fight with his other younger brother, Japusuok, who was very tall. Nakmatugi told Japusuok, "This is my place, your place is over there." Japusuok left Huwainmo for the Bele Valley, to the west across the Grand Valley. As he walked he left footprints on some of the hills in the Central Valley.

COMMENTARY. I never observed these footprints, or had them pointed out by informants.

Episode 4: Origin of Salt

Nakmatugi sent his sister Elaboke to become the brine pool at Iluekaima.

Episode 5: Separation of People from Animals

The people came out of the Huwainmo Cave, together with the *due* (birds, bats), *wato* (insects, reptiles, amphibians), and the *bpake* (forest mammals). The people and the birds were together, and the forest mammals were their pigs. Then they asked Nakmatugi who they were. He said, "You are people, you are birds, you are *bpake*, you are *wato*."

Then the birds said, "We don't like the people, we'll go off and be birds." And the *wato* said the same, and the *bpake* said the same.

COMMENTARY. This forms the basis for the association of particular sibs with particular birds, mammals, and insects. Each sib includes both men and birds. The men refer to their sib birds as *akalak*, brother, and are not supposed to eat them.

Episode 6: First Sib Men

When the people went out from the Huwainmo Cave, there were the original men of each sib. There was Busoate, the original Wilil; Halit, the original Walilo; Wamena, the original Mabel, and others.

COMMENTARY. Each sib has an original ancestor, but there is no attempt among sib members to construct specific genealogical connections with him.

Episode 7: Origin of Mountains

The mountains were originally just small stones, and then they grew to their present size. Nakmatugi gave each sib a mountain.

COMMENTARY. These sib mountains are a home of the ghosts of the sib dead. Sib members have special rights to the produce of their mountains, such as orchid fiber and pandanus nuts.

Episode 8: Ritual Direction

As the people moved out from the Huwainmo Cave, the ghosts went ahead of them.

COMMENTARY. This episode is the explanation for basic ritual directions. The Huwam Cave lies to the southeast of the Dugum Neighborhood, and that direction is called *holak wakugumo khe*, the path of coming. The opposite direction, which is more generally the up-valley arc from southwest to northwest, is called *holak lakugumo khe*, the path of going. According to this segment of the myth, the ghosts, which went ahead, are now in the western quarter. The Dugum Dani claim that the two kinds of magical objects, *hola* and *agu*, which are placed along or across paths, are supposed to prevent ghosts from approaching specific compounds. In nearly all observed cases, these objects were placed on a path from the west, and no other. Informants explained that this was sufficient because ghosts would come only from the western quarter. A similar vectoring of the landscape was observed at Jibiga, but there the lines ran not from the origin cave but from the head of the Pass Valley, and so more directly east-west than in the Dugum Neighborhood.

Episode 9: Origin of Pigs

At the beginning, there was Wamake, whose body was that of a pig but whose head was of the Wilil sib. When he died, a male and a female pig came from his body. These pigs produced pigs for all the people

COMMENTARY. The attribution of Wilil sib membership to Wamake was made by Um'ue, a Wilil, and is perhaps suspect.

Wamake means literally pig tail. Pig tails have special supernatural power and are worn by people and sewn on various ritual objects.

Episode 10: Nakmatugi and Jege (Dog)

Nakmatugi had a large garden with a house. Dog had a small garden with a house. Nakmatugi planted sweet potato, *doa* (the edible grass), yams, tobacco, and banana. Dog had fire, sugar cane, taro, cucumber, pea, and mallow. But he carried them in his ear, and he didn't know how to plant them. So he took them from his ear and gave them to Nakmatugi, who planted them. Nakmatugi taught men how to plant and build, but even today Dog just wanders around, waving his tail.

COMMENTARY. It is tempting to read into this episode a slightly muddled historical account of two cultural waves coming into the Highlands (cf. Heider 1967). The first is represented by the dog, which the Dani use only as a hunting animal. In the myth, Dog does not know how to plant. His cultural inventory includes fire, but also some domestic plants. (In 1968 the same informant repeated the two lists, and this time Dog had *doa* but not sugar cane.)

The second cultural wave is represented by the man, Nakmatugi, who is a farmer and who brings sweet potato, tobacco, banana, yams, and the edible grass *doa*.

If the Highlands of New Guinea were settled in two waves, it is not unlikely that the first wave was a basically hunting and gathering culture, living in part on the sago palm, which grows wild to about 1,200 meters altitude, and supplementing its diet with some cultivated plants. With the coming of sweet potato, the population was able to explode into the 1,200–2,000 meter zone, where the bulk of the Highland Papuans now live.

It is not known when the first people reached the Balim. It does seem probable that intensive settlements of the nature now found in such parts of the Highlands would not have been possible without the sweet potato.

At the risk of compounding speculation with speculation, it is worth mentioning an origin myth from the Trobriand Islands off the eastern tip of New Guinea, which bears a strong resemblance to this Dani myth episode.

According to Malinowski, the four main clans on the Trobriand Island of Boyowa are each represented by a totemic animal, and in the origin myth the animals emerge from a hole in a specific order: first is Iguana (Lukulabuta clan); second is Dog (Lukuba clan); third is Pig (Malasi clan); and the fourth, representing the Lukwasisiga clan, is ambiguous. It is said to be Crocodile, Snake, Opossum, or in some versions it is imply ignored. Then, after the emergence,

The Dog and Pig ran around, and the Dog, seeing the fruit of the *noku* plant, nosed it, then ate it. Said the Pig: "Thou eatest *noku*, thou eatest dirt; thou art a low-bred, a commoner; the chief, the *guya'u*, shall be I." And ever since, the highest subclan of the Malasi clan, the Tabalu, have been the real chiefs. (1954:112)

Malinowski, despite his aversion to this sort of myth analysis, does engage in it (1954:123–25). He suggests that the Lukulabuta and Lukwasisiga clans represent the "oldest layer" of Trobrianders and that the Malasi subclan, the Tabalu, are the latest, who on their arrival from the north wrested power from the Lukuba. However, Malinowski's concern is with myth as a charter or justification of a present situation, in this case the ranking of Trobriand clans, and he is not interested in pursuing historical elements in myth.

It is possible, however, to interpret the Trobriand myth, like the Dani myth, as an account of the transition from hunting and gathering to intensive horticulture. The first two creatures that emerge from the hole are Iguana, an object of foraging, and Dog, the companion of the hunt. They are followed by the animal of the horticulturist, the pig. And then Pig declares that he is chief and that Dog is a commoner, on the grounds that Dog eats *noku*.

Noku is a particularly interesting detail corroborating this analysis. Malinowski tells us that the *noku* is a "small tree growing in *odila* (the bush); fruits all year round, and in times of *molu* (famine) principal staple food" (1935b:116). Further, *noku* is "despised" and it is "hardly edible but hardly ever fails" (1935a:160). In other words, Dog is eating a despised famine food. Barrau, in his revealing article called "Witnesses of the Past" (1965), has pointed out that the famine foods of present horticultural Oceania are probably the staples of the earlier foraging stage. Unfortunately, Malinowski's interest in formal botany was slight, and it is not apparent from his account just what *noku* actually is. The major famine foods that Barrau describes are *Pueraria lobata*, which has an edible tuber; the *Cycas rumphii* a palm with edible seeds and stem starch; the *Dioscorea nummularia*, or wild yam; and the *Cordyline fruticosa*, which has an edible tuber. But none of these seem to qualify as *noku*, although it clearly is a famine food.

In short, however, it appears likely that embedded in the mythology of both the Dani and the Trobrianders are accounts of the transition from foraging to horticulture.

Episode 11: The Bird and the Snake

A snake (*balu*, the python) and a bird (*ebe bulok*, a small song bird) had an argument. The snake said that when people died and are cremated, then they should come to life again. This is called *nabutal-habutal*, my skin-your skin. The bird said, "I don't like that. They should stay dead, and I'll smear mud on myself in mourning." Then Nakmatugi, the first man, intervened, saying, "I don't like snakes," and the bird won the argument.

COMMENTARY. This explanation of human mortality is known from other Dani areas where it often takes the form of a race between a bird and a snake. Exegeses from other Dani areas suggest that the snake is a symbol of immortality because it renews itself by shedding its skin (van der Stap, Bromley, in personal communications).

Similar but fragmentary legends explaining immortality are known from other parts of New Guinea. The Daribi of East New Guinea have the same bird and snake theme (Wagner 1967:40). Blackwood reports (1939) a Kukukuku myth of a fight between a rat and a snake. The rat wins, and thus men are doomed to die. Mead (1940:362) reports two versions of an Arapesh myth involving a rat and a snake. In both cases, because the rat dies man must die, but if the snake had died man would not die. It is tempting to think of both the Kukukuku and Arapesh myths as variant fragments of a common Papuan mortality myth which has been retained in more complete from by the Dani. In fact, very similar myths are found just to the east of New Guinea. From the Melanesian Lakalai of New Britain, Valentine describes a similar pattern of immortality associated with renewable skin, opposing mortality associated with nonrenewable skin: ". . . thenceforth men could no longer live on and on by changing their skin, and death thus came into the world" (1965:165). The same theme is reported from the Trobriand Islands: Man was originally able to shed his skin and be rejuvenated, but as the result of a misunderstanding an angry old woman relinquished this ability and now all men become old and die (Malinowski 1954:127).

Episode 12: The White Man

In the beginning, everyone was together at the Huwainmo Cave, Dani, white man, dogs, and pigs. The white man emerged first, wearing clothes and carrying guns. They went far away, over the mountains. Then the Balim people emerged from the cave wearing penis gourds.

COMMENTARY. It is not known when this segment was incorporated into the body of Dani myth. The first Europeans were seen by Dani in 1909, south of the ranges. Europeans and Americans visited the Grand Valley in 1938, 1945, and have lived there continuously since 1954.

By 1968 a Cessna airplane had been incorporated into this episode, and some informants countered my attempts to learn of the distant past with, "You were here first, you flew out of the cave in your Cessna, you tell us what it was like then."

MYTH OF THE SKY PEOPLE

Another myth, which does not refer to event of origin or to the first man, Nakmatugi, is that of people in the sky called Sinegen-Munegen. Unlike the origin myth, this myth is widely known and was mentioned by many informants; it goes as follows:

People called Sinegen-Munegen live in the sky. They are humans and have compounds, gardens, and pigs. Formerly they came often to the compounds on earth, climbing down a rope, to visit and trade. But they often stole pigs, and wives ran away with them. Finally, in great anger, a man on earth cut the sky rope, and since then Sinegen-Munegen have stayed in the sky. Certain araucaria trees (*sin*) belong to them and were left behind.

COMMENTARY. There is considerable disagreement among informants as to just where the rope from the sky touched the earth and just who finally cut it, although many point to the place called Pokotigi (literally sky finger), near Jibiga.

The general pattern of this myth echoes the background of relations between alliances: two groups are friendly until increasing friction over pigs and women erupts into war.

The names of the people in the sky are suggestive. *Sinegen* are the seeds (*egen*) of the araucaria tree (*sin*) with which children make outlines of houses and compounds. The araucaria groves in the Grand Valley are not inhabited by people, and although important trade routes may cross them and pigs root in them, these groves are considered mildly sacred.

Munegen are the berries (*egen*) of the *muniga* tree (a Pittosporum), which represent warriors in miniature battles waged by boys.

The large dead araucaria trunk standing near the Mabilatma compounds was called Mabile, almost in the manner of a personal name. When it fell in a wind storm in 1963, an exchange stone was burned at its base. Informants explained that people had felt sorry for the tree and would have given the Sinegen-Munegen the stone as a kind of funeral present, but since this was no longer possible, the stone was burned.

PETRIFICATIONS

Certain curiously shaped limestone blocks are explained as petrifications of living beings.

A limestone block about forty centimeters long, lying in the middle of the trail a few hundred meters below the Iluekaima brine pool, is said to be the body of a woman, Jalige. She was returning from the brine pool when a ghost stamped on her, killed her, and then turned her to stone.

Another limestone block about the size and shape of a large reclining pig is near a path on the upper slopes of the Dugum Neighborhood. It is said to have been a pig belonging to Ajuk, a man from Dlugigin. The ghosts didn't like the pig, and they turned it to stone.

These stones do suggest the forms of a woman and a pig, respectively. However, no attention is paid the geological petrifications that occasionally appear in the limestone.

RITUAL DIVINATION

Dani behavior that attempts by ritual means to know events of past or future can properly be called divination ritual.

Sometimes when a pig is missing and thought to have been stolen, the owner will go into the fields hunting for a mouse or small rat, bring it back to his compound, cut it open, and examine the intestines. If there is blood from internal hemorrhaging, this indicates that the pig has already been eaten. If there is no blood, the search for the pig continues. The body of the rodent is hung in the men's house on a center post behind the central hearth. It apparently has no particular function any more, but often hangs there for several months.

A similar ritual is performed for a man seriously wounded in battle. Usually two rodents are examined. Bloody feces found in the body cavity are an indication that the patient will not recover.

Both these forms of rodent divination are low-level ritual in the sense that they can be performed by any man and do not involve much supernatural power.

Another type of divination involves a bundle of about two dozen sticks, five to seven centimeters long, which hangs from the rafters of men's houses with important collections of sacred objects (*ganekhe*). At the time of the ceremony for renewing and restoring these sacred objects, an important man throws the loose sticks into the air above the heads of the assembled unmarried youths. Boys who catch a stick will find a wife; those who don't, won't.

Other divinationlike behavior that does not occur in ritual contexts is described in the section concerning play (p. 197).

FUNERAL CEREMONY AND RITUAL CYCLE

The death of a person initiates a series of rites that extend over a period of several years. The immediate explicit goal of these rites is to dispose of the body by cremation, to drive the ghost of the dead person away from the dwelling areas, and subsequently to keep it placated so that it will stay away. The funeral rites also serve to reinforce ties of kinship and the local group by gathering together relatives and neighbors and, more important, by the great amount of exchange of goods that takes place in the context of the funeral rites.

All funerals follow the same basic pattern, but there is considerable variation in detail from one to another. Some events may be omitted. Some events, such as the distribution of exchange goods, may be postponed for a day or more to await the arrival of relatives from distant areas.

Many latent functions can be attributed to the funeral, but the explicit function is to appease the ghosts. This is consistent with the fact that the most elaborate funerals are those for important men and for men who have been killed by the enemy—in other words, those whose ghosts would be especially powerful and dangerous.

The funerals of very important people differ from those of unimportant people chiefly in size, as measured by numbers of mourners at the cremation, number of pigs slaughtered, and number of valuable exchange goods brought into circulation.

The first stage of the funeral follows immediately on the death, and the second stage is held a month or so later. These first two rituals are held for an individual funeral. The third stage is a combined ritual for all the funerals in one or more confederations, and the final stage terminates all the funerals in the entire alliance area, and is held in combination with the great pig feast.

The first two parts of the ceremony are carried out for a single individual and involve few people beyond the Neighborhood. The *je wakanin*, held every year or two involves one or more confederations, and is for all the deaths which have occurred in this larger area. Finally the *ebe akho*, pig feast, which takes place every few years and is the final funeral rite for all the deaths since the last pig feast, involves the entire alliance and is initiated by the most important man in the alliance.

At least seventeen deaths occurred in the Dugum Neighborhood during the twenty-six months of my field work between March 1961 and December 1963. Most funerals I observed at least in part; I observed the third phase in October 1961; preliminary activity of the fourth phase extended through 1963, but by December 1963, when the field study was terminated, the major sequence of events had not yet begun.

First Stage

On the morning after the death has occurred, the usual sequence of events is: cremation of corpse; pigs killed and eaten; goods brought; goods distributed (may be delayed a few days). On the night between the first and second days, a bundle of grass is taken outside the compound, then returned, then carried to a hilltop.

On the second day of the funeral: mutilation of fingers and/or ears (if done at all); nets distributed to women (may be delayed a few days); bony remains of corpse picked from the fire, bundled, and hung in the common cook house of the cremation compound; pig and sweet potato eaten; sweet potato distributed; ghost driven out of compound with rocks (if done at all).

On the third day: bones deposited in bone enclosure; *walon* net made (may be delayed a day or so); pig and sweeet potato eaten; mice hunted and eaten (if at all).

On the fourth day: sweet potato eaten, water poured on ashes of bones (if at all).

On the fifth day: first phase of funeral is ended by removing the *wusa* from the rocks used in the steam bundle.

The funeral takes place in the compound where death has occurred. In one instance where a person was killed in a raid, his corpse was carried back to his father's main compound. In three instances people on the verge of death moved or were brought from their own, smaller compounds to die in the compound of Um'ue, an important man. Informants explained this as a desire on the part of both the dying man and his relatives to be assured of a well-run funeral.

For the four or five days of the first phase of the funeral, the compound where it is held is usually referred to as *watekma*, place of death.

The funeral is run by the most important man of the compound or by a more important and closer relative of the dead person. This man does very little actual directing of activity, and is at most an informal master of ceremonies. Everyone is familiar with the procedure, and most of the men at the funeral help in some way with the preparation of the food and funeral pyre. Women rarely assist except in the making up of the steam bundles. The leader himself usually kills the pigs and distributes the shell bands.

The corpse of a female is arranged in the common cook house, that of a male in the men's house. The corpse sits against the rear wall, its head held up by a string under the chin and its knees drawn up toward the chest so that the angles of the legs at hip and knees are closer to 45° than to 90°.

A frame is made to hold the corpse in this position. Each frame I saw was different, but most utilized a section of banana trunk under the knees to hold them up and poles planted in the ground on either side of the knees and lashed together to hold the knees together.

In a "fresh blood" funeral for a person just killed by the enemy, the corpse is arranged in a kind of chair in the center of the courtyard before cremation (Plate 21). The corpse of a man who died of wounds several months after the battle was not "fresh blood," and so was arranged in the men's house instead of on a chair.

The chair, or *bea*, is built near the men's house in the courtyard about eight o'clock in the morning of the cremation, before the first guests arrive. It is built by the men of the compound, using available construction planks. The seat is about one meter from the ground The back rises another seventy centimeters to support the head and back of the corpse (Plate 21). Banana leaves are placed on the seat of the chair, then the corpse is lifted onto the chair facing the end of the compound and carefully adjusted. A string from the chair back runs under the chin, holding up the head. A slat is lashed across the front to draw up the knees.

The use of a chair for the fresh blood funerals was explained in terms of

PLATE 21. During the funeral of Wejakhe, who was killed in an enemy ambush, his corpse is displayed on a chair in the center of the courtyard. (Photograph by Michael Rockefeller)

the greater danger from ghosts, and particularly from the ghost of the slain man, on such occasions. By displaying the corpse more prominently, the ghosts would be more placated.

The position of corpses both in houses and in chairs resembles the fetal position, of course, although the legs are only semiflexed. There is no evidence suggesting that this is conscious symbolism on the part of the Dani.

Guests and Goods. After eight o'clock, as the rising sun burns off the early mists, the funeral guests begin to arrive, usually in small groups and usually carrying pigs or other funeral gifts.

As each group arrives, it moves toward the center of the courtyard and stands, dirging. The leader of the group sings a single line, expressing sorrow and mentioning the name of the dead person and his relationship to him. As he finishes his line, the other members of his group break in with a mourning moan. This may be repeated for several minutes and is often answered in kind by the men already in the compound. As the men dirge, they stand in stylized manner, often rubbing their eyes with one hand, rubbing a thigh with the other hand, and scratching at the ground with a foot.

Suddenly the dirge breaks off and the newcomers move forward with their gifts, which are accepted with the appropriate kin terms, and a repeated *wawawa*-ing by the men of the compound. Hands are clasped, embraces exchanged all around, and the newcomers take their seats to smoke and gossip with the others.

The women guests have joined the other women at the front end of the compound, where they sit, often with one hand against the side of the head, dirging in a swell of meaningless words.

Throughout the day the atmosphere at the women's end of the compound is subdued. But the men, except for those most closely related to the dead man, alternate abruptly between deep, tearful mourning and normal or even laughing conversation.

Various goods are brought, all of which have the primary explicit function of pleasing the ghosts. Pigs are carried, slung upside down over the shoulders of young men or, if too large, herded in. They are allowed to wander in the courtyard or are shut into a sty until the butchering. New carrying nets are draped on the corpse chair or laid by the corpse in the house. Cowrie shell bands are bound around the head and draped over the body of the corpse. Other goods that may be brought are Nassa shell chest strands, bailer shells, and feathered and furred head pieces.

Each gift can be interpreted as the contribution of an individual or a group toward the placating of the ghost of the dead person, and ghosts in general.

The basic goods involved are pigs and shell bands. The ideal pattern of circulation of these funeral gifts was stated by informants in terms of moiety affiliation. Those of the dead person's own moiety bring pigs and the people of the opposite moiety (that of his mother's brother) bring shell goods. The pigs are eaten at the ceremony, the shell goods are in part set aside for a memorial bundle and in part given to those who brought pigs.

This basic pattern also appears at a birth ceremony, when the mother's brother gives the baby shell goods, and at the time of marriage, where the individual gives pigs to his bride's family and thus to members of his mother's brother's moiety.

However, actual observation showed that this ideal pattern was often violated. Many men brought shells of the wrong type required by the ideal, and those closest to the dead person usually contributed both shell goods and pigs. It is apparent that an informal exchange based on complex networks of personal ties and previous gifts is more important than the ideal formal pattern based on moiety affiliation.

The funeral can be the occasion to settle old enmities or remove old sources of friction through goods that are given in the sense of restitution. This was observed at the funeral of Jagik, an old man who had once been very important and one of whose sons, Nilik, was then one of the important men of the Wilihiman-Walalua Confederation. Several exchange stones, carrying nets, strapless ceremonial nets, and shell bands were brought to Jagik's funeral by people who had done him an injury in the past. Those goods were spread out in the courtyard and the name of the donor shouted over them.

The Feast. Later in the morning a large wood pyre loaded with rocks is lighted to heat the rocks for the steaming of pigs and vegetables.

The pigs brought for the funeral are killed, shot with a bamboo-tipped arrow by the man leading the ceremony (Plate 11). Depending on the importance of the dead person, anywhere from two to two dozen pigs of varying sizes are killed. They are then laid side by side on a line from the men's house to the compound entrance. The ears and tails are cut off and taken to the men's house, where the ears are casually eaten and the tails saved for preparation of the *su walon* net on the third day of the funeral. The pigs are then butchered. Strips of the best meat are hung on racks, and the rest is put into the large steam bundles together with ferns and sweet potatoes.

After an hour or so of cooking the steam bundles are opened and the food distributed to all participants. The pig skins, with their thick layers of fat, are sliced with bamboo knife by the leader of the funeral. The pattern of slicing varies little. While two men hold a skin up by its snout and forelegs, the leader cuts strips alternately from side to side.

Strips of fatty skin, chunks of meat, and vegetables are passed out to everyone at the funeral. The adults of the same sib as the dead person usually refuse to eat anything, but the rest enjoy the feast. Often the young children are asked to sit together in a circle, and one man cuts meat for them. When the eating is finished, the greasy hands and some of the fatty skins are used to smear pig grease on the bodies of all.

Distribution of Shell Bands. When the meal is over, the shell bands are laid out close together on banana leaves before the men's house (Plate 58), on the line from the men's house to the compound entrance. At the funeral of the very unimportant man Ejak there were only four shell bands, while at Jagik's funeral there were about forty. The men most closely involved in the funeral now sit around the bands, conferring in whispers, deciding who is to get what.

Finally the leader stands and one by one holds the bands high above his head, shouting the name of the recipient and then handing it out to him or her (Plate 22). The recipient takes the band, replying, "*Wawawa!*"

Handling of the Corpse. When the shell bands have been distributed, the women, who have been silent, resume their dirging. The corpse is brought out from the house or lifted off the chair and smeared with pig grease, usually by several close relatives, men or women.

Once, at this moment, a small pig wrapped in a net was held with its snout to the face of the dead person. It was later explained that this was to help draw out the soul of the dead person.

The men and boys have earlier begun to build the cremation pyre with large split logs brought down from the forests earlier in the day. If there is a corpse chair, it is dismantled and its wood added to the pyre. The pyre is lit and when the wood has caught fire, the corpse is laid on the pyre, head toward the compound entrance (Plate 23). The dirge, now picked up by everyone, reaches a crescendo as the body is quickly covered with more wood, concealing it completely.

Just as the corpse is laid on the fire, a bundle of grass about one meter long and ten centimeters wide is held over the corpse by one man. Another man shouts to the ghost to leave, and he strikes the bundle with a club, stabs it with a spear, or shoots it with a bow and arrow (Plate 24). The man holding the bundle then quickly carries it to the compound entrance and either lays it on the thatch above the entrance or takes it outside.

The ideal pattern apparently demands that for a killed person, or important man, the bundle shall be shot, and for others it shall be clubbed or stabbed. In fact this was also the observed pattern.

All those who have handled the corpse must now present their hands as a man waves a feather wand over them, removing the *wusa* power, which would otherwise be dangerous (Plate 20).

DRIVING OUT THE GHOST. About 6:00 P.M. on the day of the cremation of Wejakhe, a boy killed by an enemy raid, a group of boys Wejakhe's age, accompanied by a man, raced from the back end of the compound through the courtyard and out the entrance, shouting at the ghost to leave. The man carried a bow and arrow, and the boys threw rocks wildly at houses and fences as they ran. This was explained as *mugoko*, or driving out the ghost. I do not know how generally this is a part of funerals.

Night between the First and Second Day. As dusk falls and the funeral pyre burns lower, most of the guests leave for their homes, taking pieces of meat and fatty skin which they have saved from the feast. The people of the compound and the closest relatives of the deceased prepare to spend the night awake, talking, smoking, and eating around the hearths in the common cook house.

A long bundle of grass is prepared and laid on the roof of the common cook

PLATE 22. At a funeral, Wali (Um'ue) redistributed the woven bands decorated with cowrie shells which have been brought as funeral gifts. (Photograph by Michael Rockefeller)

house. Then, around eight or nine o'clock at a signal all talk is stopped, the hearth fires are banked, and anyone in the courtyard moves inside. A man takes the grass bundle outside the courtyard, returns a few moments later, and the normal activity of the compound resumes. Informants explained that this was a moment of listening for cries from the enemy.

Shortly after 4 A.M., before the first light of morning, another ritual episode, called *wagun*, occurs. A small party of young men sometimes accompanied by women leaves the compound carrying a torch of boards, a bundle of roasted pork, an adze in a carrying net, and the grass bundle used earlier in the night. They file to a nearby hilltop and prepare a fire with the torch wood and other wood picked up on the way. Then, facing the enemy country, they sit, occasionally smoking or exchanging a word or two.

By 5:30, as dawn lights up the Grand Valley, the atmosphere of listening is broken. Those who are not of the dead person's sib eat the pig meat. Grass

PLATE 23. The corpse of an old man is laid on the funeral pyre.

PLATE 24. As Wejakhe's corpse is laid on the burning pyre, one man holds the memorial grass bundle and another shoots an arrow into it.

is laid in a ring around the group perhaps as a sort of protection from ghosts. Soon after, the people leave the hilltop, hang the net with the adze on the compound fence, and rest for a few hours.

This ritual of the first night of the funeral is obscure. Informants explained it only in the very general terms of listening for sounds of the enemy. These are apparently neither sounds of enemy ghosts nor of attacking enemy. It is difficult to understand the behavior or the ritual objects as helping to placate or to drive away the ghosts.

Second Day of the Funeral. Around dawn on the second day of a funeral of a person killed by the enemy, one or two fingers of girls who are close relatives of the deceased are chopped off (Plate 26). This is explained as part of the general presentation of funeral gifts to impress the ghosts.

In the course of the morning a woman closely related to the dead person sits by the now cold ashes of the cremation pyre slowly picking out the bony remains with tongs and placing them on a banana leaf. When this task is finished, the ashes are bundled up and hung on the wall of the common cook house to await disposition the next day.

Also during the second day nets that were brought the day before are laid out in the courtyard and distributed among the women. This is often marked by sharp arguing among the women over who should get what, but it is strictly a woman's affair, and the men ignore it (Plate 25).

Again stones are heated and steam bundles are made up with sweet potato and some of the pig remaining from the previous day. By early afternoon, when the steam bundles are opened, some guests have drifted into the compound, but only a half or a third of the number present on the previous day. The food is handed out more casually, with none of the public cutting that characterized the feast of the day before. Special large raw sweet potatoes are distributed, usually to men, who take them home in carrying nets.

Third Day. At some point during the day an older man of the compound takes the bundle of bony ashes from the compound cook house to the banana yard behind the men's house, where he pours the ashes into a low slat enclosure called *oak leget* (p. 271). This is done with no obvious ceremonialism.

A special new carrying net called *su walon* is now prepared by the leader of the funeral. The pig tails which were put aside on the first day are tied onto the net. This net, now the main tangible symbol of the dead person, is hung at the rear of the men's house. Eventually it will be wrapped with other *su walon* and, at the *ebe akho* ceremony, deposited at the chief ceremonial compound of the alliance.

Again there is feasting. Steamed bundles are made of sweet potatoes and the last of the pig, steamed, and eaten.

According to the ideal pattern, on the third day field mice are caught, steamed, and eaten with pork and sweet potatoes. This was never actually observed. Informants frequently pointed out at this time that they should do it but wouldn't because they were too tired from the previous days' activities or because it was raining.

Fourth Day. By the fourth day the ceremonial activity is nearly finished. There is less extravagant feasting; sweet potatoes are steamed and eaten.

Once in the evening of the fourth day a man was observed pouring water from a gourd over the cremation ashes in the bone enclosure behind the men's house. Informants said that this was often done at this time, but had no special explanation for it.

Fifth Day. The first phase of the funeral is over. In the courtyard, sprigs of wild raspberry are laid over the cracked rocks used to heat the steam bundles to remove or to neutralize the supernatural power which has accumulated in the rocks and in the compound in general during the ceremonies of the previous four days. The term for this is *jililik balek,* similar to the term *duesi balek* (or *balin*), the removal of *wusa* from the hands of those who have been engaged in specially sacred tasks, using a feather wand.

Depositing Bundles. Between the first two stages of the funeral or after the second stage, the grass bundle (*wagun*) representing the ghost is taken to a *wagun ai,* ghost house, in the forest. This ritual was observed once, after the second stage of several funerals. Late one afternoon about fifteen men and

PLATE 25. At a funeral, women redistribute the nets which have been brought as funeral gifts. (Photograph by Michael Rockefeller)

PLATE 26. Two girls, who have just lost fingers as funeral sacrifices, sit with bandaged hands. (Photograph by Michael Rockefeller)

boys, carrying several *wagun* bundles which had accumulated and some very old pork left over from an *ilkho* ceremony two weeks earlier, proceeded from the compound, running and singing, to a hilltop in the woods near the *wagun ai*. There they stopped, ate the pig, and then shouted in the direction of the enemy territory. Two men went on to deposit the bundles in the enclosure and hang steamed ferns and a pig mandible on the outside. When they rejoined the others, they helped make a line of brush and grass along the inside, or *wagun ai* side, of various paths skirting the area, singing as they advanced.

Supportive Funeral Ceremony (Huwi). Sometimes when word reaches the Dugum Neighborhood that a person has died in a distant area, the friends or relatives of the dead person do not go to the funeral. Perhaps it is too far or they have pressing business at home; or the cremation may have taken place already. In such cases, a kind of sympathetic ceremony is held. Sweet potatoes are steamed and eaten and dirges are sung. If shell bands have been sent from the funeral site, they are informally distributed. No pigs are killed at this time.

SECOND STAGE OF THE FUNERAL

Four to six weeks after the first stage of the funeral ceremony, the second stage is held. Like the first stage, the second has the explicit function of placating the ghost of the dead person. It also marks the end of the mourning period.

The second stage is initiated by the leader of the first stage and usually centers around the same compound. In one instance a visitor was cremated in the Dugum Neighborhood and his ashes were deposited there, but the second stage of his funeral was held in his home area.

On the day before the ceremony resumes, the leader of the funeral paints a strip on the entrance sill of his men's house using red clay. Then, holding an exchange stone also with red strip, he stands in the courtyard shouting "Wolo wetno!" (Come bring [pigs]!). At the same time men or youths are sent out to inform the neighboring compounds of the impending ceremony.

Briefly the second stage of the funeral proceeds as follows: first day: in the afternoon the *ilkho* is announced for the next day; second day: pigs killed, eaten, pig meat distributed; third day: women remove mourning mud, boys renew their penis gourds, arch ceremony, symbolic feeding of ghost, pig and sweet potato eaten; fourth day: pig and sweet potato eaten, mourning mustaches removed.

First Day—Ilkho. The main activity of the first day, the *Ilkho*, is the killing of pigs followed by a feast of pork and sweet potatoes prepared in the large courtyard in steam bundles.

The procedure of handling the pigs is much the same as that of the first day of the first stage. In two observed instances there were twice as many pigs killed at the *ilkho* as at the cremation itself. Again, the pig bodies are lined up and the names of the donors shouted over them. Then, when tails and ears have been removed and the best pork hung on racks to be saved for the next day, the rest is steamed and eaten.

Second Day. In midmorning, when several dozen guests have arrived, the women file silently out of the compound and go several hundreds of meters away, where they sit around a fire, gossiping and smoking. Shortly thereafter the boys, some carrying new penis gourds, are led out of the compound to a stream bank by a man. In half an hour or so the women and boys silently return. Informants explained that during this half hour the women replace the plain skirts which they have worn since the cremation with their usual, orchid-fiber decorated skirts, and that they wash off the mourning mud which they first put on during the cremation and have occasionally renewed since; and that the boys don new penis gourds.

In fact, changes of skirts were never observed at this time; if anything, more women returned with freshly mudded bodies; but usually some boys had new penis gourds.

VICARIOUS EATING—THE ARCH. While the women and boys are out of the compound, some men prepare a low arch in the courtyard. Two poles 1.5 meter or so high are planted in the ground, the tops slanting toward each other. A leafy branch with split stem is lashed to the two poles, forming an arch over the line from the men's house to the entrance of the compound.

The men now prepare food for the arch ritual. Several pieces of pork are browned on the coals of the fire used for heating steam bundle rocks. The pork is laid on a banana leaf segment set in a bound hoop of grass. Several sweet potatoes, baked in a cook house hearth, are laid by the arch. Clotted blood, taken from a pig killed earlier, is now smeared on the meat and sweet potatoes.

A length of sugar cane is held through the arch, and two men, one on each end, pull the cane apart, exposing a raw juicy section end. Now several adults, those most closely related by marriage or blood to the dead person, sit on one side of the arch. Through the arch a man holds a piece of pork, a sweet potato, and the sugar cane. Each person in turn takes a bite of the three foods at once, chews for a moment, and then spits the wad into the cupped hands of another man. As each chews, another man, usually an important older man, stands by, gazing upward and shouting the name of the dead person, "Jihuti, *hat nan!*" ("Jihuti, you eat!").

Now the man who has fed the mourners daubs the remaining clotted pig blood on their palms, elbows, knees, and sometimes head hair. This blood is also daubed on raw sweet potatoes which are informally handed out to the funeral guests.

Informants said the purpose of this ritual was to placate the ghost and also to restore the *edai egen,* or soul matter, of those most deeply moved by the death. Such explicitness is unusual. Although the funeral activity as a whole can be seen as a gathering of the members and resources of the community to support those closest to the dead person in their deep distress, in fact during much of the time they are tactfully ignored, left alone in the midst of the crowd of funeral guests. But at this one moment they become the focus of the ritual.

Once, a ritual episode occurred earlier in the morning before the arch ritual.

The funeral was for a young woman who had died in an influenza epidemic. Her husband and her brother had been exceptionally disturbed by her death, and as the body was laid on the cremation pyre, both tried to throw themselves onto the fire with the corpse but were pulled off by their friends. Six weeks later, at the second stage of the funeral, they sat in the courtyard facing the men's house, their backs to the compound entrance. Six or eight men walked around them four times in a silent circle. One carried a freshly killed pig, one carried three raw sweet potatoes, and the rest occasionally laid their hands on the two seated men. Informants did not explain the details, but it was clear that even more than the arch itself, this episode was directed toward restoring the *edai egen* of the two chief mourners.

Third Day. Pork left from the two previous days' ceremonies is steamed, together with vegetables. This marks the end of the second stage of the funeral.

Third Stage of the Funeral

The third phase of the funeral ceremony was observed in October 1961 when three confederations, Wilihiman-Walalua, Gosi-Alua, and Phaluk-Matian, participated. This phase was a combined ceremony incorporating all funerals since the alliancewide *ebe akho* ceremony had last taken place. The ceremony began in the individual compounds, then converged on Wakawaka, the compound of Sula, the very important ceremonial leader of the Phaluk-Matian, and finally returned to the individual compounds (Map C.3). Other confederations of the alliance, particularly the Dloko-Mabel of Gutelu, the most important man of the alliance, did not participate. It seems that this third phase is not necessarily alliancewide; but it may be that the 1961 ceremony marked the emergence of Sula as a rival to Gutelu and the beginning of a fission in the alliance.

First and Second Days. For several days previously, messages had been sent throughout the alliance area and even to people in distant areas who had some responsibility for local funerals. Then for two days there was a great coming and going as nets, cowrie shell bands, and exchange stones (*je*) were carried from one compound to another. This is *je wakanin*, carrying the *je* stones. Gradually the men responsible for each funeral collected nets, bands, and stones to make up one large bundle for each funeral.

Typically a small group of men, carrying the goods, entered a compound, massed by the entrance, and then trotted toward the men's house. They were greeted by shouts from the men of the compound, who emerged from the men's house. Then the two groups sang funeral dirges to each other, embraced, and retired into the men's house to talk, smoke, and eat. Toward the end of the first day and during the second day more groups from other alliance areas appeared with their contributions. Women generally stayed out of sight.

The exchange of goods at this time seemed to be more extensive than at the funerals themselves. The goods distributed at the earlier stages of the funeral ceremonies possibly were to assure that goods be brought at this stage. Ideally, all goods were brought by the *ami* of the dead person—that is, his mother's brothers and other men of his mother's moiety. Even when goods were brought by groups of the same sib as the dead person, the kin term *ami* was used as the greeting. In this context *ami* is not so much a genealogical term being misused as a term referring to one who gives shell and stone goods in the manner of an *ami*.

Third Day. In the early evening of the second day and during the morning of the third day, groups of men, women, and children carried bundles to Wakawaka, the compound of Sula, in the Phaluk-Matian area an hour and a half to the northwest of the Dugum Neighborhood. The groups moved in spurts, walking and running, and breaking into raucous, joyful songs of the *edai*-dancing. Women carried large nets filled with ceremonial nets, and men and youths carried flat exchange stones over their shoulders.

As large groups arrived from different areas, the women with their loaded nets stood single file in the long lower compound, each woman with her heavy net suspended from a forehead tumpline. Around them stood the men with the exchange stones. One by one, the nets were taken from the women and laid in a line in the upper courtyard, with three to seven exchange stones leaning against them. The women then retired to the women's houses and cook houses to watch the ceremony.

When all the bundles had been assembled, they were taken to the lower courtyard and spread out in two lines down the length of the courtyard (Plate 57). Each bundle of nets was folded lengthwise and placed along the long axis of the courtyard. Then the exchange stones, three to seven to a bundle, were laid across the nets. In the longer line there were about 25 piles of nets, with about 108 exchange stones; in the shorter line, about 12 piles of nets with about 59 exchange stones.

Then, one by one, shell bands were reeled out from the dark entrance of the men's house, carried carefully to the lower compound, and laid on the long lines of nets and stones.

For a few moments there was relative silence. Sula, after inspecting the goods displayed, walked slowly along the line, stopping at each bundle, touching it with a hand or a foot and shouting the name of the dead person it represented. When he was finished, he returned to the upper courtyard and shouted various kin terms, following each with an approving, grateful "*Wa!*"

Then the atmosphere suddenly reverted to normal. The men and women swooped down on their bundles, folded them up, packed them into the carrying nets, and left for home.

Fourth Day. In the compounds the bundles were again laid out, and the important man of the compound shouted the names of the dead over the bundles. Then large steam bundles were made up with vegetables, and the people of the compound ate.

Apparently this was the end of the third stage of the funeral. However, in two compounds on the following day further ceremonies began which were described as *ilkho*, the second stage ritual. These were both parts of the funerals of recently killed youths for whom the *ilkho* had not yet been held.

Among the bundles involved in this third phase were two which did not represent dead people. One was said to be for the sick pig of an important young man. The other was for a badly wounded man who died two months afterward.

FOURTH STAGE OF THE FUNERAL—THE PIG FEAST

The fourth and final stage of all funerals is one part of the *ebe akho* ceremony, which is described in its entirety below.

A ceremonial cycle of several years, climaxed by a major pig feast ceremony, is one of the most characteristic traits of Papuan societies in the New Guinea Highlands. However, the climactic Dani ceremony, *ebe akho*, is of unusual importance. Not only is the *ebe akho* the final and culminating phase of all funerals, but it is also the only time when marriages and boys' initiation rites are held.

The first step in the *ebe akho* ceremony occurred in December 1962 or January 1963, when Gutelu, the most important man of the alliance, declared that henceforth all pigs were *wusa* and thus could not be killed. (This ritual was not observed.) Informants stated firmly that pigs could not be killed even for funerals during this time. Only three deaths occurred in the Dugum Neighborhood during the eight months of observation (contrasted with fourteen deaths in fifteen months during the previous period of field work in the same Neighborhood). Two of these deaths were infants and one was an old woman, but in none of the funerals were pigs killed. It may be that if a really important person had died or been killed during this period, pigs would have been killed.

The restriction seems practical, for if a pig met an accidental death, it could be and was eaten. It seemed to me that during this period the number of accidental pig deaths increased markedly, but there are no statistics to prove it. At least one pig was eaten which had obviously died of spear wounds. Informants explained that it had been killed by ghosts.

Pig Castration. On June 27, 1963, 67 male shoats were castrated and had their ears sliced, and another 44 female shoats' ears were sliced. These shoats were all sired by the boar given to Weteklue, the most important man of the Wilihiman-Walalua Confederation, by the District Officer. The ceremony was held at Abulopak, in the Dugum Neighborhood, and involved all the pig owners of the Neighborhood and a few beyond it.

A large steam bundle with vegetables was prepared, and as it was steaming the shoats were brought into the compound and operated on by two men chosen for their skill.

One man squatted while two more held the pig upside down on his shoulder, and the operator swiftly performed the castration and then sliced the ears.

Just before the operating began the most important men took a small bundle from the men's house, went to the outer gateway of the compound, and squatted while one held the bundle just below the low pigs' entrance in the fence and shouted "*Hamep dlek*" (*ha*, your; *mep*, blood; *dlek*, no).

An informant later explained that this bundle contained a sacred stone and that the episode was to assure that the blood of the sacred pigs, which was about to be spilled, would not result in the death of any of the local people at the hands of the enemy. The cry was directed to the people themselves, saying "your blood will not be shed." The informant denied that ghosts were involved in this, but it is not at all clear just what the supernatural mechanism is.

The informant explained that among the bamboo knives used for castrating the pigs were some attributed to Nakmatugi, the first man, who had used them to cut up his brother, Phuba, before eating him. These knives are kept with Weteklue's sacred objects.

After the operations were over, the steam bundle was broken open and sweet potatoes were passed out. Before eating, the hands of all men who had had contact with the sacred pigs were ritually purified with a feather wand.

After the eating was finished, boys brought 1.5-meter lengths of cane filled with water to Weteklue, who blew over them and then sprinkled the water on such pigs as were still milling around the compound. An informant explained that the water, from several different Neighborhood streams, would make the pigs grow large for the *ebe akho* ceremony. The informant also explained that the next morning the 67 pairs of testicles which had been removed were steamed and fed to the boar who had sired the shoats.

Mock Battle. Apparently during the months preceding the *ebe akho* itself, a number of mock battles are held in connection with garden work. One was observed on October 31, 1963.

About thirty men and boys were mudding a newly planted garden area. Their singing could be heard throughout the Neighborhood. Rarely, even when in groups, do the Dani sing at work. The costumes of this group were striking and could only be called foolish. Many were smeared with mud in wild patterns. Others wore headdresses of moss, and most were decorated with leaves and reeds. At intervals they jumped from the ditches and raced back and forth along the garden beds, brandishing their digging sticks like spears, mimicking battle songs and cries. Once a group crept around through ditches and staged a noisy mock garden raid. The atmosphere was boisterously absurd.

By late November 1963, when it seemed clear that Gutelu would soon initiate the *ebe akho* ceremony, the restrictions on killing pigs were somewhat lifted and throughout the alliance area small *ilkho* ceremonies were held for those who had died since the imposition of the restrictions. The first stages of these funerals, including the cremation, had been held, but no pigs had been slaughtered. The second stages had been postponed until this time, when pigs could again be killed.

Announcing the Ceremony. By late November the leaders of several confederations in the alliance had become disturbed that Gutelu had not yet initiated the *ebe akho* proper. The leaders of the Phaluk-Matian, Sula and Polik, and the leaders of the Wilihiman-Walalua, Weteklue, Nilik, and Um'ue, decided to initiate the ceremony themselves. Sula, the only man in the alliance whose influence and supernatural power approached that of Gutelu, called a *wam edlo balin* to declare the beginning of the *ebe akho*. It was not clear whether this was a genuine attempt to wrest supremacy in the alliance from Gutelu, or to break several sibs off the alliance, forming another alliance, or merely to force Gutelu to assume the leadership of the ceremony which he was postponing. In any event, after Sula held the *wam edlo balin* on November 28, 1963, Gutelu did reluctantly agree to begin the *ebe akho* immediately. However, in early December the government required Gutelu to go to Djakarta to meet President Sukarno, and the ceremony was indefinitely postponed. My field work was then terminated on December 7 and the ceremony was not observed. And so, to my intense frustration, I never did see this, the most important of all Dani ceremonies. Peters writes (1965:115) that two months later, on February 14, 1964, Gutelu did begin the *ebe akho*. Peters was fortunate enough not only to observe two full ceremonies in the southern Grand Valley, where he did the bulk of his research, but he also followed the ceremony in the Gutelu area. His monograph contains particularly rich data on this and other Dani ceremonies. Again in 1968 I was present for the preliminary ceremonies of the *ebe akho* but had to leave before it really got under way.

Wam Edlo Balin Ceremony. On November 28, 1963, most of the people of the Dugum Neighborhood went to Wakawaka carrying pigs and *jetobo*, the arrows and other small battle trophies which had been removed from wounds or picked up from enemy corpses or on battlefields. The *jetobo* are kept permanently at the Wakawaka men's house.

Twenty-one pigs were killed and steam bundles were made up with pork and vegetables.

As the food steamed, an arch like that used in the second stage of the funerals was erected in the upper courtyard. About thirty people were lined up facing the arch, their backs to the men's house. Several men accompanied by a youth moved along the line. The youth held a live shoat wrapped in a net and above it a long-stemmed plant (*jibi*) whose roots were wrapped in bark cloth. He held the snout of the pig to the breastbone of each person, who bent over and spat onto the wrapped roots as Sula shouted "*Hamep bpeto!*" (*ha*, your; *mep*, blood; *bpeto* probably has the sense of diminish). An informant explained that these were the closest relatives of dead people, and the ritual was to pull out, to do away with dangerous bad blood.

RITUAL EATING—THE ARCH. The arch ritual was similar to that at the second stage of the funeral, but only sugar cane and pork were held for the people to chew and spit back into the hands of an old man. As the thirty people in turn chewed and spat, two important men clasped hands across the front of the arch. After each person had finished at the arch, he or she was rubbed with pig-grease-soaked leaves on palms, head, knees, elbows, and shoulders. Women were greased only on their palms and head; the men often on all the spots.

An informant explained that the hands clasped at the arch meant the shaking hands of, or greeting, the ghosts. He also said that the greasing was done to remove the mourning mud. In fact, this was symbolic, since no one was mudded.

As the arch ritual was taking place, the steam bundles were being opened and the food passed out to all in the compound. As they ate, Polik, an important Phaluk, stood near the men's house holding up strips of pig skin and shouting out names in the manner of the passing out of shell bands at a cremation.

As soon as the skin strips had been handed out, all the men stood and shouted, whooping loudly across the Grand Valley toward their enemies. Many ran back and forth across the courtyard holding the skin strips aloft. Then they ran out of the compound, taking the strips to various areas both within and beyond the alliance, announcing the beginning of the *ebe akho*.

As they left, Sula ran after them as far as the entrance carrying a small, unwrapped sacred stone (*habo*). Finally, about 6 P.M., the other participants left for their homes.

Events of the Ebe Akho Ceremony. Although the main part of the *ebe akho* was not observed, one informant, Um'ue, described the sequence of events that would take place, probably a month or more after the sending out of pig skin strips. Each event would take place on a different day: (1) *Ab Waija*, (*ab*, man; *Waija*, name of one moiety), the initiation of boys whose fathers were Waija into the Waija moiety; (2) killing of many pigs; (3) exchange stones carried to Wakawaka; (4) an arch ceremony again held at Wakawaka in connection with the funerals; (5) firewood assembled at the compounds; (6) leaves and vegetables for steaming assembled at the compounds; (7) more pigs shot; feasting; (8) marriage ceremonies in the compounds; (9) feasting for those who had died natural deaths; (10) feasting for those who had been killed by the enemy; (11) making fresh bark cloth neck strips for all; (12) pork sent to friends and relatives in other areas.

OTHER MEANS OF CORPSE DISPOSAL

In all instances observed in the Dugum Neighborhood, corpses were cremated in the ceremonial context which has been described above. However, there are rare exceptions to cremation.

Exposure. In two places in the Dugum Neighborhood and in two more places in areas just to the south, fragments of uncharred human bones were observed. In no case was there more than a few fragments. In three of these instances the bones had been placed on shelves in eroded limestone rocks; once the bones were in the hollow trunk of a tree.

Informants insisted that the bones were from enemies who had been caught and killed in the area; that their bodies had not been retrieved by relatives and had just lain on the ground, rotting, and being disturbed by pigs and dogs; and that eventually the remains had been placed in the niches. They said that this had occurred long before their time.

Certainly none of the bones were fresh, but there is no indication of just how long they have lain. There was also no indication of any supernatural power, or *wusa*, attached to the bones. At most, they seemed to be curiosities to the people.

In a large cave near Jibiga, at the center of the Gutelu Alliance, there are a few human bones from at least three different people. Again, there is no direct evidence of the age of these remains, but the local people said that they were the remains of cannibal feasts held a generation or two ago.

Desiccation. A desiccated corpse was observed in the sleeping loft of a men's house at the compound of Mitian, in the Siep-Eloktak area along the mid-Aikhe River. The corpse was male; it was seated with knees drawn up to chest, head slumped over, and arms trailing forward on either side of legs. The skin, which had drawn tightly around the bones, was stained a deep, shiny black by the smoke from the lower hearth. On the head was a new head net colored red.

According to N. Verheijen (in a personal communication), the people said that the corpse was of a man who had been so important that the survivors were reluctant to cremate it and wanted to keep it with them for supernatural aid.

Informants in the Dugum Neighborhood knew of this corpse, which was only a few kilometers away. Apparently there are a few more such desiccated corpses in men's houses elsewhere in the Grand Valley.

THE MAN-AS-BIRD THEME

The theme of man-as-bird appears repeatedly in Dani symbolism, sometimes explicitly and sometimes implicitly. Gardner used this theme as the symbol around which he built his film of the Dugum Dani called *Dead Birds* (1963). Various manifestations of this theme are summarized below.

According to one episode of the Dani origin myth, men and birds once lived together in harmony, not realizing that they were different. Later they separated. Each sib has a special relationship with one kind of bird which is considered to be a sib member.

In the episode of the origin myth which explains mortality, or failure of man to gain immortality, it is the bird who dies and who sets the pattern for man, rather than the snake, who does not die.

Especially at funerals, people often smear light-colored mud on their shoulders in imitation of the bird in the mortality episode. Also, boys may stamp clay bird's-foot designs on their bodies.

Feathers in some form are worn by most men most of the time in head-dresses, forehead bands, or on tobacco nets; feather whisks are carried in battle; feathers are occasionally attached to bows. Feathers ornament both the cowrie shell bands and the exchange stones, two valuable kinds of exchange items.

The cry of the large cuckoo dove is a call to battle, and various bird calls are imitated in battle itself. At *edai* dances after the killing of an enemy, individuals often stand on the edge of the dance area, fully feathered, flapping their hands like the wings of a slow-flying bird.

Trophies taken from killed enemy are called in the Dugum Neighborhood *ab watek*—killed, or dead, men; but in the southern Grand Valley these same trophies are called *sue watek*—killed, or dead, birds.

Another example, which I cannot verify at all, is passed on by Peters (1965:86) from a government report: The tip of the fighting spear, together with the woven band, is supposed to resemble a bird's beak. This analogy is at best valid for the southern Grand Valley, and I have never heard of it in the Dugum Neighborhood.

Some of these details are not particularly convincing in themselves. For example, feather decorations are common in all parts of the world. But the mass of evidence supports the idea of the Dani's identification of man with bird.

The symbolic importance of birds in other New Guinea cultures is apparent from even a cursory glance at New Guinea art. Examples include the prominence of the hornbill in the art of the Asmat, on the southwest coast (cf. Guiart 1963:154 ff), birds on men's heads in the sculpture of the Maprik, in northeast New Guinea (Buehler, Barrow, and Mountford 1962:114); and perhaps the long-nosed human figures of the Sepik River, also in northeast New Guinea (Linton and Wingert 1946:113 ff).

ACCULTURATION MOVEMENTS

The striking thing about acculturation movements in the Grand Valley is their absence. In the early 1960's, immediately to the northwest of the Grand Valley, the Western Dani were swept by a movement which involved the destruction of ritual objects in a massive attempt to replace the native culture with a Western-Christian culture. O'Brien and Ploeg have provided an analysis of this movement (1964), but it is not at all clear why it didn't move into the Grand Valley. There were close contacts between the Western Dani and the Grand Valley Dani. And if anything, the impact of Western culture was greater in the Grand Valley than in the Western Dani region. It would appear that the differential susceptibility to the movement reflects some basic cultural difference between the Grand Valley Dani and the Western Dani, but it is too early to say what this difference might be.

CONCLUSIONS

Much of Dani ritual activity shows considerable indeterminateness and variability. The nature of the ghosts and even their whereabouts, the vagueness of spirit categories, the variations in ceremonial details, the extemporaneous rather than precisely formulated nature of prayers, the undramatic and almost unclimactic performances of ritual events, the convenient manner in which ghosts moderate their threats, all point to the Dani's casual, almost impious approach to their dealings with the supernatural.

The climax of Dani ceremonialism, and perhaps one could say the climax of Dani culture itself, is the *ebe akho*, the great Pig Feast. Essentially every group in the New Guinea Highlands has a ritual cycle lasting for several years and climaxed by such a pig feast. This is one of the hallmarks of the Highland Papuan culture area, together with patrilineal ideology, "big man" leadership, sweet potato and taro horticulture, temperate zone adaptation, and related languages. Yet nowhere in the Highlands has the Pig Feast taken onto itself so much ritual importance as it has in the Grand Valley, where termination of the years-long funerals, the initiation of the boys, and all marriages take place only at the time of the Pig Feast.

The effects of this schedule vary. Initiation makes no immediate difference in the life of a boy. By extending the funerals, the awareness of specific ghosts is dragged out and gifts are exchanged along the particular ties which are relevant to the dead person for a longer period of time. But these effects seem minor compared to the effect of holding marriages only at five-year intervals.

Sexual activities outside marriage are apparently rare, and only occasionally does a person take advantage of the staggered schedule of pig feasts in the Grand Valley alliances to marry someone of another alliance when his own is not having a pig feast. Not only is the acquisition of sexual partners rigidly controlled by the timing of the ritual cycle, but access to sexual partners is limited by the supernaturally sanctioned five-year postpartum sexual abstinence.

This considerable limitation of sexual activity by ritual and supernatural mechanisms presents a choice of anomalies. Either the sexual regulations are an extremely powerful coercion in a culture which is remarkable for its minimal coercion, or the Dani concern with sex is much less than intuition and the general cross-cultural data would predict. If the former is correct, evidence of coercion, supernatural and otherwise, should be extremely prominent in the lives of the Dani. Since it is not, I conclude that the ritual and supernatural sanctions against sex are incidental to the Dani's rather low level of interest in sex.

5

LANGUAGE AND CATEGORIES

THE first description of a Dani dialect was the annotated word list of Pesegem Southern Dani, published by van Nouhuys (1912). This is a remarkable tour de force by an untrained but observant explorer on the basis of a few days' study of the people. This was supplemented by Snell's word list for the same group (1913).

Wirz, the anthropologist with the 1920 Kremer Expedition, has published data on the Swart Valley Western Dani dialect (1924). Huls, the medical doctor with the 1938–1939 Archbold Expedition in the Grand Valley, was responsible for the anthropological research, but apparently has never published his data.

Since 1954 the various dialects of the Dani languages have been extensively analyzed by the trained linguists of the several missionary corporations that are active in the Highlands (cf. Bromley 1961, 1968, and van der Stap 1966). My own work was greatly aided by grammars and word lists for dialects close to that of the Dugum Dani, which had been prepared by P. van der Stap and H. Myron Bromley of the Christian and Missionary Alliance. My lack of linguistic training prohibits me from attempting any sort of contribution to the analysis of the formal aspects of the language. However, it will be useful to mention here several features of the language which have general relevance to the description of Dani culture.

A prominent explorer has recently characterized the Western Dani language as primitive, very simple, and having a small vocabulary (Harrer 1963:30). Unfortunately this is far from the truth, even for Grand Valley Dani, whose language is not as complex as the Western Dani. I cannot estimate the size of the vocabulary, but it is certainly not small. As for the morphology, it is difficult to consider a language simple where there are 1,680 possible verb forms (P. van der Stap in a personal communication). Nouns, on the other hand, are morphologically simple, and only a few differentiate between singular and plural.

It is almost possible to say that Dani does not have a subjunctive aspect of verbs. Van der Stap does discuss an "Irreal Aspect Category" (1966:39 ff), but this is used primarily for something that should have happened but did not. I found the greatest difficulty in working with counter-to-fact statements. Often after having seen an act performed in a certain manner I would want to experiment with it verbally, varying some conditions in order to learn more about

that general category of act. But I had practically no success with such counter-
factual statements as, "What would have happened if X did *not* do Z?" I think
it is safe to say that the Dani are not particularly concerned with or interested
in subjunctive thought.

Another important feature of the Dani language is the apparent lack of comparative form for attribute words. One can state that something is big, or very
big, good, or very good, but there is no efficient way of indicating that X is
larger or better than Y. The entire realm of attributes is critical here. The evidence indicates that the Dani have relatively little concern with ascribing quantitative or qualitative attributes. This does *not* mean of course that they have *no*
terms for such attributes. Nor do I suggest that in their nonverbal behavior they
ignore attributes. And when I suggest that they have relatively little interest in
attributes, this is an impression rather than the result of any cross-cultural study.
But let us look at the relevant Dani vocabulary.

QUANTIFICATION

Most Dani nouns are not inflected for number, although in some contexts
the singular-plural dichotomy is indicated by the verb. When necessary, an
auxiliary word may be used to indicate quantity.

The exceptions to this general rule are certain nouns that refer for the most
part to kin or age status:

Singular Plural
son—*abut, abuti*
woman—*he, humi*
man—*ab, aguni*
boy—*jegetek, jegetugi*
girl—*hodlak, homatugi*
younger moiety-mate—*akot, akotokomi*
trading friend—*atek, atugui*
others—*abetek, abetugui*

But there are also a number of basically similar terms which do *not* indicate
number by inflection, such as "mother" and "father."

There are languages, such as Mandarin Chinese, which do not indicate quantity
in inflection of nouns or verbs. Thus, Dani noun forms, while interesting, are
in no sense unique.

More significant is the paucity of numeral or other quantity-indicating terms.
The Dugum Dani use two numerical systems. The first is, for one, *magiat;*
two, *pete;* three, *henaken.* The second seems to be basically counting by twos:
magiat, one; *pete,* two; *pete-pete,* four, but more often just *pete; pete; pete* . . .

In the course of observation and questioning about the number system, the
system described above emerged clearly. However, one informant once gave a
more extensive system: one, *magiat;* two, *pete;* three, *henaken;* four, *utut;* five,
isa (thumb) or *igetak;* ten, *igi egaga* (literally, fingers); six or twelve, *tigetak.*

These words are used by Dani in other parts of the Grand Valley; if it is indeed a pattern of the Dugum Dani, it is used very rarely. However, the informant knew some words from other Dani dialects and may well have simply transferred another system into his own dialect.

The Dugum Dani systems seem to be more systems of enumeration than of counting, and are used casually in telling of events rather than for giving an accurate description. For example, describing the results of a massacre, the narrator said, "and then women were killed, *pete, pete, pete, pete,* many." The purpose was not to give the number of women killed, but to express the extent by repetitive eloquence. This pairing of objects is common, and perhaps in the absence of an elaborated counting system the word *pete* is better translated as "a pair" rather "two"—that is, as a unit composed of two parts rather than as two separate units.

The idea of *pete* as a basic unit is supported by the way in which the term *ipitak* is used. If the things being enumerated do not come out even, the odd object is called *ipitak*, which has the sense of one extra or half a pair. There are several terms which indicate indefinite quantity, such as *hamalukat* or *abetugi,* few, and *modok* or *dabok,* many.

More complex numeral systems are used by closely related Dani groups. Van Arcken (1941–1942:38) found words for numbers up to seven used by Dani-speakers in the Saoeweri-Hablifoeri region, just north of the Pass Valley (using an orthography based on Dutch): one, *amboei;* two, *pèrè;* three, *hiengiam, pèrè amboei;* four, *pèrè pèrè;* five, *isia* (also means thumb); six, *apokdal;* seven, *sakbiot.*

Wirz reports (1924:145) a similar system from the Swart Valley Western Dani (using an orthography based on German): one, *ambuet;* two, *bere;* three, *ambuet-bere;* four, *kenera* (Wirz suggests that this may be four, but it is clearly related to other Dani forms of three); five, *enom* (also used for fist); ten, *linim-ero;* fifteen, *linim-ero-enom;* twenty, *ervoid-enom* (*erovid* also used for toes).

Although van Nouhuys and Lorentz collected some 150 words from the Pesegem Dani in 1909–1910, they got no numbers at all (van Nouhuys 1913:253). In 1913 Snell, studying the same group, found the following numbers: (using an orthography based on Dutch): one, *mediek, mesigat;* two, *biden;* three, *kenan, keneran.*

In the Dugum Neighborhood, enumeration is usually done in connection with hand gestures, counting on the fingers and arm. The count always begins with open hand, palm up, and the fingers folded in, beginning with the little finger. One, two, or three is indicated by folding the number of fingers into the palm.

Enumeration of larger amounts is done with both hands, one hand folding the fingers of the other into the palm, usually by twos. When the thumb is reached, the third pair is indicated by placing two fingers of the counting hand on the thumb of the recording hand. Subsequent pairs are indicated in the same manner, moving up the arm and, if necessary, sweeping the hand up the arm several times, saying *modok,* many.

This is clearly related to the common New Guinea Highland pattern of counting to twenty-seven or so by indicating special points along the hand, arm, shoulders, other arm, and other hand. Where this has been reported elsewhere, the terms for the anatomical points are often used for the relevant number. Thus in the Goliath Mountains the word for elbow is *toep-nang*, the word for nine is *toepnang-ge*, for nineteen, *ton toepnang ge* (de Kock 1912:170).

The Dugum Dani have no such definite system. When asked, a few informants have carried the pair enumeration around the shoulders to the opposite hand, but always saying only *pete pete* . . . and if asked to repeat it, not touching the same points.

It is hard to avoid the conclusion that the Dani counting is somehow related to a more systematic form of counting. The simple state of Dani counting can be considered a pale reflection of the general Highlands pattern, and it is even more striking when compared with the Ekagi (Kapauku) pattern.

The Ekagi live around the Tigi-Paniai (Wissel) Lakes at the western end of the Highlands, some five hundred kilometers from the Grand Valley. They resemble the Dani in many basic respects. Like the Dani, they are mountain Papuan sweet potato farmers, pig raisers, and warriors. The material objects of the Ekagi are on the same level as those of the Dani. Ekagi social and legal systems, as described by Pospisil (1958, 1963), are somewhat more formalized.

The Ekagi number system has "a decimal system which stops at sixty and starts over again, having as higher units 600 and 3,600" (Pospisil 1958:117). Pospisil refers to the Ekagi's "craving for counting" (1958:117), their "obsession with quantification," and "their quantitative world outlook" (1963:14). He describes how his informant, "when confronted with a magazine picture of a smiling girl failed completely to react to her beauty. Instead they started to count all her teeth" (1958:16). From Pospisil's accounts it would appear that the Ekagi took a kind of aesthetic pleasure in counting. In a similar fashion, the Dani seem to find the pairing of similar or identical objects aesthetically pleasing.

Despite the lack of an intricate number system, the Dani obviously survive. It is a kind of sophistry to say that since they don't have it, they don't *need* such a system. Yet the evidence seems to suggest that they once did have, or were in contact with, a somewhat more elaborate system.

Systems like that of the Ekagi are used for the exact enumeration of large quantities. In the Dani culture the largest quantities where any sort of accuracy are needed are perhaps fifteen to thirty, which would be the number of pigs in a large herd, or the number of shell bands at an important funeral. But it seems that the Dani can remember the contents of groups that large in terms of the individual units in the group.

For example, when observing funerals, I would carefully count the number of pigs killed and the number of shell bands brought. Later, I would go over the events of the funeral with an informant, who would be able accurately to recount who brought what. The total was not expressed, of course, and was not relevant. But the individual acts were held in mind.

Again, comparison with the Ekagi is striking. Pospisil says that "they may not remember the name of the parties to a trade transaction but they almost never fail to recall the exact number of shells or beads paid for the merchandise" (1963:402). In 1968 Eleanor R. Heider made systematic tests of Dani number concepts, which will be reported elsewhere.

MEASUREMENTS OF TIME AND SPACE

Dani have no exact, explicit measures of time or space. Space is described as near or far, and the trip to the Central Jalemo may be described as requiring a night at X, a night at Y, and a night at Z on the way.

This apparent spatial vagueness is perhaps understandable when one considers that nearly all an individual's behavior takes place in the thoroughly familiar home area, where particular places and the network of trails have been known from childhood.

Exact measures of space would seem to be used in other languages for giving directions to an unknown or for specifying size where exact fit is necessary or desirable. The Dani live in a world which is largely known and basically flexible. They are not compulsive quantifiers.

Perhaps the basic fact conditioning the Dani reckoning of time is that there are no significant, perceivable yearly cycles. The slight increase in rainfall during February or March is not noticed and has little effect on behavior. The same sort of life continues the year around, with continual planting and harvesting of crops.

But the Dani do not live a day-to-day existence. Planning is necessary. Crops must be planted six or nine months before they are needed. Just what the mechanism for this is, I do not know.

Time is indicated in a number of words, such as: *meta*, when; *awan*, not yet; *hane-at* long ago; *hanee-at, long* ago; *hane-mulkat*, very long ago (these three variations are used more for eloquence than to mark any special time).

The time concept found in verb inflections has been studied by van der Stap (1966) and Bromley (n.d.). The basic temporal-indicating verbs are as follows. A remote past is distinguished from an immediate past. There is a general future form. In the imperative, only, an immediate future is distinguished from a deferred future. There are two forms for repeated action, one for action that is customary, and the other for action that is repeated but is not customary.

It is difficult to infer much from the time inflection of Dani verbs. The lack of present tense as found in English and the use of the customary form invite theories. But the mere availability of forms is likely to be deceptive.

Apparently the Dani do not measure time or think of it in terms of bounded units. There are no words for hour, day, month, year, lifetime, or the like. Besides general terms for future (*akwekhe*), past (*hakane*), and very far past (*hakanelumat*), there are words which refer to broad unbounded moments in time within the daily cycle, within the few days past and future, and within the moon cycle.

The daily cycle words refer to the position of the sun or the degree of light:

huben sue-ane—time of first light (literally, probably bird voice morning)
huben—morning, forenoon
likhe-ane—midday
hiamgakhe—late afternoon and twilight
hibango—night

There are also words for days.

jokodak—today, now
hijalek—tomorrow
hiamane—yesterday
ahekhe—day after tomorrow
ahe—day before yesterday
uahekhe—day after day after tomorrow
uahe—day before day before yesterday
nokobit—day before day before day before yesterday

From this list it would appear that there are morphemes—*ane*, which refers to earlier, or past time, and *-khe* which refers to later, or future time. The *-ane* in *huben sue-ane* is explained by the Dani as the common word for song, or voice, but van der Stap (in a personal communication) feels that this may be a recent folk etymology; *-khe* is also used for "path," but this meaning in time words is not explicit.

Finally, the terms for phases of the moon are used to indicate periods in the month immediately preceding or following.

There was considerable disagreement among informants who were asked to identify the phase of the moon at any one moment. Perhaps the confusion is due to the relative unimportance of phases of the moon in planning. No behavior is specifically planned for particular phases of the moon, although on clear nights when the moon is full there is considerable outdoor activity, such as children's games and hunting in the forest.

I often attempted to force Dani informants to use days (suns) or months (full moons) as units. I wanted to know, for example, when the *ebe akho* ceremony would take place. I think that I was understood, but I was signally unsuccessful in getting answers. The *ebe akho* was always said to be four to six months (or full moons) away. The concept of time as I use it may have been understood on some level, but was basically irrelevant to Dani thinking.

In many languages the references to time use spatial analogies, implicit and explicit. In European and Arabic languages there is a basic horizontal time, indicated in such words as day after tomorrow and *Vorgestern*. (The only important exception that comes to mind in European languages is *Übermorgen*, literally "over tomorrow," the German for day after tomorrow.) In Chinese and Japanese the dominant analogy is to vertical time. There seems to be no such time-as-space analogies in Dani.

A second possible time-as-space metaphor is used in describing relative age of sibling. The term for younger brother is *opolik*, often said with the gesture of hand on small of the back. *Opolik* is also the general word for behind, in back of, when referring to a line of people.

QUALIFICATION

Basically, Dani vocabulary dealing with qualities is as vague as that dealing with quantities.

COLOR

The Dani use of color terms was extensively analyzed by Eleanor R. Heider in 1968, but the following description is based on my own, considerably more impressionistic work in 1961–1963.

Isi is occasionally used to refer to color or to surface, implying color. It is most commonly used as the word for hair, fur.

There are two common color terms which may be used in almost every color context, *modla* and *mili*. *Modla* refers to light, or bright, including red, in contrast to *mili*, dark, or dull. In skin color, *modla* is the light of Europeans or albinos versus the dark of normal Dani. But the *hibiti modla*, several kinds of sweet potatoes, have yellow to orange meat. The contrast is not explicit, because the vast majority of sweet potatoes, with white to ivory flesh, are not called *hibiti mili*. Van der Stap has told me that the golden carp which were introduced into the Grand Valley are described as *modla* by the Dani.

There are no other terms for color which are as non-object-specific as *modla* and *mili*. But on a lower, more specific level of contrast, there are a few terms which are used for more than one sort of object, and so might be considered true color terms. *Gut*, the name for the white heron, is also used sometimes to describe albinos. *Jagik*, the name for the cockatoo, is also used for a white clay. *Bima* (or sometimes *tet*) refers to the rusty color of some pigs, of the mountain dove, and to my own beard. *Getega* refers to a bluish adze stone and to a greenish feather. *Hulu* may refer to bright red. *Dakabe* means spotted.

These terms are sometimes used on the same level of contrast as *modla* and *mili*, but often, when pressed, informants would be uncertain. *Bima* is most consistently used in direct contrast to *modla* and *mili* and comes the closest to being a color term in its own right.

Color discrimination is further noted in terms for different kinds of mud used for decorating the body. A yellow mud, called *pua*, which is found at the place called *pua-ugul-oba* on the upper Aikhe River, is known from other areas of the Grand Valley by the same name (see M. Bromley's word list for the southern Grand Valley dialect).

Value Connotations of Light and Dark. Several times in the course of conversations about the Dani, missionaries who have spent years in Dani areas suggested that there was a strong value connotation to the basic colors, and that *modla* (light) was good, *mili* (dark) was bad. They referred in particular to the high value placed in light-skinned women and to the color term used with *edai-egen,* to mean "light, good, character" or "dark, bad, character." These observations about women and *edai-egen* I was not able to substantiate for the Dugum Dani. If there are value connotations in color, they are at best ambiguous.

For example, men use sooty pig grease to make their skins darker, but they also attempt to make shells lighter. Since 1954, value implications may have accreted to the terminology because of the obvious power of the light-skinned government and missionary personnel and because the pigs imported by the government were nearly white in color and significantly larger than native pigs.

Coloring Agents. There are relatively few coloring agents in Dani technology: black for body darkening is produced by pig grease mixed with charcoal or the burned berry of the *dlabu* (*Centella asiatica* (L.) Urban) tree. Blues for net thread come from the *huai* berry, a melastoma. Reds for nets, cosmetics, or paintings come from the flower of the *gibigibi* weed, an amaranth; from a local red clay called *loke;* or the baked clay imported from the Jalemo for ceremonial use, and called *bimut.* Orange-red for nets comes from the root of a curcuma called *podli.* White for the spear band comes from rotten limestone. Reds, yellows, grays, and whites for body decoration are made with local muds.

Linguistic Patterns and Ownership Relationships

Where English uses the same forms to indicate three different interpersonal or personal-thing relationships, the Dani language has three separate forms. Ownership of minor, incidental objects is indicated by the morpheme *-mege* fixed to the end of the word for the owner. Thus, *duesi an-mege* means my bird feather; *dege um'ue-mege* means Um'ue's spear. Ownerlike relationships to pigs, nets, sib hills, and relationships of kin and other status relationships are indicated by prefixing the name of the owner, or more commonly a form of the pronoun, to the object word. The normal pronouns, with special forms, are:

	Singular	Plural
First person singular:	*an* (*na-*, *n-*)	*nit* (*nin-*)
Second person singular:	*hat* (*ha-*, *h-*):	*hit* (*hin-*)
Third person singular:	*at* (*t-*):	*it* (*it-*)

Examples of this form are *nakoja,* my mother; *ninakoja,* our mother.

Two common words have special forms in this context. The carrying net is usually *su,* but when occurring with a bound possessive pronoun, it is *-jum.* Thus, your net is *hijum.* (Incidentally, the common Western Dani word for net is *jum.*) The ordinary word for pig is *wam,* but with the bound possessive it becomes *-akho.*

A third relationship form uses the postfix *wetekma,* literally "the place where," for compounds and gardens. Thus, *wen Um'ue-wetekma* means the garden where Um'ue is, or Um'ue's garden; *sili Deni-wetekma* is the compound where Deni is, or Deni's compound. This pattern corresponds to the garden and compound site ownership, which is easily transferrable and constitutes little more than usage rights.

SIZE

Size may be described by one of two relative systems. One refers to linear size, such as length or height: *bpetokat*, short; *uwan*, long, tall. The second describes gross size: *hamalukat*, small, tiny; *gog* or *muluk*, huge.

In the absence of specific verbal forms, there are nonverbal ways of indicating size. Length may be indicated on an outstretched hand and arm, with the other hand marking out the distance on the arm to the tip of the fingers. Likewise, the size of a pig may be indicated by pointing to its height on one's leg.

AESTHETICS

Aesthetic judgments seem to be unexpressed. These are apparently no words for such concepts. I often tried to elicit such statements, or to express them myself, but had little success. I could come no closer than *mutu* (or the dialect variation *hano*), which has a very general meaning of good, and its opposite *wejak;* and *warop*, which has the general meaning of "want" (rather than "like") and its opposite *a'et*.

There seemed to be no aesthetic appreciation of landscape or sunsets or other natural phenomenon. The view from a hill top is carefully observed, but primarily for the information it might yield: persons moving, new construction or gardening. When I enjoyed the landscape, the Dani would watch it.

Often I tried to get men or youths to make some statement about beauty or other desirable feminine features. I had no success. One magazine that I received regularly was especially interesting to the Dani because of its vivid photographic advertisements, often showing women with red (*bimut*) on their lips, or men with tall furred headdresses (*bpake isi*) carrying batons (*dege lu*). A beer company which holds an annual beauty contest ran advertisements with photographs of five or six girls. When Dani looked at these photographs they would express great admiration for each girl in turn, but I could not get anyone to actually express a preference. My attempts were handicapped by the lack of a comparative form for adjectives. I did notice that sometimes the men remarked on the fine *elogogen* (cheekbones) of some women. Pursuing this, I was unable to find photographs of women with bad *elogolen*. But it was stated that large cheekbones were bad. This was not particularly useful. There had been one woman with high cheekbones, but she had died long before I arrived. So was lost a chance to find, if not beauty, at least ugliness.

What is the explanation for the Dani's apparent disinterest in attributes? The linguistic evidence shows that there are relatively few attribute terms, that these are fairly vague, and that the syntactical structure does not facilitate manipulation of them. We must recognize that this is on the linguistic, or explicit level of the culture. It does not necessarily follow that in their general behavior the Dani do not make fine qualitative distinctions in many areas where these distinctions are not verbalized.

DUALISM AND PAIRING

An elaborated dualistic theme occurs in Dani culture only in the moiety system and its ramifications. All Dani are either of the Wida or the Waija moiety and can marry only into the opposite moiety. Operationally, kin terms and relationships are usually expanded to the moiety limits. Other implications of this moiety system have been described elsewhere (pp. 62-6). There is no other striking cultural dualism in the Dugum Dani behavior.

Wirz described a pervasive dualism among the Swart Valley Western Dani, based on their moiety system, in which not only every person, but every thing in the universe is ascribed to one or the other moiety (1924:46). Speaking mainly of the southern Grand Valley Dani, Bromley has described a kind of paired leadership, especially for the great pig feast (1961). There were only the barest hints of this in the Dugum Neighborhood. Van der Stap has mentioned (in a personal communication) an apparent southern Grand Valley dichotomy of all foods into the categories of *hibiti* (sweet potato) and *hute* (meaning obscure), but all my attempts to discover this in the Dugum Neighborhood were fruitless.

There is a pseudo, or near dualism in the *mili-modla* (light-dark) color distinction, but generally there are other terms on the same level of contrast, and the *mili-modla* categories do not include the entire universe of shades. Bamboo mouth harps are sometimes attached in pairs to a common string. One of the pair is *modla*, or high-pitched, and the other is *mili*, or low-pitched. Other manifestations in material objects of dualism or pairing, such as that described by Cunningham in his provocative paper, "Order in the Atoni House" (1964), were not found.

However, the theme of pairing runs strongly through Dani culture. This is sometimes the pairing of opposites, but more frequently the pairing of similar entities. Most confederations are named after the two dominant sibs or, in the case of the confederation which includes the Dugum Neighborhood, after two pairs of sibs; these paired sibs are usually of opposite moieties, but they may be of the same moiety (pp. 79-81).

Living beings are frequently paired in listings or in songs. Men and youths are paired by name, and one pair of girls' names form the refrain for many of the *silon* songs (Appendix I). Women are not paired. When eliciting lists of rodent types, it was clear that rodents were paired. Although this pairing pattern is highly suggestive of some special relationship between two individuals or types, my attempts to explain it were unsuccessful.

The importance of the term *pete* in the counting system has been mentioned

(p. 170). This follows *magiat*, one, and could be translated as "two." But especially when used repetitively in narration, it seems to have the quality of "a pair, a pair, a pair."

Certainly pairing is very important to the Dani. Although it does not appear in areas such as graphic art or in other parts of the material culture, perhaps one can still say that the Dani get an aesthetic pleasure or an intellectual satisfaction from pairing.

6

ART AND PLAY

THE PROBLEM OF DISTINCTION

THE demands of the holistic approach to culture make it impossible for the ethnographer to justify the isolation of certain types of behavior as art, and others as play.

Art is usually defined with an emphasis on two factors, formal and conceptual. Formally, art may be considered as the elaboration beyond the strictly utilitarian. Conceptually, it may be defined as the result of aesthetic intent to express something to someone. This is not very helpful in the Dani situation. According to the formal criterion, the high polish on a fighting spear or the elaborate adze binding would be art. As for the conceptual criterion, I was not able to discover even a Dani vocabulary of aesthetics, much less to discuss the subject with my informants.

Bringing the concept of play into the discussion increases the problem. One can say, with Haselberger (1961), that play like art is nonutilitarian, but unlike are it is not done to produce an effect on anyone. Again, this is of no help in illuminating the Dani culture.

Most of the graphic designs of the Dani, on arrow tips, rock shelters, and tree bark, are apparently done simply for the sake of doing them and thus strictly speaking are play.

But many of the children's games, such as hoop spearing, are blatantly educational, thus functional, and thus strictly speaking not just play.

The Dani use of language also raises problems. Dani men spend much of their time in talk, which is sometimes casual gossip, sometimes brilliantly punning dramatic stories or accounts of the incidents of everyday life. Thus talk may be considered as utilitarian communication of information; or, in the context of this gregarious society, it may be considered as interpersonal transactions; or it may be considered as the "art of conversation."

Sidestepping the issue of distinguishing art and play, we shall simply consider some of the Dani behavior which has no immediate utilitarian function.

DANI TERMINOLOGY

The Dani make a distinction between *weligat* (or *jugunat*), profane, and *wusa*, sacred. *Weligat* refers to "that which is just there," "that which has no particular significance," "that which is done for its own sake." Children's games and the charcoal rock drawings are both called *weligat*. On the other hand, *wusa* implies supernatural power or involvement, and that which is *wusa* is to some extent sacred.

Those games which have an element of mock battle are called collectively *jele*.

Various make-believe activities are described as *elege negal-negal* (*elege*, youth; *negal*, generally, lie). A syntactical construction common in play words but otherwise rare is the repetition of the noun: *wam-wam* (pig-pig) refers to a banana bud pulled around on a string like a pig; *o-o* (house-house) refers to various play houses; *jogal-jogal* (skirt-skirt) refers to the miniature skirt made by girls.

The graphic art of the Dugum Dani may be considered in two major categories, the sacred (*wusa*) and the profane (*weligat*). Charcoal drawings on rock shelters, drawings in path sand, and tree bark markings are all casual, or *weligat*. In contrast, the series of drawings in red on the far face of the Dutabut Hill, made in conjunction with the boys' initiation rites, is *wusa*, or sacred.

PROFANE ART

BLACK DRAWINGS

In the hills behind the compounds the limestone often is eroded into overhangs or rock shelters several meters high, which are frequented by men and boys playing or working in the woods. The larger shelters serve as depots where lumber cut from the surrounding forest may be stored before being carried to a construction site at one of the compounds below. Frequently there are ashes of occasional fireplaces, where men sit during rains, smoking around the fire.

On the overhanging rock face of many of these shelters are scrawled charcoal designs. Drawings are found in every shelter deep enough for protection from the rain and where the rock itself presents a firm surface neither overgrown with moss nor rotten and soft. Drawings were found at some twenty-five different sites on the upper slopes of the Dugum Neighborhood.

These drawings were usually done with charcoal against light rock, but in two places they were made with light-brown bees' wax on soot-blackened rock. They are not permanent. Some faded from sight within months. Others, in more favorable positions, shielded from rain, remained fresh for two years. Some of the sites have only one or two simple figures. Others are a clutter of figures of different ages, scrawled haphazard, often one over the other.

The drawings are usually found between one and three meters above ground level, which is the area conveniently accessible to a standing boy or man (Plate 28). At a few sites, however, the drawings are three to four meters above the ground level. These are done by someone standing on lumber leaning against the wall of the overhang. When the lumber is removed, the drawings remain at this improbable height (Plate 27). (One is reminded of the famous Punch cartoon showing three Cave Men, one standing on the shoulders of the next like a human ladder. The top man, as he draws a cave painting, says, "Now they will either think that we had ladders, or that the floor subsided.")

These charcoal drawings are done in a most casual manner by boys or men passing the rock shelter. A few of the boys ten to fifteen years old are particularly responsible and could be considered the spare-time artists of the rocks. Each drawing represents something: man, woman, ghost, pig, lizard, garden. But the drawings were invariably described as *weligat*, and all my attempts to discover some deeper ritual or communicative significance failed.

The most common designs of the charcoal series are the solid figure of a man, an outline figure of a man, a solid figure of a *buna* (lizard), and a solid figure of a *hulitna* (salamander). Other designs are the outline of *buna* or pig, araucaria tree, geometric designs representing gardens and ditches, outline figures of ghosts, and vulva designs (see Diagram 6.1).

There are never profile views; all creatures are shown full vertical body with outstretched limbs. Animal limbs are usually bent at the elbow or knee, arms forward (up) and legs backward (down). Sex of humans is always indicated by genitalia. This spread-eagle pose is not normally realistic, but it may refer to the position of the pig when, during butchering, it is laid on its back, split open down the stomach, and the skin laid out on the ground in such a manner. However, the relative width of the bodies in the drawings does not indicate that the body has been split open.

DESIGNS ON PATHS

A pig tail (*wam ake*) is made using the foot as a crude compass, rotating on the heel of the foot, dragging the toes around to dig a shallow circle in the earth. The design is finished by drawing one or two lines across the edge of the circle. The design represents the tail of a large pig as it is cut out of the hide of the pig together with a large circular patch of skin.

The rectangular design of the pig sty (*wam ai*), with its stalls, is often drawn with a stick in path dirt. The cutting of the pig skin is also drawn. An outline of the steamed pig skin is scratched into the earth with a sharp stick. Then the children cut it up, marking the cuts of the bamboo knife, and saying which piece goes to whom. Sometimes a simpler version of this is made by drawing a series of rectangles, where each rectangle represents a piece of skin. This is done in imitation of the men during important ceremonies. Occasionally a sort of X-ray representation of a pig's leg, indicating the long bones, is drawn in the earth.

These designs are drawn by children, usually boys, often while they are tending pigs. There seems to be no special significance attached to them.

By 1968 the government school program had drastically altered the pattern of casual graffiti in the Grand Valley. Both government personnel and Dani school children were printing their names on paths, trees, and rocks. New elements, such as fish and coastal-style houses, were favorite subjects. The old spread-limbed style of depicting people and animals had yielded to the school-taught single profile.

SEED COMPOUND

Elaborate diagrams of compounds are made by boys, placing the flat seeds from the araucaria cone into the ground to represent a map of the compound. Although no particular compound is usually intended, the diagram is accurate to the extent of usually having the cook house on the left side of the compound.

Dr. Toxopeus, who was in the Grand Valley with the Archbold Expedition in 1938, reported that the Dani make detailed plans of houses and compounds to guide construction (Le Roux 1948:202). This was certainly not true of the Dugum Dani twenty-five years later, and it may be that Dr. Toxopeus had misinterpreted one of these seed diagrams.

OTHER PROFANE DESIGNS

Designs have been cut into the bark of a few trees, usually by young men rather than children, using stone or iron adzes or axes. These are the vulva design, the intersected V. Other designs are carved into hard wood arrow tips and painted in mud on the body.

SACRED ART: RED DRAWINGS

Along the boundary between the Dugum Dani and their neighbors to the southeast, the Walalua, is a strip of unpopulated forest running from the mountain wall down to the Aikhe River on the floor of the Grand Valley. This political boundary is emphasized by a natural barrier, a long, steep salient ridge jutting into the center of the Grand Valley, known as the Dutabut (or Dutoba) Hill. Literally the name means son (*abut*) of the full moon (*dut*). It is also the name of a Grand Valley sib, one of the few sib names whose literal meaning is clear.

The Dutabut ridge is actually part of a line of steeply upthrust limestone strata. The northwest slope, facing the Dugum Neighborhood, is the smooth face of the upper stratum, dipping at a 45° angle. The southeast slope is the faulted ends of the layers, a jumble of boulders and overhangs falling nearly vertically back into the valley floor.

The men of the Dugum sometimes climb to the crest of the ridge, which commands a fine view of their own frontiers, and of the enemy country on the lower Aikhe River. I knew the northwest slope and the crest well, but it was not until my twenty-fifth month in the Dugum area, when exploring the southeast face, that I discovered a unique series of red drawings, including positive and negative representations of human hands.

The red figures were found in six different places on the Dutabut Hill. Some sites, with only a few drawings, are relatively accessible, lying along one of the steep trails winding down the face of the hill. The two sites with the most extensive series of drawings are isolated rock shelters, accessible only by careful negotiation of the jumble of boulders and slabs which forms the southwest face of the Dutabut.

The red series is made with *bimut*, the baked red clay found locally or imported from one of the Jalemo regions beyond the ranges to the northeast.

PLATE 27. Charcoal drawings, without cere-monial significance, are often made on accessible rock faces. Occasionally boys have stood on lumber piles to make the drawings high above a person's normal reach. (Photograph 1968, near Jibiga)

DIAGRAM 6.1
FIGURES IN BLACK

The red series of drawings has many forms not found in the ordinary black series, the charcoal drawings, and it has few of the common black figures. Representations of human hands are among the most common motifs, including two kinds of positive and two kinds of negative hands.

Most of the positive hands were made simply by smearing a hand with red and slapping it against the rock face. One solid red hand was found which had apparently been drawn onto the rock. It measured sixteen centimeters from the tip of the little finger to the tip of the thumb, considerably larger than any human hand (Plate 30). Negative hands were made by outlining with a red line a hand pressed against the rock or apparently blowing red powder against a hand held to the rock, leaving a red outline when the hand was removed (Plate 29).

PLATE 28. Black drawings.

PLATE 29. Negative hands made in red with two techniques, blowing loose powder over a hand, or tracing a hand with a chunk of red.

PLATE 30. Red figures and a positive hand.

PLATE 31. Red figures.

187

Both right and left hands are represented. None of the hands show mutilated fingers, although finger mutilation occurs with Dani men and is the rule with Dani women. The hands were all of adult size. At one site are three faint animals in left profile, with body long and arched and tail curled over the body (Plate 30). At another site is a profile of a standing long-legged bird, with neck outstretched horizontally (Plate 31). At another site are up-pointing crescents, one above the other, in a group of three and a group of two. At several sites are crosses and X's, apparently randomly placed.

The bird may be a cassowary, although it does not live in the Grand Valley itself. The crescents possibly represent the moon. The name of the ridge refers to *dut*, the full moon, however, and the crescents with upward-pointing horns would be the waxing moon of early morning.

The meaning of these red figures, which differ so from the black figures in location, style, and content is a puzzle. I never was able to observe the drawing of any of the red figures, as I did the black. In 1968 I revisited the red figures with an informant and asked many other important men about them. Those men who were of the Wida moiety professed ignorance and the Waija men simply refused to answer.

During my entire stay in the Dugum area I was seldom able to elicit accounts of events which I had not personally observed. If I had observed an event, I could go through my notes of it, asking about each point in turn. But if I asked even the best informants to describe a battle or a ceremony which I had not seen, the reply would seldom be more than, "We fought," or, "It was *wusa*." Thus, I simply do not know very much about these red designs, which are one of the few dramatic "discoveries" to be reported herein.

The red drawings are made in connection with the *waija hakasin*, the initiation of young boys into the Waija moiety. The ceremony is very *wusa*, as are the drawings. They are made by the Waija men while standing some sort of vigil on the Dutabut Hill in connection with the ceremony. The young boys are not present, and the red hands are certainly the size of adults, rather than the three- to six-year-old initiates.

The red matter is the *bimut wusa*, sacred red clay, which is brought into the Grand Valley from the Jalemo for the initiation ceremony, used to draw a red stripe down the forehead and nose of each initiate, according to informants. The use of red recalls the worldwide prominence of blood or a red blood-surrogate in initiation ceremonies. But I could find nothing to suggest that the Dugum Dani make this symbolism explicit.

OTHER DANI DESIGNS IN RED

On trips between the Dugum area and Wamena, the government post to the south, I observed red figures on the rock outcrops of the Subula Hill in the center of Widaia territory. These figures were similar in form to the red designs on the Dutabut Hill. Since the culture of the Widaia Dani is nearly the same as that of the Dugum Dani, I assume that these red designs have similar functions.

These red drawings seem to be found mainly in relatively inaccessible places, and little is known about their distribution. In 1962, A. Blokdijk and W. Westerink of the Franciscan Mission in Wamena discovered naturalistic drawings of animals in red at 3,850 meters altitude in the mountains to the southwest of the Grand Valley (Galis 1964:263).

The broad, flat exchange stones called *je*, which are imported from the Jalemo, often have traces of red *bimut* clay. One which I bought (and which is now in the Peabody Museum of Harvard University) had the remains of a red tree design covering one face. It was explained that in the Jalemo the *je* stones were decorated only with red, but when they were obtained by the Grand Valley Dani, the red was rubbed off and the stones were decorated with braided string, furs, and feathers.

MEAGERNESS OF DANI GRAPHIC ART

The meagerness of art among the Dugum Dani is particularly striking when considered in the context of New Guinea as a whole. This island has greater richness of "primitive art" than any other area in the world except possibly West Africa. To all sides of the Grand Valley, only a few hundred kilometers away, are regions with great artistic expression such as Humboldt Bay, Lake Sentani, Mimika, Asmat, Papua Gulf, Fly River, and of course the Sepik River. Even among the mountain Papuans, the Dani have less art than the people of East New Guinea.

The Dugum Dani are poorer in artistic expression than many of their immediate neighbors. To the northeast, across the ranges, the Dani of the Central and Southern Jalemo paint designs on the inside or outside of the men's round houses. The Western Dani of the Konda Valley frequently draw crude figures in charcoal on the inside walls of their round houses. These are similar to the charcoal designs found on rock shelter walls in the Dugum, but never on house walls there. It may be significant that there are few or no rock shelters in the Konda Valley. Instead of being drawn on the walls of uninhabited rock shelters, in the Konda Valley the designs are a constant background of the living space.

To the south, across the Grand Valley, the Welesi Dani decorate water flask gourds with complex geometric designs scratched into the outer skin of the green gourd. According to Welesi informants around Wamena, the designs represent garden ditch patterns and have no ritual significance.

There is no apparent reason why water flask designs should be limited to one corner of the Grand Valley. Completely analogous water flask gourds are found throughout the Grand Valley, and there is sufficient contact between the Welesi and other Grand Valley Dani groups for the trait to be diffused. R. Camps has pointed out (in a personal communication) that Welesi songs are slightly different and more complex than other Grand Valley songs. It is true that the Welesi lie at one end of a trade route that passes over the high plateau between the Western Dani on the Upper Balim and the Grand Valley Dani, and perhaps their advanced art and song represent Western Dani influence which has not yet spread through the Grand Valley.

VERBAL ART

The Dani language is impressive even at first contact. The newcomer tends to notice the speed of talk and the slurring of sounds. He also notices the Dani's almost song-like expressive range or tonality. As one learns the language, the impression persists. The speed and the slurring and the dropping of sounds remain a major hurdle to real fluency. But the beginner soon takes pleasure in mimicking the tonal expressiveness in even his first painful statements on the language.

The economic demands on the individual Dani are relatively slight, and even the women, who spend more time working than men or children, have ample opportunity to sit around gossiping. The men work hard for short periods when they are building a house or watchtower, or opening new gardens. But much of their time is spent sitting around a fire in a men's house or at a watchtower, perhaps smoking, perhaps weaving, but usually talking. Malinowski has noted the importance of idle chatter as an instrument forging interpersonal ties. Using his words, Dani talk is well described as "purposeless expressions of preference or aversion, accounts of irrelevant happening, comments on what is perfectly obvious" (1923:315).

Elsewhere in New Guinea, oratory as such is a highly developed art. Bateson describes the power and importance of the accomplished orator among the Iatmül on the Sepik River (1936:125 ff), and the Ekagi (Kapauku) of the Tigi-Paniai (Wissel) Lakes also emphasize the art of verbal expression (Pospisil 1958:15). But there is certainly none of this among the Dugum Dani. Leaders may shout advice in battle (which usually goes unheeded) or mumble incantations in rituals, but oratory is not important per se.

Another type of verbal skill, that of storytelling, is developed by the Dugum Dani. This is not the public recounting of myths or legends by wise old men but rather the dramatic relation of events and experiences. Especially after a battle or when a man has returned from a long trip, he will hold forth at great length, modulating his voice and gesturing with his hands for maximum dramatic effect while his audience sits smoking and whistling or tapping their penis gourds at appropriate moments.

Repetition is a common dramatic device in storytelling: "and then men were killed, a pair, a pair, a pair . . ." or "then they went on, and they went on, and they went on . . ."

The Dani language has resources for verbal abuse, which for the most part refer to sexual functions or genitals. These may be used in a wide range of contexts, from formal greetings, through joking insults, to serious verbal assaults.

Many of the nonkin term greetings are of the form "Let me eat your ———":

Halabok-nak—Let me eat your feces
Halobasi-nak—Let me eat your flatulence
Hagul nak—Let me eat your penis (men to men)
Heget nak—Let me eat your vulva (woman to woman)

These are usually said as pro-forma greetings with no indication of attention to the literal meaning, although once, in an intense argument, I heard them used in earnest.

Swearing Bout

Sometimes boys or men sit facing each other and exchange endless numbers of these sexual or personal insults. This is usually carried off good-naturedly, but when young boys are involved, they are often reduced to tears by the end. This resembles the American and English game called *The Dozens* (cf. Ayoub and Barnett 1965), and a Turkish pattern of verbal dueling reported by Dundes and Özkök (1968).

In the course of a battle when the fighting has momentarily ceased, the two sides may exchange good-natured insults. Since most of the men know their opponents personally, the barbs can be rather directly aimed at some personal weakness of an individual opponent, to the merriment of both sides.

Songs. The Dani sing several kinds of songs: the lullaby, called *wa-wa*, is a soothing drone sung by a woman or girl with a restless baby in her carrying net. There are no words, just "*wa, wa, wa . . .*" *Edai* and *wene pugut* are loud and boisterous types of songs which are usually sung by large groups of people at dances or at girls' puberty ceremonies. A dirge is sung at funerals or curing ceremonies, or even when greeting someone who has not been seen for a long time. A solo is usually sung by the leader of the event, a statement on a high note, dropping off at the end, which is answered by the mournful chorus: "*nai* our father has died, *aaaaaaaaaaa oh.*"

There is also a large class of incidental songs called *silon*, which are sung by boys and young men, particularly roaming the fields and woods, and the songs have no apparent purpose. These songs are short and are generally sung to one simple tune. The songs are sometimes composed by the singers, but because some of the songs include words from other dialects, these would seem to have originated in other areas. Also, many of the songs are recognized in the same or only slightly different form by Dani from the Wamena area who speak the southern Grand Valley dialect. The texts of the songs are characterized by obscure words and punning, especially on sexual matters. The sexual emphasis of the songs is especially remarkable in this culture which lays so little overt emphasis on sex.

Silon cannot conveniently be divided into types, but two main themes may be noted: sex, particularly copulation, and evocation of natural scenes. The songs are usually a simple statement of a situation or action, often with humorous overtones. The form is usually couplets alternating with a refrain. The refrain always mentions the names of two local girls. Another characteristic feature of the *silon* is the repetition of words with the change of a few morphemes.

The *silon* combines the boisterous ribaldry of the Caribbean calypso with the sensitive evocation of words characteristic of the Japanese haiku. The music itself is repetitive, an excuse for noise and a vehicle for the words. The writer has attempted to translate a few of these songs (Appendix II).

MUSICAL INSTRUMENTS

The only common Dani musical instrument is the *bigon*, or bamboo mouth harp, made from a single piece of reed and played with a string attached to one end and about ten to fifteen centimeters in overall length (Plate 32). Most men and boys carry a *bigon* at least part of the time. It is played for private amusement, and always solo, sometimes by a person sitting alone, sometimes by a person sitting in a group. There are no complicated tunes played on it, just a simple alternation of high and low tones produced by changing the size of the mouth, and resonating chamber, with the tongue. Occasionally an expert will mouth words while playing. Sometimes a player may mouth the vowels of a pair of names—one of the best-friend pairs—and see if the others can guess which pair is being mouthed. This is also done without the *bigon*, simply pronouncing the vowels, omitting the consonants of the two names.

Bigon are of two types—low-toned, called *ane mili* (dark voice) or *ane gog* (large voice); and high-toned, called *ane mola* or *ane bpuk* (no voice). Occasionally one of each kind is tied together at opposite ends of a common string and played alternately by the same man. The *bigon* are usually carried in the arm band or if possible in the earlobe hole. Usually one or more *bigon* are near the fireplace of a men's house, either hanging from a hook or slipped under the binding of the center posts. *Bigon* are never played by women or girls.

Bigon are made from the *pithe* reed (actually a *phragmites* grass). A section of the reed including one septum is cut and split in half. With flint flakes the three long pieces are shaped and scraped thin. A hole is bored in the end just beyond the septum and a string passed through, held by a knot. The two

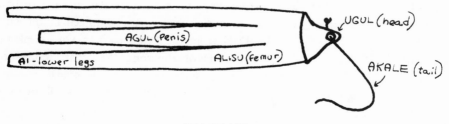

DIAGRAM 6.2
Bamboo Mouth Harp

outside strips are longer than the center vibrating one. The *bigon* is tested, scraped thinner, tested again until the desired pitch is reached.

The *bigon* is not decorated. The terminology for the parts of the mouth harp reveals some anthropomorphism (see Diagram 6.2).

Occasionally young boys use a toy one-meter bow as a kind of musical bow, holding the taut string to their mouths and hitting the string with their finger or a stick. The resonance of the bowstring in their mouths resembles the sound of the mouth harp. To play a mouthharp properly requires considerable skill, and it appears that this musical bow gives young boys practice in proper mouth positions.

A few times boys were observed with reed pipes called *widabo* or *widetabo*. They consist of one or two lengths of reed, twenty to thirty centimeters long and about one centimeter in diameter. One end is closed by leaving the septum in the reed or by holding the reed against the palm of the hand. Up to three tones are produced by blowing across the open end. Because of their rarity it seemed possible that the pipes were brought in by missionary or government personnel, but the older informants insisted that they had known such pipes when they were young.

PLAY

Play may be divided roughly into two categories: those activities which seem to have some ultimate educational effect and those which do not. Within these the following subcategories may be considered: educational: war games, hunting, house building, pigging, gardening, divination, women's things, cigarettes; noneducational: string figures, grass figures, grass knots, splat game, somersault, rhinoceros beetle, noise games.

Two striking characteristics of play may be noted here. First, educational play mirrors the entire culture of the adult Dani world, with the apparent exception of ritual. Second, except for the war games, where there is conscious development of skill, there is almost complete lack of competition in play. There are no games in which score is kept or in which there is ever a winner. This deemphasis on competition is also a characteristic of the adult culture and may be reflected in the absence of comparative words in the language.

Educational Play

War Play

GRASS-SPEAR BATTLES. Boys play this highly realistic imitation of battle. The battlefield is usually a fallow garden area. The weapons are the stalks of heavy grass, the leaves trimmed off, about thirty centimeters long. Each boy advances into battle with a handful of stalks and throws them at the "enemy," often with great accuracy. There are no tactics of battle; each side is completely uncoordinated, and individuals move forward, release their missiles, and retreat.

PLATE 32. A bamboo mouth harp.

PLATE 33. A small boy and girl try to spear the berries of each other's armies.

PLATE 34. The spear fighting game.

PLATE 35. "Kill the Hoop" game (Photograph by Michael Rockefeller)

KILL THE HOOP. This is played by two groups, standing fifteen to thirty meters apart. One group throws a hoop about forty centimeters in diameter, made of heavy intertwined vine, at the ground, and as it rolls and bounces past, the other group tries to throw spears through it, pinning it to the ground. The spears are simple sticks sharpened at the end (Plate 35).

TARGET PRACTICE. Sometimes a piece of moss, high in a tree, serves as a target, and after several weeks, when it falls down, it has many spears embedded in it.

Ant hives low on the trunks of trees are favorite targets for boys passing by with a spear.

WAIK. Longer spears, up to two meters long, are skidded along the ground, usually the hard ground of a path, in this game. Several boys play together, slowly progressing down the path; the stick is thrown hard and low, hitting the path a few meters in front of the thrower and skidding for a short distance. There is an element of competition here, but only very informally.

KILL THE BERRY. This is a miniature war game, played with the small hard yellow berry of the pittosporum tree. It is usually played by two boys, although girls also play (Plate 33).

One simple version of the game involves two armies of berries, several dozen on each side, which are rolled back and forth under the flats of the hands, representing the advances and retreats of the warriors. A more complex version of the game is played with watchtowers and spears. Each boy is responsible for one mass of warriors. Each side has several dozen berries and at least one watchtower—a stick about twenty centimeters high with a small crotch at the top, one berry warrior sitting in the tower, and a mass of berry warriors beneath it. A single spear—a short pointed stick, or a pig bone awl set in a cane handle—is thrown in turn by one boy and then the other at the enemy warriors. If the spear impales a berry, this berry is considered dead and is retired to a place behind its own lines, where the killed berries slowly accumulate. The game is usually broken up by mass movements of warriors, rolled under the flat of the hand. If the warriors of one side move toward and threaten the watchtower, the berry on the watchtower is carefully withdrawn with the other berries.

FLIP BERRY. Small hard berries or stones may be flipped from the end of a short flexible stick; sometimes one boy idly aims at a fencepost, sometimes two or more boys flip missiles at each other.

Hunting. Bows and arrows of various sorts are used by the youngest boys able to run with their older brothers; girls rarely (and women never) use them. They are often simply carried in the hand when walking around the countryside, ready to shoot at a nearby bird or other interesting target.

Children's bows are about a meter long, made in the fashion of an adult's bow, but cruder. Often they are made by boys of ten or so, sometimes with the supervision of an older man. The most common arrows are simply meter-long lengths of reed, easily found and painlessly lost. Boys between ten and fifteen sometimes make careful multipronged bird arrows, equal in quality to those used by the men. Most bird hunting even by men falls into the category of play: it is casual, nonpurposive, although an accidental kill will be eaten. (This must be distinguished from those times when men set out to kill birds for ceremonial use or specific birds for their feathers.)

House and Compound

o-o. Boys and girls often build crude imitations of long houses or round houses, two meters in diameter and 1.5 meters high, in the places where they take pigs to root. These serve briefly as shelter and play area but are soon abandoned to the elements.

A framework is made of reeds, driven into the ground, and lashed together in dome- or tunnel-shape, then covered with grass thatch.

WOOD CHIP. Once I observed that in an area where a man had been chopping wood with a steel axe and had left chips of wood lying around, a boy had made two model houses. The chips were stuck in the ground in a twenty-centimeter circle, representing the wall planks of a round house, and four sticks in the center poles.

HOUSE ON STILTS. Near a high slope garden I observed that some boys built a small domed house about one meter above the ground on stilts. It was about one meter in diameter with a dome about seventy-five centimeters high, and a thatched roof. It seems likely that this was an imitation of a sleeping place built inside his tent by the cook for our expedition, an Ambonese man.

Pigging

WAM-WAM (pig-pig). The reddish flower core of the banana stalk, which is broken off and discarded when the stalk is harvested, is sometimes attached to a length of string and given to a little girl, who drags it around as a pig on a leash, calling it *wam-wam*.

PIG CARVINGS. The *holim-holim*, a Venus flycatcher-like plant, is carved by boys with a bamboo knife as a pig. The heavy lip, removed, resembles the mandible of the pig and is strung on a stick, as is the pig mandible in the rear of the men's house; the body is opened up and laid out like a pig skin.

"Divination." Two games involve joking divination of future status.

NAKOBAK. This was observed several times on clear nights of full moon, in a compound where a ceremony with steam bundles had been held during the day.

A group of boys sit around the coals of the fire used to heat rocks for the steam bundle. Each has several fifty-centimeter wooden splints. A boy places the splint upright in the coals. As the base of the splint burns through and falls, the boy says to the boy to whom the splint points, *nakobak*, brother-in-law. The implication is that the first boy will marry a sister or other member of the second boy's sib. All the boys laugh, and another one plants a splint in the coals as the game continues. The game is not taken seriously, and even when the splint falls to a boy of the same moiety, where marriage would be incestuous, there is no change in the atmosphere of the play.

HODLAK-WETAK (girl-boy). Young children often throw nets into the air as high as they can and try to catch them before they hit the ground. If they succeed they say *wetak* (boy) if not, *hodlak* (girl).

Women's Things

JOGAL-JOGAL (skirt-skirt). Older girls often make miniature women's skirts of a sedge around their hand or around a stick a couple of centimeters in diameter. This, like the girls' play with spears, may be a rare example of play incongruous with the adult life, since these women's skirts are made by men, or it could be that they represent the simple version of the skirts, which are indeed made by women.

SU-SU (net-net). I once observed a young girl imitate the women's nets (*su*) with half a dozen leaves, held by the stem; the outer one was bright red, representing the decorative outer net; the inner one doubled up to hold a small stick she called "baby."

Gardening. Sometimes children will scratch grids in the ground representing garden ditch systems. Sometimes boys play at making cigarettes. They take a *lisaniga* leaf, fold it over like a cigarette without tobacco, light it, and smoke it.

String Figures. String figures, called *hele-mule*, are sometimes made by girls or boys. Apparently few people know how to make more than ten or so kinds, and even groups of boys and girls could think of only fifteen or so. The string loop is about sixty centimeters long. The children use both hands, the mouth, and sometimes a leg or foot or twig to form the figures; some figures require two operators. No real experts, who could swiftly and surely perform a large repertoire, were found.

Some figures are static, built to a specific figure, and are then undone. Others involve acting out a brief scene. The doubling of the noun, characteristic of words for games, is common in the names of the figures: (1) *daluga-daluga* (pandanus-pandanus) represents the pandanus tree with spreading roots, trunk, and spreading leaves. One person makes it with two hands, the other "climbs" it with her fingers, then smashes it to the ground; (2) *sin-sin* (araucaria-araucaria) represents the araucaria tree. One person makes it with two hands and a foot; (3) *bpake-hele* (rodent snare)—one girl makes it with two hands and the other girl demonstrates by letting her fingers be caught in the snare; (4) *aigape* (ambush)—like the rodent snare, above; (5) *beagi* (the chair on which the corpse sits)—one girl makes it with two hands and the string running under her thigh; (6) *sue laka* (cassowary feather dance whisk)—one girl makes it with two hands, and loose loops flop like the dance whisk; (7) *gu* (bridge)—one girl makes it with two hands, and it represents the single pole bridge with hand rails; (8) *jali he* (Jalemo woman)—one girl makes it with two hands, and two loose loops represent the breasts; (9) *hali udluk* (carry wood on head)—one girl makes it with two hands, another girl puts a piece of wood into the design, which is then worked from one side to the other; (10) *oati* (copulation)—one girl makes it with two hands. Two loops, representing a man and a woman, are moved in from each side to meet and "copulate" in the middle; (11) *helegin* (bee hive); 12) *puna-puna* lizard-lizard) 13) *olie-olie* (garden shelter-garden shelter).

Grass Designs. Boys and young men construct complicated three-dimensional figures by knotting the stalks of grass to form nets. One design is reminiscent of the Fadenkreuz or string cross: three cane diagonals crossing at a common point, with grass wound to make concentric circumferences. This design seems to have no symbolic meaning.

Frequently the tall grass beside a path is knotted: two clumps are bent toward each other and tied together to form an arch. I once observed a grass cross, a 130-centimeter upright clump, with a second clump 78 centimeters long bound as a crosspiece. Informants invariably denied that these had any special significance.

Splat Game. I once observed a boy making pancakes of mud, raising them above his head, and throwing them down on a shallow hole in the ground. If aimed right, the center of the pancake would blow out with a loud pop.

Mud Mogat. A boy on the side of a hill made a little cave in the mud, put in a mushroom, and covered it with leaves, saying that this represented his father who had died. (In fact, his father was still alive.)

Somersault. Boys often roll down the side of a hill lengthwise; or standing at the top with arms spread, they whirl around and around, moving down hill until finally they fall down.

Rhinoceros Beetle. Rhinoceros beetles may be captured, their horns broken off, an end of grass stalk forced in, and the beetles led around as if on a leash.

Pop Mouth. Children make popping noises by holding one forefinger inside a closed mouth, then flipping it out with a pop. This may also be done by holding the forefinger at the chin and quickly flipping it past the everted lips, jiggling them and getting a pop.

Anewu-anewu. (*Ane*, voice, noise; *wu*, apparently the imitation of the noise. *Anewu* is the term now used for airplane.) I once observed a boy make a "bull-roarer" of a chip of wood at the end of a thin vine: the vine was threaded through a hole in the chip and knotted. A whirring sound was produced by whirling the chip around the head. Informants generally said this had no ritual significance, but one said it was to make the boy grow larger.

PART II

7

THE NATURAL ENVIRONMENT

T HE natural environment of any cultural group may be described from several standpoints. There are such modern scientists as structural geologists, meteorologists, and cartographers, whose scientific descriptions will use such terms as anticline, beech forest, and milimeters of rainfall. The scientific description has the advantage of being readily understandable to most readers. It also has a comfortable illusion of reality, using the tools of the exact sciences.

We must also consider the native perception of the environment. This is ultimately of more cultural significance than the scientific perception. The scientifically described environment is useful for understanding in broad terms the limitations or the possibilities of the environment, stripped of all cultural meaning. But here we are interested in the culture of the Dugum Dani and in the environment as it forms a part of that symbolic system that we call culture.

The distinction between scientific and natural perceptions of the environment is well illustrated in the case of rainfall. Rainfall charts for the Grand Valley show a regular yearly variation of rainfall, with a peak from January to March.

Culturally this variation is irrelevant, and indeed nonexistent. The Dani do not perceive the variation. Of course, the Dani act differently on dry days than on rainy days, but their explicit and apparently also their implicit behavior does not reflect or accommodate to the regularity of this variation. Scientifically we may describe regular climate cycles; culturally they are nonexistent.

In addition to the scientific and the native perceptions of the environment, there is the middle-level perception of the ethnographer, which combines relevant aspects of both scientific and native systems.

For example, let us consider the distance between the Dugum Neighborhood and the Balim River to the southwest, and the Iluekaima brine pool to the north. The scientific description of the distance in each case is about five kilometers. From the Dani standpoint, the path to the brine pool lies through friendly country, and the round trip, which takes a laden woman about an hour, can be made in the early morning, before the day's work begins. But the Balim lies across a war frontier; to cross it is tantamount to suicide.

The following pages give a broad general view of native and scientific statements about the Dani environment.

TOPOGRAPHY

The Balim River flows in a great arc through the Highlands before breaking out onto the low-lying southern swamplands of New Guinea (Map C.2, p. 299). The East Balim River begins at Lake Habbema, which lies 3,225 meters high on the northern side of the Central Highlands of West New Guinea. Although an important trade route crosses this high plateau, there is no permanent occupation here. The East Balim flows westward and then swings to the north, where it joins the West Balim, flowing in from the west along the Ilaka-Tiom valley system. This is the land of the Western Dani, a land of narrow valleys where the scattered settlements cling to the sides of the slopes.

The river, now the Balim proper, flows eastward for another fifty kilometers before angling off to the southeast. As it enters the Grand Valley, which lies on a northwest-southeast axis, the river changes from a swift mountain stream to a slow river meandering its way through the broad plain of the Grand Valley. At the southeast end of the Valley, the Balim breaks through the central mountain chain in a series of gorges, zigzagging in white-water torrents for another fifty kilometers before it finally emerges into the flat jungle land of southern New Guinea. Now the river splits, and is called the Vriendschap and Eilanden Rivers, then again joins into the Vriendschap River, seeping through the mangrove swamps of the Asmat Coast into the Arafura Sea.

The Grand Valley of the Balim is unusual in the generally rugged highlands of New Guinea and is comparable only to the Waghi and Chimbu valleys of East New Guinea and the Wissel Lake region of West New Guinea in size and opportunity for dense population.

The Grand Valley is some forty-five kilometers long and up to fifteen kilometers wide, less valley than plain, 1,600 meters above sea level. The surrounding mountains rise abruptly from the floor of the valley to a height of 2,500 to 3,000 meters. In the distance, Wilhelmina Top (Trikora), 4,750 meters high and occasionally snow-streaked, can be seen.

The surrounding mountains are primarily limestone, with some quartz sandstone layers (Schroo 1961:85). Sinklike depressions and underground streams, emerging and disappearing, are common, and in the southeastern corner of the Grand Valley there is an extensive area of karst topography, pitted with sinks and almost uninhabited. Caves are rare, although there are two in the northwestern part of the Gutelu Alliance. One lies near the government and mission post at Jibiga and another beyond it at a place called Gondilula. Also, two of the eastern tributaries of the Balim, the Huwam and the Minimo in the southern Grand Valley, emerge from caves. The cave of the Huwam is considered by the Mid-Valley Dani to be the point at which the original people emerged into the world (p. 140).

GEOMORPHOLOGY

The geomorphology of the Central Highlands of West New Guinea and of the Balim drainage in particular has been the subject of only preliminary study. Although the Balim drainage area lies on the north side of the line that generally marks the central divide of New Guinea, it actually drains through the divide out to the south coast. Verstappen (1953), on the basis of his examination of aerial photographs, suggests that the West, East, and North Balim rivers and the Grand Valley formerly drained to the north into the Hablifuri River and eventually the Idenburg River system, but that the Vriendschap River breached the central divide and captured the Balim system, diverting it to the south.

The Dugum Neighborhood lies away from the Balim River, against the eastern mountain wall of the Grand Valley (Map. C.3, p. 300). Most of the Dugum compounds hug the edge of the valley floor or straggle up the flanking slopes. In front of them are the low-lying gardens of the valley floor and beyond is the deserted no-man's-land separating the Dugum area from the lands of the enemy Widaia Alliance, which occupies the east banks of the Balim in the midvalley.

Most of the Dugum Neighborhood lies within the upthrust arc of the mountain wall, a great faulted anticline, where the beds of limestone have been bowed up and sheared off (Plate 13). The western end of this anticline curves out into the valley, forming the hill known as the Dugum, before it drops off abruptly to the valley floor.

On the southern edge of the neighborhood is a steep salient jutting from the mountain wall, bisecting it, and extending out into the valley floor. This ridge, the Dutoba, forms a line with the low Dogolik and the higher Siobaka in the Widaia country in the center of the Valley. Schroo suggests that

these limestone ridges used to form single continuous barriers across the plain, causing parts of the valley to be transformed into temporary swamps or lakes. The dammed-up water then rose until a spillway was found in this barrier where it could overflow and carve a new outlet through the limestone ridge. (1961:85)

Several permanent streams issue from the mountain slopes and flow through the Dugum Neighborhood on their way to the Balim River. A number of these flow into the networks of garden ditches.

COGNITIVE ORGANIZATION OF THE ENVIRONMENT

Names of Features

The Dani have no maps or other graphic representations of their landscape. However, each different area has a particular name. Suffixes common in place names are: *-ma, -mo, -baka,* meaning at the place of; *-ai,* a bound form referring to water, commonly used as *-aima*, the area around a spring or stream; *ugul*, a point or promontory, also a large area and a person's head.

There are two generic names for places. *Sili* indicates a relatively small area of only a few thousand square meters. The specific names for these areas refer to outstanding characteristics of the area. For example: Wubakaima, the place of the gardenia springs, from *wubak*, gardenia; *-ai*, water; *-ma*, place of; Abugulmo, the place of the skull, from *ab*, man; *-ugul*, head; *-mo*, place of.

Compounds or gardens are called after the areas where they lie. The compound itself does not have a name other than the area name, nor does a cluster of adjoining compounds. In fact, in cases where two or even three separate compound clusters lie in the same area, they are all called by the same name. They are distinguished from one another in cases of potential ambiguity by reference to a person living in a particular compound.

On a more inclusive level than *sili* is *ugul*, an area of several square kilometers, often where a confederation or part of a confederation lives. However, the *ugul* is a geographical area with no necessary correlation to a territorial political unit. Among various named Grand Valley *ugul*, Pugima and Solimo are both discrete valleys; Subula is an area on the mid-Aikhe River; Iluekaima is the area around the brine pool of that name; and Bpetobaka is the area around the hill slope of that name. Although the names for distant *ugul* were used in a fairly consistent manner by the Dugum Dani, informants could not agree on a name for the *ugul* of or including what I call the Dugum Neighborhood. The areas so named are not strictly bounded, and often there is ambiguity about a specific spot, which may be considered in either of two different areas by the same person at different times.

The knowledge of *sili* names is generally limited to areas where members of the Neighborhood have traveled. The Neighborhood itself is thoroughly known, and compounds and areas in the neighboring confederations are also known. But the high mountains which dominate the southern and western skyline are not known by name. However, the word for snow, *bpikagup*, and its coldness are known from the tales of long-range traders. Snow is visible from the Neighborhood at times on Wilhelmina Top (Trikora).

Place names seem almost exclusively to be used on only one level of contrast. Thus, there are names for specific areas, but there are rarely names for larger, inclusive, or collective areas. For example, the long hill which dominates the Widaia country I considered "a hill"—a unit, albeit with different parts—and I called the entire hill by the name Siobaka. It later became clear that this was the name for one specific part of it. The Dani would refer to it as a *dom*, hill, or mountain, but when naming it in narration they would refer only to that part relevant to the narrative.

This can be explained, perhaps, by the circumstances that although in a photograph (for example, Plate 2) the Siobaka appears as a discrete entity, there is no behavior in which it figures as a totality. In fact, in English, where I used Siobaka for the entire hill instead of loading the narrative down with the names of the parts, I otherwise would have had to use a clumsy circumlocution: Tulem is at "the far end of the Siobaka"; lookouts lit fires on "the top ridge of this end of the Siobaka." This lack of specific name for an entire feature was also true of the mountain wall behind the Dugum Neighborhood, of the Pass Valley, and of the Grand Valley itself.

Named areas and features may be described as being in the territory of a specific named confederation. However, there seems to have been no Dani name for the specific alliance or alliance area. For convenience, the Dutch administration used the name of the most important man, Gutelu, for the alliance and the territory of which the Dugum Neighborhood is a part. This usage has been adopted by many of the Dani themselves but does not seem to be original with them.

Dani stream terminology is the same as in English: separate streams have specific names, and when two streams join, the resulting stream bears the name of the larger tributary.

DIRECTIONS

The Dani do not speak of the cardinal points of the compass or in terms of the sun's path; however, the terms *opu-khe*, uphill or upward, and *uwema-khe*, downhill or downward, are frequently used in a relative sense. These generally refer to the valley itself: roughly downstream, out toward the center of the valley, is "down"; back toward the hills is "up." The area toward the north, the valley floor which is actually upstream in terms of drainage, is usually referred to as down, but sometimes as up.

The Dani do not necessarily maintain a strict sense of direction when inside a house. Very often when telling a story or giving directions, the narrator will indicate a direction with the hand which is far off the direction of place referred to and also not related to the direction of the path necessary to take to reach it. The naming of the place is sufficient for the narrative, and indicating the direction with the hand is a superfluous gesture.

THE KNOWN WORLD

The known Dani world includes first of all the Grand Valley itself, most of which can be seen from vantage points in the hills behind the villages; the Jalemo, the valley system beyond uninhabited forest to the northeast, where related groups live and with which there is considerable trading; and the rather more vague Balim Elesimo (source of the Balim) beyond the valley to the west, from whence come the stones for adzes and axes.

In recent years the Dugum Dani have become aware of the world beyond the Dani area in a vague way. They understand that there is a greater world beyond the mountains. During the Dutch rule they called it Holadia, a corruption of Hollandia, the capital of Netherlands New Guinea which was in fact the point of departure for goods and people flying into the Highlands. By 1968, after five years of Indonesian rule, most were using the new name, Sugatanaputa (Sukarnapura). They understood that most of the members of the expedition lived in Ametiga, but it was generally considered that this place had some connection with Holadia. There was little curiosity about Ametiga. When questions were asked, it was about my pigs or wives or other relatives. I often showed people magazines with illustrations of exotic scenes in Paris and New York, but the only subjects which really aroused any interest were pictures of people.

P. van der Stap has reported (in a personal communication) that the Dani living along the Balim in the vicinity of Wamena, where he was carrying out linguistic research, believe that the Balim River flows in a great clockwise circle. This is an understandable error: Map C.2, p. 299, shows that from Lake Habbema, one of its sources, to the gorges below the Grand Valley, the Balim does in fact nearly complete a circle.

Even more striking is the fact that the Wamena and the East Balim rivers rise only a few hundred meters apart on the northern flank of Wilhelmina Top (Trikora). The East Balim flows westward, the Wamena eastward, and after flowing a combined total of some 250 kilometers they meet again at the junction of the Wamena and the Balim Rivers in the Grand Valley. However, the Dugum Dani say that the source, or spring of the Balim (Balim *Elesimo*) lies somewhere to the northwest, and after leaving the Grand Valley it continues to flow toward the south.

I was never able to elicit a definite picture of the world from the Dugum Dani. Apparently they do not consider the universe bounded. Beyond the regions which they know best, the Grand Valley and the Central Jalemo, there are other, similar regions with people who speak strange but not incomprehensible languages. They know of the Hoop Jale (Delok Jale), who sometimes come into the Grand Valley on trading trips from the east, wearing their broad waistbands of multiple bamboo hoops; they also know of the Gem peoples who sometimes come as far as the Pass Valley. But there is no contact with either of these people except when they visit the Grand Valley.

The men around Jibiga were better informed. They live much closer to the Pass Valley and seem generally more involved in trading beyond the Grand Valley than are the people of the Dugum. They described a people called Maikbok who live beyond the Gem people, apparently at a much lower altitude and perhaps even in the Lake Plains, where they eat sago, red pandanus, taro, cucumber, and greens, but no sweet potato. The Maikbok people trade cowrie shells for salt and tobacco with the Gem people, meeting them on paths, making quick exchanges, and then retreating. At Jibiga in 1968 informants also described the Juaijuk people who sometimes wander into the Grand Valley from the southwest. They are said to be naked and to walk around with their hands joined behind their backs, munching grasses, fruits, and seeds with their mouths. It is hard to tell to what exent this is ethnocentric myth and to what extent it is a distorted description of people from the interior Asmat, who might well have made contact with Dani groups.

The sky is the home of several kinds of supernatural creatures; the sun and moon pass through it invisibly on their journeys back to their homes in the east, and the stars and planets are recognized. But there seems to be no definite conception of the sky that would explain such questions of the anthropologist as, "Why does one not see the sun at night when she returns?" The fact that the larger stars are described as the heads of important (big) men suggests a material conception, but I was not able to elicit it nor to determine satisfactorily whether these are just symbols of the big men or signs of the heads of the big men in contact with some physical sky.

COSMOLOGY

Stars and Planets

The Dani do not explicitly group the stars into constellations and in fact do not seem to observe them with any care. There may be a number of reasons. First, it is unusual for a Dani to spend much time outdoors at night, except during nights of the full moon, when stars are not visible. Clear nights, when the stars are most impressive, are the coldest nights and just the time when the Dani prefer to stay indoors because of the cold and the ghosts. The one exception is the night after a cremation, when for an hour or two before dawn a few young men hold a watch on a vantage point near the village of the cremation. It might be suspected that at this time of ritual stress, when there is special danger from ghosts, the stars would be especially observed, but this does not seem to be true.

Another explanation lies in the fact that for the Dugum Dani the stars are never necessary for orientation. A seafaring people could hardly be casual about the positions of stars. But the Grand Valley Dani are not only landbound, they live in an area dominated by distinctive mountain ridges, beyond which they rarely go and which therefore present unchanging points of reference. The occasional trips beyond the familiar Grand Valley are along the well-trodden trail to the Central Jalemo, where there is little chance of becoming lost. Of course, the necessity for accurate land or sea navigation is not the only motivation for elaborating constellations. The "aesthetic-intellectual" motive is probably important in many cases. The Dani show strikingly few signs of this sort of activity.

Stars and planets are lumped together. The larger ones are called *wap*, and they are said to be the heads of the most important men (*ab gogtek*, big man) touching the sky. Specific *wap* are attributed to specific important men over whose area the *wap* happens to be at the moment. The inconsistency arising from the constant shift of the stars in the sky is not taken into account.

The majority of the stars and planets are called *husakal*. They have no special significance. A falling star is called *husakal idako* (*idako*, being born) and represents a particular rodent, the *bpake pugale*, falling to the earth, and being born.

THE SUN

The sun is called *mo* and is a woman of terrible aspect: she has long hair, which is uncommon for Dani women; wears a married woman's skirt; carries a spear, and wears men's decorations. In the *edai* dancing after the killing of an enemy, Dani women carry spears and wear men's decorations, but this does not seem to be explicit sun symbolism. The sun is potentially dangerous to living people, but the exact conditions of this danger were not learned. Occasionally the sun is referred to as *ninakoja*, our mother.

During the day the sun moves across the underneath of the sky. At sunset she sits down on a *dabul* (the dried grass on the floor of a house) and retraces her steps above the sky to her home. In the winter months, when the sun is in the south, her home is in the Jalemo; during the summer months at Wadlagu, in the Pass Valley. This seems to be the only recognition of a yearly cycle.

Most questions about the sun were met with professions of ignorance; people said that only Maikmo (and sometimes Maikmo and Alum) of the Wilil-Himan really know about the sun.

The Sun's House. The Pass Valley is about ten kilometers long, running from east to west, where it opens onto the northern Grand Valley.

The Wadlagu compounds lie at the far eastern end of the Pass Valley, and it is here that the sun is said to spend the night between roughly March and September, when it is north of the Dani areas and the Equator. For the viewer in the Grand Valley looking up the Pass Valley, this illusion is strengthened by the fact that the sun does seem to rise at the head of the Pass Valley and traverse its length as it moves westward.

At the end of one of the Wadlagu compounds, where the men's house would normally stand, is the square, bark-roofed house of the sun, called *mo-baka*, or *ninakoja ai*, our mother's house.

Although I visited Wadlagu with Gutelu, I was not allowed to examine the house carefully, and I took photographs only with difficulty. This attitude is very different from the general casualness about all except the most sacred objects in the Dugum, and it suggests the great *wusa*, or power, of the house.

The house is about 2.5 meters high at the roof's ridge. It stands on stilts one meter above the ground. The wall and floor construction is of wood slabs. A small structure hangs from the center of the house, like the dropped hearth pit of a normal woman's house. The entrance is closely boarded. The roof is of two-meter semicircular bark strips, apparently from the trunk of pandanus trees, laid so as to interlock with each other. The entrance faces west, but other buildings in the compound block a clear view in that direction.

Gutelu explained that inside the house were nets, skirts, and other such feminine paraphernalia of the sun. This was confirmed by informants in the Dugum area. However, F. Verheijen, who visited the house after I did, reported (in a personal communication) that when he saw it, it was empty. It was not possible to learn more of the ritual or symbolism surrounding the sun.

The form of the house raises historical problems. At first glance the square bark-roofed house on stilts appears unique in the Grand Valley—Pass Valley context. However, the structures hidden in the forests that hold the sacred bundles symbolic of the dead are often square, of about the same dimensions as the sun's house and, when they are not nestled against a rock overhang, are roofed with bark slabs or grass.

Also, the women's round houses found in every Grand Valley Dani compound are essentially raised houses, although they are raised above the ground only ten or twenty centimeters instead of the meter of the sun's house. Calling the sun's house *ninakoja ai*, our mother's house, evokes the standard woman's house. Thus, the sun's house could be simply a derivation of other, more common Grand Valley house forms. On the other hand, raised square living houses are known from the Kapauku to the west (Pospisil 1963:258); Phillip Temple, a member of Harrer's 1962 expedition, described (in a personal communication) such houses in the Nogolo Basin to the north of the Dani region; they are common in the Star Mountains to the east (Brongersma and Venema 1960); and Snell has described them from the Pesegem Southern Dani (1913:62). So it is possible that the Dani sun's house may represent a general Highlands trait.

THE MOON

Unlike the sun and stars, the moon is hardly a factor in Dani symbolism. There is no single Dani word for moon, but rather different words are used for the different phases in its cycle: *ape goto*, the new crescent; *dut*, the waxing half-moon (and sometimes the full moon); *dugi*, the full moon; *dut oak*, the waning half-moon; *dauok, oak a sik*, the last-quarter crescent.

There seems to be considerable variation in the use of the above terms, and informants would often disagree. I first thought that there must be another factor in moon terminology which would explain this apparent disagreement, but I was not able to discover such a factor. The lack of a generic term for moon might suggest that the Dani perceive each phase as a different entity, but this is definitely not so. Informants agreed that the moon is a single man, and they describe it as aging during the cycle. The new crescent is described as young, or new, and by the last quarter it is old. This was not elaborated, nor an explanation given of how the transition was made from old to young. The moon follows a path similar to the sun, the Dani said, crossing beneath the sky, sitting down in the west, and then returning through or above the sky to the east. In the east it shares the house of the sun. No animal or face is seen in the moon.

There was considerable disagreement over the relationship between the sun and the moon, some people saying that they are brother and sister, others that they are husband and wife.

CLIMATE

The striking thing about the climate of the Grand Valley is its temperateness. Lying at an altitude of 1,600 meters and protected by the central ranges, the valley is not subject to the heat and monsoons of the tropics. But perhaps even more important is the fact that yearly variations of climate are so slight and irregular that they are not perceived by the Dani. In fact, they are not even perceived by outsiders who come from tropical or temperate zones where seasons are an inescapable part of life. In most other world areas, seasonal variations are culturally influential, for they effect growing seasons and availability of different foodstuffs, and they demand changes of attire and shelter. In short, they demand regular alterations in behavior through a yearly cycle. And this effect is seen not just in subsistence activities but also in social and religious activities. It is normal for a ritual cycle to be closely tied to the subsistence cycle. What is notable about the Grand Valley is the lack of both yearly subsistence cycle and yearly ritual cycle. The concept of the year has no cognitive reality for the Dani at all. Thus, the Grand Valley of the Balim is a significant exception to Oliver's general statement (1964:6) that all cultures recognize seasons.

RAIN

Brookfield states that the Grand Valley "has only a short season of heavy rain and cloud, and evaporation is high during the rest of the year" (1964:36). The rainfall charts (Diagrams 7.1, 7.2) were compiled from official data collected at Wamena, the government station ten kilometers south of the Dugum Neighborhood. The charts indicate a peak of 240–350 millimeters per month around February and March, falling off during the rest of the year to around 100–200 millimeters of rain per month. Yearly rainfall is remarkably steady, with a mean of around 2082 millimeters (78.5 inches) per year. Rainy days (with 0.6 millimeters or more of rain) occur about 65 per cent of the year, and no month during the three-year period measured has less than eleven rainy days.

On the chart of monthly rainfall (Diagram 7.1), the yearly cycle is clear, and the erratic differences from year to year is also well shown. The number of rainy days per month (Diagram 7.2) for the same period shows even more erraticism. A more complete scientific statement about the effect of rain on soil would demand data on wind, sun, and evaporation, which are not available. But one can say that the seasonal variation so apparent in measured rainfall is not perceived by the Dani. In fact, even the government and missionary personnel in the Grand Valley, all of whom came from regions with marked seasonal variation and who were accustomed to think in terms of seasons, did not perceive a seasonal variation in the Grand Valley.

Even though there is no anticipation of wet or dry periods to effect behavior, rainfall itself of course does effect what the Dani do. Rainy days are likely to be

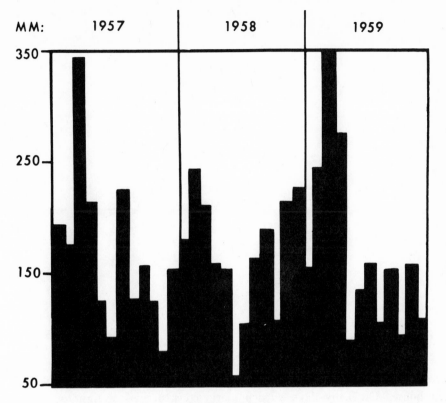

DIAGRAM 7.1

MONTHLY RAINFALL IN MILLIMETERS AT WAMENA, 1957–1959

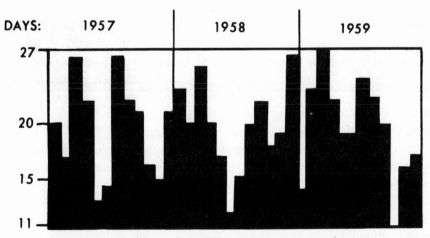

DIAGRAM 7.2

DAYS PER MONTH OF RAIN AT WAMENA, 1957–1959

TABLE 7.1
RAINFALL IN MILLIMETERS PER YEAR MEASURED AT WAMENA

1957	2,002
1958	2,062
1959	2,030
1960	2,233
1961	2,139
mean	2,082

TABLE 7.2
RAINY DAYS [1] PER YEAR MEASURED AT WAMENA

1957	233
1958	237
1959	234
1960	242
1961	241
mean	237.4 (or 65 per cent of the year)

1. 0.6 millimeters rain or more.

overcast and chilly, and the Dani are not likely to go far from the warmth of their houses. On many days, garden work, construction, or fighting is done in the warm period between the rising of the morning mists, by eight or nine o'clock, and the closing in of the midafternoon rain.

One informant said that when the sun was in the north (March to September) the weather was dry, and when she was in the south (September to March) the weather was wet. In fact, it *is* about March that the rain drops back to normal. If this was a recognition of seasons, it was not otherwise apparent in the behavior.

Cause of Rain. Rain is attributed to ghosts who come in the clouds and splash water with the insteps of their feet, the way boys do in play. These ghosts are the same ghosts of local people who are also said to stay in the nearby forests.

There is a special term for morning rain, *o sit.* Rain at other times of the day or night is called *o mio.* Urine is called *a mio,* but there is no explicit symbolic connection between rain and urine. There are also specific terms for rain coming from different directions. Most of the rain comes from the east, over the mountain wall, and is called *dliligen;* rain from the southwest, down-valley, is called *wam aik* (literally, pig tusk); and rain from the northwest, up-valley, is called *gog mio* (literally, great rain).

Rain Magic. When rain interrupts a cremation or other ceremony, an important man, usually the man in charge of the ceremony, stands up and with his arms wrapped around his neck in the typical posture reaction to cold, shouts or mumbles at the ghosts: "You go away, you don't come here, we are burning your relative, you go away . . ."

The effect of extremes of rainfall on sweet potato crops is mitigated by the garden ditches, which drain as well as irrigate. However, extended rainy or dry spells can cause crises by threatening to rot or parch the tubers. At such times the Dani perform rituals to encourage or discourage the rain.

TEMPERATURE AND HUMIDITY

Temperature and humidity as measured at Wamena are shown in Tables 7.3 and 7.4. The mean range of temperature is from 26° C (78.8° F) to about 15° C (59° F); the absolute range is from 29.5° C (85° F) to 6° C (42° F). Thus, during the day it is rarely too hot to work comfortably, and at night by generally staying indoors the Dani do not suffer from cold.

OTHER NATURAL EVENTS

Earthquakes strong enough to be noticed occur perhaps once a month; sometimes they have the force to shake houses. Called *dlugul*, earthquakes are said to be frequent during rainy periods, although they do not have any explicit symbolic association with rain or sun. Earthquakes are certainly not considered to be alarming, and they are said to be beneficial to the sweet potatoes and to be caused by the moving of certain sacred objects (*sugan*, or *ganekhe*) in distant areas. There was considerable disagreement over whose objects these were, and even in what direction they were. Most people thought that they were up-valley, to the west. One informant said that the sacred objects were passed from father to son.

The rainbow is called *wato baik* and is considered to be the reflection of a snake. The body itself is apparently nonexistent. There is no particular association between the rainbow and rain.

Thunderstorms often pass across the neighborhood. The thunder is called *pokot ane* (literally, sky noise or voice) or *dele pele*. Lightning is called *ojabok* and is considered simply an accompaniment of rain and thunderstorms.

Heat lightning is called *dokagup* or *ab amok* (literally, man grease, fluid, or in this case, blood, which is usually *mep*). It is considered to be the blood of recently killed men rising into the sky. In fact, where blood has been spilled on the ground by a dead or dying man the grass is burned repeatedly to remove

TABLE 7.3
MEAN TEMPERATURE (CENTIGRADE) AT WAMENA

	6:30 A.M.	12:30 P.M.	6:30 P.M.	Mean Max.	Mean Min.	Abs. Max.	Min.
1960	15.1	23.8	19.1	25.9	14.6	29.2	9.2
1959	15.0	24.0	19.4	25.0	14.7	29.5	9.4
1958	15.4	24.1	19.6	26.0	14.9	29.2	7.3
1957	14.9	24.1	19.3	25.9	14.5	29.1	6.0

TABLE 7.4
MEAN RELATIVE HUMIDITY AT WAMENA

	6:30 A.M.	12:30 P.M.	6:30 P.M.
1960	98%	61%	83%
1959	97%	59%	79%
1958	97%	61%	81%
1957	98%	60%	82%

the traces of the blood and to cleanse the area. Heat lightning represents the smoke from such burning in distant areas.

FLORA

According to the observations made by Brass in the Grand Valley during the visit of the Archbold Expedition of 1938–1939, the flora of the Grand Valley of the Balim represents several different vegetation zones.

Scattered surviving examples suggest that rain-forest flora, spreading up from the coastal lowlands, once was well established on the lowest places of the Grand Valley floor and "probably reached several hundred meters higher in branch valleys and ravines" (Archbold, Rand, and Brass 1942:281).

The midmountain forest, dominated by oak, Castanopsis, and Engelhardia, with some of the great coniferous araucaria, was probably the most important on the higher portions of the Grand Valley floor (Archbold, Rand, and Brass 1942:282). Brass remarks that "in the mountains of New Guinea, man follows the oaks" (1941a:303).

Savanna grasses, which are especially characteristic of lowland treeless areas with marked wet and dry seasons, have forced their way into the seasonless Grand Valley, where they have taken over abandoned garden areas and burned-off slopes (Brass 1941a:338).

The beech forest zone, with moss-laden beech and pandanus, begins above the rain forest and midmountain forest zones, at about the 2,000-meter level, which is the lower limit of the midafternoon clouds in the Grand Valley (Brass 1941a:337).

The subalpine forest zone, which is confined to about 3,000–4,000 meters (Archbold, Rand, and Brass 1942:283), is represented in the lower flanking slopes of the Grand Valley floor by scattered rhododendrons and tree ferns.

The Dugum Neighborhood lies partly on the 1,600-meter-high floor of the Grand Valley and extends up the flanking slopes. One compound lies above the face (Matthiessen's "Mountain Wall" [1962]), at the edge of the mossy beech forest, and the people of the Dugum make frequent trips into this zone for lumber, pandanus fruit, and fiber plants. The lower part of the neighborhood is dominated by secondary growth of the midmountain forest type, and the valley floor itself, by sweet potato gardens and savanna grasses.

Most of the flora is useful to the Dani. Wood is used for tools, weapons, houses, and fire; grass for thatching; vines for lashing; and some shrubs for fiber. The pressure of the Grand Valley population has resulted in the virtual disappearance of the best woods and fiber plants from the valley floor and even from the flanking hills. Now the finest spear wood and the best fibers must be imported from the Jalemo.

The only restriction against the use of flora is that against burning araucaria wood. But the bark is used for ornaments and the seeds of the cone for games. Brass mentions that in the southern Grand Valley, "some species" (which he does not name) seem to be protected by taboo (1941a:281). This did not seem to be the case in the Dugum Neighborhood.

However, the one grove of araucaria and the few trees of this type do have some special supernatural power (*wusa*), and when one great old dead araucaria trunk fell, it was the subject of special ritual.

Dani Classification of Flora

A generic term *oga* is sometimes used for all wild flora, and *oga-ma*, the *oga*-place, is the term for forest or woods. The Dani have at least 334 names for specific kinds of plants. By the time a boy is ten years old he has learned the names of most of the plants around him. Apparently the children learn in a casual way by accompanying older people on their frequent trips into the forest. Since so many of the material objects of Dani culture come from the forest, this expertise is not surprising.

In addition to the specific names for plants, there are generic names for some groups of plants: *o*, trees and many woody shrubs; *etesiga*, grasses; *we*, orchids, whose inner brightly colored fiber is used for decorating string goods and arrow points; *sip*, mosses; *duk*, mushrooms. Some eighteen kinds of mushrooms are known and eaten casually. Three of these are *wusa*, or taboo, and not to be eaten because of supernatural sanction. The story is told of one boy who ate a *wusa duk* and died, vomiting blood, so it seems likely that these three kinds may in fact be poisonous.

Other plants are just given their specific names, or occasionally lumped as *oga*.

Trees, in the category *o*, may be classed in one of two groups on the basis of their value for construction purposes and the ease with which they can be split. The word for difficulty in splitting is *abum*, and the trees described as *o abum wejak* (with much *abum*) are such trees as araucaria and Casuarina. Trees described as *o abum dlek* (no *abum*) are oak, myrtle, laurel, and soapberry.

FAUNA

New Guinea, lying to the east of the Wallace Line, was cut off from the mainland of Asia before the development of placental mammals and, like Australia, abounds in the more primitive marsupial forms of mammal life. The only pre-European placental mammals are man, his dogs and pigs, bats and flying foxes, and small rodents which came with man or found their way across the sea.

Larger marsupials such as the tree kangaroo and the bandicoot have long since been hunted out of the Grand Valley floor, even as the forests which once sheltered them have been chopped down for lumber and garden land. Some of the larger marsupials, whose fur is prized by the Dani for headpieces, live in the forests flanking the Grand Valley, but they are found only by the most determined hunters.

Small rodents are common in the fields and gardens and compounds, but they are rarely hunted except for use in ceremonies. The thumping of the wings of the great flying foxes coming to eat bananas at the compounds is heard nightly.

The Grand Valley is alive with birds: mountain birds, savanna birds, a few soaring birds of prey; two kinds of herons, a large gray-blue one called the white-faced heron, and a white heron; and, on the streams, ducks and the zoologically atavistic cormorant. However, the ground-running cassowary and the cockatoo no longer live in the Grand Valley, and only once in twenty-six months did I see a bird-of-paradise there. (For a fuller account of the birds of the Grand Valley, see Matthiessen 1963; Archbold, Rand, and Brass 1942; and Ripley 1964.) Cassowary, cockatoo, and birds-of-paradise are plentiful in the Jalemo, the thinly populated valley system northeast of the Grand Valley, from whence their feathers are imported.

Birds play a major role in Dani life. The men wear a wide variety of ornaments made from the feathers of both local and Jalemo birds. The birds figure prominently in Dani ceremonies and mythology, much of which is based on the identification of man with bird. (Birds serve only incidentally for food.)

There are a variety of other creatures in the Grand Valley. Snakes are rare, but there are two sorts of nonpoisonous ones. The Dani do not hesitate to roast and eat them. The only amphibians are small frogs which generally live in the garden ditches and are ignored by the Dani. Insect life is only slightly annoying. House flies swarm around any occupied area. Mosquitoes are small, their bite does not annoy the Dani, and in the early 1960's they did not yet carry malaria. Fleas live in the thick matted hair of the Dani, and much time is spent searching friends' heads for the creatures. It is not clear just how fleas are passed from head to head. I spent countless hours awake and asleep in Dani houses without acquiring a flea population of my own.

A few insects are eaten, but only casually. Sometimes rotting logs are chopped apart for wood grubs, which are roasted and eaten. The large green stinkbug, common in the *pabi* trees which form secondary growth on fallow gardens, is often eaten by children, who wrap it in leaves and munch on it, apparently enjoying the heavy odor that hangs about them for hours afterwards. The hive and larvae of a small native bee is also eaten.

Bee wax is imported from the Jalemo and used to give a fine finish to spears. Large pieces of material, ten or twenty centimeters in diameter, said to be from a cocoon, are also imported from the Jalemo and used to wrap valuables.

Smaller cocoon sacks, three to four centimeters long, are occasionally used to store flint flakes. The flat, attenuated cocoon of the case moth, which has often incorporated small twig spikes and thus looks like the tail of some spiny anteater, is found in the local forests and used extensively by men as neck or penis gourd ornaments. It is supposed to have the magical quality of attracting women.

A large spider, called *muligak*, is almost a third domestic animal of the Dani, along with the pig and the dog. These spiders are collected in the forest and brought to the compounds, where they construct elaborate webs on frames. The webs, matted into fabric, are used for men's caps and for magical strips suspended from the throat.

Fish are totally absent from the Balim and its tributaries. In the streams of the Dugum Neighborhood there are small crayfish, rarely more than three or four centimeters long, but they are rarely caught. On the Balim, where they grow to ten or fifteen centimeters long and contain considerable flesh, the Dani hunt them with special traps.

The Dani divide the wild fauna into three categories, within which the different types are named:

(1) *due:* primarily birds, but also furred flying creatures, bats and flying foxes. At least seventy-one different types are named. Most of these are local birds. A few are known only from their feathers, which are imported from the Jalemo.

(2) *bpake:* nonflying furred creatures (marsupials and rodents). At least thirty-two different types of these are named.

(3) *wato:* insects, reptiles, and amphibians. At least sixty-seven different types are named.

Both generic and specific names are used, as, for example, *due gut* (*gut*, the white heron).

Pigs, dogs, human beings, and the recently introduced cats are not included in any of these categories.

MINERALS

There are two broad categories of local rock: *hegit*, common field rock, which includes limestones and sandstones; and *moli*, flint. There are also stones not found locally but imported as finished objects. The names for these objects refer in part to the stone type and in part to the finished object. The chief categories of these objects are: *jaka*, adze, axe, and chisel blades; *je*, large slaty exchange stones; *habo*, sacred stones apparently of the same rock as *je*.

Other mineral substances are white sand, mud, and red clays used for coloring.

8

THE BODY

Pᴴʏꜱɪᴄᴀʟ anthropological measurements of the Dugum Dani were not made, and there is only scanty information on other Dani groups. Van den Broek, using materials from the 1909 Lorentz Expedition, attempted a physical anthropological description of the people of the Oroh Valley (1913a), called Pesegem, Morup, and Lokmere, all of whom are probably Southern Dani. Van den Broek also studied the skeleton of a Papuan who was killed in an attack on the Lorentz base camp. At the time it was thought that this man was a Pesegem, but Franssen Herderschee, who visited the area four years later, reported that he was probably of the Util group (1913b:14). It is not known if the Util are also Dani.

Here we will consider the physical aspects of the Dani in a general way and the cultural meaning of the body, its forms, and its normal and pathological states. For a general impression of Dani features and physique, the accompanying photographs are more useful than any description.

BODY SHAPE

Children usually have protruding stomachs. This characteristic seems to be in part because of the high starch in the predominantly sweet potato diet and the fact that when pork is eaten, children get less pig meat than adults. Another reason for prominence of the stomach is Dani posture: Typically the lumbar region is arched forward and the pelvis is rocked down and back.

Women range from slender and flat-stomached to heavy-set with protruding stomachs. Youths and young men are well muscled, but by middle age they tend to become flabby. There is a remarkable absence of body fat on all but the older Dani. The Dani recognize two body types: *bunu*, thick, which refers to the fat-bellied children and to mesomorphic adults; and *butuk*, thin, which refers to slender, ectomorphic adults.

The height of adult males ranges from about 4 feet 10 inches (149 Centimeters) to about 5 feet 10½ inches. (179 Centimeters). The average is probably between 5 feet 2 inches and 5 feet 4 inches. Because of their slim, muscular bodies, many of the men seem on first impression to be considerably taller. Tall people are called *uwan*, short people *bpetokat*. (The word for important man, which involves a symbolic size, is *gog*, the general term for big, large; but it is not a term which is used in connection with physical types.) Physical height seems to be unimportant to the Dani. Although I am 193 Centimeters (6 feet 4 inches tall, no Dani ever indicated that he found my size unusual or noteworthy. Perhaps more significant, one of the Dutch patrol officers was about two meters (6 feet 6 inches) tall; to distinguish him from other patrol officers the Dani never referred to his height but invariably to his name, his hair color, or his mustache.

Nose shape varies from relatively flat to high. Flatter noses seem to be preferred in the sense that the higher ones are considered somewhat comical.

SKIN COLOR

The Dani's skin is basically brown, with considerable range from light to dark shades. Skin color, especially of males, is darkened by liberal and frequent application of pig grease mixed with ashes. Albinism occurs among the Grand Valley Dani, although no albinos lived or were seen in the confederation area during my study. The Dugum Dani are aware of albinism and know that albinos are bothered by sunburn and glare. They have no explanation for albinism, saying that it is just *welegat*, it just occurs. Although it is obviously inconvenient, there seems to be no strong positive or negative value attached to albinism.

The Dani refer to skin color with the basic color terms, *modla*, light, and *mili*, dark. These terms are used to express contrast in several situations: *modla* may refer to a man at the light-skinned end of the normal range; it may refer to an albino in contrast to a normal Dani; recently it has also come to be used for people at the light-skinned end of the range of *tuans*—people who wear clothes—those of predominantly European, Indonesian, or Chinese descent.

Value may be placed by the Dani on different skin shades. A few missionairies claim that the lighter-skinned Dani, particularly the women, are especially esteemed. I found no sign of this. There seems to be no particular standard of beauty for women at all. Among men there is also no particularly noticeable trend. The most important man in the alliance, Gutelu, is light-skinned. His name apparently refers to this: *gut*, the white heron; *elu*, knowing; thus, the wise white heron. But other important men of the alliance are quite dark-skinned. The effect of the male cosmetic of pig grease mixed with charcoal is to darken the face and body. This might indicate, if anything, preference for darker skin. However, I could find no explicit evidence one way or the other.

HAIR

Dani hair is naturally curly, and on some of the younger children it even curls into tight whorls, with bare scalp showing between the whorls. The hair of younger children is often reddish, a sign of protein deficiency. However, ash-

PLATE 36. Asikhanedlek, a young married man, his face and hair smeared with ash-blackened pig grease.

PLATE 37. An old man.

PLATE 38. A young married woman.

PLATE 39. Aneakhe, the old mother of Um'ue and Jege Asuk.

blackened pig grease which is rubbed into the hair of Dani of all ages usually obscures any traces of the red.

HANDEDNESS

The incidence of left-handedness seems to be high. Of the 148 males in the Dugum Neighborhood, some half-dozen were observed to be left-handed. It is more difficult to determine female handedness, since it would tend to be effected by the ritual chopping off of the fingers of young girls.

The general term for the right hand is *inigi ebe*, literally main hand; for the left hand *hatobpak*. However, when specifically referring to the left hand of the left-handed person, it is called *inigi ebe* and the right hand is called *hatobpak*.

There is no pressure to make a child right-handed and no stigma attached to to a left-handed person. There are no acts that must or should be performed with one hand or the other, and no artifacts that are specifically made to be used by one hand rather than the other. Unlike many cultures, the Dani have no cosmological or other symbolism based on the opposition of right and left.

KNOWLEDGE OF REPRODUCTION

I was not very successful in eliciting information about sex, even from Dani male informants. However, it appears that there is a fairly accurate idea that the male sperm, released during copulation, is responsible for conception. It was not possible to determine exactly what role the Dani attribute to the father and the mother in conception. Although no distinction is made in kinship terminology between father, father's brother, and so on, or between mother, mother's sister, and in fact relatively little behavioral distinction exists, there is no confusion as to a person's biological father and mother. To distinguish the biological father from other men called *opase*, one can use the term *opase ampusu bpin*, this is, the *opase* who put in the semen.

When I was inquiring about premarital sexual intercourse, several informants insisted that it was very common. When I asked if any unmarried girls had had babies, they replied no, that conception required a great deal of sexual intercourse and these premarital affairs were too brief for that. On the basis of my own observations, I doubt that there is much premarital intercourse, but the Dani's replies may indicate something of the Dani knowledge of reproduction.

HEALTH, SICKNESS, AND DEATH

To an observer untrained in medical observation, the Dani seem surprisingly healthy, strong, and active despite their lack of internal medicines and their unbalanced diet, heavy in starch and light in protein. To some extent this health may be due to the favorable location of the Grand Valley. It lies 4° south of the Equator but more than 1,600 meters above sea level, and the climate is more temperate than tropical. The anopheles mosquito does live in the Grand Valley, but apparently the cold nights inhibit malaria from invading the area. By 1968, however, malaria was entering the Grand Valley, and there is danger that soon it will be a major Dani disease. The only serious endemic disease that is obvious is framboesia, or yaws, a spirochete skin ulcer that particularly infects children and occasionally their mothers. In rare cases, advanced states of yaws have caused serious deformations, such as loss of feet or nose. But in most cases the ulcers disappear by the time an individual is about ten, leaving no external trace.

Occasionally epidemics sweep the Dani area. An example was the influenza epidemic of early 1962, which apparently started in the vicinity of the Ilaka mission posts and, after causing many deaths in the Western Dani area, was brought over the high plateau trade route, entering the Grand Valley from the south and sweeping up the Grand Valley. It passed through the Dugum Neighborhood, where three or four people died from it.

ABNORMALITIES

Physical. The most common physical deformities are those of the feet and legs. Several Dani have badly bowed tibia, and a few have splayed toes or club feet. One woman has no feet and shuffles along on her knees; another has only one foot and limps with a crutch. The Dani attribute both of cases to severe yaws. One man has a shriveled arm. One woman is deaf and dumb. Several men and boys are blind in one eye, apparently as a result of mock or real battle. Many Dani have scars from burns suffered when as children they rolled into the open hearths.

A few men have peculiar lateral scars across their upper sternums (Plate 14). Informants insisted that these were ordinary burn scars or arrow wounds. Le Roux states that scarification has never been reported from the Highland Papuans of West New Guinea (1948:118). However, there is some faint suggestion of ritual scarification among the Swart Valley Western Dani (Denise O'Brien, in a personal communication). And since in the Grand Valley the scars do seem to be more common on important men, I suspect that they may *not* be accidental.

There is no indication of infanticide. However, the crippling of one young boy is attributed to an attempted abortion. With the exception of the two foot-less women, all those with deformities lead normal social lives, and their activities are limited only by the physical limitations imposed by their deformities. For example, Alheto, who limps badly, is an outstanding warrior, as is the short, bandy-legged Jege Asuk; Bumega, with the shriveled arm, is an active and important man.

The two badly crippled women, each about thirty to thirty-five years of age, both still wear girl's skirts are called *hodlak* (girl, unmarried woman) rather than *he* (married woman), and it is said that no one wants to marry them, apparently on aesthetic grounds. On the other hand, the deaf and dumb woman is married and has a normal baby. However, she is the only married woman with all her fingers intact.

Seizure. Twice I observed a patterned type of individual seizure called *sinuknuk* or *hunuk balin*. The seizure is said to be caused by the dislodgement of the individual's *edai-egen*, or soul matter. Apparently seizures are unpredictable, and informants claimed that any adult is subject to them.

One time a young man ran through several compounds, threatening people with his spear, shouting, shaking his hair, and eventually loosing his penis gourd. After an hour or so he was caught by friends who took him, struggling, into a men's house, held him down, warmed his extremities at the fire, and blew on his chest and head to restore his *edai-egen*. After another hour he was quiet, and by the next day he was quite normal, and the people were no longer discussing the incident.

In another instance, an older woman came from outside the Neighborhood as a visitor during a funeral. She was well known for having seizures, and as she stormed through fallow gardens outside the funeral compound, boys and girls followed her, shouting, laughing, and falling back in mock alarm when she threatened them with a bow and arrow. Eventually she calmed down of her own accord and came into the compound. Women brought her steamed sweet potatoes which she broke, spit into, and handed back to be fed to pigs to make them grow; during this last, she kept her arms deeply crossed.

Similar but culturally much more significant seizures have been reported from elsewhere in the New Guinea Highlands; and even among the closely related people of the Southern Jalemo, seizures are much more common than in the Grand Valley (cf. Koch 1968b).

Edai-egen CONCEPT

Western civilization considers the relative health or relative sickness of an individual in terms of three distinct but interrelated entities, the body, the soul, and the spirit. Men have differed over the relative importance and degree of interrelatedness of these entities, but as basic concepts they have persisted. The Dugum Dani conceptualize health and sickness in terms of *edai-egen*, which is more psychical than physical. Minor and sometimes relatively major physical wounds or ailments are practically ignored until they threaten an individual's *edai-egen*.

The strength of an individual lies in his *edai-egen*, and the state of his physical and psychical health is indicated by the state of his *edai-egen*.

In one sense, the *edai-egen* is an actual physical organ, the heart. Although the Dani have little knowledge of internal human anatomy, they do know the innards of pigs in detail, consider that human organs are analogous to those of pigs, and point out the pig heart as the pig's *edai-egen*. But in humans the *edai-egen* has the broader implications of soul, seat of the personality, spirit. The term may be literally translated as "seed of singing." The *edai* is a ceremony, the first day of singing and dancing after killing an enemy that announces the death of the enemy to the ghosts. *Edai* is also the special song sung at this ceremony. *Egen* is used in various contexts to mean seed, pith, core, egg, or essence.

When the individual is in a physically and emotionally normal, healthy state, his *edai-egen* is about the size of his fist and is situated forward in the body just under the base of the sternum, where it may be seen pulsing. But when a person is seriously ill or wounded, or is mourning for a dead relative, the *edai-egen* becomes small and slips back toward the vertebral column. In this condition the *edai-egen* is described as *wejak*, bad, or *hamalukat*, small. Frequently the words are accompanied by the gesture of fist held near base of sternum, rotated down and toward the sternum.

The unfavorable condition of the *edai-egen* is caused by the ghosts, and at the same time the individual is particularly vulnerable to further damage from the ghosts. The individual is in a weakened state, he is out of joint with the world.

There is an analogy between the sick and the very young that is not explicitly elaborated by the Dani. When a child is born, he has no *edai-egen*. During the first two years the *edai-egen* appears near the backbone, grows in size, and moves forward to its normal position at the sternum. The development of the *edai-egen* parallels the development of rational speech, and by the time a child is three or four years old he has a full *edai-egen*, can take part in conversations, and is ready to be initiated at the next *ebe akho* ceremony.

In addition to *edai-egen*, the term *akotakun* is used to refer to some soul-like entity. The *akotakun* may be the same as the *edai-egen*, but it is probably a separate entity. There is some suggestion that when a person dies the *akotakun* becomes the *mogat*, or ghost, and leaves the body. Under stress the *edai-egen* diminishes and retreats into the body while the *akotakun* is in danger of flying out of the body. People sometimes cry, "*Hakotakma!*" (*h-*, your; *akotakun*; *-ma*, place of), "Your *akotakun* stay in place!" to a person who falls on a path.

It must be stressed throughout this discussion of the Dani that most of this conceptualization is done with anthropological license. The Dani do not use explicit concepts of health, or the state of normal, well-being, such as those which permeate casual American conversation: "How are you?" "Fine, thank you, how are you?" Yet, the abnormal physical and mental states of sickness, wounds, grieving, or the *sinuknuk* seizure are noted by the Dani. Both cause and effect of all such abnormal states are described in the same terms, the action of the ghosts on the *edai-egen*. Further, although the Dani have no sophisticated conceptualization of healing, various steps are taken to counter sickness, which will be described below.

Causes of Sickness

Illness and death are always considered to be more or less directly caused by ghosts, but the nature of the ghost's action may take several forms.

When a person is killed by enemy spears or arrows, his wounds are recognized the immediate cause of death; but the Dani feel that the wounds are possible only because an enemy ghost has already "killed" the person with ghostly weapons (p. 113). In some cases, illness or death is considered to be the sanction taken by ghosts because the person has knowingly or unknowingly violated a *wusa* restriction. In other instances, informants gave no particular reason for illness or death but said that it was due to ghosts who for some unknown reason were unhappy with the people.

Black Magic. In many instances illness or death was attributed to black magic perpetrated by persons who, with special techniques and objects, induced the ghosts to attack the subject.

There are three important types of black magic. The black magic most commonly mentioned by informants is *imak*, which is administered by an *imak he*, or *imak* woman. Informants described the *imak he*'s behavior with a jabbing motion of their forefinger, representing an object which she carries in her *imak su*, or *imak* net. Jabbing this object toward her victim, she directs a ghost in the form of a particular rat-like animal (some say *bpake pugale*, others say it is a *bpake widlo*) to enter the body of the victim through the testicles or vulva and nibble at the victim's *edai-egen*, or soul matter, causing death.

A second form of black magic is *guakap*, a white powder used by men to the southeast of the Dugum Neighborhood. They sprinkle this powder into a cigarette or on sweet potato, and when the victim smokes or eats, his stomach swells and he dies. People are warned, when traveling to other areas, not to take food or tobacco from strangers for fear of *guakap*. However, when I made trips beyond the Dugum Neighborhood, none of my companions hesitated to eat sweet potato offered by strangers.

Another danger which resembles black magic is *dugun su*, which resides in an object kept in a net (*su*) with the sacred objects of a man on the Balim River. This object apparently works by itself, coming to a sleeping person, causing sickness, and then returning to its place. A woman in the Dugum Neighborhood, recently come from the Balim, decided that she had been attacked by this *dugun su* and was cured by another woman in the Neighborhood, also originally from the Balim and a daughter of the owner of the *dugun su*.

A minor sort of black magic is the *pipon*, a piece of grass laid across a path by a women. A person must step over the grass, for if he touches it he gets foot pains. On paths leading south from the Dugum Neighborhood such grass was often encountered, and my companions always warned me of it.

The center of the practice of black magic are invariably said to be in regions distant from the Dugum. The *imak* is practiced by the Dloko-Mabel, to the northwest; *guakap* by men in the Solimo, to the southeast; and *dugun su* is practiced on the Balim River. This suggests the classic projection of aggression by accusing foreigners of black magic. However, in 1968, when I questioned the Dloko-Mabel around Jibiga about *imak*, they quite openly admitted, even to the point of bragging, that indeed *imak* was a Dloko-Mabel speciality. It is not a matter of one area accusing others of practicing withcraft; there seems to be general agreement about which areas do and which do not. When informants in the Dugum Neighborhood were asked about magic, they invariably added that two local women, one living in Wubakaima, in the Dugum Neighborhood, and the other in Dagulobok, just outside the Dugum Neighborhood, were practitioners of *imak*. This was said in a completely matter-of-fact manner. There was no apparent fear of or hostility toward these witches, and little interest or concern in what they may have been doing. In several cases, when asked about specific deaths, informants attributed them to one or the other of these witches. A woman said that one of the witches had caused the death of a daughter of her husband. The utter calmness of the Dugum Dani in the face of widely accepted witchcraft in their midst contrasts vividly—and inexplicably—with the behavior of the Western Dani. Denise O'Brien reports (in a personal communication) that in the Konda Valley the people kill accused witches by various violent means, and Ploeg, writing about the Bokondini area, also stresses the importance of sorcery, specifically in contrast to the Grand Valley situation (1966:268).

The only action taken by the Dugum Dani against black magic is defensive. Black magic is especially powerful at night, and then the doors of the compound entrance and of the houses are closed, partly for privacy, but also, the Dani say, to prevent the witches or their ghostly assistants to enter.

CONCEPT OF DEATH

During life the vital essence of the individual is his *edai-egen*, whose state fluctuates as the individual's health fluctuates. After death the essence is the *mogat*, the ghost, which is basically malevolent and must be driven, coerced, persuaded, and induced to leave the corpse, the compound, and the general area, and to stay in the forest.

The precise details of the transition from life to death, or of the relationship between a person's *edai-egen* and his *mogat*, are not of great concern to the Dani. It appears that in some cases, when a person is critically ill or perhaps barely conscious, those around him consider that his *edai-egen* has gone and that he is in fact dead. Thus, he may be dead culturally some time before his physiological death. Two cases were observed that suggest this.

Uaklilu, a man of about thirty-eight, slowly wasted away over a period of several months from the infection of an arrow tip lodged deep in his groin. During this period, as he became more immobile, he was increasingly ignored. Some food and water was brought to him, but his hair and nails were allowed to grow long and unkempt. When he finally died, it was probably as much from neglect as from the infection.

A few weeks before his death I attempted to treat him with penicillin, but it had no effect. Then a government doctor who happened to be in the area looked at him and said that he could be cured if he was carried to the hospital in

Wamena, a few hours' walk away. At the last moment his kinsmen refused to let him go, saying that he would surely die and that it was important he be given a proper funeral at home. My arguments were ignored, and he did in fact die a few days later.

A robustly healthy woman, Jihuti, about twenty, was stricken by influenza in the epedemic of 1962. She then contracted pneumonia and died. During her last day or two, neither food nor water was brought to her because her *edai-egen* was so small. Again, it seems likely that a cultural death, or premature cultural acceptance of death, did in fact speed or even cause biological death.

Immediate causes of death are attributed to the observable wound, or sickness, or just old age. But when pushed for further explanation, people will say that the ghosts are responsible. The immediate causes so weaken the *edai-egen* that ghosts may successfully attack and kill the person.

INCIDENCE OF DEATH

Death rates can be roughly estimated on the basis of twenty-six months' observation of about 350 people. I feel fairly confident that I was aware of the deaths which took place in the compounds of the Dugum Neighborhood during the time that I lived there, but it is quite possible that some births or deaths of infants may have escaped my attention.

During this twenty-six-month period nineteen deaths were noted: 6 were infants about six months to two years of age; 5 were people over sixty, old or even senile; 4 were adults of twenty, thirty, thirty-five, and fifty years of age; 3 were boys or youths of eight, fifteen, and sixteen killed in warfare; 1 was a thirty-eight-year-old man who died of a wound received several months earlier.

The ages at death are of course only crude estimates. The war deaths occurred over only five months of the period, since in September 1961 the government successfully pacified the area. In the thirty-two months from April 1961 to December 1963 about eighteen births occurred in the Dugum Neighborhood; no mothers or children died at birth, but three of the eighteen infants, or about 16.7 per cent, died before they reached the age of two. Of the eight people who died between infancy and old age, four died as a result of war, and two in the influenza epidemic of May 1962.

The death rate of warfare is difficult to estimate. Certainly the population is too small and the time involved too short to produce much of a valid figure. Also, the 350 people of the Dugum Neighborhood live in a particularly vulnerable position, close to the enemy. Two of the war deaths were caused by enemy raids into the Neighborhood. Other neighborhoods not so immediately engaged in the war suffered less loss; during the five months of wartime observation in 1961, no other war deaths occurred in the entire Wilihiman-Walalua Confederation, and there was only one death in the contiguous friendly Gosi-Alua Confederation. Assuming the combined population of the two confederations to be about 2,000, four of the 2,000 were killed in five months of ritual war. This gives a figure for ritual war deaths of .48 per cent per year, which may serve as a rough and slightly spurious estimate of war deaths. (This is comparable to Bromley's estimate of 1 per cent per year for war deaths in the southern Grand Valley [1962:23]). However, if one also computes the deaths during the attack of June 4, 1966, when about 125 (or 6.25 per cent) of 2,000 people in three confederations were killed in one morning, the picture is very different.

An attempt to estimate war mortality—that is, deaths resulting from either raids or battles—was also made on the basis of genealogical data gathered in 1961–1963. The genealogies could be pushed back for one or two deceased generations, and when they were recorded, the causes of death were noted. Of 350 deceased males, 100, or 28.5 per cent, were reported to have been killed in war; of 201 deceased females, five, or 2.4 per cent, were reported to have been killed in war.

Since one can safely assume a bias toward remembering people who were killed and forgetting those who died natural deaths, especially infants, these figures are certainly inflated in favor of war deaths. But the ratio of male to female war deaths is probably fairly accurate.

TREATMENT OF ILLNESS

There are three main sorts of actions that can be taken to restore health of the individual, if he is not to die. First, he must be hidden from the ghosts, at least in the sense that his presence, or his being, is muted so as not to draw the attentions of the ghosts. Also, he is strengthened by food, especially pig meat, and by various medical and magical treatments of the body. And finally, the ghosts, who have some particular if unknown reason for attacking the individual, are placated with a ceremony.

CONCEALMENT

When an individual's *edai-egen* is weak, he is particularly vulnerable to the ghosts. The Dani use several strategems to conceal the person from ghosts. A man or boy who is sick or wounded will often wear a large woman's carrying net draped loosely over his head. This is also done when traveling into strange territory and is more of a modest muting of the personality than any real attempt to hide. Perhaps the sick woman's action of putting away her elaborate decorated skirt for a plain one may be interpreted as the same sort of modesty.

A sick person is generally ignored by those around him. There is an almost studied turning away from him, and he gets no special attention or sympathy. In cases of severe sickness or wounds, the friends and relatives of a man may come for an hour or more to sit in the men's house with him, implicitly offering him their support while he sits quietly back in the shadows, rarely speaking. Even during ceremony purposely to cure him and relieve him of the ghostly pressure, he is allowed to sit in silence. No one ever asks of his health.

When a man is sick or wounded, or during the first few weeks after the death of a particularly close friend or relative, he will neglect his body, allowing body and facial hair to grow. Thus, the only men with mustaches are those whose *edai-egen* are in a perilous state. This self-neglect is also seen as a kind of self-abasement to escape the special attention of the ghosts.

In addition to muting the presence of the sick or especially vulnerable person, steps are taken to prevent ghosts from approaching the compound where he is. One of a variety of magical barriers called *hola* is placed on or across a path leading to the compound. Although there is usually more than one path leading to the compound, only one path is "blocked" by the *hola*. In reply to questions, informants would say that the present danger was from specific ghosts coming from a specific direction. This is clearly related to the origin myth, which states that as people moved west from the point of emergence, the ghosts traveled ahead of them and are now in the western quarter. Most *hola* are placed on paths leading from the west.

The *hola* is prepared by an important man in the compound and then taken to the proper place with a minimum of ritual. While the *hola* is being prepared, the people engage in ordinary talk and even casual shouting. There is no particular reference to the ghosts but also no particular attempt to conceal the proceedings from ghosts.

One common kind of *hola* is prepared from the stem of the *dlogop* reed (*Phragmites karka*). The stem is about one meter high and the branching twigs are broken off a few centimeters from the stem. A dozen or so feathers are inserted into the hollow butts. One or two of these feathered reed stems are erected near a path, with some things laid at the base—taro greens, grasses, or leaves from the *pabi* tree (a soapberry, *Dodonaea viscosa*). In one case (shown in Gardner's film *Dead Birds*) a bundle containing grass, bamboo strips, hearth ashes, string from an old net, a pig tusk, and some tobacco was placed by the feathered reed.

A similar *hola* is made with a vine hoop, fifteen to twenty-five centimeters in diameter, hung on a one- or two-meter pole. The hoop is studded with feathers inserted between the wound loops of the hoop. Again, greens are placed at the base of the pole.

A form of *hola* made by a visitor to the Dugum Neighborhood, a man from the Gosi-Alua region to the west, was observed only once. Taro leaves draped with grass were laid on either side of the path, and a line of hearth ashes led across the path between them.

Treatment of Wounded

If a man cannot walk away from the battle, he may be carried back to his compound sitting on the shoulders of another man or on a stretcher built for him, and he is covered to conceal him from ghosts. Any blood that has been spilled on the ground is removed by burning grass at the spot at least once, and several times if a person has died. Heat lightning as noted before, is said to be the blood of a killed man rising into the sky.

If the arrow that caused the wound is still lodged in a man, it is taken out at the earliest opportunity, usually at a safe place just behind the battle lines. Some men are considered to be experts at removing arrows and if they are in the vicinity, they are summoned. Otherwise, any man may try to take out the arrow. The most difficult to remove is a barbed point that has broken off deep inside the body. A bone awl or perhaps a bamboo knife, often made on the spot from the tip of a bamboo arrow, is used to probe the wound, to try to draw out the arrow. The hole of the wound may be opened a bit and attempts made to grasp the broken end of the arrow with the fingernails or with the teeth. If possible, the arrow tip may be pushed on through the flesh. Sometimes arrows are simply left in the body and are eventually fatal. If the arrow tip is removed, it is carefully saved as magic to be put over the men's house fireplace.

Any serious wound, arrow or spear, is usually treated by bleeding the victim. The bleeding is done by a specialist. The wounded man is supported upright; a piece of skin from his stomach just below the rib cage is lifted and with a bamboo knife the skin is cut through; then the point of the bamboo knife is forced in and up under the rib cage two or three centimeters and withdrawn; this is usually repeated at several points along the lower line of the rib cage and often in the center of the stomach, under the sternum. Then the wounds are sealed with *egenbuga* (*Centella asiatica* (L.) Urban) leaf, the standard dressing for a small open wound. This is a small leaf which is simply licked and pasted over the wound; the plant is common around the villages, so the dressing may be replaced whenever the old one falls off. The Dani say that this bleeding operation removes the bad, dark blood.

More elaborate wounds, burns, or sores, are commonly covered or wrapped with leaves and then bound with the soft outer bark of the banana, *gisakpel*. A sore on the underside of a toe may be protected with a fragment of gourd tied on with string. A crutch is commonly made for a person with a disabled leg: a heavy stick with a short-crosspiece lashed near the bottom for the foot to rest on; or the L-shaped shaft of an adze may be lashed on.

The skull of the *wato bolo*, which is apparently a fish traded from the Jalemo to the east, is used to speed recovery from arrow wounds. A bit of the fish bone is eaten together with steamed *doa*, the cultivated thick-stemmed grass. Often the fish skull is worn on a loose string around the neck of a recuperating man.

A common weed growing around the fallow gardens called *dogo* (*Alternanthera sessilis* (Bl.) DC.) is smoked as a cure for vomiting. The stems and leaves of several *dogo* plants are wrapped into a ball, tied with fiber, and placed in the coals of a fire in the common cook house. When the ball is red-hot, it is removed with tongs and laid in a leaf dish. The leaf is folded over the ball, and a short sucking tube of bamboo, the end of which has been dipped into salty ash, is inserted into the packet. The salt and the fumes are taken in simultaneously with a series of loud slurpings. The ball cools in a few minutes and is laid back in the coals, the mouthpiece is dipped into the salt again, and the process continues. Both men and women were observed smoking *dogo*.

The bark of the *gami* tree, which has a slight cinnamonlike taste, is traded from the Jalemo. It is said to be a cure for general sickness. Adults may carry a small piece of the bark on a string suspended from their neck cord. The edge of the bark is nibbled as the person eats steamed vegetables.

In case of pain in a limb, a string is tied around the limb above the pain in an attempt to force the pain down and out, or at least to prevent it from reaching the torso. The spiny leaf of a bush called *jabi* may be rubbed on the skin, for relief of headache or stomach-ache. The leaf severely irritates the skin. Pain is often eased by soaking in water. A cut finger may be held in water. The boy Wejakhe, as he was dying from spear wounds, was held in a stream to ease his last moments. A man who was recovering from an arrow wound made daily trips to a stream, where he sat for an hour or so in a small pool. Women are said to sit in a pool to ease labor pains.

Curing Ritual. All curing ritual has the double purpose of restoring the *edai-egen*, or soul matter, of the individual and of protecting him in his weakened condition from the potentially inimical ghosts. Such ritual usually involves feeding pork to the sick man, in a ritual similar to that at a funeral, to induce the ghosts to leave. Rappaport has pointed out that the physiological value of such a ceremony is to get more nourishment into the systems of those who most need it (1968:84 ff). The more complicated curing rituals last several days and are led by a man or woman who is supposed to have special curing powers. However, when the ritual is not successful there seems to be no particular blame attached to the would-be curer.

TOILET

In addition to attire and medication, there is a broad range of treatments of the body that may be termed toilet or mutilation. Toilet includes applications, rearrangements, and minor removals such as hair cutting; mutilations are more drastic and bloody alterations of the body.

GREASING

The most common cosmetic is pig grease, which is smeared frequently on the bodies of Dani of all ages. When pigs are butchered and cooked during ceremonies, the skin and fat are separated from the meat. After the pig meat is eaten, each person wipes his greasy hands on himself and on his neighbor's back. Some of the chunks of pig fat, distributed with the meat, are squeezed between the palms and rubbed on the body; some are saved after the feasts and kept for more casual use. They are stored in gourds in men's and women's houses. Perhaps because they have been cooked, they last for several weeks.

Men often grease themselves as part of the general preparations before a battle or an *edai* dance. Greasing may also be done for no particular reason other than to beautify the body. Women grease themselves less frequently than do men.

A fat chunk is prepared for use by heating it slightly over a fire or coal. At the same time, a handful of the fine, dry grass laid on the floor for sitting is set afire. As the warmed fat chunk is squeezed between the palms, the grass ashes are mixed in to blacken the grease. The man slaps and rubs the grease over those parts of his body he can reach and then often asks an onlooker to spread it across his back. Any small child standing around is grabbed and greased at the same time. The face is often specially treated with stripes or areas of black for ceremonies, battles, or just casually. The most common pattern is a horizontal black stripe from the nose across the cheekbones. Sometimes only the forehead is blackened. A few men occasionally smear the reddish *bimut* clay under their eyes. There seems to be no symbolism involved in either the general greasing or the patterns. The most important motive seems to be cosmetic, to beautify body and face.

Thoroughly greased skins must help the Dani, especially the men, to withstand the chilly nights and mornings. No specific tests were made, but it was obvious that the Dani were effected less by extremes of temperature than I was. Probably the greasing of the skin also contributes to the general health and healing ability of the skin, the latter being especially important for people who are nearly naked and continually exposed to grasping branches and thorns.

MUDDING

Often, instead of greasing, the Dani smear mud on their bodies. Mudding was observed under three kinds of circumstances. Mud-covered bodies are particular signs of mourning and are seen during cremations and in the following days of the funeral ceremony. Often people on their way to a funeral will stop at a particular mudhole to smear their bodies and their hair. The mud dries and remains on the body until it gradually flakes off.

One particular mudding pattern is explicitly related to the immortality myth. The bird in the myth, who lost the argument with the snake and thus caused men's mortality, is a small black bird with white epaulettes. Men and women sometimes smear light-colored mud across their shoulders in imitation of this bird. I was not able to find any deeper implication of this action or learn effects it might be expected to have. Although never stated by the Dani, it seems reasonable that the general mudding of the funeral is symbolic of the bird, and thus of death.

People also mud themselves for events connected with war, for battles and *edai* dances. In these events in general, there is considerable bird-man symbolism, of which the mudding may be a part. The patterns of war-related mudding are more elaborate than those of the funerals. Many people smear their entire legs, and frequently boys draw circles or square designs on their bodies.

Three particular patterns were noted on boys in battle and *edai*, and only in these contexts.

The first was a broad grid of vertical and horizontal lines. Some informants said that it represented the cutting of the steamed pig skin; others that it represented an object wrapped in a net.

The second pattern was circles about ten centimeters in diameter, often with dots in the centers, called *bpake hiluk*. *Hiluk* is a fiber in the tail of various forest mammals (*bpake*) that might cause sickness if eaten. The design is said to cure or to avert cramps that might result from the dancing.

Third were designs like the tracks of a large bird, made with the stem of the *boduk* plant. The leaves are plucked off, leaving a number of leaf stems radiating from the main stem. This is pressed in mud and then applied to the body, leaving bird foot tracks. There is apparently no specific symbolism in these marks, but they are clearly part of the general Dani symbolism associating man with bird.

Finally, people often seem to smear mud on their bodies for no particular reason at all, when working in the gardens or on impulse when passing a mudhole. Perhaps this helps to cut the heat of the midday sun.

BATHING

The Dani occasionally swim but practically never bathe in the sense of washing the entire body with water. However, they are not particularly odoriferous. Though grease or mud is often smeared on the body as cosmetics, at least for adults there seems to be a real aversion to dirt, that is, accidental mud on the body. When passing a puddle, a man often drags his feet through the water to clean off dirt that may have been picked up since the last puddle.

HAIR TREATMENT

Both men and women wear hair long or short, although women more often have short hair and men more often have long hair. A woman's long hair may hang down to her eyebrows in front, and can be decorated with small snail shells tied onto the locks; men's hair may hang down to the shoulders, and men are often very proud of their hair, treating it carefully with pig grease. During particularly dirty work it may be protected by a head net or a taro leaf cap.

Especially before a ceremony or battle, men prepare their hair with pig grease, or have someone else do it for them. Grass is burned to produce a fine charcoal dust. Chunks of pig grease are taken out of the gourd where they have been stored, heated over a fire, then crushed between the hands to squeeze out the grease. The greasy hands are then rubbed in the charcoal dust, and then over the hair. When the hair has reached the proper degree of greasiness, the curls are separated and sometimes tied up in curls with a plant fiber. It is left this way for a few hours or overnight before being shaken out.

HEAD HAIR CUTTING AND DISPOSAL

Sometimes a man cuts his head hair a few centimeters shorter with a bamboo knife, or he asks a friend to do it. Cutting may apparently be done as a whim, or it may be done as a symbol of mourning or other distress. The cut hair is set aside and within a few days is stuffed inside the stem of a growing banana plant. Informants are vague about the reasons for this but say that the ghosts may cause the individual trouble if he leaves his hair lying around.

DEPILATION

Normally both men and women remove all visible body hair. Women's pubic hair in the area covered by the low-slung skirt is not removed. During mourning or when near death, men allow their body hair to grow out (p. 232).

Hair is plucked out with forefinger and thumb smeared with araucaria pitch. A man usually removes the hair from his arms, legs, and front of his torso himself. Then friends work on his back and buttocks as he lies on his stomach during leisure periods in the men's house or by a watchtower. Depilation, like defleaing, is a social event. The reasons for it seem primarily aesthetic. Practically speaking, however, it would be difficult for a man or a woman to roll fiber into thread on a thigh that was hairy.

Under most circumstances, Dani men wear a ring-beard but no mustache. The hair is carefully removed from the region of the mouth by tweezers made from the partially broken-through twig of the araucaria. A man may do this himself, or another man or boy may pluck him. Reasons for not wearing a mustache are varied; some say that the women do not like it, or that it would become messy when eating sweet potato. Another possibility is that many Dani have chronically dripping noses, and a mustache would seriously complicate matters. Youths do have mustaches, but by the time their beards are noticeable, they pluck the lip hair. A man in mourning or near death allows his mustache to grow as a sign that his *edai-egen* is small and weak.

DEFLEAING

Although fleas are not a major problem, most Dani have some in their hair. (I assume that these vermin are fleas, but they may be lice.) Often when sitting in groups, one person will deflea another, searching through the hair, capturing the flea, smashing it between the backs of the fingernails, and then crushing it between the teeth, usually swallowing it afterward.

Defleaing is usually done by older people on younger people, or by peers on each other. Adults do it for other adults of the same sex, but, at least in public, no one does it for a member of the opposite sex who is not considerably younger.

MUTILATION

The Dani mutilate ears, nose, and fingers. Chopping off fingers is particularly common, and nearly every female above the age of about ten has lost four or six fingers. The thumbs are never removed, nor are at least the first two fingers on at least one hand.

FINGER MUTILATION OF GIRLS

Fingers are removed from girls, usually when they are between the ages of three and six, in connection with funerals. This is a part of the two major, interrelated themes of the funeral: extensive exchange of valuables on the part of the deceased person's sib or moiety and on the part of his mother's (that is, his mother's brother's) sib or moiety; and efforts to impress, placate, and drive away the ghost of the deceased.

Of the goods brought by mourners to the funeral, some are redistributed, some are put away in a memorial bundle to be used later to impress the ghost, and some, like the pigs, are consumed. One explanation the Dani give of finger chopping is in terms of these goods: They say that some people bring shell bands, some bring pigs, and the little girls give their fingers. The various kinds of valuables are used to impress the ghosts. So in a sense the fingers may be called sacrifices, but there is no specific act of presenting the severed fingers to the ghost.

Girls usually lose fingers at the funeral of a close relative of their own sib who has been killed by the enemy—in other words, when the ghosts are particularly threatening. Apparently no more than two or three girls are involved in any one funeral, and they lose only one or two fingers at a time. Although such operations were performed during my stay, I did not actually observe any. Informants describe the procedure as follows.

Early in the morning after the cremation, the girls are brought by their mothers to the place of the funeral. One man in the Wilihiman-Walalua Confederation, a specialist, is called upon to perform the operation. Just what his qualifications are and what the nature of this specialist status is, I did not discover.

The operator ties off the arm with a constricting string just above the elbow. Then he raps the nerve at the olecranon process (the "funny bone"), deadening nerves in the fingers. Laying the hand on a board, he cuts off the finger with a single blow of a stone adze, striking through the proximal joint of the finger. When one or two fingers have been chopped off, the hand is bound in leaves and held up, the elbow resting in grass in the unharmed hand, catching the blood. The girls sit in this posture throughout the ceremonies of the second day, stunned (Plate 26).

After a week or two the bandages come off and the healed stumps are used. The few cases I could observe healed without incident, but undoubtedly infections do sometimes occur.

Meanwhile, the finger that has been removed is tied in a bundle and hung on the wall of the long common cook house of the place of the funeral, where the ghosts become aware of it. There seems to be no special ritual connected with it, and after a few days the piece of finger is simply burned in a fire in the compound and the ashes thrown away, but not into the enclosure with the ashes of cremated bodies.

Attitude toward Finger Chopping. The Dani treat finger chopping as normal.

Of some 120 females of ten or over, only two had all ten fingers intact. One was a twenty-five-year-old woman, deaf and dumb, but married and with a young, normal, child. No particular reason was given for the exception in her case.

The second exception was a nubile unmarried girl of about fourteen. The explanation in her case was always simply that she did not want her fingers chopped off. If this is indeed the explanation, I cannot explain the explanation. Missionaries have suggested that daughters of important men are exempt from finger chopping, but this certainly did not hold for this girl, since her father was rather unimportant, and the daughters of the most important men had lost fingers. This girl did indeed have a strong character, but so did other girls and women who had lost their fingers. In short, she did not seem to be exceptional in any matter except this. Also, it seems unlikely that all those girls who had their fingers chopped were really willing. Once I heard a girl screaming hysterically, and was later told that she was objecting to losing fingers.

The loss of fingers does not drastically limit a woman's activities. With both thumbs and two fingers on at least one hand, and in most cases usable stumps on the other, the women are able to manipulate the woman's thin digging sticks in garden work. They also roll string and make nets and do other fine work. Comments on the lack of fingers were rare, but once an older woman remarked, more in joke than complaint, that she could not wield the heavy men's digging stick.

Activities that require ten fingers, such as shooting with bow and arrow or handling heavy digging sticks or axes, are generally reserved for men, but these are just the activities that are characteristically masculine in most cultures.

Finger Mutilation of Men

Men may also lose fingers, but this has quite a different aspect from the finger chopping of women. No boys are forcibly mutilated. A few men, at the cremation for a favorite wife killed by the enemy, or at some other funeral with high emotional effect, chop off one or more of their own fingers. This seems to be a sign of deep personal grief, and a thoroughly individual gesture, rather than a means of placating the ghosts for the benefit of the group.

The age pattern of such men is remarkable. Apparently the only two men of thirty or under who have lost fingers were victims of angry pigs rather than of their own sorrow. Otherwise, all the men who are missing fingers were mature or old men. Perhaps the pattern of male finger mutilation is dying out. At any rate, no fresh mutilations were observed during my stay.

Ear Slicing

Many people have sliced off the upper edge of one or both ears. This was observed after funerals of close relatives killed by the enemy. It is said to be done also in grief or disturbance at relatively minor losses, such as the stealing of a boy's favorite pig. The ear top is sliced off with a bamboo knife and the wound smeared with mud.

Casual Mutilation

Men and boys casually puncture their own earlobes and nasal septum to be able to carry objects in the holes. Most men have punctured nasal septums, in which they wear pig tusk ornaments in battle or dance. Small bones or cigarettes are carried in earlobe holes.

ARTIFACTS OF CULTURE

THE artifacts of a culture pose a real problem to the ethnographer: How is he to bring them into his description? Undeniably they are an important aspect of culture and form integral parts of the most esoteric nonmaterial behavior. But to describe them with anything like the necessary detail would result in an unreadable catalogue. I first went to the Dani with high hopes of being able to solve the problem, but it proved more intractable than I had imagined. In short, the problem has not been solved, but in this chapter, we examine five realms of artifacts—attire, construction, tools, weapons, and sacred objects—whose analysis yields particularly relevant information about the non-material aspects of Dani culture. (Cf. also Heider 1969a.)

ATTIRE

The objects of Dani attire may be discussed in terms of their function and in terms of the circumstances of situation and status.

The minimal effect of status on Dani attire reflects the minimal status differentiation in Dani society as a whole. Male versus female role behavior is clearly differentiated, as is male versus female attire. The only attire normally shared by men and women is the neck piece protecting the base of the throat from ghostly attack, and the bark "breech cloth" which may be worn by babies of either sex. The other examples prove the rule: Young girls who have not yet begun to take on female roles and so can enter men's houses, also wear the men's woven arm bands; men in time of spiritual crisis may conceal themselves from ghosts by draping a woman's net over their heads; and women at the *edai* may wear men's ornaments. In the first example, the little girl's status has not yet been firmly defined; in the second, the man's status is in jeopardy. The explanation for the third exception is not so clear, but it does seem that in the high emotional and ritual intensity of the dance, the normal rules are suspended.

Age is also reflected in attire in a similar but less decisive way. The major age break for the Dani occurs around two or three, when the child begins to walk and talk more or less competently, and when his soul matter is considered to have achieved normal size. Within a few years the child will begin to regularly wear a penis gourd or skirt, but these are not directly connected with the achievement of "person-hood." Boys' initiations occur sometime between three and ten, and a girl goes through a minor ceremony at puberty, but neither of these are marked by changes of attire. The only major change of attire directly related to change of status takes place at a girl's marriage, when she begins to wear the woman's wound skirt in place of the girl's hanging skirt.

Other than age, sex, and marital status, there are virtually no major status distinctions in Dani society. There are leaders and spare-time specialists, but neither can be predictably recognized by their attire. (Some informants suggested that Nassa-shell forehead bands were worn by big [important] men. Although there are many big men who do not wear them, they are not worn by men of average or little importance.) The attire of the Dani reflects and even goes beyond the general egalitarianism of Dani society. There are individual differences in attitude, but these are more sartorial than status-linked. Generally speaking, there is no important differentiation of attire within the group of, say adult men, just as there is minimal status differentiation within this group.

The nature of a situation has only minor effect on what attire a Dani wears. The most obvious situations that require special attire are battle and the *edai* dance, when the participants wear their finest furs, feathers, and shells. Also, the mourners at funerals are usually smeared with mud. But otherwise there is little variation in attire connected with particular behavoral situations.

Functionally, Dani attire serves as: protection of the body against the elements; concealment of parts of the body; expressive decoration, including ornamentation; symbols of status; magical effects; and transportation of other items. These functions are not mutually exclusive. Most objects that belong to the class of attire can be described in terms of more than one of these functional attributes.

BODY PROTECTION

The climate of the Grand Valley of the Balim is remarkably temperate. Daytime temperatures rarely exceed 80° F. and the coldest nights never get below 40° F. Pig grease rubbed on the body may give some protection against chilly days, and men's taro leaf caps and women's matted rain capes give some protection against rain.

But for the most part, the Dani protect themselves from rain and cold in ways other than attire: Simple shelters in the gardens and rock overhangs in the forests provide shelter for people caught abroad in a rain; most Dani carry coals or fire-making equipment when they go to the gardens or into the forests, and they kindle a small fire near their temporary base of operations to light cigarettes, and for warmth. The well-built round sleeping houses provide warmth throughout the nights.

BODY CONCEALMENT

For the Dugum Dani the pattern of body coverage varies by sex and age. Very young children are not restricted at all, but between the ages of four to six they begin to conform to the pattern of adults of the appropriate sex.

The Dani woman's immediate genital area is covered by skirts at all times (except during sexual intercourse and childbirth). Her back is covered (but not really concealed) at all times in public by nets hanging from the forehead. The nets may be removed for coolness in midday or to bask in the early morning sun in the relative privacy of a garden or compound. Her upper sternum area is usually covered by ornaments or magic paraphernalia hanging from neck cords. This is explained as protection against ghosts.

Dress for the Dani man dictates that the penis be covered by a penis gourd at all times after he reaches the age of four to six, except occasionally when he is working in muddy garden ditches or during *sinuknuk* seizures. Feebleminded men who customarily go about naked, as reported from the lower Grand Valley and from the Western Dani region (Carel Schneider, in a personal communication), were never observed in the Mid-Valley. The anal region is sometimes covered (but only in a token manner) by a "tail," a long leaf of Cordyline or a bark strip that hangs from the waist string. Like the women, Dani men wear ornaments and magic paraphernalia on neck cords over their upper sternum area to protect against ghosts.

Closely related to the Dani pattern of modesty is the removal of all exposed body hair with a pitch depilatory and, by men, of the facial hair around the mouth, leaving a ring beard. This was explained in terms of general, nonmagical norms.

DECORATION

Feathers, furs, mud, and ash-blackened pig grease are the main elements of Dani decoration. Just as the Dani have relatively little status differentiation beyond that based on sex and age, so there is little in the way of status-specific ornamentation. There are no insignia of rank, and important men rarely wear finer ornaments than lesser men do. Men often wear ornamentation, but women practically never do. Men tend to be most elaborately ornamented in battle and at the *edai* dance and least ornamented while doing manual labor, but there are many exceptions even to these generalizations. Individual differences seem to stem from personal inclination to elegance rather than from status or other norms.

Much attire has only ornamental function, but it is difficult to draw a line between the feather and body-mud designs explicitly referring to the bird of the mortality myth, and those worn for nonritual display. Most objects of attire can be enhanced ornamentally by the addition of furs, feathers, mud, flowers, or vegetal coloring.

MAGICAL PURPOSES

Some Dani attire serves to conceal and protect parts of the body from ghosts, but it is often difficult to separate this supernatural function from the general purposes mentioned above. The base of the throat and, secondarily, the anal region are most vulnerable to ghostly attack. The former is usually concealed, and the latter (with men) only sometimes concealed, by objects with ritual power, such as the bark cloth neck strips, or the Cordyline leaf anal strip. (Women's anal regions are always concealed by their skirts.)

Other objects of attire, such as pig scrotum arm bands, give a more generalized protection against the ghosts. Wounded or sick men—that is, those with weakened soul matter—wear large nets loosely draped over their heads to conceal their presence from the ghosts. In ceremonies people smear clay on their bodies in symbolic identification with the bird of the mortality myth.

TRANSPORT

Transport is a minor function of Dani attire. Women's back nets are used to carry babies, shoats, or garden produce. Men sometimes use small tobacco nets to carry cigarette material and small tools. Some small tools, such as needles, awls, and pig tusk scrapers, may be slipped under an arm band or through an earlobe. But most objects are simply carried in the hands or, if they are too large, over the shoulder or on top of the head.

OBJECTS OF ATTIRE

Table 9.1 outlines the objects of attire. It will be immediately obvious that women have few objects of attire compared with men.

Male Attire

PENIS GOURD. The *holim*, or penis gourd, is the only essential men's garment. It is a narrow gourd tube about the diameter of the penis, which is slipped all the way inside it, covered, and held erect. The gourd is held in place by two strings: a small loop tied through holes in the lower end of the gourd, which encircles part of the scrotum and often at least one testicle; and an upper string which passes around the waist and is fixed to the upper end of the gourd or, if it is a long gourd, to the middle.

Penis gourds are of several shapes and sizes. A small token gourd is sometimes worn dangling from the waist string of a male baby or infant. Gourds worn by boys or men may be short and straight, about ten to twenty centimeters long. These are sometimes worn in battle or during vigorous work because of the ease of keeping them on; longer straight gourds may rise to an elegant length of sixty centimeters or more, rising above the shoulder; gourds of middle length may be curved or even curled at the end.

The Grand Valley Dani gourds are distinctive: long, narrow, and worn nearly vertically. Visitors to the Grand Valley from the Western Dani areas are particularly noticeable with their short, thick penis gourds, often ten centimeters in diameter, standing out at a 45° angle from the wearer's body.

Gourds are grown near compounds and are carefully shaped as they grow. The vine is trained up a framework which holds it about 1.5 meters above the ground. If a long straight gourd is desired, a stone weight is tied to the end of the gourd, drawing it out. Later, if a curve or curl is desired, the gourd is

TABLE 9.1
Dani Personal Attire

	Male	*Female*
Essential	Nothing to about three years Penis gourd	Nothing to about two years Girl's hanging skirt or woman's wound skirt
Usual	Woven arm bands Buttocks leaf "tail" Neck gear	Carrying nets Neck gear
	Baby: Bark cloth "breech cloth"	
Accessory	Arm bands: fur, pig scrotum Wrist bands Bailer shell Nassa-shell "bib" Other neck gear Cane belt Head net Spider web cap Leaf cap Seed wig Forehead band Headdress Feathers, in hair Tobacco net Back "shield" Feather whisk Feather wand	Rain cape Girls: woven arm band (In *edai* dance: much male ornamentation)

bent to the horizontal or turned upside down and lashed to the frame. Often the gourd is wrapped with *gisakpel*, the outer banana bark, to prevent its darkening in the sun.

When a gourd is grown to desired size, its tips are cut off; it is roasted over coals to harden the shell and soften the meat; the meat is gouged out with a bamboo knife; the outer skin is scraped off; and the gourd is carefully wrapped and hung to dry behind the fire of the men's house. After a few days, when it is dry and before it has begun to discolor from the smoke of the fire, it is removed to be stored on the wall of the men's house. When it is needed, the gourd is unwrapped; two holes are bored near the base for the scrotum string; if necessary, a hole is bored at the tip for the waist string; then the man, carefully turning his back, fixes the new gourd in position.

Gourds, especially long ones, are frequently broken. If only the tip is broken, it may simply be reinserted, wedged into the opening, or a new hole bored and the waist band moved down to the new tip. If the base is broken, the gourd will be replaced, but the broken piece is put aside for possible future use.

The penis gourd may be ornamented in several ways. A forest marsupial's tail fur twenty to thirty centimeters long, held rigid by a stick inside, may be stuck upright into the end hole of the gourd. Another sort of fur tassel is limp and hangs loose, with the bare prehensile tip of the tail inserted into the tip of the gourd. Tassels are usually of dark fur, but occasionally are embellished by an end piece of light fur of another animal. The spiked cocoon of the case moth, called *pumpalep*, may serve as a dangling tassel at the end of a straight gourd or be fixed to the middle of a long or a curled gourd. *Pumpalep*, considered magic lures for women, are usually worn by older men. Also, a few greased strips of bark cloth or strings may dangle from the middle of the gourd.

Although the tip of a curled penis gourd may simply be the natural end of the gourd, on a straight gourd this end has been cut off, and the end hole is plugged with a stopper. If there is no tassel, a wad of dried banana bark is used.

We may now use the attributes discussed above to analyze the gourd and its place in Dani culture. As already mentioned, each Dani male over about six years of age wears a penis gourd in all public situations. No Dani female ever wears a penis gourd, although in victory dances women often wear other specifically male objects, such as shell neckpieces and feather headdresses.

The penis gourd certainly does not protect the body against the elements in any discernable way. Neither is it good protection against arrows, since it is so brittle. In fact, by holding the penis upright, it increases the genital area exposed to arrows. But the penis gourd does conceal the penis, and this sexual modesty is the only reason given by the Dani themselves for the gourd.

The great variety of lengths and shapes of gourds seemed to offer cues about the personalities of the wearers. The gourds are so obviously extensions of the penis that it would seem at first glance that there must be some personality or status differences reflected in the differences between straight shoulder-length gourds, gourds with a drooping curl, and the short finger-length gourds. In fact, however, each man has a wardrobe of several sizes and shapes of gourds which he wears alternately. It is conceivable that a man picks his gourd according to his mood of the day, but I found no evidence of this. At best it seems that old men often wear tightly curled gourds, but even this is far from regular. The fur tassels sometimes worn on the gourds showed no more correlation with status or personality than did the shapes of the gourds themselves.

There are some other symbolic uses of the gourd worth mentioning. The gourd is used by men as a symbol for a fellow sib member; the word for penis gourd may be used, or the gourd may be tapped, indicating the agnatic relationship. During the *pelabi*, the renewal ceremony marking the end of the mourning period, the stated norm is for all people involved to discard their mourning skirts or penis gourds for new ones. In fact, in the instances I observed, only a few of the boys did this. The noisy flicking of the gourd by the fingernail of a forefinger punctuates the more dramatic conversations. This flicking has the same range of meanings as the word *naijuk*—I am afraid, I am impressed, Wow!

The penis gourd does not seem to serve any magical purpose, and except for an occasional needle stuck in the wadding at the tip of the gourd, penis gourds are not used for transporting other items.

Although it is tempting to make psychological explanations of the penis gourd, it is difficult to see the pertinence of any such explanation in the Dani case. Explicit sexual activity, sexual concern, and phallic emphasis are remarkably low in Dani culture. It is, of course, possible that psychological or psycho-analytical investigations of the Dani would be more revealing, but no such studies have been carried out. For example, the psychological interpretation of the gourd as a symbolic erection and the fur tassel as a symbolic orgasm has been suggested (Le Roux 1948:148), but I observed nothing in the Dani culture to support this interpretation. Perhaps the most remarkable aspect of the Dani penis gourd is that it is not, in any explicit way, a focus of Dani sexuality or eroticism.

ARM BANDS. Most Dani males wear arm bands just above the elbow most of the time. Occasionally young girls also wear arm bands. The most common arm bands are woven from fibers. A common variant is a pig scrotum arm band, made of the penis, seminal duct, and scrotum of a boar which have been removed in one piece. The woven bands are mainly decorative, but the pig scrotum bands, which are made from pigs killed in important ceremonies, have general power to protect the wearer from ghosts. The bands also serve as convenient carrying devices; cigarettes, pig tusks, a needle, or other small objects are often slipped beneath the band.

It was never possible to elicit any statement suggesting that this pig scrotum arm band might be a symbol of masculinity. The wearing of arm bands correlates well with those people who are allowed to enter the men's house, namely all males and younger girls who have not yet begun to show signs of womanhood. Thus it seems to be not so much a sign of masculinity as evidence of non-femininity. However, this linking together of males and neutral girls does not seem to be explicitly noted by the Dani themselves. Informants deny that there is any special significance to the bands. One often sees a man whose old bands have worn off, walking around for several weeks unconcerned before bothering to make new ones. And finally, although the arm band resembles the band around the fighting spear, there seems to be no conscious analogy, and the names for the two are different.

NECK GEAR. Most Dani, most of the time, wear some objects suspended from a string around the neck. Neck gear, which often includes ornaments, magical objects, and tools, is collectively called *wopok*. An important function of *wopok* is to conceal the upper sternum area from the gaze of ghosts. At curing ceremonies the subjects of the ceremonies tie on new *wopok* strips to strengthen their souls, or *edai-egen*, and to protect themselves from the ghosts. However, the *edai-egen* itself is said to reside somewhat lower, at the base of the sternum.

Neck gear includes: matted spider web strips; bark cloth strands, which have *wusa*, or magical power, and are made as ghost protectors at ceremonies; bailer shells; bibs of small ocean snail shells; and occasionally marsupial tails, which serve as sheaths for carrying needles or awls.

HEAD GEAR. Net caps or, rarely, caps made of matted spider webs may be worn by men for decoration. Sometimes to protect their hair from dirt or rain, men fashion temporary caps from large taro leaves. One man, who was balding and rather vain, would occasionally wear a magnificent wig made of the tiny red and black seeds of a vine strung on threads that were attached to a base made of an ordinary head net. Headdresses are made of a band of pandanus leaf and are often spectacularly set with bright feathers and furs.

OTHER MALE ATTIRE. Men, especially older men, may carry small net pouches slung from their shoulders. These are called *hanom su*, tobacco net, and hold the makings of cigarettes. In battle men wear pig tusks in the holes of their nasal septums. Other ornamental battle attire includes hand-held cassowary feather whisks and feather wands.

Female Attire

GIRL'S SKIRT. The dress worn by girls from about one year to the time of marriage is the *dali*, made of reed or string hanging from a string around the waist to midthigh. Except for the youngest girls, below the age of two or three, who often have trouble keping their *dali* on, all girls wear it all the time.

WOMAN'S SKIRT. The skirt worn by all married women, which is to say all normal adult women, of the central Grand Valley, is the *jogal*, made of some twenty-five to thirty meters of braided cord wound around the hips. The skirt gives minimal coverage to the pubic region and is held in place by pressure around the hips, producing, in time, callouses at the contact points. The tenuous placement of the *jogal* may influence the straight-legged bending posture of women when doing garden work. When a woman sits, her skirt often slips a bit out of place, and it is necessary to give it a jiggling adjustment when standing up.

The *jogal* is a braided cord made of five to eight strands of fiber, with red or yellow orchid fibers braided in to form a brightly colored upper surface. The cord is wound around the hips, the upper part tied together into a tube and the lower lengths caught up on either side at the hips but draped down in front and behind.

The cords are braided by the husband of a married woman, or by the father of a girl about to be married. Only on two occasions were women themselves observed braiding *jogal*. Both these women grew up in other areas, where they learned to braid; local women were said not to know how. There are apparently no restrictions against their braiding, however. (Often lengths of skirt material are traded from the Jalemo, together with nets.)

A crude version of the *jogal*, made by women themselves from braided *gem*, looped and tied like the normal *jogal*, is sometimes worn by old women and by women when they are very sick.

A different sort of woman's skirt, the *jali*, is worn in the Jalemo, and by women who have moved into the Neighborhood from the Jalemo. This is made of *gem* reeds, basically two big brushes tied fore and aft.

THE WOMAN'S CARRYING NET. The woman's carrying net, *su*, is a large string bag about seventy-five centimeters square with a wide mouth and a forehead strap. Similar nets are the men's tobacco net (*hanom su*), a small netted pouch worn over the shoulder by men and used to carry cigarette makings and miscellaneous small tools, and the head net (*ugul su*), a net cap worn by some men.

The Dani net is not knotted but knitted with loose open loops. Nets are made by women or older girls. The maker alternately knits the net and adds to the string by rolling fibers into it on her thigh, so that each net is made of a single string. A split stick shuttle may be used to draw the loose string through the loops (Plate 40). Before netting, the string may be colored by a red clay, a blue-purple flower base, or a yellow-to-orange root. The string may also be decorated by winding strips of brightly colored orchid fiber around it.

Although the general term *su* is used for all nets, there are several names for specific kinds of carrying nets. Though repeated questioning of women and girls failed to produce a consistent system of net classification, three names were used with some consistency. Nets with orchid-fiber decoration are generally not made in the Dugum Neighborhood but are traded in from the Gutima area in the southern Grand Valley, and they are called *Gutima su*. Nets traded in from the Jalemo are called *Jale su*. Long rectangular nets, open along two sides, which are usually reserved for the funeral exchange but are sometimes worn by women, are called *tegetagi*. The apparent absence of subclassification of women's nets in the Dugum Neighborhood contrasts with the situation in the Konda Valley Western Dani area, where Denise O'Brien found an elaborate and consistent scheme of net classification (personal communication).

Old, frayed nets are sometimes mended with new string. When they are no longer mendable, they may still be worn for cover or they may be unraveled for string. When a net is beyond use, it is hung on a convenient tree limb outside the compound to rot. Informants insisted that this had no particular significance.

Names for the parts of a carrying net suggest some anthropomorphic symbolism, corresponding roughly to the English terminology. The body of the net is *ebe*, body; the mouth is *ape*, mouth; the carrying strap is *adle*, which is also the term for bow string and tendon. All nets have a free-ended string several centimeters long, hanging somewhere along the carrying strap. This string is called *ilaka*, which also means eyebrow. No informant was able—or willing—to explain this string.

It is convenient to call a *su* a woman's carrying net because the *su* is used by women for carrying things. The only times a man uses a *su* is to carry sacred objects to a ceremony, or, when his soul matter is diminished and in danger because of a wound or the death of a friend, to drape over his head to mute his presence, to conceal himself from the ghosts.

Women use the nets constantly for carrying babies, garden produce, or small pigs. But the *su* is much more than just a device for transport. Women wear nets constantly; only rarely, in the privacy of their own houses or a deserted garden, does a woman take off her nets. Although a woman's net does not

PLATE 40. Egabu, one of Wali's wives, netting in her cook house.

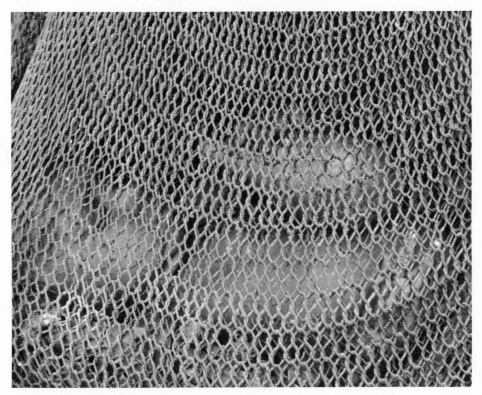

PLATE 41. A baby in a net clutches a small water gourd.

completely conceal her back, a stranger is as likely to see the fully naked back of a Dani woman as he is to see the naked breasts of an American woman. (However, the Dani do not seem to find a decolletage eroticism associated with nets and backs.)

Women usually wear two to six nets, of which only one or two are actually used for transport. The outer net is usually decorated, either with the soft colorings of the string of a local net, or the more garish orchid fiber of imported nets.

The nets do afford some protection against sun. When a woman has given birth, she uses a set of new nets. The baby lies horizontally on a soft grass "nest" in the bottom net, against its mother's back; while the outer nets lie over it, shielding the child from the light. A child spends most of its first year in the net, cradled against the back of its mother or a young girl babysitter.

Nets, like pigs and shells, are commonly used in ceremonial exchange and are given out to women in the funeral ceremony, on the day after the cremation.

NECK GEAR. Women generally wear the same neck ornaments as men, except for shells, although some women wear one or two strands of Nassa shells and occasionally a few cowrie shells. A few women with long hair have Nassa shells tied at the ends of the front-hanging strands.

Rain Cape. A crude cape, made of matted or felted grasses, is usually carried by a woman to the gardens when rain threatens. The cape is made by girls, who pick the grass in fallow garden ditches and then felt it by stamping and jumping on it. It is held around the neck with a string. Men never wear such capes. They say that they do not need to, since when it rains they have access to the watchtower shelters (which, especially in time of war, are taboo, for women).

Ceremonial Dress. During dances, and only then, women wear many men's ornaments—apparently they just take them from husbands. This includes all men's neck and head ornaments, feather whisks, and tobacco nets.

CONSTRUCTIONS

The homes of the Dani are grouped in compounds. The elements of the compound, and the order in which they will be discussed are: men's house (*bilai*), woman's house (*ebeai*), common cook house (*hunu, lise*), fences (*leget*), central courtyard (*silimo*), pig sty (*wam ai, dlabu,*) banana yard (*hagiloma*), bone depository enclosure (*oak leget*), ghost enclosure (*wadlo leget*).

Men's House

The men's house is a round structure with a domed, thatched roof where men and boys usually sleep and spend parts of the day. In the midvalley area, which includes the Dugum Neighborhood, the term *bilai* is used for the men's house. Also known and recognized is the Southern Valley term *honai* (apparently from *hun*, a slightly honorific name for older men, and *ai*, house).

In every compound there is at least one men's house. This is the largest of the round structures and is located approximately opposite the compound entrance, at the far end of the central courtyard.

Most men's houses are 4 to 4.5 meters in inside diameter, but the range is 2.8 to 4.75 meters. (For a cross-sectional view of a men's house see Diag. 9.2.) The height of the lower room is usually about one meter from floor to rafters. The lower room of the men's house is directly on the ground. It is entered through a narrow antechamber, the *miobulak*. The plank walls of the lower part rise about 1.5 meters, and across these is laid the structure which serves as ceiling of the lower room and floor for the sleeping loft. The sleeping loft is reached through a narrow opening. It is a semispherical room, dark and warm under the tight thatch roof. It is smoky from the fire that usually smolders in the center of the lower room, and fragrant from the dried grass laid on the reeds, and the pig grease in gourd containers and smeared on the bodies of the occupants. Occasionally objects are hung from the four center posts that reach from the ground through the loft to support the center of the dome. Flat objects may be slipped under the floor grass. The floor of the loft, like the floor of the ground room, is laid with a sweet-smelling grass which, when it dries and becomes dirty from tracked-in mud, is renewed.

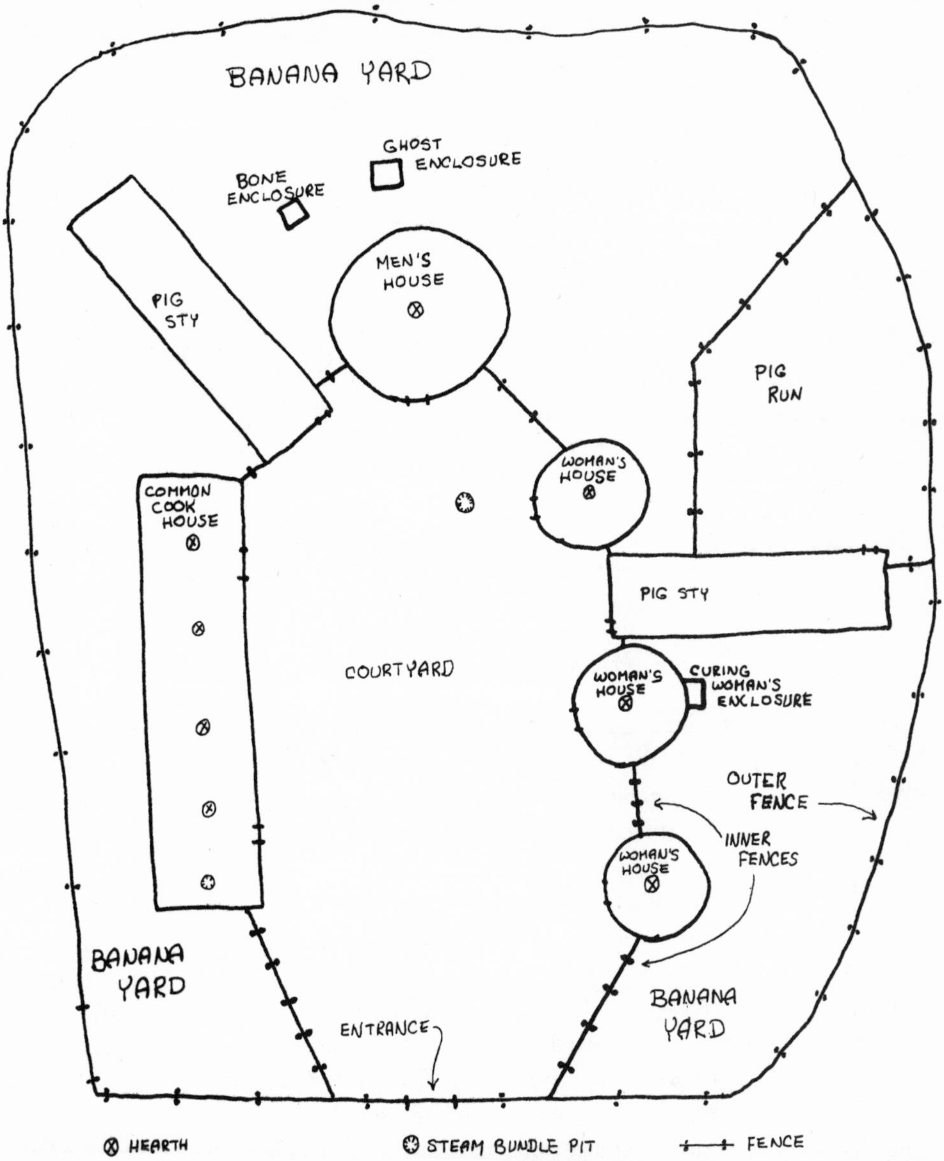

DIAGRAM 9.1
COMPOUND PLAN

The men's house is the main living quarters for the men and boys of the compound. Here they sleep, nap, talk with the other men, and store their personal ornaments, valuables, or tools. Two of the men's houses are occupied by the sole male in their compound; others are occupied by as many as a dozen males. Men's houses are referred to in terms of the most important man who lives there: *bilai* Um'ue *mege* (Um'ue's men's house), or *bilai* Um'ue *wetekma* (the men's house where Um'ue is). There is some sense of ownership involved, but the men's house is not the exclusive domain of its residents. Men from other compounds make almost as much use of the men's house as do the regular

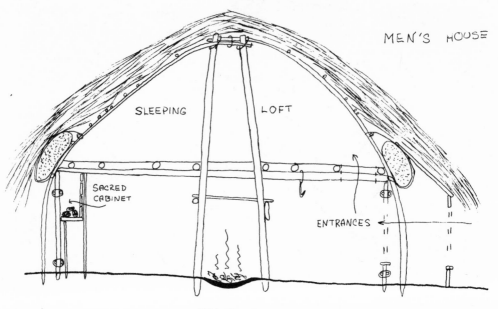

MEN'S HOUSE

SLEEPING LOFT

SACRED CABINET

ENTRANCES

DIAGRAM 9.2
MEN'S ROUND HOUSE (*Bilai*)

residents, dropping into talk, eat, and even sleep; and no permission is asked before entering. (Still, the problems of negotiating the low double entrance do give those inside a moment to size up the man entering.)

Normally, women are prohibited from entering the men's house. No special reason is given, and there is even disagreement as to whether this would be taboo or not. Under only four circumstances did I see a grown woman inside a *bilai:* a young boy had been mortally wounded in an ambush, had been brought inside a men's house as he was dying, and two women who were close relatives followed him in, sitting in the shadows to the rear, mourning; during a lull in a very important ceremony the wife of the most important man, Weteklue, was seen in his men's house; and at the funeral of an old man, formerly a very important man, the wife of one of his sons who was also an important man stayed in the men's house with the corpse, mourning, during most of the morning; and once an important woman curer entered a men's house to conduct part of a curing ceremony.

However, young girls frequently enter a men's house either with their fathers, or to bring potatoes or fetch things. Older girls and women, when bringing food or talking with the men in the men's house, may squat briefly in the forechamber, and on occasion may even reach a hand inside. The oldest girl observed in a men's house was about eight years old, well before puberty. No girl with even a slightest hint of breasts was seen inside.

Much of the ceremonial activity is focused in the men's house. During a cremation, if the dead person is a man, his corpse is usually kept in the men's house, sitting flexed against a side wall, until it is time to bring it into the

PLATE 42. Aerial view of Abulopak. On the right, pigs stand in the *wam lal;* the cook house of the central compound is being rethatched. (Photograph 1968)

PLATE 43. Abugulmo, where a new pig sty is being built in preparation for the reopening of the nearest compound, which has been empty for some time.

yard, grease it, and lay it on the pyre. Wounded men usually remain in the men's house, and thus away from women. Curing ceremonies take place to a great extent in the men's house. And in ceremonies that involve shell bands and exchange stones, these are brought first to the men's house, where they collect until time to lay them in the yard and redistribute them.

The lower room of the men's house escapes the dense gloom of the sleeping loft. During the day some light and even occasionally the bright sun comes through the double doorway. At night the interior may be briefly lit up by a blazing fire. In the center of the room is the fireplace, sunk into the ground, and surrounded by the inward-slanting four center posts. Firewood is kept ready just to the rear, or lies drying in the rack above.

The two sets of rafters of the *bilai* afford nooks to wedge things in. Often wooden hooks dangle from the ceiling and on them are hung neck ornaments, shells or throat strips, and men's small tobacco nets. Between the center posts are lashed the platforms for drying firewood. On these platforms and in the lashing are stuck and hung chunks of rolled tobacco, bamboo knives, feathers for ritual purification; mandibles of the small marsupials and rodents killed in the hunt, now slowly turning black from the sooty smoke of the fire.

Since only a few men's houses have really tight walls, the smoke of the fire may seep out through the cracks between the wall slabs and drift out the doors above the cool clean incoming air. But most of the soot is deposited on the rafters. They and any objects hung near the fireplace turn a shiny black after a few months. If a pig-killing arrow is stored in the rafters near the fire, it is necessary to wrap its point with a leaf to avoid the black deposit.

The most important objects of the rafter space are the weapons and symbols of fighting, stored between the fireplace and the entrance. These are usually one or more arrows that have wounded a resident of the men's house, have been drawn out, and now serve as countermagic, laid with its tip toward the door; and one or more sets of miniature bows and arrows, like those used by the smallest of the children or those set into the base of a newly finished watchtower. These are also used in ceremonies related to battle.

Minor fighting trophies are kept in the two most important men's houses. These have been taken from the killed enemy and are called *ab watek,* dead men.

The four center posts serve as back rests; men relax against them, backs to the warming fire, as they talk or work or smoke. When a man is wounded, or very ill, a cord is tied between two side posts, halfway down, for the man to hang on, to support himself over the fire. The old man Ejak spent most of his last months hanging on the strap in his son's men's house.

Higher up, between the rear center posts, a permanent strap is fixed from which things can be suspended to dry: a fresh tobacco roll; a green gourd destined to become a penis gourd; small rodents which have been used for illness, wound, or stolen pig augury, and then hung up to dry for months.

On the floor in front of the fireplace are a bark or wood dish for depositing sweet potato skins before they are tossed to the pigs and usually several lengths of thin cane that are reamed out and used as cigarette holders.

PLATE 44. Asukdlokoima (1963)

PLATE 45. Wubakaima (1963), with the author's house.

A fire is kept going most of the time. In the morning the last coals are dug out of the ashes and the first warming fire is built to cut the cold of the early morning for the naked men who have spent the night in the comfort of the sleeping loft. This fire, like most Dani fires, serves two main functions: warmth and cigarette lighting. Occasionally a potato may be baked in the fire, but food is usually brought in from the common cook house. As the men drift off for the day's activities, the fire is banked, to be re-stoked whenever a man returns to the compound. If the fire should die, fresh coals are fetched from one of the other fires in the compound. By late afternoon, most of the men have returned, and the fire receives regular attention as long as the men stay awake, until nine or ten o'clock on most evenings. A final stock of wood is laid on by the last man to crawl into the loft, and the fire slowly dies down through the night, maintaining a comfortable temperature in the sleeping loft above.

Each man who frequents the men's house has an area for his belongings. The wall itself is used for storage: axes and adzes may be leaned against it; things may be wedged between the horizontal stringers and the upright wall planks; and often a long stick is so wedged that between it and the wall an envelope of feathers or cigarette leaves can be placed; a new penis gourd or other object may be wrapped in the dried outer bark of the banana plant and hung on the rafters near the wall. At any time there are numerous secret wrapped bundles of all sizes and shapes hanging from the rafters; now and then one will be taken down, and a new gourd unwrapped or a necessary feather extracted to complete a hairdo. Large fur headpieces may also be stored in tall cylindrical bark containers standing against the wall.

Usually on each side, near the wall, a long pole is suspended from the rafters. Here may be hung drying tobacco leaves; during a ceremony, pig meat which is held over to be eaten the next day may be hung as well.

The ceremonial focus of the men's house is the rear wall, where a cabinet (*gagok*) runs across the wall (Plate 59). This cabinet is usually raised above the ground. It has a sliding door like that of the house itself and is used to store sacred objects, *ganekhe*.

The front of the cabinet is often festooned with the steamed, dried ferns and other leaves from an important ceremony. Under the cabinet on a pole hang mandibles of pigs killed in important ceremonies. In the lashings of the front of the cabinet are stuck the feathers on wands used to ritually cleanse the hands of those who have come in contact with *wusa*, or taboo, objects.

Cabinets are not found in every men's house, only in those where there is a need to store sacred objects. Although spears are rarely brought into the house, bows and arrows are usually stored here. They may be wrapped in banana bark and hung from the rafters to the rear of the fireplace; or they may be leaned against the rear wall—or, if there is a cabinet, against the cabinet, and indeed sometimes even sticking into the open door of the cabinet.

Symbolism of the Men's House. Different areas of the floors of the lower

PLATE 46. Abulopak (1963)

PLATE 47. Mabilatma (1963)

area and the loft have special names, and the following ideal pattern for seating is stated: in the *dugam*, the front area between the entrance and the fire, sit the most important men and the warriors, ready to spring out at the first signs of enemy attack; in the *idikmo*, the rear area, sit the boys and the *gebu* men; other men sit at the sides. In practice this arrangement is hardly ever observed, although there is a tendency for the more important men to sit toward the front while the less important men and boys sink back into the shadows at the sides or the rear of the room. But if even the most worthless man is working on knitting or some other activity that demands light, he will not hesitate to move into the *dugam* and then, when he is finished, retire to the shadows. There is an apparent discrepancy between the ideal statement that the rear sitting area is the least important and the fact that the sacred objects are stored in the cabinet at the rear of the house. In fact, during ceremonies the older important men tend to sit in the rear, behind the fireplace, even when the sacred objects are not directly involved.

The antechamber is called the *miobulak* (the word includes *mio*, rain) or the *mogat ai* (ghost house), referring to its two important aspects. In daily life, it is a handy place to drop an axe or tool not immediately being used, or to toss a rattan strip which may someday be of use; during ceremonies, when the men's house is likely to be filled to capacity, it serves as an additional shelter from sun or rain. It is also considered to be a place for the ghosts to sit when they come on a visit to the compound seeking food. The idea is that if the ghosts can have this place to sit, they will not find it necessary to actually enter the men's house and perhaps cause trouble.

The four center poles of the men's house are consciously anthropomorphized, the front two being considered important men and the rear two being old men or youths. The planks lashed across the uprights, on which firewood is laid to dry over the fire, are called *hali igi* (*hali*, firewood: *igi*, fingers, lower arms). This symbolism is supported by the paraphernalia: the crossbar usually has bamboo wound around it in which knives or pig tusks are often kept and which corresponds to the form and function of the men's arm band. The uprights themselves are decorated with the same objects worn as *wopok*, neck gear: pig tails, cocoons, bark or spider web strips. Often there are also bunches of steamed fern from the steam bundle of a past ceremony. All this seems to be to strengthen the house vis-à-vis the ghosts.

In some men's houses there is a layer of ashes, a hearth, under the grass of the sleeping loft. This hearth is just above the hearth in the lower room, and is called *mogat wuligan*, ghost hearth. It is for the convenience of ghosts who visit the house at night. They can come in, use the hearth to light their cigarettes, and go away happy.

Thus, protection against ghosts is achieved on several perimeters of defense. First, they are lured by the front porch, to stay there; then the power of the anthropomorphized uprights and their magical paraphernalia intimidates and neutralizes ghosts that do enter the house; and finally, ghosts that penetrate to the sleeping loft are appeased with their own hearth.

Construction. The main part of the construction is done by the men and boys who will live in the men's house. Chopping of lumber and actual construction is done only by men; women carry wood and thatch grass to the site. Often other men will casually drop by to assist in the construction. During thatching, men will be called to assist as part of a semiformalized exchange of labor.

The first step in making a men's house is clearing the ground, removing grass and tree roots with digging sticks. Then materials, which have usually been completed before actual construction, are assembled: new planks, cut and shaped in the forests (if an old structure is available, it is dismantled and the best planks are used); bundles of vines, often thrown into a convenient ditch to soak to soften.

A circle of heavy vines is laid on the ground and carefully rounded out. This is used as a guide for placing the wall uprights. The two largest rafters, which will run from front to back on either side of the fireplace, are laid directly on the circle. The wall uprights are then set into the ground around the outside of the guide circle: shallow holes about twenty centimeters deep are dug with digging sticks, then the uprights set into them. When the uprights are in position, horizontal circles of rattan are used to tie the frame together. These circles are paired, one on the inside, one on the outside, and lashed together with vines through the cracks between the wall slats.

Rafters are now laid on across the tops of the wall uprights closing off the lower chamber. There are two sets, one runing front to back, the other side to side. The four centerposts are set in, one in each quadrant of the floor, surrounding the area where the fireplace will be dug. The centerposts are about eighty centimeters apart at their bases but meet at about three meters above the ground; their combined point will represent the peak of the roof. The reed floor is laid

PLATE 48. Men are about to thatch a woman's house in a new compound.

down across the upper layer of rafters. The reeds are laid tight against each other, each one lashed with thin vine to the rafters beneath.

The frame for the domed roof is made with supple saplings four to six meters long. Their butt ends are jammed into the earth at the outside circle of the walls, then curved to the center poles (Pl. 48). As the men on the ground fix the poles and bend them over, a man standing on the reed floor of the sleeping loft grasps the ends and lashes them together where they cross at the center. The dome framework is made of dozens of such poles ten or more centimeters apart. On the outside of this dome, reeds are lashed horizontally at small distances to form a base for the thatch. The *miobulak*, antechamber, is added at the front of the structure: upright slats are driven into the ground, then more slats are lashed across them to form a low roof. The *jitne*, a thick pad of grass, is lashed on around the structure extending about fifty centimeters above and below the level of the sleeping floor to assure that the sleeping loft will be draft-free.

Now thatch is laid on the roof. The day before, both men and women will have gone to a grassy area, usually a fallow garden or abandoned compound site, where the grass has grown to a meter in height. Usually the men of the compound have some right to that land. The grass, grasped by the bare hand just above the roots, is plucked in handfuls, laid in a heap, and finally, when a bundle of about fifty centimeters in diameter is collected, it is bound. A rope twisted of the same grass is wound around the bundle. The two free ends are twisted together and tucked back under the rope. Women complain that they cannot pluck grass well because they have so few fingers; and after they have helped the men with the first plucking, they carry the bundles, one or two at a time on their heads, back to the construction site.

The thatching is laid from the bottom up. One man or more stands on the sleeping floor, his head and shoulders through the holes in the frame, catching the bundles as other men throw them up to him. Discarding the ropes that bound the bundles, he lays out the grass. One man may follow him around, beating the grass, matting it as it is laid down. Gradually he works around one level, then around the next higher level, until he is forced to stand on the frame itself to thatch the top of the dome. By careful laying and judicious beating of the thatch, the grass usually stays in place even on the steepest portion of the dome. (Sometimes thatching will be done in two steps—an underlayer laid, its roots pointing toward the ground, and then a second layer, with the tops of the leaves pointing downward, laid over it.) When all the thatch is laid, the twisted grass ropes of the bundles are thrown on the finished house.

The doorways are finished off by low uprights, twenty centimeters high, which are put as sills, and boards are wedged inside the opening, making a frame.

The fireplace is dug out in the center of the ground floor, between the four centerposts. First, with a digging stick, a depression deeper than the intended fireplace is dug and lined with clay. Usually women carry the clay to the construction site, where a man mixes it with water to a sticky texture, then carefully plasters the hole, lining it several centimeters thick. The fire pit is then allowed to dry for a couple of days before the first fire, which will eventually bake it to a sort of pottery core. The last phase of construction is to gather sweet, tender grass and lay it on the floor of the new house.

MAGIC ASSOCIATED WITH HOUSEBUILDING. Various forms of magic were observed in connection with the construction of the men's house. At Anisimo a knot of grass was tied around an upright wall plank at the inside rear of the house. This was to draw the smoke out the rear, through the cracks between the slats, so it would not get in the eyes of those inside. At Biem, dried banana leaf was wrapped around the base of the broad upright at the center of the rear as protection against ghosts and rodents. At Musanima, after the wall planks were put in, a banana leaf smeared with pig grease, on which were laid sprigs of the *pholopholo* weed, was tied to the rear center plank. This was done swiftly and with no apparent other ritual. The purpose was to protect the house from ghosts.

In several men's houses, small bundles of grass called *isia* are tied to the base of the center poles to protect the poles from ghosts who, in the form of rodents, might chew the poles through and bring the house down.

RENEWAL AND REPAIR. The men's house is used for as long as the compound is occupied and is often repaired. The most frequent repairs are to the thatch of the roof. This is renewed every year or so, whenever it begins to leak. The outer thatch is removed, but the inner layer is usually left as a base for the new thatch. When a compound is abandoned, the structures are usually left standing until the former occupants need the wood for other construction. Then it is torn down. The frame of the men's house dome usually is transported intact to the new site; those boards that have not rotted at their bases are also transported to the new site.

Often when a compound is deserted for a short time and then reoccupied, the men's house will merely be rethatched; if it is completely rebuilt, as much of the old wood as possible will be used.

WOMAN'S ROUND HOUSE (*Ebeai*)

The *ebeai* is the smaller round house in which one or more women sleep (see diagram 9.3). *Ebe* most commonly means body, often in the sense of presence, but also has implications of main, or central; *ai* means house. Structurally the *ebeai* resembles the men's house in most respects. However, it tends to be smaller in diameter than all but the smallest men's houses. The lower room, rather than being directly on the ground, has a reed floor structurally like the loft of the men's house, raised about thirty centimeters above the ground. It extends to the outside antechamber. Between the four center posts there is a hole in the floor, and the fireplace is built up from planks about fifteen centimeters from the ground.

The rear third or quarter of the lower room is blocked off by boards to form

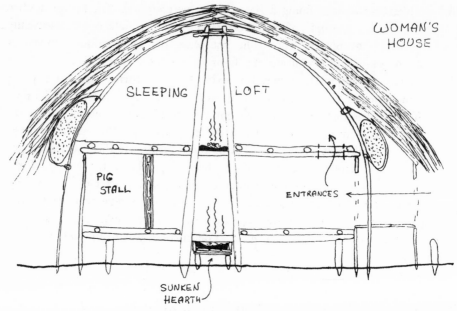

WOMAN'S
HOUSE

SLEEPING LOFT

PIG
STALL

ENTRANCES

SUNKEN
HEARTH

DIAGRAM 9.3
WOMEN'S ROUND HOUSE (*Ebeai*)

a separate place for pigs, the small pigs or sick pigs which the women care for, to stay at night. This has the name (*gagok*) as the sacred object cabinet in the analogous position in the men's house.

Some women's houses have a fireplace in the loft, with the clay laid directly on the reed floor.

Although the men of a compound all use the men's house, each woman generally has her own house, which is referred to in terms of the woman, or most important woman, sleeping in it. Two women who are good friends may share the same house. They may be two cowives, but since cowives usually find it hard to get along together, one more often finds a woman and her unmarried daughter living together, or an older woman who has moved into a compound with her married daughter or daughter-in-law.

Men are not barred access to the women's houses, but these structures have in no sense the common-house quality of the men's house and the cook house. Husbands and sons of the resident woman enter freely and may even store goods and tools there. Husbands occasionally sleep in the women's house and this is where at least some of the conjugal sexual intercourse takes place. It is possible for an unwilling wife to bar the door of her house, refusing access to her husband.

The woman's house of Egabue at Wubakaima was gradually changed into a men's house. Egabue moved into her mother-in-law's house in the same compound, and Loliluk's wife, Modokoluk, moved into Egabue's house. A few months later Motokoluk died, but Loliluk continued to frequent the house. Gradually ceremonial goods that were accumulating in the regular men's house because of cremations in the compound were moved into the house. By this time the structure was functionally, if not by name, a men's house. Women no longer entered, and it served as a sort of secondary men's house for Loliluk.

COMMON COOK HOUSE (*Hunu*)

The common house, or *hunu*, is the site of much ordinary family activity, where men and women sit together, talking, cooking, working, eating.

The cook house is long and rectangular, stretching along one side of the compound—usually the left side. Several entrances open onto the courtyard. Along the center axis of the house lie the fireplaces; the length of the house depends on the number of fireplaces necessary for the compound when it is built.

Most cook houses are two meters wide and from 7.1 to 18.1 meters long. The walls are not constructed simply of broad upright slats, as are the round houses, but of pairs of upright stakes, between which are wedged horizontal stringers which form the body of the wall. (See diagram 9.4.)

Down the center run ridge poles, and between these are the fireplaces. Usually at one or both ends of the house is a steam bundle pit, with rocks for heating, and the leafy remains of the last steaming.

Above the fireplaces, on boards lashed between roof struts, firewood is stored and dried. Each woman has her own fireplace; or sometimes they double up, on the pattern of shared women's houses. Against the back will is dried brush for firewood; materials for making string; vegetables brought in from the gardens that day; perhaps a young pig or two whose mothers have been killed, and which are in the charge of a woman until the time when they are able to join the other pigs; assorted water gourds; a matted grass rain cape; and the women's digging sticks.

A cook house is occupied rather than owned. Each woman in the compound has one fireplace, and here she sits most of the time, retiring to her house only briefly during the day to fetch things, or at night to sleep. Men have free access to the cook house and usually sit with one of their wives or their mother.

Most of the daily cooking is done in the cook house. Here the sweet potatoes are roasted and every few days a steam pit is made up to cook sweet potatoes and leaves of various edible plants.

This is a common house. People of all ages drift in and out, usually gravitating to the fires of those women to whom they are related. Women do most of their work here, making thread, weaving nets, making girl's skirts (Plate 40). Children play up and down the length of the house with complete freedom; occasionally a child falls into one of the unshielded floor-level fires and is seriously burned.

Ceremonial Use. The cook house has only a peripheral role in most ceremonies. When the compound is filled with visitors at a cremation or other event, women crowd into it to escape the rain or sun. If it is a woman who has died, the corpse is usually placed against the center of the rear cook house wall during the morning, surrounded by mourning women.

The night of the first day of the cremation, as the pyre is slowly burning down to coals and then ashes, some people, especially women and children, stay up through the night in a sort of wake. The men's house is closed on the sleeping men by about midnight, and even in the cook house some women and girls lie down to doze for a while. But the fires are kept going, and sweet potatoes and even meat from the pigs slaughtered that day are occasionally cooked for those still awake. The atmosphere is light after the strain of the day, and there is much joking.

At the funeral the men who carry the bundle to the hilltop leave from the cook house, and late the next day the adze in the net is hung on the back wall (pp. 155-6). The bundle containing the bony remains of the corpse picked out of of the ashes the second morning is also hung on the back wall of the cook house.

Construction of the Cook House. The long houses are in some respects constructed as the round houses. There is similar division of labor: the men do all the work except carry material, especially thatch, to the construction site.

The ground is cleared and leveled with digging sticks, and construction materials are assembled. Then poles are laid and pegged down to indicate the positions of the side walls; pairs of narrow uprights are planted into the ground. Sometimes a shallow hole is dug, and the pole is grasped, raised above the head, aimed at the hole, and slammed into the ground. If it does not go deep enough on the first try, it is wiggled back and forth until it can be removed, and again raised and slammed in. When it is fixed, the earth around it is tamped down by the foot. Pairs of poles, one inside the guide pole, one outside, are inserted. Then horizontal boards are wedged between the uprights, gradually building up the wall. The first boards fit easily between the uprights. The building up of the wall continues, leaving gaps between the uprights which will side the doorways. It becomes necessary to force many of the thicker boards into position, often with a heavy wooden club. The end walls are put in as a single line of uprights implanted in the ground. Across the top, a horizontal pole is lashed, holding the whole wall of end poles together.

The centerposts are either cut so as to have a natural crotch at the top, or a crotch is carefully carved with an adze. A hole is dug and the pole is thrown into it again and again until it is sunk to the proper depth. If the ground becomes too hard after successive poundings, water is poured in to loosen the soil. The ridge pole or, if the house is too long, overlapping ridge poles, is laid along the line of crotches. At each crotch, the ridge pole is lashed to the side walls by vine stays. Now the roof slats are laid on—narrow boards, often slightly rotten lumber from a dismantled house. The roof slats are lashed at the ridge pole and often where they overhang the side walls. The ridge pole extends approximately fifty centimeters beyond the end walls. To accomodate the general roof overhang, struts are extended from the tops of the side walls the same distance. On these are laid the end roof slats. Sometimes a separate eave pole like the center poles, as high as the side wall poles but planted twenty centimeters out from them, supports the ends of the roof slats that overhang the structure.

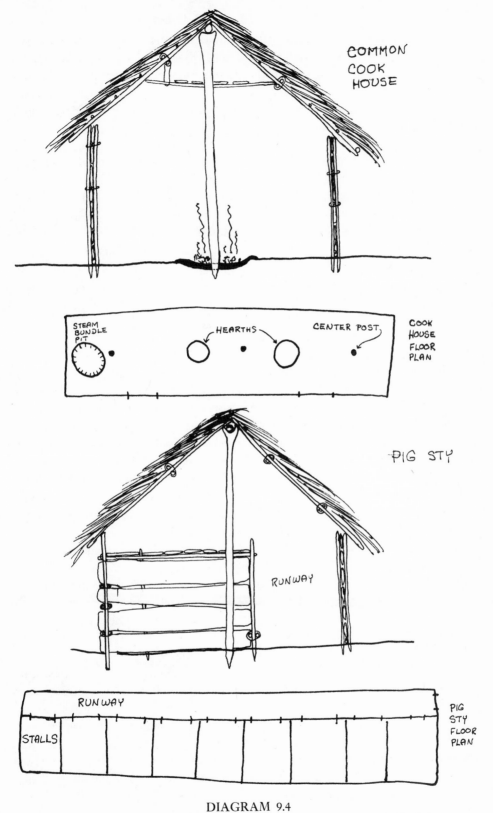

COMMON
COOK
HOUSE

STEAM
BUNDLE
PIT

HEARTHS

CENTER POST

COOK
HOUSE
FLOOR
PLAN

PIG STY

RUNWAY

RUNWAY

STALLS

PIG
STY
FLOOR
PLAN

DIAGRAM 9.4
THE COMMON COOK HOUSE (*Hunu*) AND THE PIG STY (*Wam dla bu*)

Thatch is laid on top in a manner similar to the thatching of the round houses (Plate 42). When thatching is finished, the last bundles of grass are laid out along the ridge pole to seal up the ridge area from leakage. As the finishing touches, fireplaces are dug by the men; cross-struts are laid across the horizontal stringers of the roof, making an A shape and providing storage and drying space below the ridge. The doorways are finished like those of the round houses.

Every year or so, the house must be rethatched and the walls may be rebuilt. The roof edge is raised off the side walls and held up by stick supports while the side walls are dismantled and completely rebuilt.

The *lise* is a shorter version of the *hunu*, apparently distinguished primarily by name. It has only one entrance, one fireplace, and one steam pit. The *lise* serves the same function as the *hunu* and is a secondary *hunu*. In a Wubakaima compound, when a man extended the compound outside the regular walls, he built a *lise* there for his wife; in another Wubakaima compound, the wife of Egali has a *lise* to herself and is never seen inside the *hunu*, although Egali frequents the men's house.

FENCES

A compound is enclosed by two fences: an inner fence, or sections of fence connecting the various structures and enclosing the yard; and an outer fence, which encloses the banana gardens behind the houses.

Fences may be constructed in two ways: like the front walls of the long houses with horizontal boards held together by pairs of uprights lashed together through the slats; and with upright palings held together by an upper and lower pair of horizontal stringers. Fences are usually topped by thatch grass, sometimes simply laid on top, sometimes supported as a narrow rooflet by short cross-bars.

The thatchings on fence tops are convenient places for laying things: drying plant stems and brine-soaked banana bark and so forth.

The inner fences are about 1.5 meter high; the outer fences are more elaborate. About two meters high, they have the additional support of diagonal struts. The lower fences can be crossed at several points where there is no thatch. The top of the fence has been lowered to a convenient height, and there are low steps on either side of the fence, forming a stile. Steps allow access to the banana yard at one or more places from the courtyard.

The main entrance to the compound is more elaborate. Here the fence rises to about three meters. The thatched roof is supported out from the fence by two uprights on either side of the fence, and there is actually a narrow roof, like that of the *hunu*. In this entrance structure are two entrance ways. One of them is high enough to allow a person with bulging back nets to pass through without bending over. The step up to this entrance is more elaborate and often adds an unexpected, almost Japanese touch—a water-worn boulder, or a twisted root or branch. The second entrance is small and near the ground, used by pigs and occasionally small children.

Both entrances are closed at night, and during the day when the compound is deserted, by broad boards that fit into slots at the top and bottom and are barred across the middle by a pole.

During cremation ceremonies the front entrance structure is used: the symbolic ghost-releasing bundle is carried from the pyre, where it has been shot or hit, and laid on the top thatch. The next morning, as the adze net and the bundle are carried back from the *wagun* (ghost) watch, they are hung on the outside of the entrance for a day before being brought in to the *hunu* (p. 154).

COURTYARD

The central courtyard is called the *silimo*, or settlement place. All the structures open onto it, and during a rainy spell it is churned into mud by the constant traffic between houses and entrances. Except during ceremonies, the courtyard is more of a passage than a place.

The areas of the yard are named: the areas directly before the entrance and the pig sties are called *hutagola*, or passage. The body of the yard is divided like that of the houses: the back, near the men's house, is the *idikmo*; the half near the entrance is the *dugam*. Ideally, when the yard is filled during a ceremony, the men sit in the rear half, the women in the front half. This is done except when the women's area is overcrowded and they are sometimes allowed to move to the rear. In most compounds, where the men's house occupies the back and the women's houses and cook house the middle, women seldom have need to go into the *idikmo* area, but there is no prohibition against it. The area around the houses and under their eaves, where there is often a shallow ditch to drain the thatch run-off, is called the *maikmo*.

In every yard there are one or more *bpakte*, or pits for steam bundle. These pits are roughly conical, dug with a digging stick, about two meters at the mouth and one meter deep. When the pits are not being used, the grass lining that spills out over their sides is flipped back into the holes, and often someone will sit on the grass edge while working in the sun. During a rainy spell the pit fills with water and is used to wash off muddy feet, or small children may splash about in it, using it as a wading pool.

The populous compounds have no trouble keeping the yard free of grass and weeds, but in those with less people, men often use a digging stick to cut the grass down to root level. Only in Asikanodlek's compound is the yard allowed to grow wild with weeds. Other men note this and remark that he is a careless man.

During a rainy spell, one of the men may take it upon himself to scrape the surface mud off to the side of the courtyard with the side of his foot. This is only a temporary solution, for the new surface is quickly churned up by feet, human and pig. Pigs and small children may defecate in the yard, but older people always step outside the courtyard.

Around the houses and along the fences grow single plants of tobacco, taro, mallow, and sometimes gourds. The vines may be allowed to climb up the thatch of a nearby roof, or a gourd frame may be built out into the yard for a few months until the gourds are ripe.

Although most of the daily life takes place indoors, on a chilly day a man or woman will often move into the yard to work in the warmth of the sun. Children play freely indoors and out. On nights when there is a full moon, young people and adults congregate in the yard, often sitting around a low fire talking or playing games.

During important ceremonies, such as cremation, the yard fills up with visitors who sit on the ground, the men to the rear, the women to the front. The cremation ceremony is focused on the yard: here the pigs are slaughtered and eaten, the shell bands received and later distributed, and the corpse burned. Subsequent ceremonies in the funeral cycle, curing ceremonies, and others take place primarily in the yard.

PIG STY

The pig sty is a long rectangular structure opening onto the yard but extending back into the banana yard (Plate 43). It is called either *wam ai* (*wam*, pig; *ai*, house) or *dlabu*.

Externally the sty resembles the cook house—the same long rectangular structure, and the same wall and roof construction. Inside there are individual stalls, about 1.25 meters high and roofed with planks. On top is a storage area for fire or construction wood, vines, fighting spears, and digging sticks. Each stall opens onto a passage which in turn opens onto the yard, and each has an individual plank door (see Diagram 9.4).

Pigs spend nights in the stalls, and the days when, because of rain or fighting or a ceremony, they are not taken out to root. Each stall is occupied by a single pig or a sow with shoats, or, occasionally, immature siblings. Grass is laid on the ground of the stalls. Generally there is little problem with feces, since even on rainy days the pigs are usually led out of the compound for a few moments, and they seem to be more or less housebroken.

The sty is constructed by those men who will keep pigs there. First the ground is cleared and construction materials assembled. Then guide poles are laid down for the rear wall and the front line of the stalls, and the rear wall and front wall of stalls are erected. Dividing walls between the stalls are laid horizontally and the side walls erected. The center posts are planted, and the roof over the stalls is laid down and lashed. Then ridge poles are laid on center pole crotches and anchored to the outer walls with diagonal lashing. The roof is constructed in the same manner as on the common cook house, and the doorway finished.

As the sty walls gradually rot, it becomes easy for mice and rats to get to the pigs at night and injure them (p. 56). Sometimes a sty is moved and rebuilt with new boards to discourage rodents. (Once I observed a dried banana leaf wrapped around the center posts as magical protection against rats and ghosts.)

Banana Yard

The area behind the compound structures, enclosed by the outer fence, is called the *hagiloma* (*hagi*, banana; *lo* and *ma*, place of). This is the only area where bananas are grown. There may also be a few pandanus trees; occasionally a large tree for shade, to cut wind, and on which a spider web may be encouraged; gourd frames; and often taro, yam, and sometimes a small patch of sweet potato.

During a ceremony when the yard is filled beyond capacity, visitors who are least central, least related to the dead man, will slip into the banana yard where they will sit out of sight but within hearing distance of the activity in the yard. Pig meat is always passed out to them.

Within many banana yards is an area separately fenced, called the *wam lal*, where pigs can be let run without taking them out of the compound proper. In some cases, the pig sty will have a secondary entrance directly into the *wam lal* (Plate 42).

Ritual Enclosures

Behind some men's houses are two important ceremonial structures: the *oak leget* and the *wadlo leget*. The *oak leget* (*oak*, bone; *leget*, fence) is a low enclosure about a meter square, built in the style of the front wall of the cook house. Its walls seldom rise more than fifty centimeters, although the uprights may be a meter high. Here the ashy remains of a cremation are deposited after they have been plucked from the fire and kept in the cook house for a day (p. 156). Remains of everyone cremated in the compound, regardless of sib or home compound, are deposited here with little ceremony and no attempt to distinguish one from the other. The uprights are generally decorated with dried ferns and banana leaves from the steam pit.

The *wadlo leget* (insect fence) is considered to be the house of ghosts. It is a low enclosure like the *oak leget;* in one wall it has a square entrance chopped in the bottom of the lowest board; it is divided across the center by a wall about forty centimeters high. When built, or "renewed" in an important ceremony, fresh mud is smeared on the ground around it. Nothing is laid inside, but greens from the steam pit may be draped on the uprights.

During a curing ceremony for an old man—the third, following two unsuccessful ceremonies—the old enclosure, which was felt to be inefficacious, was dismantled and a new one was built.

A similar structure, but smaller, is found behind the house of the most important *he phatphale*, curing women, and is used in certain curing ceremonies which were not observed by me.

Variations

Several compounds in the Neighborhood have slight variations on this general plan of structures.

In Wubakaima, Asokmege, who has several wives, built an annex for one in the banana yard of his compound consisting of one woman's house and a small cook house (Plate 45). After this was abandoned, he built in the same general area a pig sty, at the end of which was attached a cook house. The sty has two entrances, one through the *lise*, the other opening into a fenced pig run.

In the compound at Asukdlokoima, where the Wilil *ganekhe* (sacred objects) are kept and which is thus often the scene of important ceremonies, there is a back yard with a steam pit for handling overflow from the courtyard. (Plate 44). In Weteklue's compound at Abulopak there is a similar back yard with steam pit and a single woman's house (Plate 46).

In addition to special structures, there are some specialized compounds. Padosagi was a compound built high on the ridge above the Neighborhood, primarily for pigs, at a time when the war frontier with the Widaia was too dangerous to allow pigs near it. It offered easy access to fresh rooting grounds, and its strategic position made the casual theft of pigs more difficult for a raiding party of Widaia. This special compound consists of a single men's house, a single women's house, and four stys. It was built by a dozen men from several different compounds in the Dugum Neighborhood. By late 1961, when the Widaia frontier had cooled off, it was abandoned. The stys were dismantled and their lumber used for stys in the other compounds. There are several such pig compounds in the Neighborhood.

Wakawaka, the compound of Sula, is an important ceremonial compound. It lies two hours' walk from the Dugum Neighborhood to the northwest, against the mountain wall. It has an exceptionally long courtyard, along which nets and stones were laid during the *je wakanin* ceremony (p. 139). The men's house, where important trophies of battles are kept, is separated from the womens' part of the compound by a fence.

TOOLS

The Dani have a small repertory of stone, bone, and bamboo tools.

Ground Stone Tools (Plates 50–56)

The stone adze, *jaka*, is the general tool of the Dugum Dani. It is used for chopping down trees, for shaping such things as digging sticks, for smoothing planks, for breaking pig bones during butchering. The stone axe, *jakabiliga*, is also common, used primarily for splitting logs into planks or firewood.

Stones for these tools are not obtainable locally and must be imported. There is apparently only one source for the stones: quarries in the bed of the Jelime River, some 150 kilometers to the northwest of the Dugum, in the Nogolo Basin.

There is little population in the immediate vicinity of the Jelime, but Western Dani come from areas several days' walk to quarry the stone, which occurs in the raw state as large boulders in the stream bed. This quarry area was first

PLATE 49. A man sits in a watchtower while others are in the shelter below.

visited by the Harrer Expedition in 1962. According to Harrer's description (1963:155ff), fires are built on wooden platforms against the large boulders, which are then broken up into convenient pieces and carried in nets back to the villages. There the men grind the stones down into blades. These blades are traded over several hundreds of kilometers in the Highlands. They reach the Grand Valley by various trade routes from the west. Only once was a blank, unground stone observed in the Dugum Neighborhood. Otherwise, the blades are finished by the time they reach the Dugum Dani.

By the early 1960's there was no longer much trade in stone blades in the Grand Valley, in part because metal blades were trickling into the valley, and perhaps also because of near-saturation of blades from long years of trading.

The general Dani term for adze stone, as well as for the implement itself, is *jaka*. There are two major types of stone, *jaka gu* and *ebe jaka*. The *gu* is a dull

PLATE 50. A stump cut with a stone adze.

PLATE 51. A tree cut with a
stone adze.

PLATE 52. A stump cut with a steel axe.

PLATE 53. Sharpening a stone
adze blade.

PLATES 54, 55. Chopping a tree with a stone adze. (Photograph directed in 1968)

PLATE 56. Splitting wood with a stone axe; one boy chops while the other wedges the wood open with a stick.

black stone too soft to hold a good edge for long, and is described as *aik dlek* (*aik*, tooth; *dlek*, none). *Ebe jaka* is a term used for several different kinds of stone, considerably harder than *gu* and appearing in a variety of colors: green, blue, mottled, streaked, and plain. Samples of the harder stone, *ebe jaka*, were analyzed by W. Valk, head of the Netherlands New Guinea Bureau of Geology and Mining in 1962. He reported (in a letter of May 2) that the stone is

a metamorphic rock consisting of the minerals epidote and clorite as major constituents, accompanied by small amounts of glaucophane, titanite, albite (?), free silica (chalcedony or quartz), calcite, and opaque minerals.

The distinction between *jaka gu* and *ebe jaka* is obvious from the color. Distinctions among the different sorts of *ebe jaka* are unclear. Eight different names were elicited: *dlelaka, deneli, busu, onagen, dedok, dipo,* and *hipitiga.* When informants were presented with a stone, a name was immediately given with the greatest confidence. But when the same stone was checked with other informants, or rechecked later with the original informant, the names seldom agreed. This disparity was an ever increasing puzzle. As the months of the field investigation wore on, and other systems of the Dani culture became clearer, the *ebe jaka* types became less and less so. Obvious cues of color and shape, which I thought would be used in the typology, were ignored by the Dani. Attempts to check this data with P. van der Stap and his informants at Wamena were fruitless, for in that region the Dani recognize only *ebe jaka* and no subdivision.

The stones are basically oval in cross-section, with a few samples squaring off to a near-rectangular cross-section. In outline they are generally elliptical, but the broader end, with the cutting edge, may be nearly straight. Variations in shape are not considered significant to the Dani. They do distinguish between the *jaka* proper and the lighter, smaller stones, which are called *huonge* and are used for such delicate tasks as finishing spears. The haft of a *huonge* may be in fact larger than that of the regular *jaka*.

Generally the difference between an adze and an axe blade is shape. The adze blade is symmetrical vertically (its outline is a regular ellipse) but the cutting edge is crescent-form when looked at head on. The axe blade is asymmetrical along the long axis, but the cutting edge tends to be straight or S-curved. However, there were several cases where a straight-edged stone has been hafted as an adze, and the other way around.

Most blades are ten to twenty-five centimeters long, but one axe blade thirty-four centimeters long was observed, and the *huonge* blades can be short as five centimeters.

Hafting. The adze is hafted on a piece of wood shaped like a figure 7, cut from a tree at the point where a branch makes a proper angle with the trunk, usually an acute angle between 80° and 45° (Diagram 9.5). The branch forms the handle, the trunk section is the crosspiece on which the stone is hafted. A short butt is left to stick out behind. The handle is carefully smoothed down like a spear, with pig tusk and sanding. The overall length of the haft from tip of handle to butt ranges from about forty to sixty-eight centimeters; from butt to tip of the blade, about thirty-five to fifty centimeters.

The tip of the crosspiece on which the stone rests is flattened. The stone's butt is wrapped in banana trunk tissue and then bound with bamboo rattan or braided cord, or a combination of the two, in an intricate pattern using several meters of material. It usually covers all except the very butt end of the cross-bar of the haft. It would seem that this binding is far more elaborate and extensive than necessary for securing the blade to the crosspiece. Perhaps it also serves to keep the handle from splitting off the crosspiece during use.

The form of the adze haft shows considerable variation. In the southern Grand Valley there is rarely any butt behind the joining of the handle to the crosspiece. In the Dugum Neighborhood, and elsewhere in the central Grand Valley, the butt is about one-third the length of the piece in front of the handle; and in the Western Dani region, the butt is often as long as the forepiece.

The axe blade is hafted in a hole made by a chisel in a long straight or curved piece of wood (Diagram 9.6). The stone is set with the pitch of the araucaria tree. The end of the axe is usually straight and squared off, and is used to wedge wood apart.

Efficiency. The relative efficiency of stone and metal tools is a matter of considerable theoretical interest, and I made an attempt to gauge the efficiency of stone adzes. This was not very successful. Two observations of the same

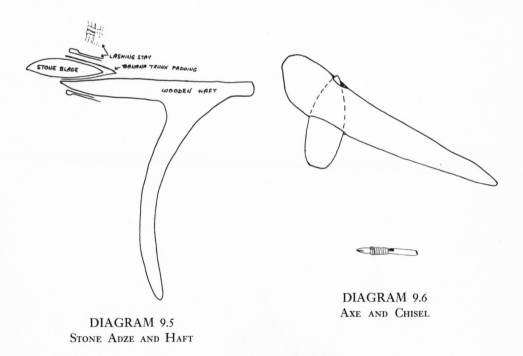

DIAGRAM 9.5
STONE ADZE AND HAFT

DIAGRAM 9.6
AXE AND CHISEL

man chopping down oak trees with an adze showed that a twenty-two-centi-
meter-diameter tree was felled in five minutes and fifteen seconds, and a tree
with a diameter of twenty-two to twenty-five centimeters in seven minutes fifteen seconds. But the subject did the work casually, with several long pauses
to think, or to look around, or to shout to friends in other parts of the forest.
In other words, while this experiment gave an indication of how long it takes
a man to chop down a tree, it gave virtually no information about the stone
adze. Unfortunately I did not pursue this line of investigation.

Use. Both adzes and axes are used almost exclusively by men. Although there
are no specific restrictions against women using them, I rarely saw it. Dani
explained that since women have lost most of their fingers, they were not able
to manipulate the tools well.

When chopping down a tree, a man stands square to the tree and takes short
downward blows, mainly with a wrist action. Chips are removed by alternating
high and low blows some ten centimeters apart.

Axes are used primarily for splitting wood. The log to be split is attacked first
from the end. As soon as the axe has opened a split, a wedge or pole sharpened
at the end is set into it before the axe blade is withdrawn. Then the wood is
struck further down, and the wedge moved down after it. One man working
alone will use a short wedge. If two or more men are helping him, longer sticks
may be used. The sticks first hold the log open, and then are used for prying
the split wider, putting pressure on the splitting wood and making the subsequent chops more effective.

Sharpening. When an adze or axe becomes dull, it is knocked loose from the
haft and ground on sandstone, preferably near water, which is sprinkled on
the rock to increase the grinding power (Plate 53). In several places along the
trails leading from the compounds to the forests on the upper slopes of the
Dugum Neighborhood, large exposed areas of bedrock show innumerable grooves
from years of sharpening.

TOOL KITS

Many men have tool kits, which are usually wrapped in bark cloth and kept
either in a small carrying net or an old head net. These kits contain the basic
small tools of the Dani. The contents of tool kits are pig tusk, bone awls and
needles, flint chips, and bamboo knives.

The tusk of the boar (*wam aik*) is used as an all-purpose concave-edge
scraping tool to smooth down the many poles and handles of Dani tools and
weapons. The back side of the tusk is removed and the inner, concave edge is
scraped down with a flint flake. When the edge is dulled, the flake is used to
resharpen it.

The bone awl (*dlisu*) is made from the femur of a pig; the bone is splintered
and a suitable fragment is ground down on sandstone into a point. The awl
is used in knitting shell bands and for probing for arrows in bodies. The awl is
used interchangeably with the needle, though usually heavier than the needle.

The bone needle (also, like the awl, called *dlisu*) is made in the same way as the awl, but with a hole at the butt end drilled with a piece of flint. Both needle and awl are sometimes carried in a woven sleeve hung from a man's neck, or they may simply be pushed into the man's hair.

Small flint concretions are found in the limestone throughout the Grand Valley. Flint nodules are smashed into small flakes and used, without retouching the edge, for working and sharpening tusks and bone and for engraving wood arrow tips. Some flint is local and some is traded from other parts of the valley.

Finally, in the tool kit is carried a simple bamboo splint knife used for butchering and castrating pigs, for cutting hair, and for other general cutting. The knife is a longitudinal strip of bamboo cut with a flint flake and then usually pointed at the end. When the point is dull, it is easily resharpened by stripping off a strand from the side of the point. Bamboo knives are also carried in the arm band; or in a special holder made of the tail of a large forest marsupial, hung from the neck.

Garden Implements

The only tools used in gardening, beyond the adze used in clearing trees, are digging sticks.

The heavy digging stick is a rough-hewn pole 1.5 to 2 meters long, about eight centimeters thick, and pointed at both ends (Pl. 7). It is made from a tree trunk of roughly the right diameter, the outer wood cut off with an adze. The end is fire-hardened by sticking it in a fire and chopping it down to a point. The paddle digging stick cut down from a plank, is the same length as the heavy stick, but one end splays out to a thin paddle ten to fifteen centimeters wide, which is fire-hardened. It is used exclusively for slicing the ditch mud into chunks that can be easily lifted onto the fields by hand.

These two digging sticks are usually left in the water of the ditches when not used, soaking, to weight them for use. Then, before being used again, their edge or point is sharpened with an adze.

The woman's digging stick, carried by most women when they leave the compound, is seldom more than a meter long and usually only two to four centimeters thick. It is used to break the soil, to plant and harvest sweet potatoes; it is also a defensive weapon in case of a garden raid. This digging stick is finely finished like a man's spear; it is made and resharpened by a man.

Children are often given a small digging stick, usually made from the broken end of a normal digging stick. They use them to play at gardening and to help the women in minor jobs such as breaking the soil in the gardens after the mud has been smeared and dried.

In the early 1960's one man was using steel shovels which he had obtained from the police, but no one else showed any interest in obtaining them. By 1968, however, steel shovels had nearly replaced the men's digging sticks and were one of the most desired trade items.

WEAPONS

The Dani use two kinds of weapons in war, spears and bows and arrows. The men at a battle are about evenly divided between spearmen and archers. There seems to be no reason other than personal preference for carrying one or the other.

SPEARS

The spearmen carry a long jabbing spear and often smaller throwing spears. The jabbing spears are carefully made weapons two to three meters long. A third of the way down the spear is a broad band, woven or wound around the shaft. This is the *hiba*, which separates the blade from the handle. Above it is the flattened, diamond-shaped blade; below it the rounded shaft of the spear, ending in a point used to stick the spear in the ground when it is not being used.

Spears are either light-colored, made of *dlubu*, or laurel, wood, with a dark band, or dark with a deep red shaft, blue-purple blade, and white band, made of *joli*, or myrtle, wood.

In time of war a man carries his spear whenever he leaves his compound. When entering another compound, he leaves the spear outside. If he is doing garden work, the spear is stuck upright in the ground, ready to be grabbed at the first alarm. At a watchtower, the spear is leaned against the shelter. When walking, a man carries his spear over his shoulder, not balanced, but the butt end held in the hand, two thirds of the spear behind pointing out of the way of anyone following him on the path.

Smaller spears are sometimes carried instead of a regular long spear, usually by younger men and youths. These are simply sharpened thin sticks about two meters long.

Manufacture. A spear is made by its owner. The best spear wood comes from the Jalemo and is bought usually from Jale people who come into the Grand Valley on trading trips. Inferior wood for shorter spears may be cut in the mountains to the east of the Neighborhood. If the wood is freshly cut, the first step is to strip off the bark. The pole is held briefly in fire, then the bark is stripped off with an adze. Then the pole is cut down to the approximate size desired for the spear. Short, careful strokes with an adze gradually thin the shaft, keeping it round but cutting the blade into a flattened diamond shape. Now the pole is soaked in a stream and the surfaces sanded with freshly broken sandstone to smooth out the adze marks. Finally, the sharpened concave edge of a pig tusk is used as a scraper, shaping the spear down even further.

If the spear is not satisfactory, the adze, sandstone, and pig tusk will be used again until the proper shape and diameter is reached. Final smoothing is done with *leno*, a rough, abrasive grassy reed (*Equisetum debile* Roxb.) that serves as a fine-grain sandpaper.

The spear is then bent to take out curves in the wood. The maker sights along its length to locate the warp; the spear is held briefly over a fire, then rubbed with beeswax. The wax fills in minor cracks in the wood and prepares it for bending. For the actual bending, the man usually has assistance. The two men may kneel on the opposite ends of the spear, the middle over a lump of earth, or the tip may be wedged in a fence or the crotch of a tree while the shaft is bent. Bending alternates with waxing until the spear is straight.

If the spear is of *dlubu* (laurel) wood, it is left a natural color under the wax; if of *joli* (myrtle) wood, it is colored. The shaft section, which is to be blackened, is laid in the mud of a ditch for a day or so. When it is removed and again polished, a dark, almost purplish black has soaked into the wood. If this process has discolored the blade, the blade is scraped off with a pig tusk and dyed reddish by rubbing with *bimut*, a chunk of baked red clay. The *hiba*, or band, is now put on in one of several ways. The simplest is to wind a strip of araucaria bark around the shaft; or a braided cord may be wound around it, or the band woven on like an arm band. If the spear is the light-colored *dlubu*, the band is left dark; if the spear is the darkened *joli*, the band is caked with white chalklike paste from rotten limestone. Nearly every spear has a band, although new spears are sometimes carried for weeks before being fitted out with a band.

The short spears are made from a pole two or three centimeters in diameter. A diamond-shaped blade is carved at one end, but the shaft of the spear is not carved down. The spear is straightened, but often has a crook or zigzag in the shaft. The spears are not given a band, although they may be mud-blackened.

Use. Normally a man will carry only one spear, but in battle he frequently carries two, one long and one short. When he reaches the front lines, he may throw the short one into the enemy ranks. If it is thrown back, he can retrieve it. If not, it is expendable. The long spear is too valuable to be thrown except when a kill seems certain. It is used primarily as a jabbing, threatening weapon. In both battles and raids, spearmen and archers work together, the spearmen ready to kill a man whom the archer has disabled. Arrows are ineffective for killing but have a longer range than the heavy spear, and considerably more accuracy than a thrown light spear.

Since battles rarely involve hand-to-hand, and therefore spear, fighting, spear wounds are rare. However, when a spear blade is blooded, the blood is carefully scraped off with a pig tusk.

BOW AND ARROW

The bow and arrow are used by the Dani for fighting, hunting, and killing pigs.

The bow is short—rarely more than 1.5 meter long. The bowstring is a bamboo band about one centimeter broad. The arrows are composite, a plain reed shaft and a hardwood point. They are neither notched nor feathered and are relatively inaccurate.

Bow and arrows, like spears, are carried by men whenever they leave their compound for a dangerous area, an area subject to enemy attack. When working in such an area, weapons are never far from their hands.

The arrows are carried, loose or tied together with a string, in the same hand as the bow. The bow is carried unweaponed, except when about to be used. To weapon the bow, the base of the bow is rested on the ground; one knee flexes into the back of the bow, bending it, while the loop of the string is slipped over the top.

When shooting, the extra arrows are held with the bow; the butt of the arrow is held between the thumb and first joint of the forefinger and pulled back against the tension of the bow string; the shaft of the arrow is held under the crook of the forefinger of the bow hand. The bow is held vertically, the arrow at eye level. Occasionally, close-range during battles, the bow is held at a slant and shot from the hips. The bow arm is held straight; and the string is pulled back to just beyond the elbow of the bow arm.

Arrows account for the majority of battle wounds. But even at close range, where they are relatively accurate, they do not have the force to penetrate deeply. Unless they hit a particularly vulnerable spot, they are rarely fatal.

The maximum range of arrows, measured on a level windless field, is about ninety meters. But at ranges beyond ten or twenty meters they must be shot in a high arc. The high-shot arrows, with no feathers to steady their wobbling flight, are easily seen and avoided. If the arrows were shot in volleys, they would be much harder to dodge and thus much more deadly. However, this is never done. Each man fights more or less on his own, with little coordination with his comrades.

Arrows are shot back and forth on the battlefield. The archers arrive at the battle with a dozen or so arrows, and at the end of the day leave with about the same number, but all are different from those he brought. Arrows shot by the enemy are followed in their flight, snatched up, and quickly shot back into the enemy ranks. I watched one arrow make four such trips until it was finally retired from battle in the body of an archer.

There is no special significance attached to an enemy arrow that hits the ground. It may be shot back or eventually carried off the field to be used in a later battle. However, an arrow that causes a wound is carefully saved by the victim and placed in the rafters of the men's house in front of the fireplace. If the arrow cannot be removed and eventually results in death, it is removed from the corpse before cremation.

Of all the killings that took place during my field work, no immediate deaths were caused by arrows. Two men did eventually die from arrow wounds received in battle—one man ten days after the battle, the other some months afterwards.

Bow Manufacture. Bows are made of several different woods, most of which can be obtained from the local forests. Shaping the bow involves the same processes as that of the spear: rough shaping with the adze, finer smoothing with sandstone and finally with *leno* grass. In cross-section, the bow may be either plano-convex or concavo-convex, the back side of the bow being only slightly concave. Cracks in the wood are filled with wax, but there is no special attempt to straighten out the bow, and some are noticeably out of perfect line. Several centimeters from either tip, rattan is wound around; often below this is a centimeter or so of *degan* (arm bandlike) braidwork which serves to anchor the bow string. The bow string is made of a strip of bamboo. It usually includes one or two of the thick node ridges. It is scraped down with a pig tusk to a thickness of about one half centimeter. Loops are made at either end and lashed back on themselves. Although neither end of the string is fixed to the bow, when the bow is unweaponed, one loop is usually left on the bow. Occasionally the bow is decorated with a knot of feathers tied loosely to the upper bow string anchor.

Classification of Arrows. All Dani arrows have certain things in common: They are shot with the same hand positions; there are no specialized bows, so all may be shot from the same bow; all have an unfeathered and unnotched reed shaft; most have a striking head which is separate and set into the shaft; none are more than 170 centimeters long, so that compared with other New Guinea arrows they are relatively short. But there are many aspects in which Dani arrows differ from one another. These variable aspects can mostly usefully be described in terms of three interrelated systems of classification, which are: (1) functional, in terms of the different observed uses of arrows; (2) linguistic, that native classification expressed by the Dani names for types and subtypes of arrows; and (3) physical, in terms of certain physical dimensions.

The functional and physical classifications are analytical classifications made by the ethnographer. They are based on observation of behavior and the results of behavior (that is, behavior objects), and so they could be called implicit native classifications, in contrast to the linguistic classification which is the explicit native classification and is merely reported by the ethnographer. To the extent that the physical classification uses dimensions chosen by the ethnographer without regard for what the natives consider relevant, it is more properly an ethnographic, rather than a native, classification.

The three systems of classification and their interrelationships are described by Diagram 9.7. Two potential problems that could complicate this sort of diagrammatic description do not happen to arise in the case of Dani arrows. First, there is relatively little overlap in functions of different named types. The *mate* group are never used for fighting or pig killing; the hunting arrows are never used for fighting or pig killing; only the single-blade bamboo arrow has two functions, pig killing and fighting. Second, there is only one linguistic classification used for arrows, and its terms do not refer to function and only in a few instances to physical characteristics. The Dani have words for the physical characteristics, of course, and would describe a certain type of arrow as having a barbed, hardwood point. The *mate* arrows are all of hardwood, but so are other types not included under *mate*. In short, there is no evidence to suggest secondary linguistic classification of arrows such as barbed versus unbarbed, or hardwood versus bamboo, or even hunting versus fighting arrows.

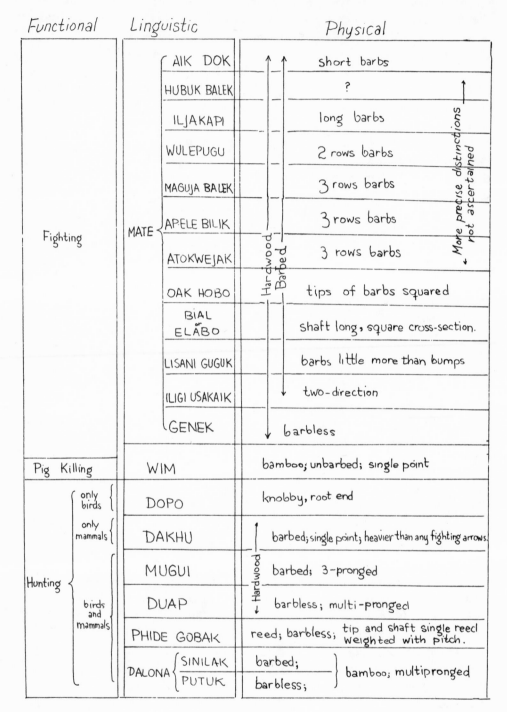

DIAGRAM 9.7

THE CLASSIFICATIONS OF DANI ARROWS: FUNCTIONAL, LINGUISTIC, AND PHYSICAL

These classifications refer only to arrow-tips, since the shafts are all alike.

Hardwood Fighting Arrows. The basic fighting arrow has a hardwood tip, set into the reed shaft (Diagram 9.8). The tip is never more than ½ centimeter in diameter. The arrow tip may be plain, or it may have one to three rows of barbs, carved and gouged out with rodent incisors. Usually the tip has a deep ring notch; if barbed, the barbs are cut deep so the tip of the arrow will break off inside the body. Removal is complicated by barbs. Fighting arrows are often daubed in grease or mud to irritate a wound. Narrow strips of orchid fiber are often wound around the tip near the point; they often are left in the wound when the point is removed and cause irritation. Beyond these irritants, no specific poison is used on arrows.

The shafts of fighting arrows are often decorated with crudely incised designs scratched in with rodent incisors. The tip of the arrow is often decorated with lines and dots. But apparently these designs have no particular meaning.

Although every man and boy can make arrows, some men are known for their ability to make especially fine barbed and decorated ones. However, there are no individual styles in arrows. No one can identify the maker of a particular arrow.

Bamboo Arrows. Bamboo-tipped arrows are used primarily for killing pigs but are also carried and shot in battles. These arrows are tipped with a long blade (about fifty centimeters) made of an arc-section of bamboo, with a sharp point (Diagram 9.9). The concave face of the arrow is often decorated with notches or dots cut in the soft inner side of the bamboo.

There is considerable variation in the way these arrows are fixed to the shaft. They may be simply bound on by many irregular windings of a threadlike fiber; or they may be bound by a tight, bumpy woven sleeve. Often the binding is smeared with the white limestone paste that is also used on the band of the dark long spear. Although these arrows do not break off in the wound and are easily pulled out, their broad blade makes a wide wound which, if encountering a major vein or artery, can be quite serious.

Arrow Variation. The variation in design of fighting arrows in terms of barb patterns, notches, and decoration of tip and shaft is particularly striking. There is tremendous within-group variation but remarkably little between-group variation—the group here being the arrows carried by any one man. Although a man usually carries a dozen or so arrows, rarely are two of them similar. Exceptions occur when a man has just made a set of arrows. But after the first battle these have been shot out over the battlefield, picked up by various fighters and carried to different villages.

The between-group variation is even more striking. Throughout the Dani area, with a population of about 100,000 people covering some 2,000 square kilometers, arrows vary in the same manner within the same limits. There are a few regionally characteristic variations. But most of the arrows from the Tenolome area (Konda [Swart] Valley Western Dani) seventy-five kilometers away could be presented to a Gutelu Dani and he would not think them unusual. It is clear from Wirz's drawings made in the Swart in 1920 (1924:Pl. XI) that there has been little change in arrow variations over time.

This pattern of low variation over both time and space is especially striking in light of the considerable variations in other aspects of culture and language within the Dani area. What are the probable causes for such variation? There seems to be no magical or religious aspect to arrow design which might promote conservatism here. Perhaps the answer lies in the rapid diffusion of arrows during battles over the very war frontiers that perhaps have contributed to regional isolation and variation in other aspects of the Dani culture. Arrows are the one item rapidly diffused, because of warfare. Men come together from kilometers apart to fight each other and incidentally exchange arrows. The next week each may be fighting and exchanging arrows on other fronts, more kilometers apart. There is, to be sure, peaceful trading in arrows; but the constant state of war throughout the Dani area assures that arrows will be in constant movement from one region to another.

RITUAL OBJECTS

Symbolic Stones

The many stones used primarily for symbolic purposes can usefully be considered in terms of the three classification systems applied to arrows: functional,

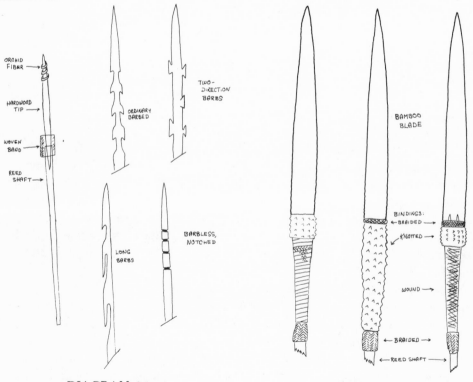

DIAGRAM 9.8
Hardwood-Tip Fighting Arrows

DIAGRAM 9.9
Pig-Killing and Fighting Arrows

Functional	Linguistic	Physical
Sacred stones (WUSA)	HABO	(not inspected)
Exchange stones, profane (WELIGAT) — JE OAK ("bone") laid in center on net display; JE AIE ("leg") laid near center on net display.	JE — EDAIEGEN, IBAL, JU, DABA, BUNUON, GAKALEK (split), DUMA (also a banana), WETENE (a parrot), POLOM, DIDO, WULUM, WAM GOLAK, POLOKHE	long, 40~70 cm.
OGOSI laid at ends on net display.	HOLI	short, under 40 cm. in length

DIAGRAM 9.10
CLASSIFICATIONS OF SYMBOLIC STONES

linguistic, and physical. Diagram 9.10 shows the relationships of these three systems.

All symbolic stones are of a hard slaty rock imported from the east and south; they are all ground smooth into one- to two-centimeter-thick elongated ovals ranging in length from twenty-five to seventy centimeters and in width from ten to thirty-five centimeters.

One type of symbolic stones are used only for the sacred collections of objects kept in certain men's houses and may be called sacred stones; the other are used primarily for exchange at funeral ceremonies and may be called exchange stones. Sacred stones are *wusa*, sacred or powerful, in contrast to exchange stones which are *weligat*, or profane. Sacred stones are kept wrapped up in the cabinet of the men's house as part of the *ganekhe*, are never seen by women, and are handled only by the most important men at certain ceremonies (Plate 59). Exchange stones are often carried unwrapped to and from ceremonies, and attention is publicly called to them at the moment of exchange and when they are arranged on piles of folded nets.

Exchange stones are further described in terms of their positions on these net piles (Plate 57). The largest and most important, which are laid in the center, are called *je oak* (*je* bone) (all exchange stones are called *je*); those slightly less important, laid on either side of the center stones, are called *je ai* (*je* leg); and the small stones at the ends of the net piles are called *ogosi*. The significance of this anthropomorphic terminology is not clear.

All sacred stones are called *habo*. All exchange stones are called *je*, and there are at least fourteen specific names for different kinds of *je*. (Van Nouhuys reports that the Pesegem Southern Dani use *ije* for the stone axe [1913:255].)

The principles of the physical classification are not at all clear. It was not possible to inspect the sacred stones. Informants did not hesitate to give a specific name to each exchange stone inspected, but relatively few of each type were seen and there was a good deal of variation when different informants were asked about the same stone. *Je holi* were definitely smaller than the others, never measuring more than forty centimeters in length; the thirteen other *je* types ranged in length from forty to sixty-eight centimeters, but the basis on which they were distinguished by the Dani was not at all apparent. *Holi*, the name for the small *je*, is also the term for female pig. The small *je* are said to be female, and the large *je* male.

Exchange Stone Parts. The exchange stone is usually slightly bowed along the long axis and slightly elliptical in outline. The concave surface is called *elokhegen*, cheekbone or face, and the convex side is called *opolikhe*, back. The narrow end is called *uguloak*, head or skull bone; the long edges are called *elak*, side or edge; and the broader end is called *alokhe*, anus.

Exchange Stone Decoration. Many *je* have traces of red paint (*bimut*). Often they have elaborate decorations tied around the center of the stone. Informants say that the *je* come from the Jalemo, to the east and southeast, where they are decorated only with the red paint. When they reach the Grand Valley, most of the red is wiped off and the other decorations bound on. Absence or presence of decorations has no correlation with the classification systems mentioned above.

The decorations of the exchange stones are called in general *etani* and consist of: *jogal*, lengths of braided bark fibre and bightly colored orchid fiber (this braided material is also used in married women's skirts, which are also called *jogal*); *dibat*, strands of bark cloth similar to those hanging from people's neck strings; *gem dadli*, a short "skirt" of flattened reeds similar to the girls' skirt of the same name; *akotati*, which in this context is a general name for *due isi*, bird feathers, and *bpake isi*, furs.

Anthropomorphism of the Exchange Stones. The terms for size, parts, and decorations of the exchange stones indicate an elaborate anthropomorphic symbolism. There are minor inconsistencies in the fact that it is especially the larger, or male, stones which "wear" the decorations, made of female skirt material. And, of course, a Dani female wears either a *jogal* skirt or a *dadli* skirt, while the exchange stones often have both.

The explicit function of the exchange stone is for display at funerals to placate the ghosts by showing them how much the people are undertaking on their behalf. Thus, it is very tempting to interpret these stones as symbolic humanoid beings who mediate between people and ghosts. However, there is no specific evidence to support this hypothesis.

COWRIE SHELLS AND SHELL BANDS

Of the three kinds of seashells used by the Dani, the small snail shell (Nassa) and the large bailer shell (Cymbium) are used primarily for personal ornamentation. The cowrie shell, however, is used primarily for decorating the long knitted bands that are exchanged at funeral ceremonies; the backs of the shells are ground off and the shells sewn to the knitted bands. Cowries are occasionally worn on neck strands, but this is a minor use. The importance of the cowrie shell for shell-band decoration is indicated in the terminology: The shell band itself is called *jetak;* the cowrie shell is called *jetak-egen,* the seed or principle core element of the *jetak.*

Classification of Cowrie Shells. The cowrie shells used by the Dani reached the Highlands in precontact time by an intricate trade network (pp. 28-9).

There are several terms used to describe color or shape of cowrie shells: *haboke*, white; *gusa*, discolored; *gut*, ivory; (*ili*) *jako*, elongated, "hipless"; *hepugen*, small, knobby; *mogen*, broad split. However, these terms are rarely used, and the Dani have no system of classification at all comparable to the complexities of the system used by the Ekagi (Kapauku), some five hundred kilometers to the west, which involves four different levels of contrast to describe five different types of shells, each of which has a precise value. (Pospisil [1963:304] describes a Kamu Valley Ekagi [Kapauku] system, and Dubbeldam, who observed Ekagi around Enarotali, describes a similar but slightly more elaborate system [1964:295, 298].)

Anthropomorphism of Cowrie Shells. Large cowrie shells are said to be female, the smaller ones male, and the smallest ones children. All informants

PLATE 57. At important ceremonies, the large decorated exchange stones are laid out on new nets; the whole unit is presented and displayed as a memorial bundle.

PLATE 58. At funerals, the woven bands decorated with cowrie shells, job's tears, orchid fiber, feathers, and furs are displayed on banana leaves in the courtyard before redistribution.

PLATE 59. At the renewal ceremony, men remove the carefully guarded sacred stones from the cabinet in the rear of the men's house. The stones will be unwrapped and smeared with pig grease. (Photograph by Jan Th. Broekhuijse)

agreed on these general principles. However, when asked about specific collections of shells, there was little consensus about the precise cut-off point between
female and male or between male and child. The system is the reverse of that
used for exchange stones, where the larger ones are called male and the smaller
female.

The names for the separate parts of the shell indicate that the shell is seen as
a complete torso and head. The side that is cut off is *amun*, navel, or *elabut*,
belly; the jagged lips are backbone with *apelep*, lips, at one end and *amoto*,
intestine, or anus, at the other end. The inner coil of the shell is the *edai-egen*,
the heart or soul matter. The precise significance of this anthropomorphic
symbolism is not clear. Although shells are usually sewn onto a band all pointing
in one direction, it is not uncommon for a few to be reversed.

The similarities of these part names to the names for the parts of the exchange
stone is apparent. However, while the broader end of the cowrie is the "head"
end, the broader part of the exchange stone is the "tail" end.

Shell Bands. Shell bands are basically long, knitted strips decorated with
cowrie shells and usually furs, feathers, pig tails, and orchid fiber (Plate 58).
They are about two meters long and from one to three centimeters wide. They
are knitted by adult men in their leisure moments, sitting in a men's house or
at a watchtower.

The bands are knit from one continuous string. Keeping the fibers at hand, the
men make a meter or so of thread by rolling the fibers on the thigh; then, with
a needle or awl they knit the thread into interlocking loops. As the thread
is used up, more is rolled onto the end. When a band is not being worked on, it
is kept rolled up and protected from dirt with a leaf covering.

The band has a certain amount of *wusa*, or supernatural power. After knitting,
before eating or smoking, a man removes the *wusa* that has transferred to his
hands with a feather wand. But those same informants who insisted on this
as an ideal rule were often observed violating it.

Many shell bands have segments of different colors. Sometimes one- or two-
meter lengths of thread are dyed red or blue or yellow before being knitted
into the band. After the band is completed, strips of brightly colored orchid
fiber may be threaded into it, dividing the band into irregular segments.

The Archbold Expedition reported the use of a band as a measuring device
to determine the price of pigs. From the description (Uittreksel 1940:417) it
would appear that a cowrie shell band was meant. The band was wrapped
around the pig's body just behind the forelegs, and payment of one cowrie shell
was demanded for each marked segment of the band it took to circle the pig.
Nothing comparable was observed in the Dugum Neighborhood.

The bands are decorated on one side with cowrie shells sewn at ten- to fifteen-
centimeter intervals and usually tufts of fur and feathers at either end and
a few places along the band. Occasionally shiny gray seeds are sewn in a line
along either edge.

CONCLUSIONS

CONCLUSIONS

I T is easy to claim too much for the holistic approach. I have tried to show its usefulness as a descriptive principle, which is a prerequisite for specific theoretical formulations. As used here, holism is based on the assumption that various aspects of culture are interrelated and that at the beginning of research it is useful to consider as broad a range of these interrelationships as possible. In this sense, this work does represent only the beginning of research on the Dani. It is not complete holism, for the description of the interrelationship of everything with everything else is not humanly possible. It does not purport to be harmonious holism, for the interrelationships within a culture are not necessarily neat and consistent, especially in the New Guinea Highlands, where there seems to be some dissonance between the dominant horticultural patterns and what are probably the survivals of prehorticultural, hunting and gathering patterns. And finally, the use of holistic description does not necessarily lead to a statement of the uniqueness of each culture, which would preclude any cross-cultural comparisons and the development of theories. But it does seem to be a way to consider traits in their complex contexts.

One of the most pressing problems of general theoretical interest emerging from New Guinea Highland studies is that of variation, or flexibility of pattern. I have indicated some of the areas in which the Dani seem to have relatively great flexibility.

Related to the alternative patterns of behavior implied in the concept of flexibility is the degree of development of cognitive patterns which I have called intellectual elaboration. Judgment of intellectual elaboration, like that of flexibility, demands cross-cultural comparison. In some cases, the Dani clearly have relatively little intellectual elaboration: the use of *mili* and *modla* almost to the exclusion of other color terms; the use of only two or three numbers; the lack of stellar constellations; the scanty plastic or graphic art; and the scarcity of explicit rules and formal socialization techniques. Also, the apparently in-consistent applications of terms in areas where there is an elaborated vocabulary, such as for adze stones, spirits, and sweet potatoes, suggest unconcern for existing intellectual elaboration.

In short, Dani culture as a whole can possibly be characterized as relatively

295

flexible, certainly with low intellectual elaboration, and low interest in sex and competition, which has been described in earlier chapters. A further generalization, which seems relevant to the others and may well have some explanatory power, concerns the cultural isolation and environmental regularity of the Dugum Dani. They have had little challenge to their own cultural patterns from exposure to other cultures (at least until the 1960's); minimal threat to their food and general physical comfort from climate and disease; and none of the cognitive pacing that a strong yearly seasonal round might provide. When a U. S. Army airplane crashed in the Pass Valley in 1945, the Dani region was dubbed Shangri-La by the press. Ironically, it does have the benevolent isolation of a Shangri-La.

I am reluctant to press such gross, unprovable generalizations too far. However, it does seem reasonable to suggest that this low level of stimulation from either the cultural or the natural environment has played an important role in creating what can be called a general blandness of Dani culture.

But of course no Dani group was completely isolated, even in the days before European contact. It might be hypothesized that flexibility of pattern would be related to receptivity of outside influences. The many closely related cultures of the New Guinea Highlands, and particularly those of the greater Dani area, would offer an ideal opportunity to explore this hypothesis. For example, when the Grand Valley Dani are compared with the Western Dani, who are their closest neighbors both geographically and culturally, the former seem relatively impervious to innovation. Despite the close relations that link the two areas, a number of items of material culture that are widespread among the Western Dani have not been accepted by the Grand Valley Dani. Among the apparently trivial are tobacco pipes and woven chest armor. Both of these are known to the Grand Valley Dani, are within their technological competence, and would be as useful in the Grand Valley as they are in the western valleys. Yet they have not spread to the Grand Valley. Among the more culturally significant items is maize, which spread through the Western Dani region before the first missionaries arrived in the early 1950's, but did not enter the Grand Valley. In the early 1960's there was no interest in maize, and even by the late 1960's it was grown only by the most acculturated of the Grand Valley Dani. Also, the nativistic-Christian movement that swept the Western Dani in the late 1950's and early 1960's, often moving into areas where no missionaries had been, stopped short at the head of the Grand Valley (cf. O'Brien and Ploeg 1965). In 1968 the Indonesian government was impressed by how much more successful its schools and economic projects were in the Western Dani region than in the Grand Valley, and the Protestant missionaries who were trying to carry out fundamental changes in Dani life remarked on the tremendously greater receptivity of the Western and Southern Dani in comparison with the Grand Valley Dani.

Why the Western Dani are so receptive and the Grand Valley Dani not is a legitimate and intriguing question which seems to point to basic differences between the two cultures. The most obvious difference is that the Western Dani live scattered along their steep valley slopes, while the Grand Valley Dani are more densely settled on their flat valley floor. But while ecological determinism may be the main clue, a detailed comparative study would be necessary to provide a satisfactory answer.

Until 1960 the Dani of the Gutelu Alliance and the Dugum Neighborhood had experienced little direct outside influence. A police patrol had effected a brief peace, and some material goods were seeping in from missionary and government centers elsewhere in the Grand Valley. Then late in 1960 a mission post was established at Jibiga in the Gutelu Alliance region an hour from the Dugum Neighborhood; in early 1961 the Harvard-Peabody Expedition came to the Dugum Neighborhood, and in September 1961 a police post was set up just outside the Neighborhood. After the attack of June 4, 1966, which split the alliance, the police post was moved to Jibiga, and by 1968 Jibiga had become a center of government power. Within a kilometer of Gutelu's large settlement there was not only the police post and the Roman Catholic mission with its airstrip and school, but also a first-aid station, a civil government official's house, and a small military detachment. Throughout the area were schools run by the mission in cooperation with the government. In theory all children were attending the schools. In 1968 only three grades were taught, and a few boys went to Wamena for further training, but higher grades were planned to be taught at Jibiga in 1969.

Change is under way. To return the Dani to their pre-1954 state is impossible, and its desirability a subject only for philosophical speculation. In one way or another they will be brought into the modern world socially, politically, economically, and religiously. Yet there are major obstacles to their development. They are decades behind most of the other peoples of West Irian, and their main rivals in the Highlands, the Ekagi (Kapauku) have the added advantage of a sophisticated pseudocapitalistic economic system which the Dani lack. The terrain is against them, for a road into the Grand Valley from the coast would be a major engineering feat, far more difficult to build than the roads that now service the population centers in the East New Guinea Highlands.

In 1968 the Indonesian government generously invited my reactions to their present Dani policy and my advice for the future. I could talk at length about the former but had little to offer of the latter. The Dani have nothing and produce nothing which the world wants. No mineral resources have been discovered, and the lumber is where the people aren't. Even tobacco, which they do grow, or coffee which could be introduced, would probably always have to depend on air transport to reach their markets. The Indonesians would find it difficult enough to develop the Dani even with plentiful resources of their own, and a Grand Valley rich in natural resources and easily accessible. But all these are lacking, and the chances are slim indeed for the Dani to become other than detribalized parasites.

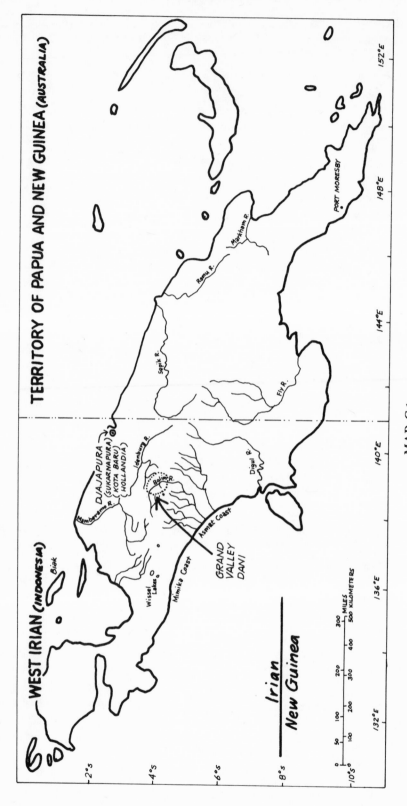

MAP C.1
IRIAN (NEW GUINEA)

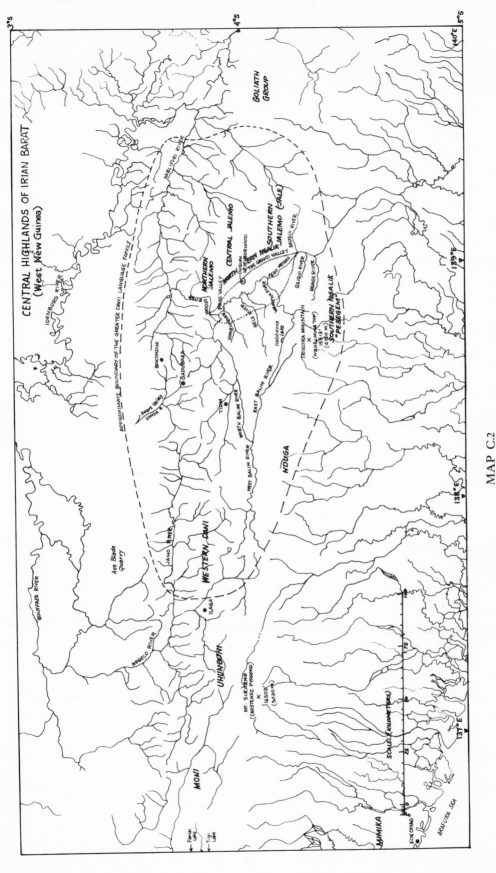

MAP C.2

THE CENTRAL HIGHLANDS OF WEST IRIAN (WEST NEW GUINEA)

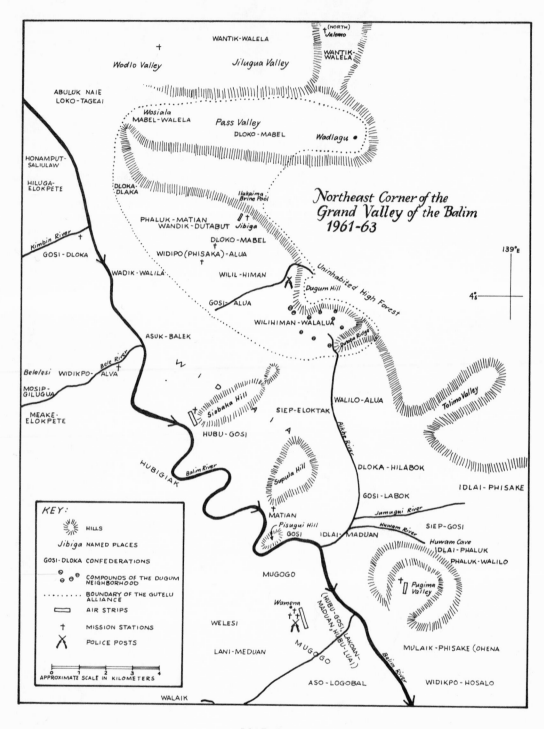

MAP C.3

NORTHEAST CORNER OF THE GRAND VALLEY OF THE BALIM, 1961–1963

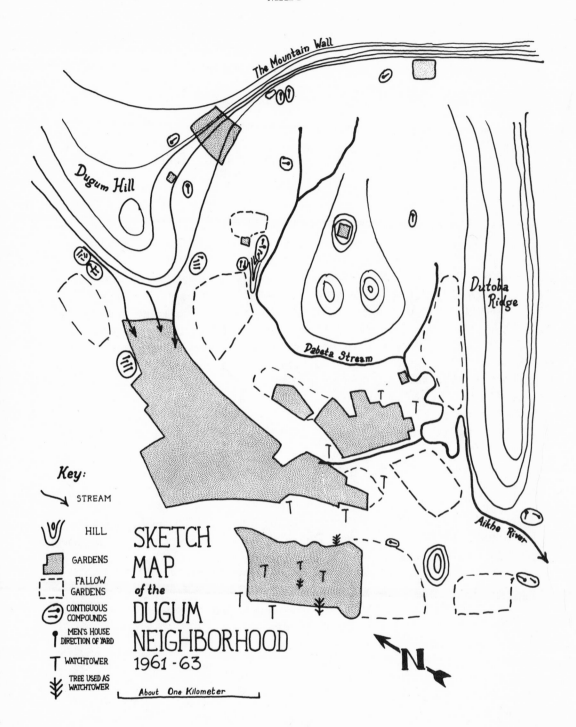

Key:

→ STREAM

HILL

GARDENS

FALLOW GARDENS

CONTIGUOUS COMPOUNDS

MEN'S HOUSE DIRECTION OF YARD

T WATCHTOWER

TREE USED AS WATCHTOWER

SKETCH MAP *of the* DUGUM NEIGHBORHOOD 1961-63

About One Kilometer

The Mountain Wall

Dugum Hill

Dutoba Ridge

Pabeta Stream

Aikhe River

N

MAP C.4
THE DUGUM NEIGHBORHOOD, 1961–1963

EXPLORATION AND RESEARCH IN THE DANI AREA

A comprehensive survey of exploration in the Central Highlands of West New Guinea is given by Le Roux in his three-volume work on "The Mountain Papuans of New Guinea and Their Habitat" (1948:1–18). Of the forty-four expeditions before 1945 mentioned by Le Roux, six contacted Dani groups.

The first Highland Papuan group in West New Guinea to be contacted was a small group of Dani living on the southern slopes of the ranges just south of Wilhelmina Top (Trikora). The Lorentz Expedition of 1909–1910 encountered a few settlements of Dani-speaking people who called themselves Pesegem, a name which is cognate to the sib name Hesekem, found among the Dani of the lower Grand Valley and the Gilugui Valley.

The Lorentz Expedition spent about forty hours in the Pesegem compounds in October and December 1909, and in January 1910 some of these Pesegem visited the expedition base camp on the Lorentz River for two days. The amount of data collected during these four days' contact with the Pesegem is truly impressive both in quantity and quality and must set some record for instant ethnography (van Nouhuys 1912, 1913; Lorentz 1913; van den Broek 1913a, 1913b; Fischer 1915; and van Eerde 1911).

In 1912 and 1913 an expedition led by Captain A. Franssen Herderschee retraced the route of the Lorentz Expedition to Wilhelmina Top and again made contact with the Pesegem (Pulle n.d.; Franssen Herderschee 1913). L. A. Snell spent three weeks among the Pesegem and his report (1913) adds many important details to the knowledge of the language and culture of these Southern Dani.

In 1920 an expedition led by van Overeem reached the Swart Valley Western Dani from the north. The Swart Valley groups were called Oeringoep, or Timorini. Jongejans and Bijlmer spent seven weeks, and Lam one week, among these groups (Le Roux 1948:7; Jongejans ms.; 1921–1922; Bijlmer 1923a, 1923b; Lam 1922, 1927–1929).

In 1921 the Kremer Expedition reached Wilhelmina Top from the north. They met several different Western Dani groups as they passed through the Swart Valley and crossed the North and East Balim rivers. For the first time a trained ethnologist, Paul Wirz, studied a Dani group. He spent about two months in the Swart Valley (Wirz 1924, 1925, 1931; Kremer 1922–1923, n.d.). Wirz recognized the close relationship between the people of the Swart Valley and the Pesegem which had been described by earlier expeditions.

In 1926 a Netherlands-American expedition led by M. W. Stirling came into the Nogolo Basin, where they apparently met Dani groups living among the Dem and Moni. Le Roux, in his report on the expedition, used the Moni name Ndani for the first time (Le Roux n.d.).

In June 1938 the Archbold Expedition of 1938–1939, from the American Museum of Natural History, was flying reconnaissance flights between Lake Sentani and Lake Habbema, and on June 23, 1938, discovered the Grand Valley of the Balim.

In mid-July the expedition established a camp at Lake Habbema, where they met some Dani from the Bele River. In August two expedition patrols, one from Lake Habbema and the other from the Idenburg River Camp, met in the Grand Valley. A few days later were flown out by the pontoon plane which landed on the Balim River. During November and December a collecting camp was maintained at 2,200 meters in the upper Bele Valley. For about seven weeks in November and December another camp was maintained in the Grand Valley itself. The ethnographic research was to have been done by G. Huls, but apparently none of his material is available (Le Roux 1948:15). However, the military and natural historians of the expedition give considerable incidental ethnographic data on the Grand Valley, Bele Valley, and Sauweri-Hablifuri Dani in their reports: Archbold 1941; Archbold and Rand 1941; Archbold, Rand, and Brass 1942; Brass 1941a, 1941b; Uittreksel 1940.

In 1945 a U. S. Army aircraft based on Lake Sentani crashed at the outer (eastern) end of the Pass Valley. To help rescue the three survivors, Philippine troops were parachuted in. A glider strip was built in the Grand Valley at the mouth of the Pass Valley and survivors and parachutists were taken out (Hastings 1945; Elsmore 1945).

During the early 1950's American Protestant missionaries had been pushing from the Wissel Lakes eastward to the Grand Valley. In April 1954 members of the Christian and Missionary Alliance (CAMA) were landed in the southern Grand Valley by pontoon plane and the first permanent Caucasian settlement began. In 1956 the Netherlands government established a post at Wamena in the southern Grand Valley, and in 1958 Dutch members of the Franciscan Order entered the Grand Valley. Since then the several missionary corporations have built stations with airstrips in most parts of the Dani area. The mission and government activity in recent years is too extensive to detail here, but Hitt (1962) describes some of this work from the Protestant point of view. The first major anthropological data to appear from this have been Bromley's papers on law (1960) and linguistics (1961, 1967); the mimeographed Working Papers of the Conference on Dani Ethnography, which was held in Wamena in August 1962 and was attended by government and missionary personnel and anthropologists (Bureau of Native Affairs 1962); Peters' doctoral dissertation (1965); and van der Stap's outline of Dani morphology (1966).

Since 1960, D. Carleton Gajdusek, M.D., of the United States National Institute of Neurological Diseases and Blindness, and others have made a number of trips to the Western Dani of the Mulia region to study the endemic goiter which occurs in a remarkably high percentage of the population there (cf. Gajdusek 1962; Kidson and Gajdusek 1962; and Sorenson and Gajdusek 1966).

Anton Ploeg, a Research Scholar in Anthropology at the Australia National University, carried out field work for eighteen months in 1960–1962 among the Western Dani of the Bokondini area, north of the Grand Valley (cf. O'Brien and Ploeg 1964; Ploeg 1966).

From 1961 through 1963 the Harvard University Peabody Museum Expedition, of which I was a member, carried out anthropological research among the Dugum Dani of the Grand Valley. In 1968 Eleanor R. Heider and I returned briefly to the Grand Valley. (For research information on the Dugum Dani, see the author's publications; Matthiessen 1962; Gardner 1963; Putnam 1963; Versteegh 1961; Broekhuijse 1967; and Gardner and Heider 1969.)

In 1961 a New Zealand alpine expedition attempted to climb the Carstensz Pyramid (Mt. Sukarno), and Temple's account (1962) gives some details of the Western Dani groups they encountered.

From 1961 to 1963 Denise O'Brien, a doctoral candidate in the Department of Anthropology at Yale University, spent twenty-one months among the Western Dani of the Swart (Konda) Valley, who had been briefly described in the reports of the 1920 and 1921 expeditions. (O'Brien and Ploeg 1964, O'Brien 1966, 1969)

In 1962 an expedition led by Heinrich Harrer, and which included Philip Temple, visited the important axe-blade quarry in the Nogolo Basin; later Harrer followed the course of the Balim River from the Grand Valley to its mouth on the Asmat Coast (Harrer 1963).

Since 1963 two Indonesian anthropologists have done work in the Dani area. Dr. Anwas Iskandar, of Universitas Tjenderawasih, studied acculturation and education among the Mugogo group of the Grand Valley near Wamena (1964); and Herman Lantang, an M.A. candidate at the University of Indonesia, studied a multiethic community in the Heage Valley to the south of the Grand Valley.

Between October 1964 and July 1966 Klaus-Friedrich Koch, then a doctoral candidate at the University of California at Berkeley, worked among the Jale, to the east of the Grand Valley (1968a, 1968b).

TEXTS OF SONGS

1.

Walikhe	*walikhe*	*Na'et-o-e au!*
far away	far away	I dislike
Hitikhe	*hotokhe*	*Na'et-o-e au!*
nearby	nearby	I dislike

Walking far away, walking far away,
I don't like it.
Staying nearby, staying nearby,
I don't like it.

2.

Walik	*ligin,*	*Walek*	*legen,*
far	(I) shall go,		
Hane-mege	*ege laken*		
long ago	you were saying		

Hodlak Giluge, *hodlak* Jaiige

Wuligin	*hotokan*	*higi goko*
hearth	near to	next to

Walik ligin, etc.
Hodlak Giluge, etc.

Hisekhe	*notoken,*	*nigigoko*	*notokat*	*agegatek*
fireplace poles	near to	next to	near	sit next to

"I shall go far away, I shall go far away,"
You were saying long ago.
Giluge girl, Jaiige girl.
You are sitting close to the hearth.

"I shall go far away, I shall go far away,"
You were saying long ago.
Giluge girl, Jaiige girl.
You are sitting next to the poles of the fire place.

3.

Duan	*widioko*	*eden*	*phaden*
Tuan, non-Dani	comes over	twisting	turning

Modla Malik	*widioko*	*egen*	*phaden*
(name for	comes over	twisting	turning
M. Bromley)			

Hodlak Giluge, *Hodlak* Jaiige

Je isok phagakonem	*Wetati wetatipo*	
(there are no exchange stones?)	swiftlet	

Wam isok phagamonem	*bulel*	*pokotoba*
(there are no pigs?)	(a bird)	in the sky

The Tuan flies over, twisting and turning
Bromley flies over, twisting and turning
Giluge girl, Jaiige girl
We don't have any exchange stones. The swift, the swiftlet.
We don't have any pigs. The *bulel* bird in the sky.

4.

Walimogen	*ogo balin*	*igo ege*	*Na'eto e*
Nassa shells	buy		I dislike

Jetakegen	*ogo balin*	*igo ege*	*Na'eto e.*
Cowrie shells	buy		I dislike

Hodlak Giluge	*Hodlak* Jaiige		
girl	girl		

Mili bokot	*opu ji de*	*higi-nen*	*debeganhe*
blue sky	up there	your hand-by	grasped

Modla bokot	*wema ji de*	hijok-en	*debeganhe.*
white cloud	down there	your foot-by	stepped on.

I don't want to buy Nassa shells,
I don't want to buy cowrie shells.
Giluge girl, Jaiige girl.
The blue sky up there, your hand grasped it,
The white cloud down there, your foot stepped on it.

5.

Homuak	phi	igi	dokogoko,	wakei adi de o.
(a place)	(a tree)	leaves	falling	I am going

Abulobak, etc.	
(a place) etc.	

Hodlak Legak,	Hodlak Alilion.
girl	girl

Legak	bpigako	wako-mege,	wisiga	lobaknekhe.
(a girl)	look at	we come	(a rat)	eat

At Homuak the *phi* leaves fall; I am coming.
At Abulobak the *phi* leaves fall; I am coming.
Legak girl, Alilion girl.
We come to watch Legak, she eats the rat.
We come to watch Alilion, she eats the vulva.

6.

Widaia	dlukal hunem	i aikhe	bibitegen.
(an enemy group)	mass of warriors	(the river)	leaves

Wilihiman	dlukal hunem	hetake	bibitegen.
(a friendly group)	mass of warriors	(a swamp)	leaves

Hodlak Legak, *Hodlak* Alilion.

Watoko	bpigasinem,	aouak	hutu	adi de o.
killing	looking	nose	twisted	

Segeloko	bpigasinem,	aouak	mane	adi de o.
cannibalizing	looking	nose	twisted	

(the feathers of) the Widaia warriors (look like) *bibitegen* leaves along the
    Aikhe River.
(the feathers of) the Wilihiman warriors (look like) *bibitegen* leaves in the
    Hetake Swamp.
Legak girl, Alilion girl.
Watching them kill, the (man with the) twisted nose.
Watching them eat the dead (is) (the man with the) twisted nose.

7.

Bunuti		atoto
Gentle slope		climb up

| *Nena-mege* | | | *Negatek dlek.* | |
| what | | | is eaten not | |

| *Jomate* | *Wio-mege,* | | *Jomate Dolimo-mege.* | |
| here | Wio people, from south, | | here Dolimo people, from South | |

| *Jomate* | *ilue* | *heatik,* | *maiju* | *heatik.* |
| here | local salt | seek | trade salt | seek |

We walk up the gentle slope (to look around).
What is it that is not eaten?
Here (come) the Wio people,
Here (come) the Dolimo people,
Here I'll look for salt,
Here I'll look for trade salt.

8.

| *Duan* | *iok-oba* | *gut-adi* | *misak-adi.* |
| Tuan | footprints | (an insult) | (an insult). |

| *Modla* | *malik* | *iok-oba* | *gut-adi* | *misak-adi.* |
| Myron | Bromley | etc. | | |

Hodlak Giluge, *Hodlak* Jaiige.

| *Jetakegen* | | *igatek* | |
| cowrie shell | | worn (at the neck) | |

| *Inugul balek* | *halok* | | *igatek* |
| (birth ceremony) | because of | | worn |

| *Walimogen* | | *igatek* | |
| Nassa shells | | worn | |

| *Inogo wakanek* | | *halok* | *igatek* |
| (part of wedding ceremony) | | because of | worn |

The Tuan's footprints? You liar, you fool.
Bromley's footprints? You liar, you fool.
Giluge girl, Jaiige girl.
Cowrie shells at the neck,
Because of the birth ceremony, at the neck.
Nassa shells at the neck,
Because of the marriage ceremony, at the neck.

9.

| *Okega* | *Wakanuokoluk.* |
| Steam leaf | let's go get |

Inebe	*bete*	*gilik*	*lan*	*ote.*
body	two	together	go!	

Ega			*wakanuokoluk.*	
steam leaf			let's go get	

Inebe	*henaken*	*gilik*	*lan*	*ote.*
body	three	together	go!	

Hodlak Galu, *Hodlak* Iliekhe.

Halukmo	*jagudega*	*etnoko*	*labedakoluk.*
in anus	copulate	this	hidden.

Huakma	*jagudega*	*etnoko*	*labedakoluk.*
in hip	copulate	this	hidden.

Let's go get leaves for the steam bundle.
You two go together!
Let's go get leaves for the steam bundle.
You three go together!
Galu girl, Iliekhe girl.
Let's go ourselves, and I'll make love to you in your anus.
Let's go off by ourselves, and I'll make love to you in your hip.

10.

Wigiga	*mili*	*mulumo*	*lelo*	*aie*	
(leaves)	dark	good	go		

Bakhoga	*modla*	*mulumo*	*lelo*	*uai*	
(leaves)	light	good	go		

Nilik	*hutek*	*wetek*	*mate*	*lelo*	*e*
(a man)	sitting	there is	arrow	go	

Elabotok	*hutek*	*wetek*	*mate*	*lelo*	*aie*
(a man)	sitting	there is	arrow	go	

The dark leaves of the *wigi* trees are good, let's go.
The light leaves of the *bakho* tree are good, let's go.
Where Nilik sits, there are fighting arrows, let's go.
Where Elabotok sits, there are fighting arrows, let's go.

AN ACCOUNT OF BATTLES AND RAIDS,
APRIL–SEPTEMBER, 1961

THE southern frontier of the Gutelu Alliance lies in the Dugum Neighborhood of the Wilihiman-Walalua Confederation. The major battlefields are the Dogolik and the Watabaka (Map C.1). The Gutelu in the following description are men of the Gutelu Alliance, but for the most part only men from the Wilihiman-Walalua, Gosi-Alua, and Wilil-Himan confederations of the Alliance are involved in the fighting on this front. The following events have also been described by Matthiessen (1962) and Gardner (1963). Broekhuijse's account (1967:232–78) is by far the most extensive, for he was able to make extensive and efficient use of informants during the crucial months of the battle. He describes immediate details of battle and participants' opinions that could not be replicated after the events were long past.

10 April. Battle called by the Widaia, challenge accepted by Husuk, a young Gosi-Alua leader. Fought on the Watabaka. Fighting commenced early, about 8 A.M. By 9:30, wounded men being carried back. Fighting ended by rain, 4:30.

15 April. Battle called by the Gutelu. Fought on Dogolik. About noon, fighting was broken off by the appearance of a white man (one of the expedition party returning from Wamena). By two o'clock, many men were leaving the field. A few stayed, shouting insults at the Widaia. By three o'clock, the insults were too much to bear in silence, and the Gutelu streamed back onto the field. Fighting was resumed for another two hours until ended by dusk. (One Widaia died six weeks later from wounds.)

4 May. Battle called by the Gutelu but challenge was not taken up by Widaia. One group of Gutelu waited on the Watabaka, another along the Aikhe River. By noon, when no Widaia had appeared, they gave up and returned home.

11 May. Raid on Widaia gardens by Gosi-Alua under Husuk. One Widaia killed in his watchtower. After the kill, the Gosi-Alua massed on the Watabaka, were joined by other Gutelu, and waited for Widaia to appear for a normal battle. They didn't.

25 May. On a northern front the Gutelu killed an Asuk Balek, an ally of the Widaia. People of the southern front prepared for dance to celebrate death.

26 May. Battle initiated by early-morning Widaia raid up the Aikhe River.

Gutelu quickly responded, and the Widaia withdrew to the Dogolik, where they asked for battle. Gutelu refused, saying they had to dance for the man killed the previous day. Widaia made a second thrust up the Aikhe River. The Gutelu finally accepted the battle. Battle was to be fought on the Watabaka, which by this time the Widaia controlled in total. As the Gutelu moved into the swamp to approach the Watabaka, the Widaia withdrew from sight. The Gutelu, fearing an ambush, approached the hill carefully, finally massed at the base and rushed the summit of the short arm of the L, took it without opposition, finding the Widaia properly withdrawn to the long arm of the L. Sporadic fighting. By two o'clock both sides withdrawn a bit, sitting, shouting, taunting. Then half an hour of fighting around the bend of the L. Then disengagement, the Gutelu withdrawing to middle of short arm of L. As the Widaia moved away, along the long arm of the L, the Gutelu, led by Husuk, began triumphal singing. Suddenly the Widaia turned and charged at full speed. The Gutelu held them for a time, and then, in unusually close and fierce fighting, the Gutelu dropped back and finally were pushed off the hill completely into the swamp and bushes. The Widaia stood on the crest of the last knoll, taunting in their turn. Finally they dropped back and both sides went home.

29 May. Widaia announce that man has just died from wounds received on the Dogolik (battle of April 15). Dance begun but abruptly terminated about 1:30 when report of Widaia raid on northern frontier is shouted in.

4 June. Widaia sent in raiding party, set up ambush at edge of gardens. No one was caught, so at 5:30 they raided the then deserted gardens and burned the Uwenebaka watchtower shelter. Then they withdrew to the Dogolik, where the Gutelu rushed, and fought for fifteen minutes before both sides went home at dusk.

5 June. Widaia massed on the Dogolik and called battle in early afternoon. Those Gutelu men within hearing responded immediately but were far outnumbered, so stopped at point on Dogolik where the strip is very narrow. Thus the front would be narrow and the numerical advantage of the Widaia could not be exploited. At the same time, a group of about fifty Gutelu faded into the swamp, prepared to attack the Widaia flank. The Widaia did not advance to meet the Gutelu, and the afternoon rain sent both sides running for home.

7 June. Morning raid by the Widaia, who burn a shelter, uproot potato vines, trample tobacco, and break a dam, letting water run out of a duck pond on the Dogolik. The Gutelu came to meet them on the Dogolik, and by eleven o'clock a battle had developed here.

8 June. Tracks of unsuccessful Widaia raid discovered. Apparently they had come up the Aikhe River and penetrated as far as the Anelatak, found no one, and returned home.

10 June. Widaia raid up the Aikhe River, kill Wejakhe, young boy. Wilil *ganekhe* ceremony had left the gardens and watchtowers deserted. Wejakhe, two other boys, and one man went to the river to drink, were surprised by Widaia ambushed; Wejakhe was killed, others escaped.

22 June. Battle called by Widaia on Watabaka. Some Gutelu crept through the swamp and waited on the east slope of the Watabaka in hopes that the Widaia would walk over the crest into the ambush. Nothing happened. Finally the Gutelu broke the ambush and occupied the short arm of the L. Fighting began at the bend of the L. One hundred Gutelu crept into the woods on the inside of the L, and those in the open tried to draw the Widaia back into an ambush. This was also unsuccessful. Finally the ambush broke and the mass of the Gutelu rushed the Widaia. Shouting and cheering, the Gutelu pushed the Widaia back up the long arm of the L and finally off the hill altogether. By 5:00 the Gutelu stood on the hill, taunting the Widaia. There was no further engagement, and both sides finally went home.

5 July. Raid on the Widaia gardens, called by Weteklue. The raiding party was apparently spotted by Widaia lookouts; a counterambush was set up, and one Gutelu, Jenokma, was killed.

2 August. A Widaia pig turned up on the Gutelu side of the no-man's-land: perhaps strayed, perhaps stolen, perhaps a bit of both. The Gutelu, expecting retaliation, went to the Watabaka, and a battle developed on the flat ground between the Watabaka and the Siobaka hills. Desultory fighting, with relatively few men on either side. The high point of the day when a *jo koik*, the large cuckoo dove whose cry is the signal for battle, flew low over the Gutelu warriors. Everyone dropped his weapons and tried to hit the bird with all available missiles. It flew away but returned to be greeted by a large supply of sticks. It escaped uninjured.

6 August. Gutelu attempted raid on gardens beyond Watabaka. This failed, and battle developed on fields between Watabaka and Siobaka hills. Along the banks of the stream, a boys' front. Boys as young as six, standing on either side of the stream, shooting arrows at each other, coached by older men. About noon the skirmishing became desultory, and Nilik, in angry disgust with his men, called them back to the Watabaka Hill. By 3:00 the Widaia had occupied the field and were taunting the Gutelu. The Gutelu charged down the slope and fighting resumed. But once again Nilik was disgusted and called his men back. Then both sides withdrew to their hills—the Widaia to the Siobaka, the Gutelu on the Watabaka. For an hour or two they exchanged words rather than weaons: derogatory references to individual enemy's wives, to the stolen pig; a choice phrase would bring forth a peal of laughter from the comrades; a good blow from the other side would be met with jeers of derision. The Widaia, who had a wider repertoire of bird calls than the Gutelu, used trilling, jeering calls to good advantage. No one made any further attempt to fight. They sat in the setting sun, shouting. A good time was had by all.

16 August. Early morning raid by the Gutelu to the Widaia gardens near the Subula. One watchtower overturned. Battle developed on the strip, far beyond the Dogolik. Desultory fighting, with a two-hour rest in the early afternoon.

24 August. Widaia woman crossed the no-man's-land seeking refuge in Abulopak. Weteklue decided to kill her, but she was escorted out of the region by a member of the expedition.

25 August. Four Asuk Balek men, allied to the Widaia, visited Abulopak. Two have relatives there. The other two were attacked in the early evening. One escaped, the other was killed.

Early September: Widaia raid deep into Gutelu territory, killing one young boy. Gutelu raid into Widaia territory, killing two Widaia. The next day a government police post is established between Abulopak and Dagulobok, effectively pacifying the southern frontier. Warfare continues unabated on the northern frontier of the Gutelu territory.

BIBLIOGRAPHY

ABERLE, DAVID F.

1963. Some sources of flexibility in Navaho social organization. *Southwestern Journal of Anthropology* 19.1:1–8.

ARCHBOLD, RICHARD

1941. Unknown New Guinea. *National Geographic* 79.3:315–44.

ARCHBOLD, RICHARD, AND A. L. RAND

1941. Latchkey to a savage tribe. *Natural History* 47.4:193–99.

ARCHBOLD, RICHARD, A. L. RAND, AND L. J. BRASS

1942. Results of the Archbold expeditions. No. 41. Summary of the 1938–1939 New Guinea Expedition. *Bulletin of the American Museum of Natural History* 89.3:197–288.

AYOUB, MILLICENT R., AND STEPHEN A. BURNETT

1965. Ritualized verbal insult in white high school culture. *Journal of American Folklore* 78.310:337–44.

BARNES, J. A.

1962. African models in the New Guinea Highlands. *Man* 62.2:5–9.

BARRAU, JACQUES

1965. Witnesses of the past: Notes on some food plants of Oceania. *Ethnology* 4.3:282–94.

BATESON, GREGORY

1936. *Naven. A survey of the problems suggested by a composite picture of the culture of a New Guinea tribe drawn from three points of view*, 2d ed., (1958). Stanford: Stanford University Press.

BERNDT, RONALD M.

1964. Warfare in the New Guinea Highlands. *American Anthropologist* 66.4.2:183–203.

BIJLMER, H. J. T.

1923a. Anthropological results of the Dutch scientific Central New Guinea a° 1920, followed by an essay on the anthropology of the Papuans. *Nova Guinea* 7.4.

1923b. Met de Centraal Nieuw-Guinea-expeditie a° 1920 naar een onbekenden volkstam in het hooggebergte. *De aarde en haar Volken*, Nos. 5-9. 4°.

1923c. Uit de geneeskundige verslagen der Wetenschappelijke Centraal Nieuw-Guinea-expedite 1920-1921. De Malaria. *Geneesk. Tijdschr. v. Ned. Indie* 64:600.

1923d. De vitamine-rantsoeneering. *Geneesk. Tijdschr. v. Ned. Indie*, 64:657.

BIJLMER, H. J. T., AND H. DE ROOK

1923. Medisch Verslag van den bergtocht en slot-beschouwingen. *Geneesk. Tijdschr. v. Ned. Indie*, 64:670.

BLACKWOOD, BEATRICE

1939. Folk-stories of a stone age people in New Guinea. *Folk-Lore*, 50.3:209–42.

BOHANNAN, PAUL
 1963. *Social anthropology.* New York: Holt, Rinehart and Winston.
BRASS, L. J.
 1941a. The 1938–39 expedition to the Snow Mountains, Netherlands New Guinea. *Journal of the Arnold Arboretum* 22:272–342.
 1941b. Stone age agriculture in New Guinea. *Geographical Review* 31:555–69.
BROEKHUIJSE, J. TH.
 1967. *De Wiligiman-Dani. Een cultureel-anthropologische studie over religie en oorlogvoering in de Baliem-vallei.* Tilburg: H. Gianotten N.V.
BROMLEY, H. MYRON
 1960. A preliminary report on law among the Grand Valley Dani of Netherlands New Guinea, *Nieuw-Guinea Studien,* 4.3:235–59. Reprinted 1965: Reprint Series No. 8. Southeast Asia Studies. New Haven: Yale University Press.
 n.d. Short guide to the grammar of Mid-Valley Dani. Duplicated. Christian and Missionary Alliance.
 1961. The phonology of Lower Grand Valley Dani. A comparative structural study of skewed phonemic patterns. *Verhandelingen van het Koninklijk Instituut voor Taal-, Land- en Volkenkunde.* Deel 34. -s-Gravenhage. Martinus Nijhoff.
 1962. The function of fighting in Grand Valley Dani Society, in *Working papers in Dani ethnology,* No. 1. Bureau of Native Affairs, Hollandia-Kota Baru.
 1967. The linguistic relationships of Grand Valley Dani: A lexico-statistical classification. *Oceania* 37.4:286–308.
BRONGERSMA, L. D. AND G. F. VENEMA
 1960. *Het Witte Hart van Nieuw-Guinea.* Amsterdam, Scheltens & Giltay. English translation 1962. *To the mountains of the stars.* London: Hodder and Stoughton.
BROOKFIELD, H. C.
 1964. The ecology of highland settlement: Some suggestions. *American Anthropologist* 66.4.2:20–38.
BROOKFIELD, H. C. AND PAULA BROWN
 1963. *Struggle for land. Agriculture and group territories among the Chimbu of the New Guinea Highlands.* Melbourne: Oxford University Press.
BROWN, PAULA
 1963. From Anarchy to Satrapy. *American Anthropologist* 65.1:1–15.
BUEHLER, ALFRED, TERRY BARROW, AND CHARLES P. MOUNTFORD
 1962. *The art of the South Sea Islands, including Australia and New Zealand.* New York: Crown.
BUREAU OF NATIVE AFFAIRS
 1962. *Working papers in Dani ethnology,* No. 1. Bureau of Native Affairs hectograph, United Nations Temporary Executive Authority in West New Guinea-West Irian.
CUNNINGHAM, C. E.
 1964. Order in the Atoni house. *Bijdragen tot de Taab, Land- en Volkenkunde* 120:34-68.
DE KOCK, A. C.
 1912. Eenige ethnologische en anthropologische gegevens omtrent een dwergstam in het bergland van Zuid Nieuw-Guinea. *Tijdschrift Koninklike Nederlandsche Aardrijks Genootschap,* 29:154–70.
DUBBELDAM, L. F. B.
 1964. The devaluation of the Kapauku-cowrie as a factor of social disintegration. *American Anthropologist* 66.4.2:293–303.
DUNDES, ALAN, AND BORA OZKÖK
 1968. Penis and anus in the strategy of Turkish male verbal dueling rhymes. Paper

presented at the American Anthropological Association Meetings, Seattle, November 24, 1968.

ELLENBERGER, JOHN D.
1962. On leadership amongst the Damals (Uhundunis) north of the Carstensz Mountain Range, in *Working papers in Dani ethnography*, No. 1. Bureau of Native Affairs, Hollandia, pp. 10–15.

ELSMORE, RAY T.
1945. New Guinea's mountain and swampland dwellers. *National Geographic* 88.6:671–94.

FISCHER, H. W.
1915. Ethnographica von den pesechem und aus Südwest-Neu-Guinea. *Nova Guinea* 7.2:145:160.

GAJDUSEK, D. CARLETON
1962. Congenital defects of the central nervous system associated with hyperendemic goiter in a neolithic society of Netherlands New Guinea. *Pediatrics* 29.3:345–63.

GALIS, K. W.
1964. Oudheidkundig Nieuws uit Westelijk Nieuw-Guinea. *Bijdragen tot de Taal-, Land-en Volkenkunde.* 120:2.

GARDNER, ROBERT G.
1963. *Dead birds.* A film produced by the Film Study Center, Peabody Museum, Harvard University. Dist.: Contemporary Films, Inc., New York.

GARDNER, ROBERT, AND KARL G. HEIDER
1969. *Gardens of war. Life and death in the New Guinea stone age.* New York: Random House.

GRINNELL, GEORGE BIRD
1924. *The Cheyenne Indians. Their history and ways of life*, Vol. 1. New Haven: Yale University Press.

GUIART, JEAN
1963. *The arts of the South Pacific.* New York: Golden.

HARRER, HEINRICH
1963. *Ich komme aus der Steinzeit. Ewiges eis im Dschungel der Sudsee.* Frankfurt/M. Ullstein. English translation by Edward Fitzgerald. *I come from the stone age.* 1965. New York: Dutton.

HASELBERGER, HERTA
1961. Method of studying ethnological art. *Current Anthropology* 2.4:342–84.

HASTINGS, MARGARET
1945. A WAC in Shangrila. *Reader's Digest* (November, 1945).

HEIDER, KARL G.
1965. The Dugum Dani. A Papuan culture in the West New Guinea highlands. Unpublished doctoral dissertation. Department of Anthropology, Harvard University.
1967a. Archaeological assumptions and ethnographical facts: A cautionary tale from New Guinea. *Southwestern Journal of Anthropology* 23.1:52–64.
1967b. Speculative functionalism: Archaic elements in New Guinea Dani culture. *Anthropos* 62:833–40.
n.d.a. Functional matrix analysis for alternate behavior. Paper read at the American Anthropological Association Meetings, November 22, 1968. Seattle.
1969a. Attributes and Categories in the Study of Material Culture. New Guinea Dani Attire. *Man*, 4.3:379–91.
1969b. The Dongson and the Dani; A Skeuomorph from the West Irian Highlands. *Mankind*, 7:147–8.

HELD, G. J.
1951. *De Papoea. Cultuurimprovisator.* 's-Gravenhage/Bandung: N.V. Uitgeverij W. van Hoeve.

HERDERSCHEE, FRANSSEN A.
1913. Verslag der 3de Zuid-Nieuw-Guinea-expeditie van af 5 December 1912, in Bulletin 68, *Maatschappij ter bevordering van het Natuurkundig Onderzoek der Nederlandsche Koloniën.*

HIATT, L. R.
1965. *Kinship and conflict. A study of an aboriginal community in Northern Arnhem Land.* Canberra: Australian National University Press.

HITT, RUSSELL T.
1962. *Cannibal valley.* New York, Harper & Row.

HOEBEL, E. ADAMSON
1954. *The law of primitive man. A study in comparative legal dynamics.* Cambridge: Harvard University Press.

ISKANDAR, ANWAS
1964. Irian Barat. Pembangunan Suku Mukoko. Diterbitkan oleh *Projek Penerbitan. Sekretariat Koordinator Urusan.* Irian Barat. Kodam XVII.

JONGEJANS, J.
1921. Naar Centraal-Nieuw Guinea. Eenige mededelingen omtrent den stam der 'Oeringoep.' ('s-Graven. Juni-July 1921. *ms. in Archief Ind. Con. v Wetenschap. Onderzoekinge.*)
1921/22. Eeenige mededeelingen omtrent don onbekenden stam der "Oeringoep" in Centraal-Nieuw-Guinea. *Inie, Geill. Weekbl. voor Ned. en Kil.,* 5:565, 588, 597, 634, 664.

KIDSON, C. AND D. C. GAJDUSEK
1962. Congenital defects of the central nervous system associated with hyperendemic goiter in a neolithic highland society of Netherlands New Guinea. II. Glucose-6-phosphate dehydrogenase in the Mulia population. *Pediatrics* 29. 3:364–368.

KOCH, KLAUS-FRIEDRICH
1968a. Marriage in Jalémo. *Oceania* 39. 2:85–109.
1968b. On "Possession" Behaviour in New Guinea. *Journal of the Polynesian Society* 77. 2:135–146.

KREMER, J. H. G.
1922/23. De expedite naar het centraal gebergte van Nieuw-Guinea (den Wilheminatop) 1920-22 (*onze Vloot.* 14, 15).
n.d. Verslag: Eenige opmerkingen omtrent de bevolking. Bijlage IV bij Ethnografisch Expeditie. by P. Wirz, *m.s. in the Archief Ind. Com. voor Wetensch. Onderzoekinge Batavia.*

LAM, H. J.
1922. Iets over den akkerbouw bij een Papoeastam in Centraal Nieuw-Guinea, Benevens eenige opmerkingen over land en flora van dat eiland. *Handel v.h. tweede Ned. Ind. nat. wetensch. congr. geh. te Bandoeng,* Mei 1922.
1927/29. Fragmenta Papuana. *Natuurk. Tijdschr. v. Ned. Indie.* 87:110–86; 88:187–227; 252–324; 89:67–140; 292–388.

LARSON, GORDON F.
1962. Warfare and feuding in the Ilaga Valley, in *Working papers in Dani ethnology* No. 1, pp. 32–39. Bureau of Native Affairs, Hollandia-Kota Baru.

LAWRENCE, P., AND M. J. MEGGITT
1965. Introduction, in *Gods, ghosts and men in Melanesia.* P. Lawrence and M. J. Meggitt, eds. Melbourne: Oxford University Press. pp. 1–25.

Le Roux, C. C. F. M.

n.d. Dagboek van de topograaf en ethnograaf der Nederlandsch-Americaansche expedities 1926 (Stenciled. Archief Ind. Com. v. W. O.).

1948. *De Bergpapoea's van Nieuw-Guinea en hun Woongebied.* Leiden: E. J. Brill.

LeVine, Robert A., and Donald T. Campbell

1965. Ethnocentrism field manual. (Mimeo.) Evanston: Northwestern University.

Lévi-Strauss, Claude

1963. *Totemism.* Transl. by Rodney Needham. Boston: Beacon Press.

Linton, Ralph, and Paul S. Wingert

1946. *Arts of the South Seas.* New York: The Museum of Modern Art, Simon and Schuster.

Lorentz, H. A.

1913. *Zwarte Menschen-Witte Bergen. Verhaal van den Tocht naar het Sneeuwgebergte van Nieuw-Guinea.* Leiden: Brill.

Malinowski, Bronislaw

1922. *Argonauts of the Western Pacific.* Paperback ed. 1962. New York: Dutton.

1923. The problem of meaning in primitive languages. Supp. I, pp. 296–336, in C. K. Ogden and I. A. Richard, *The meaning of meaning.* New York: Harcourt.

1935a. *Coral gardens and their magic,* Vol. I. *Soil-tilling and agricultural rites in the Trobriand Islands.* London: Allen and Unwin.

1935b. *Coral gardens and their magic,* Vol. II. *The Language of magic and gardening.* London: Allen and Unwin.

1954. *Myth in primitive psychology* (originally published 1927 by W. W. Norton and Co.) pp. 93–149 in *Magic, science, and religion and other essays.* Garden City: Doubleday Anchor Books.

Matthiessen, Peter

1962. *Under the mountain wall. A chronicle of two seasons in the stone age.* New York: Viking.

Mauss, Marcel

1925. Essai sur le Don. *L'Annee sociologique* n.s. 1:30–186.

1954. English translation by Ian Cunningham. New York: The Free Press.

Mead, Margaret

1938. The mountain Arapesh. I. An importing culture. *Anthropological Papers of the American Museum of Natural History,* 36.3.

1940. The mountain Arapesh. II. Supernaturalism. *Anthropological Papers of the American Museum of Natural History,* 37.3.

Meggitt, M. J.

1964. Male-female relationships in the highlands of Australian New Guinea. *American Anthropologist* 66.4.2:204–24.

1965. *The lineage system of the Mae-Enga of New Guinea.* Edinburgh: Oliver and Boyd.

Mitchell, Clyde

1964. Foreword, in J. van Velsen, *The politics of kinship.* Manchester: Manchester University Press.

Murdock, George Peter

1949. *Social structure.* New York: Macmillan.

Newman, Philip L.

1964. "Wild man" behavior in a New Guinea highlands community. *American Anthropologist* 66.1:1–19.

O'Brien, Denise, and Anton Ploeg

1964. Acculturation movements among the Western Dani. *American Anthropologist* 66.4.2:281–92.

O'BRIEN, DENISE
1966. A twentieth-century stone-age culture. *Discovery* 1.2:31–37.
1969. The economics of Dani marriage. Unpublished Doctoral dissertation. Department of Anthropology, Yale University.

OLIVER, DOUGLAS L.
1955. *A Solomon Island society. Kinship and leadership among the Siuai of Bougainville.* Cambridge: Harvard University Press.
1964. *Introduction to anthropology. A guide to basic concepts.* American Museum Science Books, Garden City: The Natural History Press.

PETERS, H. L.
1965. *Enkele Hoofdstukken uit het Sociaal-Religieuze Leven van een Dani-Groep.* Venlo: Dagblad voor Noord-Limburg N. V.

PHILLIPS, HERBERT P.
1969. The scope and limits of the "loose structure" concept, in Hans-Dieter Evers, ed., *Loosely structured social systems: Thailand in comparative perspective.* New Haven: Yale University Southeast Asia Studies. Cultural Report Series #17, pp. 25–38.

PLOEG, A.
1966. Some comparative remarks about the Dani of the Baliem Valley and the Dani at Bokondini. *Bijdragen tot de Taal-, Land- en Volkenkunde.* 122.2:254–73.

POSPISIL, LEOPOLD
1958. *Kapauku Papuans and their law.* New Haven: Yale University Publications in Anthropology, 54.
1963. *Kapauku Papuan economy.* New Haven: Yale University Publications in Anthropology, 67.

POUWER, J.
1960a. "Loosely structured societies" in Netherlands New Guinea. *Bijdragen tot de Taal-, Land- en Volkenkunde* 116.1:109–18.
1960b. Social structure in the western interior of Sarmi (Northern Netherlands New Guinea): A response to a response. *Bijdragen tot de Taal-, Land- en Volkenkunde* 116.3:365–72.
1961. New Guinea as a field for ethnological study. *Bijdragen tot de Taal-, Land- en Volkenkunde* 117.1:1–24.

PULLE, A.
n.d. Naar het Sneeuwgebergte van Nieuw-Guinea met de derde Nederlandsche expeditie. *Amsterdam z.j.* 8°.

PUTNAM, SAMUEL
1963. Under the mountain wall, in Harvard Medical School. *Alumni Bulletin,* Winter 1963:28–33.

RAPPAPORT, ROY A.
1967. *Pigs for the ancestors. Ritual in the ecology of a New Guinea people.* New Haven: Yale University Press.

READ, K. E.
1954. Cultures of the Central Highlands, New Guinea. *Southwestern Journal of Anthropology* 10.1:1–43.

RICHARDS, AUDREY I.
1957. The Concept of culture in Malinowski's work. pp. 15–32 in Raymond Firth, ed., *Man and culture. An evaluation of the work of Bronislaw Malinowski.* London: Routledge and Kegan Paul.

RIPLEY, S. DILLON
1964. *A systematic and ecological study of birds of New Guinea.* Peabody Museum of Natural History. Yale University. Bulletin 19.

SAHLINS, MARSHALL

1963. Poor man, rich man, big-man, chief: Political types in Melanesia and Polynesia. *Comparative Studies in Society and History* 5.3:285–303.

SALISBURY, RICHARD F.

1964. Despotism and Australian administration in the New Guinea Highlands.
American Anthropologist 66.4.2:225–39.

SCHNEIDER, JOSEPH

1950. Primitive warfare: A methodological note. *American Sociological Review*
15:772–77.

SCHROO, H.

1961. Some pedological data concerning soils in the Balim Valley, Netherlands
New Guinea. *Boor en Spade. Mededelingen van de Stichting voor Bodemkartering.*
11:84–103.

SNELL, L. A.

1913. Eenige gegevens betreffende de kennis der zeden, gewoonten en taal der
Pesechem van Centraal-Nieuw-Guinea. Bull. 68 der *Maatschappij ter bevord. v.h.
natuurk. onderz. der Ned. Koloniën.* pp. 57–86.

SORENSON, E. RICHARD AND D. CARLETON GAJDUSEK

1966. The study of child behavior and development in primitive cultures. A research archive for ethnopediatric film investigations of styles in the patterning of
the nervous system. *Pediatrics* 27.1.II.

TEMPLE, PHILIP

1962. *Nawok! The New Zealand expedition to New Guinea's highest mountains.*
London: J. M. Dent & Sons.

TURNEY-HIGH, HARRY HOBART

1949. *Primitive war, its practice and concepts.* Columbia: University of South
Carolina Press.

UITTREKSEL . . .

1940. Uittreksel van het algemeen verslag van de Nederlandsch-Indische-Ameri-
kaansche Expeditie naar Nieuw-Guinea 1938–1939. (Archbold Expeditie) door de
Redactie. *Tijdschrift Koninklike Nederlandsche Aardrijks Genootschap* 57:233–47,
404–22.

VALENTINE, C. A.

1965. The Lakalai of New Britain, in P. Lawrence and M. J. Meggitt, eds., *Gods,
ghosts and men in Melanesia.* Melbourne: Oxford University Press. pp. 162–97.

VAN ARCKEN, V. J. E. M.

1941/1942. Verslag Betreffende het Bewoonde Gebied Gelegen Pl.M. Twintig
Kilometer Ten Zuidwester van het Bernhardkamp. *Tijdschrift "Nieuw Guinea"*
6:33–41.

VAN DEN BROEK, PROF. A. J. P.

1913a. Zur Anthropologie des Bergstammes Pesegem im innern von Niederländisch-
Neu-Guinea. *Nova Guinea* 7.233–76.

1913b. Das Skelett eines Pesechem. Ein Beitrag zur Anthropologie der Papuanen
von Niederländisch Sudwest-Neu-Guinea. *Nova Guinea* 7.3:281–353.

VAN DER LEEDEN, A. C.

1960. Social Structure in New Guinea. *Bijdragen tot de Taal-, Land- en Volkenkunde* 116.1:119–49.

VAN DER STAP, P. A. M.

1966. Outline of Dani Morphology. *Verhandeligen van het Koninklijk Instituut voor
Taal-, Land- en Volkenkunde.* Deel 48. 's-Gravenhage: Martinus Nijhoff.

VAN EERDE, J. C.
1911. Vingermutilatie in Centraal Nieuw-Guinea. *Tijdschrift Koninklike Neder-landsche Aardrijks Genootschap*, 2.28:1 49–65.

VAN NOUHUYS, J. W.
1912. Eerste bijdrage tot de kennis van de taal der "Pesegem" van Centraal Nieuw-Guinea, in *Bijd, T. L., en Vk.*, 66:266–73.
1913a. Appendix B in Lorentz, H. A. 1913 *Zwarte Menschen-Witte Bergen.* Leiden. pp. 252–59.
1913b. Der Bergstamm Pesegem im Innern von Niederlandisch-Neu-Guinea. *Nova Guinea* 7.1:1–33.

VAN NUNEN, B. O.
1966. The community of Kugapa. Report of a research conducted in 1957/1958 amongst a group of Moni in the Central Highlands of West New Guinea. Unpublished M.A. Thesis. Anthropology Department, University of Sydney.

VAN VELSEN, J.
1964. *The politics of kinship. A study in social manipulation among the Lakeside Tonga of Nyasaland.* Manchester: University Press.

VAYDA, ANDREW P.
1968a. Hypotheses about functions of war, in Morton Fried, Marvin Harris, and Robert Murphy, eds., *War: The anthropology of armed conflict and aggression*, pp. 85–91, 102–05, Garden City: The Natural History Press.
1968b. Primitive warfare, in David L. Sills, ed., *International encyclopedia of the social sciences*, Vol. 16. pp. 468–72. New York: Macmillan and The Free Press.

VERSTAPPEN, H. TH.
1953. Luchtfotostudies over het Centrale Bergland van Nederlands Nieuw-Guinea. *Tijdschrift Koninklike Nederlandsche Aardrijks Genootschap*, 2.59.3:336–63; 4:425–31.

VERSTEEGH, C.
1961. List of plant names in the Dani language. (Mimeo.) Boswezen. Bosplantologie & Bosexploratie. Manokwari.

WAGNER, ROY
1967. *The curse of Souw. Principles of Daribi clan definition and alliance.* Chicago: The University of Chicago Press.

WATSON, JAMES B.
1965a. The significance of a recent ecological change in the Central Highlands of New Guinea. *Journal of the Polynesian Society* 74.4:438–50.
1965b. From hunting to horticulture in the New Guinea Highlands. *Ethnology* 4.3:295–309.

WHITING, JOHN W. M.
1964. Effects of climate on certain cultural practices, in *Exploration in cultural anthropology, Essays in honor of George Peter Murdock*, pp. 511–44. New York: McGraw-Hill.

WIRZ, PAUL
1924. Anthropologische und Ethnologische Ergebnisse der Central Neu-Guinea Expedition 1921–1922. *Nova Guinea* 14.1:148.
1925. *Im Herzen von Neu-Guinea. Tagebuch einer Reise ins Innere von Holländisch Neu-Guinea.* Zurich.
1931. *Im Lande des Schneckengeldes. Errinerungen und Erlebnisse einer Forschungsreise ins Innere von Holländish-Neuguinea.* Stuttgart.

WURM, S. A.
1964. Australian New Guinea Highlands languages and the distribution of their typological features. *American Anthropologist* 66.4.2:77–97.

INDEX

INDEX

Page numbers in italics refer to illustrations or diagrams